PUBLIC EDUCATION
IN
AMERICAN SOCIETY

PRENTICE-HALL INTERNATIONAL, INC., *London*
PRENTICE-HALL OF AUSTRALIA, PTY., LTD., *Sydney*
PRENTICE-HALL OF CANADA, LTD., *Toronto*
PRENTICE-HALL FRANCE, S.A.R.L., *Paris*
PRENTICE-HALL OF JAPAN, INC., *Tokyo*
PRENTICE-HALL DE MEXICO, S.A., *Mexico City*

KENNETH H. HANSEN

Director of the School of Education
Western State College of Colorado

PRENTICE-HALL, INC.,

Second Edition

PUBLIC EDUCATION
IN
AMERICAN SOCIETY

ENGLEWOOD CLIFFS, N. J.   1963

PRENTICE-HALL EDUCATION SERIES

JOHN S. BRUBACHER, *Editor*

PUBLIC EDUCATION IN AMERICAN SOCIETY

KENNETH H. HANSEN

LIBRARY OF CONGRESS CATALOG CARD NO.:
63-11103

PRINTED IN THE UNITED STATES OF AMERICA
73645-C

Early in the sixteenth century, Thomas Elyot, author of a pioneer book on educational principles, exclaimed somewhat intemperately, "Lorde god, howe many good and clene wittes of children be nowe a days perisshed by ignoraint scholemaisters." In less explosive language, the same charge is heard today.

Perhaps seemingly dull-witted children may reflect the dull-wittedness of some of their teachers—not really "ignoraint scholesmaisters," but ones whose own "good and clene wittes" have been in part "perisshed" by the dull and didactic way we have introduced them to one of the most interesting and important subjects they study as prospective teachers: the American educational system.

The introduction to American education should not be dull, but we have often made it so by pedestrian writing, by assuming that prospective-teacher readers have a simple-minded, "student" viewpoint instead of adult interests and analytical abilities, by focusing on the problems of the teacher himself rather than on the problems of the American educational enterprise, and by trying to give the beginning student in the field the entire teacher education program in one introductory book.

To avoid each of these errors was my attempt in the first edition, and in this second edition I have had the same goals. Therefore I have written

PREFACE

to and for beginning teachers as intelligent and critical adults, ones who
want to consider analytically some of the major problems in American
education and who want guidance—not didactic answers—in attempting
solution of some of these problems. Since these educational issues have
backgrounds in the historical, social, and philosophical roots of our
society, each of the background areas is treated as part of the contemporary problems of education, not as a separate discipline. Moreover,
since those who are most likely to read this book will have ample later
opportunity to study human growth and development, educational psychology, methods of teaching, evaluation, and similar major educational
problems, a consistent attempt has been made only to introduce these
topics into the problems being discussed, not to give a short course in
each of them.

No one book can provide complete coverage of the vastly complex
American education system, nor can a single text provide answers to the
many educational problems we face today. Therefore, each chapter is
followed by a list of suggested readings, to provide more detailed coverage of the chapter topics and to suggest divergent viewpoints, and a list
of suggested thought-and-action topics which will lead the reader to work
out some partial answers for himself.

Since, in any fast-moving society, the educational system itself changes
at a rapid pace, this new edition has been extensively rewritten to reflect
the latest school statistics, organizational practices, and operationally
effective educational theories.

The primary audience is still prospective teachers, but I hope that this
will not make the many in-service teachers and administrators, interested
laymen, and others who read the first edition shy away from this one.

My indebtedness to the countless persons who have helped, in one way
or another and over a period of a couple of decades, in providing the
teaching experiences and factual background materials on which this
book is based can never be repaid; but if the book can serve indirectly
to help keep alive in our schools the "good and clene wittes" of children,
down payment will have been made on the debt I owe to all who work
in American public education.

KENNETH H. HANSEN

CONTENTS

vii

PART TWO   THE WORK OF THE SCHOOL

PART ONE

BACKGROUNDS

Alameda County Curriculum Materials
Center, Hayward, California

Physical education class. *What would
have been the Puritan reaction to this
"education"?*

CHAPTER ONE

This is the day after Labor Day, the first week in September. Today (and every school day for the rest of the year) nearly 40 million boys and girls, young men and women, have left their homes to attend the public schools of the United States. They have walked, ridden the subway, train, bus, or trolley systems, come on horseback, by wagon, by convertible, or arrived on one of the thousands of school buses that daily bring children to school. They have come from pretentious homes and mere hovels, from gleaming aluminum-and-glass apartment buildings and crude packing-box shelters—all of them headed for school. Their parents are of every occupation or are unemployed; they have fed their children well or poorly, or not at all, as the family's economic conditions determine; they have sent the children off with words of affection and encouragement, or they have dispatched them to school without a word, or with a profane sigh of relief.

The boys and girls are of all physical sizes, mental abilities, colors, and backgrounds. A few of them actually detest school and will try to make life miserable for the teacher and for their schoolmates. For others, each day of school is a new, exciting adventure. Many of them—too many of them—are simply bored and indifferent. Yet,

SCHOOLS IN
OUR SOCIETY

whatever their origins and attitudes, they have a common destination this September day—the school.

What Is the American Public School?

What is this American public school that daily serves as the focal point for the activities of American children, the daily destination of so many of them, the pride of so many communities, and, in some cases, the object of the distrust of "puzzled parents and tired taxpayers"? What is this institution that, directly or indirectly, costs the American people billions of dollars annually, employs over a million teachers and other educational workers, and is alternately praised as the citadel of freedom and damned as a subversive influence?

The American public school cannot be very accurately described in terms of its buildings, because they vary from log or tarpaper or painted-board shacks (there are still 23,000 one-room schools) to multi-storied or ranch-type buildings of the most imposing architectural style. They may be located in isolated mountain mining towns; out on the barren, sunbaked desert; amid cool, pleasant, well-kept farms; or in the crowded city streets. The structure may house a total of two or three students, or it may be overflowing with thousands of boys and girls.

Nor can the American public school be described adequately in terms of its organization, for this, too, varies from a rather casual mingling of eight grades under the supervision of a single teacher, with the business, legal, and instructional matters under the general surveillance of a loosely organized board of laymen, to a highly complex hierarchy of closely-graded classes supervised by a line-and-staff organization of professional workers who operate under a clearly defined set of educational policies set up by the board of education.

Not even in terms of a single idea or ideal can we describe just what is the essence of the American public school system. In some towns or communities, the school is the expression of the highest sort of educational, political, and humanitarian idealism, and is supported generously by the tax-paying public. Elsewhere the school, unfortunately, represents a harsh, authoritarian, prison-like atmosphere, or a mere carrying-on of an almost meaningless tradition of "schooling" as a necessary evil, an expense to be borne grudgingly and supported with extreme reluctance.

A Common Denominator: The Society

Yet, somewhere beneath this mass of confusion and conflict which so often seems to characterize the American public-school system, there is a common denominator of meaning which can be used to describe the place of schools in our society. That common denomminator is the *society itself:* in our case, the democratic society or culture which finds its expression in that phrase which sometimes seems so hackneyed—"the American way of life." For there *is* such a thing as "the American way of life"; not even the shallow oratory of the political campaigner or the tired platitudes of the commencement speaker can entirely dim the reality of what that phrase denotes. "The American way of life" does exist, and our schools are an expression of it.

In any culture and in any time, the educational system of a society, whether it is a system specifically designed, merely tolerated, or constantly revised—that educational system is an outgrowth, an expression, a reflection (and even, though rarely, a leader) of the society which gives it nurture. For the educational system (or as we usually say it more simply and directly, the *schools*) of any country is the one designated agency whose sole function and purpose is to train the youth so that the life of that society may be carried on.

Therefore, as we attempt to understand what public education in our country means, how it is carried on, its relation to the community as a whole, and the part the teacher plays in the educative process—in studying these things it is of greatest importance that we try to see the school and "education" itself as a part of society, and understand the truth of the assertion that the school and the educational system have no meaning and no existence in themselves; they have meaning and importance only in terms of the society which they serve.

American Schools in the Puritan Period

It is quite possible that we can get a clearer perspective of the American educational system today by looking briefly at our schools as they operated in the early days of our country's history, the Puritan period. As we consider the schools of Puritan times, two cautions must be observed. First, this is by no means a complete account of the educational system of that era; detailed, accurate, and interesting historical accounts can be found in the standard works on educational history that are listed at the close of the chapter. Second, any comparison between the old and the new in education is likely to seem somewhat exaggerated; the old ways will seem unaccountably strange and the new ways just naturally better. But in actuality, the schools of the Puritan period in the early history of our country served the people of that time remarkably well. They were not necessarily inferior schools, but different; different because the times were different, and the culture, and the people's needs and desires.

A Theocratic Society

Puritan New England was a theocracy, not a democracy. Rule of the people and provision for their welfare was, pretty much by common consent, left to the leaders or "theocrats" alleged to be directly appointed and chosen by God himself. Democracy, in this new and struggling country, peopled by those who had been used to more autocratic governments, was quite widely viewed with suspicion. One of the great Puritan divines, John Cotton, a recognized leader in contemporary political and intellectual life, as well as in religion, spoke for many of the more "liberal" and thoughtful people of his day when he said, "Democracy, I do not believe God did ever ordain as fit government for either church or commonwealth. If the people be governors, who shall be governed? As for monarchy and aristocracy, they are both clearly approved and directed in the Scriptures . . . He setteth up theocracy . . . as the best form of government in the commonwealth as in the church." John Winthrop, another of the great Puritan leaders, spoke as forcefully and directly when he described democracy as "that meanest and worst of all forms of Government." True, these were spokesmen for the upper class, the ruling class of "theocrats," but they echoed sentiments that were much more generally popular than were the beliefs of democracy.

Religious Orientation

Is it at all strange, then, that the schools of Puritan times reflected what we would consider today the harshest of disciplinarian and authoritarian practices? Students often sat long hours in chilly and poorly-lit rooms, with no freedom of movement of either tongue or body, drearily memorizing the lessons set forth by the master. Since religion was the very basis and center of Puritan life, religion was also the "core" of the curriculum. The books, insofar as there were any at all, were basically religious. The *New England Primer,* one of the earliest of the American textbooks, was one of the basic texts used for teaching the alphabet. But in that primer there was nothing so worldly as "A is for Apple," or "Z is for Zebra," as we might find today. No, the ponderous religious tone was felt even through the alphabet. The Puritan school child was taught to memorize such solemn phrases as these: "In *A*dam's fall we sinned all," and so on down the alphabet to "*Z*acheus he did climb a tree his Lord to see."

It would be unfair for us to laugh, although we can't help smiling, at this rather primitive approach to the teaching of reading. Religion *was* life, and if the Puritan schools were to prepare for life, if they were to reflect their society and try to preserve their culture, they could do no other than make their interpretation of religion central in the curriculum.

Furthermore, the Puritan belief that all children were "born in sin" and were inherently evil—the doctrine of "innate depravity of infants," as they called it—was quite rightly reflected in the school discipline of the day. The great Puritan theologian and preacher, Jonathan Edwards, preaching what became one of the popular sermons of the day, entitled "Sinners in the Hands of an Angry God," recounted his vision of the delight which the Almighty took in sniffing the holy incense of little children who had died before baptism roasting over the fires of hell. It is no wonder that the schools of the day reflected this popular Puritan view: children were naturally full of the Devil; the only way to get rid of it was to beat it out of them.

Nowhere is the debt of the Puritan school to the society which supported it better seen than in one of the first compulsory school-support measures to be enacted in this country, the "Old Deluder Satan Act," passed in 1647 in Massachusetts. This act takes its name from the opening sentence:

> It being one chief project of that old deluder Satan to keep men from the knowledge of the scriptures . . . (to the end) that learning may not be buried in the graves of our fathers in the church and commonwealth, the Lord assisting our endeavors,
> IT IS THEREFORE ORDERED, that every township in this jurisdiction, after the Lord hath increased them to the number

of 50 householders, shall forthwith appoint one within their town to teach all such children as shall resort to him, to write and read . . . *Provided* that if any town neglect the performance hereof above one year, that every such town shall pay five pounds to the next school till they shall perform this order.[1]

You will notice that the motivation for establishing schools and providing penalties, however slight, for the failure to establish schools, was not basically educational but religious. Schools were not designed, as they are today, to meet basic needs of youth or to preserve and advance the welfare of society; they were merely to thwart the evil designs of that old deluder, Satan.

Quite naturally, then, the schools were not looked upon by the Puritan populace as an independent educational enterprise, but as an arm of the governing church organization. Support of the schools was largely a matter of Christian charity, rather than a civic duty fulfilled by the payment of school taxes. The curriculum was centered in the teachings of the church. Teachers, most of whom (except in advanced "Latin Grammar Schools" and the colleges) had little formal education themselves, were chosen by ecclesiastical authorities for their religious conformity and orthodoxy rather than for their scholarship and professional training.

Contrast with Today's Schools

Contrast these Puritan schools with the ordinary public school of our own time. Today, to meet the needs and desires of a quite different type of society, schools of entirely different pattern and purpose have been established. The public schools of today are supported and controlled by the secular government rather than by a religious body. The curriculum is primarily secular, with formal instruction in religion relegated to the teaching of the churches during out-of-school hours or on Sundays. Teachers are certified and appointed on the basis of their professional qualifications rather than on grounds of their degree of conformity to religious orthodoxy. What is perhaps most important, the entire educational enterprise today is based not on the assumption of the wickedness of child nature, but on the child's natural human goodness and almost infinite improvability.

Thus, we can see clearly that in Puritan times or modern times,

---

[1] Edited and distributed by Committee on Publications, Harvard University. Reprinted by permission.

our public schools are part of the very social fabric which gives them being and support; they reflect the basic beliefs, hopes, and aspirations of the society whose representatives they are. Further example of the interdependence of the school and its society may be seen as we sketch in brief the rise of the American school system in the post-Puritan period, the time of the emergence of America as a nation.

Schools in an Emerging American Nation

In the broad period of American history covering roughly the years from the pre-Revolutionary to the post-Civil War eras, the formulation, founding, and development of the American school system was not a conscious educational effort divorced from the other major problems of an emerging nation. Rather, the educational development took place slowly and sometimes almost unconsciously as a result of social forces quite outside the strictly educational enterprise. As the new American nation fought through its external revolution with an overseas government that had long held the colonies in subjugation, as the new nation established its own con- stitutional form of government, and as it went through the rigors and traumas of an internal Civil War, schools developed in different parts of this new nation in response to the peculiar needs of the geographic and social area to which they were indigenous. Generalizations cov- ering so long an historical period and so great a geographical area can never be wholly accurate or complete, but it is certainly not mis- leading to note that during the period from before the Revolutionary War until after the Civil War the earlier religious motivation which had so dominated the Puritan period was no longer felt either in the society as a whole or in the schools. Rather, the motivation for edu- cation during this period of the emergence of America as a nation was no longer predominantly religious but essentially economic and governmental. That is, the problem of the new nation was to establish itself and its people in economic independence and governmental stability.

The Common or Elementary Schools

For half a century after the Revolutionary War, there was little distinct change in the nature of the elementary school in the American culture from that which had obtained in the period prior to the Revolution, except that the strong Puritan religious motivation was no longer so evident. Elementary schooling continued to be offered as a purely local responsibility, with the parents of the school children paying the major cost of education in direct proportion to their ability to do so. Limited curriculum, short school terms, and relatively untrained teachers still were the dominant characteristics of the schools of this time.

It was not until about 1830 that the realization grew that a country which was to be a free and independent republic must give major concern to the revamping of the entire system of elementary education. If everyone was to vote and have a voice in the government, then it was a governmental responsibility that everyone have education sufficient to enable him to carry out the duties of citizenship. If the society was to be free in the sense that there was no peasant class or inherited economic disadvantage, then the common people must have enough education to enable them to become independent, self-supporting, and self-determining members of the economic community. It was the realization that the new country could not survive either economically or governmentally without an educated populace that led to the battle for schools that would be free, compulsory, tax-supported, state-controlled, and non-sectarian—American educational ideals which will be mentioned in another context later in this chapter.

By the time of the Civil War, free schools, in which no tuition charge was assessed against the parents on the basis of their supposed ability to pay, became nearly universal in the emerging nation. However, it was not until a decade after the Civil War, in 1874, that the famous Kalamazoo decision rendered by the Supreme Court of the United States decided, once and for all, that not only elementary but secondary education could properly be supported out of public funds.

Only gradually did it dawn on the people of the emerging American nation that it was not enough to provide free schools with at least some tax support; providing these schools without insisting that the children attend them would not meet the needs for an enlightened and economically secure people. Compulsion to attend these schools must be instituted, through the police power of the state or commonwealth. Beginning in about 1852 the battle to enact legislation in each state requiring compulsory school attendance was carried on for over half a century, for it was not until 1918 that all the states had enacted a compulsory school attendance law.

It will be seen that all of these changes toward building a strong and effective school system in the emerging American nation were motivated not by educational principles per se, but largely by the urgency of the need to have an entire nation of independent and self-governing people qualified by educational background to discharge the duties of a free and enlightened citizenry.

The Emergence of Secondary Education

The development of secondary education in America, like the development of the elementary school, represents a long historical process which our purposes here do not require that we give in great detail. Clearly, a skeletal outline of the development of secondary education is sufficient to show that, as with the elementary school, the secondary school in America developed primarily out of the changing social needs of the American society.

The earliest distinctive form of secondary education, the Latin Grammar School, was probably quite adequate for the needs of its time. The first of such schools, the Boston Latin Grammar School, established in 1635, became the prototype for this form of secondary education. The enrollment was limited primarily to students who aspired to college or one of the learned professions. The teachers were well and properly trained for giving instruction in Latin grammar and related subjects to a limited clientele. Because the schools of this sort were in no sense designed for everyone of adolescent years, it was thought quite proper that they should be supported entirely by private donations and tuition charges, with only rarely a very small grant of tax funds contributed to their operation. The Latin Grammar School, under this or a similar name, was the dominant form of secondary education until the time of the American Revolution. Not only was it the dominant form, but it was probably quite correctly designed to meet the needs of secondary education as they were seen and understood in this period.

The academy, an extension of the Latin Grammar School which included many of the same functions of the earlier secondary school but added additional subject matters of a more practical utilitarian nature, and emphasized English rather than Latin grammar as the basic core of the curriculum, owes its initial establishment to Benjamin Franklin, who in 1751 founded such a school in Philadelphia. From approximately the time of the American Revolution, a century of secondary education in America was dominated by this academy.

Some of the academies were given tax support, particularly after 1800, but most of them continued to be schools supported out of private funds and tuition monies intended for a somewhat broader class of students than had been served by the Latin Grammar Schools, but still not in any sense intended for the vast multitude of American youth of secondary school age. It was still assumed that while an emerging nation which required a constant supply of educated leadership would need a very substantial portion of its youth educated beyond the common or grammar school, elementary education would still suffice for the great multitude. It was further assumed that even though the growing economy required further training for some in the fine and practical arts, this need could be met by providing such secondary education for a relatively small proportion of the population. The fundamental curriculum of the common school would suffice for the majority of American youth.

While the academy was still in its prime, however, indications of its inadequacy to prepare youth for the responsibilities of citizenship in an emerging America became evident. In 1828 the first "English Classical School," a few years later renamed the English High School, was established. It existed as a parallel form of secondary education, along with the still popular academy, and for fifty years served as the basic form of secondary education for those who could not afford to or did not wish to attend the more formal private academy. It was not until the close of the 19th century that the academy virtually disappeared and the common American high school became the dominant form of secondary education.

But even as late as 1885, only seven or eight per cent of American youth of high school age actually attended high school. By the standards of today, with nearly 90 per cent of high-school-age youth in secondary school, this indeed seems a minimal educational opportunity. We must remember, however, that even toward the end of the 19th and the beginning of the 20th century, neither the demands of citizenship nor the demands of the economy made it at all evident that secondary education should become an inviolable birthright of every American youngster.

In summary, the development of both secondary and elementary education, during the period when America was forging ahead as an independent nation and ultimately taking its place as a leader among the family of nations, illustrated an educational system gradually changing as the needs of the society changed. In retrospect, it may

seem to us today that the changes were far too slow and the educational system far too limited both in curriculum and in its making
educational opportunity available on a widespread basis. But, as seen
by the social and educational leaders of its time, the school was simply
trying to reflect the needs of society as they were understood. It
remained for a more dramatic change in the American society—
one overlapping some of the period we have just discussed and continuing on into the present—to point up the need for even more
drastic changes in the educational system. This movement was the
industrial revolution.

American Schools and the Industrial Revolution

Religious forces in the Puritan period and broadly political
forces in the pre-Revolutionary to post-Civil War periods had a strong
impact on American education. But not only political or religious
forces find reflection in the schools; economic forces, too, play a
significant part in determining the kind of schools the nation will
have.

One of the most notable of the economic forces in our own national history has been the industrial revolution. No very accurate
set of dates for the occurrence of this great "revolution" can be
given; it was a gradual process, extending over several generations,
and is by no means wholly completed today.

From an Agrarian to an Industrial Society

Basically, the industrial revolution in America meant a change
from an agrarian to an industrialized and mechanized society. For
the American public schools, this change was significant in many ways.
It brought about a mass movement of people from the farms to the
cities; today, more than one-half the population of the United States
is crowded into fewer than one hundred metropolitan centers. The
one-room "little red schoolhouse" has not gone into a decline because of changing educational theories or the natural evolution of
schools from small to large; it has disappeared because the children
no longer live on small nearby farms within easy walking distance.
The one-room school is a casualty of technological change.

Urbanization

The vast development of the cities, as a consequence of the urbanization brought about by the industrial revolution, has meant a tremendous shift in the location of the wealth of the nation. Now, our national wealth tends to be concentrated in the cities; the majority of personal income is earned in the towns and the cities, and the majority of taxable property is found there. Obviously, the older system of financial support of the schools which depended on each local district to pay for its own schools with the wealth locally available, while completely logical and workable in an agrarian society, is no longer appropriate to a highly urbanized society. The trend toward more school support from state and national levels is another change that has been brought about not primarily by a shift in educational theory but as a direct result of new developments in our economic way of life.

More Schooling for All Youth

Another direct result of the changes in American life brought about or strongly influenced by the industrial revolution is seen in the increased percentage of our boys and girls who now customarily attend school, and the increased amount of time they spend there. No longer do parents find it generally necessary to keep children at home to work on the farm for a major portion of the year. A three-month school during the winter—a very common arrangement during the agrarian period of our nation's development—has been lengthened in almost every area of the country to nine or even ten months. Moreover, stringent child labor laws, enacted in the earlier days of the industrial revolution, both to prevent the cruel exploitation of children in the factories and to provide more work for adult laborers by making it illegal for children to work during their school-age years, made it imperative to increase both the length of the school year and the number of years that children would be in school. What else besides school did we have to offer the unemployed youth?

A Changed Curricular Emphasis

Still another development brought about in American education by the impact of the industrial revolution is seen in the changing concept of the curriculum. More time in school, plus increased leisure time created by shorter working hours, made it practical, even mandatory, that the school broaden its offerings, particularly in areas which would provide training in the worthy use of leisure time. Subjects and areas like art, music, and physical education could now have a larger place in the curriculum. Moreover, there was now both *time* for and *need* for an enlarged program of "extracurricular" activities. Many "subjects" formerly taught in the home—cooking and sewing for girls, and the agricultural and mechanical arts for boys—were now provided by the public schools. This was a necessary change forced on the schools; the home, formerly an independent, self-sufficient economic unit, had been changed by the industrial revolution until it no longer offered the wide variety of work experience it had once provided. The schools stepped in to fill this gap.

From Laissez-Faire to Planning

One more effect of the economic changes in our way of life and our system of education brought about by the industrial revolution might be given. This may be expressed as the change from a *laissez-faire* to a *planned* economy. Whether one accepts or deplores this trend, it exists as a matter of fact and seems likely to continue. A society that has come to accept municipally-owned utilities, public health services, unemployment and old-age insurance, government support of farm prices, and many state and federal controls over private business is likely to accept similar forms of planning in the educational system it supports. There has been, therefore, for several decades a notable trend toward increasing state and even federal participation in the educational enterprise. At least some of the public schools in two-thirds of the states now provide free or partially free textbooks. State-supported programs of health service are common in many schools. Subsidized school lunch programs are found in at least some of the cities and towns in a majority of the states. Tax money is almost universally used to provide school bus transportation for public school children.

It would be difficult to argue convincingly that all of the changes mentioned in the previous paragraphs are unmixed blessings, absolutely and unequivocally good. It would be erroneous to suggest that economic forces were alone responsible for these educational developments. The fact remains, however, that these changes in our schools in the United States *have* occurred, and the basic reason for the change has been in many instances more economic than educational.

We have attempted to make clear, by comparing our schools today with schools of previous times and by analyzing the changes that a great social and economic movement like the industrial revolution has brought to the schools, that the American educational system can be understood only in its cultural context. The cultural context includes influences that are not only religious, political, and economic, but ideological as well. So, let us turn briefly to examine one of the most interesting ideological phenomena that has affected our American schools today, the rise of the movement known as "Progressive Education," as a means of understanding even more fully how the school system is conditioned by the society which sets it up and gives it support.

Cultural Background of Progressive Education

Not all schools in the United States, by any means, could be accurately called "progressive," but this term, which is used by its proponents as the ultimate of praise, and by its critics as the last word in opprobrium, is often uncritically applied to all modern American education. In many ways, the terms "modern" and "progressive" are used interchangeably to describe American education in the twentieth century. Let us examine briefly the background of this "progressive" movement in the American educational scene.

The New Progressive Emphases

A more detailed study of progressive education will be made in a later chapter. Since the term is in such widespread use, however, it should be sufficient to use it here in the general, uncritical sense in which laymen usually employ it when speaking of the schools. "Progressive" education ordinarily implies several distinct emphases:

1. A relatively large measure of freedom in the classroom
2. Much opportunity for self-activity and self-expression
3. A strong belief in the importance of *interest* as precedent to effective *effort*
4. The use of the entire school experience as a means of furthering the social development and personality adjustment of the child

Without attempting at the moment to evaluate these emphases of progressive education at all critically, we may readily accept the fact that they have made a terrific impact on modern American education. What was there about this "progressive" movement that made possible its introduction into American schools in the face of educational traditions of long standing which were in striking opposition to these new ideas?

The answer is quite clear. At the time these new "progressive" ideas were first being introduced by such leaders as Col. Francis W. Parker and Professor John Dewey, in the late 1890's and early 1900's, our American society, our culture, was undergoing changes that made the introduction of new educational ideas not only possible but necessary. Our society was ready for an educational revolution. Fifty years earlier or fifty years later the progressive movement might have had an entirely different reception in American schools. But, coming as it did at the turn of the twentieth century, it found a fairly ready and widespread reception.

The beginning of the present century found American society in many respects ready for a change, and not in education alone. It was a society which was beginning to question the validity of established and inherited institutions, such as the home and the church; it was questioning the validity of established ideals of honesty in public and private life, of justice and honor and fairness and patriotism; a society questioning the validity of established social patterns of marriage and family life, of rank and class in "society." Why not a time for questioning traditional educational ideals and patterns, too?

The same turn-of-the-century American society had affirmations as well as questions. There was an affirmation of faith in a physiological, rather than a spiritual, concept of the nature of man. This was a rather rabidly democratic regard for individual differences, even individual eccentricities. There was a frankly experimentalist outlook, running from the Gay Nineties through the Roaring Twenties and the Jazz Age—an experimentalist outlook in social, economic, and moral questions as well. Why not, then, a new, experimental education, dedicated to the freedom of man as an adjustable physiological mechanism, man free of past restraints, man an individual in his own right, accountable to no one?

What we are saying is simply that progressive education was not just an "educational" movement, but part of a social and cultural pattern much larger than its manifestation in educational affairs. And this social and cultural pattern, this new groping for freedom, this denial of established mores and morals, was by no means well-conceived or well-disciplined. The "new education" it begot had the same faults.

Progressive education, then, had the virtues and faults of the society into which it was born, illustrating again the relationship between our society and our schools. But we still do not have a complete or clear answer to our question, "What is this institution called the American public school? What is this social institution called 'education'?" Perhaps, however, as we look still further at the interrelationships between education and our society we can come closer to a satisfactory answer. And a large part of this answer, as well as a better understanding of how the American school is an outgrowth of American society, may be found as we consider next another aspect of the public schools of our country.

American Education as an Expression of Ideals

A few years ago an eminent American scholar, Professor Henry Steele Commager, wrote an historian's summary of the impact of public schools on American life, using the challenging, thought-provoking title, "Our Schools Have Kept Us Free." [2] This title, it is true, may perhaps sound overly idealistic, but it is equally true that American ideals and American idealism provide one of the best answers to the question, "What is the American public school?"

The "Democratic" Educational Ideals

There are six basic principles of American education that underlie all of the virtues, faults, and variations that go together to make up our total educational enterprise. Ideally, yet practically, the American school system tries with all its power to bring to full realization these goals:

1. Our schools are free to all.
2. Our schools are universal.
3. Our schools are publicly supported.
4. Our schools are publicly controlled.
5. Our schools are compulsory.
6. Our schools are nonsectarian. [3]

[2] Henry S. Commager, "Our Schools Have Kept Us Free," *Life,* Vol. 29 (October 16, 1950), 46 f.
[3] See Edgar W. Knight, *Education in the United States,* 3rd ed. (Boston: Ginn and Co., 1951), pp. 2 ff. Reprinted by permission.

The history of the struggle for the realization of these basic principles of American education is a long and interesting one. It has been skillfully recounted and thoroughly documented in many very readable books on the history of education in the United States and need not be repeated here. It is a story resplendent with the names of many of the greatest leaders in the educational and political life of our country: Benjamin Franklin, Thomas Jefferson, Horace Mann, Henry Barnard, John Dewey, and a host of others. Throughout the story runs the bright thread of American idealism, which like most idealism is made up of many conflicting ideas.

Equalitarianism and Ethical Idealism

Basic to all of these principles of American education is that of *equalitarianism:* ". . . all men are created equal . . . they are endowed by their Creator with certain unalienable Rights. . . ." Equal education for all has never been achieved, but it has stood for generations as one of our most cherished dreams. A strong core of *ethical idealism* has also served to guide the development of American education; universal education has been conceived of as a moral obligation, not just a political expediency or an economic desirability. The early American concept, imported from Europe with our first settlers, of a good education as a vested right of the wellborn, with a few dry and vapid crumbs of education to be cast down carelessly as a matter of charity for the poor—this European concept did not long endure in a growing, democratic America.

Rugged Individualism

But along with the principles of equalitarianism and ethical idealism, other strong American ideals of lesser worth educationally have often been as readily accepted. One of these is the type of "rugged individualism" which, however appropriate to a rude, frontier society, has remained to plague most sorely our attempts to secure a more efficient centralized management of the school system. Extreme and excessive localism in education, a direct outgrowth of the belief in rugged individualism, has remained to throttle the natural development of our educational system long after its time of greatest usefulness was past. Another American ideal of long historical tradition, but of little present usefulness, has been our extreme suspicion of taxation. From the time of the Boston Tea Party and the Whiskey

Rebellion, the American people have been almost as much opposed to taxation per se as to "taxation without representation," that old rallying cry of Revolutionary days. Small wonder, therefore, that our schools have had to struggle so long and, it sometimes seems, so ineffectually against the natural American disinclination to consolidate schools, centralize educational authority in more workable units, and support the schools with adequate and fairly distributed tax funds.

The American School in a Changing Culture

Critics Don't Agree

The American public school system today is frequently under severe criticism from many sources and on many counts. The schools are accused by some of failure to teach the three R's, the solid academic fundamentals; other critics see the schools as overly concerned with mere bookish learning. Some persons criticize the schools for not teaching "Americanism"; others, for teaching a narrow nationalism. Certain critics think that the schools should teach more religion, and others decry the continuation of some religious influences still found in our avowedly secular schools. Some taxpayers complain that school costs are too high, yet defenders of the schools say that we are literally starving public education. There are people who think that the school tries to include too much in the curriculum, and others who believe that the school is leaving out things it ought to teach. Some of our citizens call the schools too "progressive"; others disparage the schools for being subservient to a narrow academic traditionalism. Some say that there is too much provincial local control in our school sytem; others, that the schools are coming more and more under state and federal control and being led down the ruinous road to socialism.

What is the truth about American public education? The succeeding chapters of this book will try to assess, directly or indirectly, the validity of some of these criticisms, but this much should be clear at once: the schools of America, we have said, are a reflection of the society they represent; and like this society, they may sometimes appear to be in a confused, even chaotic state. The American people are not always sure of their cultural, social, and national goals or confident of the road they should take to reach these goals. As a product of the American culture, our schools, naturally enough, have some faults, exhibit some hesitations, and reflect some failures. This is not surprising. What is surprising is that our American public schools are as good as they are—and they *are* good schools! Let us note very briefly some of the difficulties under which our public schools have labored in the relatively brief period of their development, some of the cultural confusions and social problems that continue to affect them today.

First, the early schools in America were transplanted almost bodily from a European culture in which were entrenched long traditions of academic exclusiveness, mental training for a privileged class, and subservience to ecclesiastical or royal authority. Our early settlers were not trying at first to set up a new and better educational system; they were merely trying to carry on, as best they could in a new and unfamiliar setting, a tradition of education that had worked out fairly well in the Old Country. That our schools have developed—almost by sheer chance and the grace of Providence, it sometimes seems— into a modern, liberal, reasonably progressive, and forward-looking system is a tremendous tribute to their adaptability to the changing American culture.

The American public school system has not had an easy, comfortable, uninterrupted growth. We have mentioned before the industrial revolution and some of its effects on the public schools. These schools have lived through not only this tremendous social upheaval affecting every segment of American life, but through other major changes as well—cultural and social changes which might conceivably have proved devastating to an educational system less closely responsive to the culture which supports it. A costly Revolutionary War which severed our ties with the mother country; the rapid development of a new, independent nation and the expansion of the Western frontier across a vast unexplored continent; a bloody Civil War; and two major World Wars through which the United States emerged as a major world power with grave international responsibilities—all of these events have greatly affected the educational system of our country, but have not seriously curtailed the growth or hampered the steady development of our nation's schools.

Moreover, even when great social changes affecting education have not at a given time been taking place—even in the relatively peaceful periods between recurring crises—the public schools of our country have never had a clear mandate from the American people as to what they should be and do. We have wanted moral and spiritual values to be upheld by the schools, but have shied away from any sectarian religious influences in education. We have wanted a degree of uniformity in our schools, but have insisted on local autonomy in running the schools. We have desired good schools, but have been reluctant to pay for them. We want our schools to reflect the American way of life, but we are not always sure just what this way of life is.

Is it any wonder, therefore, that the American public school system has often shared the upheavals, the doubts, the uncertainties, and sometimes the contradictions and confusions that have typified the American culture itself? Yet our schools—reflecting the past history, the present development, and the changing aspirations of our society— have been for the most part a strong and healthy expression of American society at its best, and a convincing embodiment of the greatest of American ideals: free schools for free men.

ONE: TOPICS FOR STUDY, REPORT, AND DISCUSSION

1. In what ways were the schools (elementary and secondary) you attended a specific expression of the cultural pattern of the community where you lived?
2. What are some of the conflicting ideals of our American society that are reflected in conflicting viewpoints about the purpose of public education?
3. In what ways can it be said that the industrial revolution is still going on in our country? What effects are currently being felt in the schools?
4. Secure the basic statement of the philosophy of the public school you are best acquainted with (or from some other school that has such a statement available). Analyze this statement from the standpoint of how well it expresses the basic ideas of our modern American culture.
5. How would you define the phrase, "the American way of life"?
6. How can we justify compulsory education and compulsory support of the public school system in a democracy, where we value so highly freedom from compulsion?
7. In what ways have our public schools failed to live up to the highest ideals of American democracy?

ONE: BIBLIOGRAPHY

Association for Supervision and Curriculum Development, *Forces Affecting American Education,* 1953 Yearbook. Washington, D. C.: National Education Association, 1953. Excellent chapters by leading authorities on several phases of the impact of modern American culture on the schools. See especially chap. 3, "Groups Affecting Education," and chap. 4, "Communication Affecting Education." Even though written in the 1950's, it is still pertinent.

Bartky, John A., *Social Issues in Public Education*. Boston: Houghton Mifflin Co., 1961. A complex but rewarding analysis of the social nature of public education.

Butts, R. Freeman, "Search for Freedom—the Story of American Education," *NEA Journal,* Vol. 49, No. 3 (March, 1960), 33-48. Perhaps the best brief summary of the development of the American system of education extant.

Commager, Henry Steele, "Our Schools Have Kept Us Free," *Life,* Vol. 29, No. 16 (October 16, 1950), 46 f. A powerful statement of the effect American public schools have had on our development as a free nation.

Cox, Philip W. L., and Blaine E. Mercer, *Education in Democracy: Social Foundations of Education*. New York: McGraw-Hill Book Co., Inc., 1961. See chaps. 1 and 2 for a sound discussion of the social roots of our educational system.

Cremin, Lawrence A., *Transformation of the School*. New York: Alfred A. Knopf, Inc., 1961. An extremely thorough, highly accurate historical interpretation of the genesis and growth of progressive education.

Drake, William E., *The American School in Transition*. Englewood Cliffs, N.J.: Prentice-Hall, Inc., 1955. An authoritative, well-documented, very interesting interpretation of the development of the American schools as an outgrowth of American society.

Good, Harry G., *A History of American Education,* 2d ed. New York: The Macmillan Co., 1962. Comprehensive, chronological treatment of the development of American education.

Knight, Edgar W., and Clifton L. Hall, *Readings in American Educational History*. New York: Appleton-Century-Crofts, Inc., 1951. This is one of the few books of readings in any academic field that actually makes enjoyable reading—not from cover to cover, but on any phase of the development of our schools that you might be interested in. Well worth sampling.

Meyer, Adolphe E., *An Educational History of the American People*. New York: McGraw-Hill Book Co., Inc., 1957. For those students interested in a scholarly documentation of the broad sweep of American educational history, this is an excellent account.

Pounds, Ralph L., and James R. Bryner, *The School in American Society*. New York: The Macmillan Co., 1959. These authors consider the question of school-societal relationships from an interesting and informed sociological viewpoint. See especially, Part II, "Social and Economic Trends in America," for a clear discussion of the ways in which social change affects educational institutions.

Woody, Thomas, *Life and Education in Early Societies*. New York: The Macmillan Co., 1949. A very interesting account of how early education changed along with cultural patterns. See especially chap. 2.

Language laboratory. *Does federal provision of funds for language laboratories imply possible federal control of education?*

CHAPTER TWO

In Chapter One we tried to gain a better understanding of the American school system by exploring its relation to the culture that supports it and gives it life and meaning. Another useful approach to this understanding of our schools may be found in answering this question: who controls our schools? Our schools are, of course, partly an expression of cultural, political, and economic forces, but even more concretely they are part of a vast organization, a system of public education. Teachers and other professional educational workers, as well as the ordinary layman, the man in the street, are often surprisingly unaware of just how the American public educational system is put together, organized, and controlled.

Is There an American School System?

One of the difficulties is that our schools are not really organized according to any *one* uniform system, as are those of many other countries. In France, for example, schools are very neatly arranged and tightly organized in a hierarchy of educational plan and control that runs from the smallest village school, on through the intermediate

WHO CONTROLS
OUR SCHOOLS?

levels of control, and up finally to a national Minister of Education. Germany, likewise, has a national system of education that can be neatly charted and clearly explained. Every totalitarian government, of course, has its educational system as thoroughly and logically organized as is any other part of the governmental enterprise under a dictator-controlled way of life. But the schools in the United States are quite different. They appear to present a hopeless confusion of types of organization, overlapping local, county, state, and federal authorities, and a mixture of kinds of administrative control so varied and perplexing that they are indescribable in any clear and concise fashion.

Really, however, there *is* an American educational system. Its apparent disorganization is the result of two major factors: first, the wholly unplanned historical development of education in this country from semiprivate, short-term, low-cost schooling for a relatively small proportion of the children to the gigantic enterprise it is today. Second, throughout the history of educational growth in this country has run the persistent American belief that the best government is that which governs least, a laissez-faire attitude that has encouraged local initiative and regional differences in educational planning rather than any over-all state or national pattern.

Strangely enough, this confusion in our educational system, this lack of uniformity in organizational pattern and adminstrative control, so confusing not only to the beginning student in education but to the educational specialist as well—this apparently disorganized, haphazard, planless development of education is perhaps the great, unique strength of our schools today. Because we are not committed to the inflexible plan or strict control of education that characterizes so many modern nations, we have been able to build a system that with all of its many faults is rich, varied, experimental, unfettered, surprisingly successful: in short, an educational system which can at its best command the respect, enthusiasm, and devotion of the American people.

With a frank understanding of the complexities of the problem, then, let us return to our original question: who controls our schools? In the simplest possible terms, education is controlled by each of the 50 states; it is primarily a *state* function, some of the responsibilities for which have been delegated to local school districts. The Federal government plays only a relatively minor part in the control or administration of the public school system.

Like any brief or simple answer to a complex question, the answer above is oversimplified. Without attempting in any sense to arrive at a complete picture of the total function of local, state, or national educational authorities, let us look in some detail at each of these levels of governmental control in education.

Educational Control at the Local Level

School Boards and Local Administration

It is perhaps best to start with the local school board, since that is the most common and familiar of all the formal agencies of educational control. If we were to ask the average citizen our question, "Who controls our schools?" he might well say, "Why, the school board, of course!" His answer would, in many respects, be correct. For almost every local public school in this country, regardless of size or location, is under the direct legal control of one of the some 37,000 school boards now operating in our nation.

Today, there are approximately 160,000 laymen serving on the local school boards of our country—more than ten per cent as many board members as there are teachers. The number of boards is steadily decreasing as districts are consolidated (there were 423,974 school board members about three decades ago—1933), but very small districts quite frequently have as large school boards as do much more populous districts. Thus, in 1961, 91 per cent of the school boards in the United States had jurisdiction over less than 20 per cent of the school children of the nation.

Approximately 86 per cent of the school boards in the country are chosen by direct, usually nonpartisan, election for terms averaging four to six years; the rest are appointed by other elective officials or legally constituted bodies—judges, special appointing boards, county superintendents, or the governor and the state legislature.

Fortunately, from the standpoint of good democratic practice, the appointive system for selecting school boards is rapidly being replaced by the system of direct election. This method of securing school board members is sometimes held to be inferior to a system of appointment, for the latter is alleged to make it possible to secure the services of highly qualified persons who would not consent to "run" for an elective office. Furthermore, it is sometimes said, greater continuity of service distinguishes the appointed board, and less possibility of political influence is felt in such an appointive system. Nevertheless, direct election is largely preferred; but whether elected or appointed, board members serve as special representatives of the people, chosen to oversee the people's schools.

These boards are not mere debating societies or deliberative bodies. They are legislative bodies, with many very specific and many very broad duties—duties legally prescribed by constitutional authority of the state in which they serve. School board members are, legally, *state* officers—locally elected representatives of the *state* school authority. The local board, then, is a very important and generally quite autonomous body.

Duties and responsibilities. Typically, the local "school board" or "board of education" or whatever it may be called is charged with such responsibilities as these:

1. Determining over-all educational policies for the local school
2. Setting local tax levies high enough to secure sufficient money to run the schools
3. Appointing, assigning and dismissing superintendents, principals, and other school employees according to legal procedures
4. Deciding what kind of curricular and extracurricular program the schools will have
5. Determining the type of grade organization which will be used (*e.g.,* shall there be a junior high school, an 8-4 organization, or still another plan?)
6. Approving the daily schedule for the school
7. Securing school sites and approving construction of buildings
8. Determining what kinds of special services will be offered— kindergarten, vocational training, health services, guidance services, and the like
9. Approving budgets, setting staff salaries, approving purchases, authorizing payment of bills, and performing a host of other fiscal duties

All of these decisions, and many others that must be made, are of course subject to the general laws and school laws of the state in which the boards operate. More will be said regarding this point a little later. It is obvious, however, that the local board has great responsibilities and real power. The very range and complexity of the problems which a board faces is staggering. Ideally, each board member should not only be an honest, courageous, well-informed representative of the people of his district, but he should also be reasonably familiar with school law, school finance, school building construction and materials, curriculum, educational objectives, the problems of classroom teaching, the selection and in-service training of professional personnel—there is simply no end to the list. Actually, of course, the typical school board wisely leaves the details of many of the problems to *its* chosen administrative representatives, the school superintendent or principal.

Delegation of local authority.   Thus, a large share of the direct responsibility for running the schools devolves upon the local school administrator selected by the school board. This person, usually called "superintendent of schools," holds his office by appointment of the board; that is, he is directly responsible to the school board. His job is to carry out educational policies and practices adopted by the board; to administer the day-by-day routine of school operation; to coordinate the educational efforts of other administrators and teachers in the system; and, with the assistance of his staff, to formulate for board approval new and improved educational policies. (The administrative function will be discussed in greater detail in Chapter Twelve.) In brief, the administrator's job is just what his title implies; he *administers* or *superintends* the local school system under the direction of the board of education.

Nature of a local board membership.   So, the local board is a very important part of the American educational system. Upon the intelligence and good judgment of these boards rests the effectiveness of our public schools.

Just how good are these boards? This question, like others we have raised, is very difficult to answer adequately, but a generally true answer can easily be given: the lay school boards of America are most encouragingly able, conscientious, and effective in operating our public schools. Many studies have been made of the membership of school boards, studies which indicate that these boards are often heavily weighted with people from the upper classes, with members of labor and minority groups conspicuously absent.

The occupational classification of board members, taken over the country as a whole, is approximately as follows, in order of descending frequency, with the first two categories named comprising approximately 60 per cent of the total membership:

1. Business owners, managers, and officials
2. Professional and technical personnel
3. Farmers
4. Housewives
5. Sales and clerical personnel
6. Skilled craftsmen and other skilled workers
7. Retired persons
8. Semiskilled operatives and unskilled workers
9. Service workers

Women represent approximately only ten per cent of total board membership in the United States. Except on rural boards of education, where farmers tend to predominate, the board membership usually represents a rather select group of people educationally as well as economically. Although the average adult American has completed only about 9-plus years of schooling, three-fourths of the boards of education in the United States have no members who have not completed high school or college.[1]

Lack of any guarantee that the board members will know their educational business or attend to the public interest is, of course, detrimental to the service that the board may render. Board members, it is true, may be ultraconservative, overly progressive, and in some cases untrustworthy or just unwise. The heartening thing is that despite all of these difficulties, the 160,000 laymen who run the affairs of so many of our schools do a highly commendable job.

When one considers that board members are, almost without exception, unpaid, that the work is very time-consuming, and that public appreciation for their services is much less common than public complaint, it would not be surprising if board members did only what was required of them and let it go at that. But an increasingly large number of school board members have joined and taken an active part in their state and national School Board Associations in order to school themselves in how to be better public servants; many of them subscribe regularly to educational periodicals such as the *American School Board Journal* so that they may become better acquainted with school problems and their solutions; and in other ways these public servants have gone well beyond the call of duty in working for better schools at local, state, and national levels.

[1] Alpheus L. White, "Survey of School Board Organization and Practices," paper presented at meeting of National School Board Association, Philadelphia, Pennsylvania, May 4, 1961.

Educational Control at the State Level

Again, a complete, concise, and definite account of educational control at the state level is just as difficult to give as a complete account of the local level of educational control. There are many variant patterns among the 50 states of the nation; each state has a somewhat, and sometimes markedly, different approach to its educational problems. But some sufficiently inclusive and accurate generalizations can be made to help us arrive at the answer to our question: who *does* control our schools?

Development of State Control

At the time of the very beginnings of our national educational system, in the New England colonies, education was almost entirely a matter of local option; local interest or local indifference determined what kind of school each village, town, or district would have. When state governments became more firmly established, it was the general practice of each state to encourage and strengthen *local* control of schools, rather than to assume state control of schools. Beginning with the early nineteenth century, however, each of the states, led by New York, Massachusetts, and Connecticut, gradually assumed more state-level control of their educational systems and vested more authority in *state* boards or departments of education. State constitutions were written or revised to give the state the legal responsibility for all education of *all* of its children. Today, all but nine of the states have a state board of education, and every state has some sort of state educational authority. According to experts in the field of constitutional law, the state has always *possessed* the authority to take over education as a state responsibility; only the actual *assertion* of this authority was slow in developing.

Chief State School Officer

Although many different types of state organization of educational control are found today, in nearly every state the voters have enacted constitutional provisions for choosing their chief state school officer in one of these four ways:

(a) through direct election of the officer (usually called Commissioner of Education, State Superintendent of Public Instruction, or by a similar title)

(b) through direct election of the members of the State Board of Education, who then appoint the chief school officer

(c) through the election of a governor who appoints the state board and/or the chief state school officer

(d) through the election of a legislature which in turn appoints the state board of education

This sounds complicated, but it really means just one thing: the voters of the state, directly or indirectly, see to it that a person or a board is appointed who will carry out the state's legal educational responsibility to the satisfaction of the people. It is generally believed by educators that the best method of expressing the people's choice is through the direct election of a nonpartisan lay board of education, which in turn appoints a professionally qualified state school officer to head the state department of education. The poorest method is to elect the chief state school officer on a partisan basis, thus making it possible, even probable, that a political hack who has served his party faithfully will be elected, regardless of whether or not he has any experience or educational qualifications for the position. A few years ago, one of the midwestern states did in fact elect to the position of State Superintendent of Public Instruction a political "nobody" who, the day before the election, in anticipation of his possible defeat, had taken and *failed* an extremely elementary examination for a fourth-class postmastership! Thus, a man of distinctly mediocre ability and dubious literacy became the titular head of the educational system of that state.

State Department of Education

Fortunately, these older practices of selecting political hacks to head the state school system are fast disappearing. Most chief state school officers today are qualified professional educators. The state departments of education which they head are generally staffed with a corps of professionally trained and experienced consultants, specialists, and administrative officers who carry on the educational work of the department. Specifically, in most states the official state educational agency performs three major functions:

1. *Leadership and advisory functions* such as initiating and encouraging better school practices through publications, conferences, workshops, and consultations with teachers and school officials

2. *Statistical and research functions* such as keeping official school records for the state, compiling and coordinating statistical data, issuing reports on educational affairs, and computing and distributing school monies
3. *Supervisory and regulatory functions* such as insuring enforcement of state school laws, issuing teachers' certificates, and accrediting schools

Fortunately, the latter two areas of state department of education functions—providing statistical and research services and enforcing of legal controls—are largely being subordinated to the performance of the first function, that of providing leadership for and encouraging the improvement of educational programs. Thus, the alert and effective state department of education is most deeply concerned with the raising of educational standards and the broadening of educational opportunities for all of the children of the state.

State Educational Responsibilities

Under some sort of centralized state control, then, each state sets up a department or division to carry out the state's legal, constitutionally—or legislatively—determined responsibilities for education. Remember that these duties are self-imposed by each state; no federal law *requires* the state to have an educational system. What are these responsibilities?

First, each state must provide a system of free public schools open to all children. These schools must meet the minimum educational standards which are set by the state. Second, the state must see that these schools are free from any sectarian bias or pressure-group influence and that they represent in spirit, as well as in fact, the real will of the people.

It is at once apparent that many of the states, either on occasion or as a matter of practice, have failed in some ways to fulfill their obligations to their own educational systems. In some cases, the state has not stepped in to maintain a public school in the event that the local authorities have failed to act. Some states make little provision for financial support of schools. In other instances, the schools have not been open to all children and free to all; nor have the schools been kept free of sectarian or other pressure influences. But the legal responsibility and the ideal have been maintained: the state is ultimately responsible for its own school system.

The states have, typically, concentrated their educational efforts in a relatively few areas and have been quite content to delegate to local boards, either directly or by default, direct responsibility for most other educational problems. The typical state has, to a greater or lesser degree, taken these responsibilities directly upon itself:

1. Some responsibility for financial support of all public schools (a rather extended discussion of this problem will be found in the following chapter)
2. Legislative or constitutional provision for compulsory attendance of school children
3. Enabling acts to legalize the establishment, operation, and financing of local schools
4. Certification of teachers and other educational personnel
5. Enforcement of standards designed to provide for the health, welfare, and safety of the school child
6. Legislative provisions for the *mandatory* content of the curriculum—for example, insistence in almost every state upon the teaching of American citizenship
7. Provisions for certain school services (either legalizing the local board's actions or giving direct state-level help): free textbooks; free bus transportation; help toward the cost of new buildings; consultative help or supervision from the state department of education

This list is, of course, incomplete; in the case of some of the more backward or conservative states, it may be too complete. Generally speaking, however, these are the areas of educational control usually operative at the state level. We will consider later in this chapter whether the state should curtail or expand its area of educational service and control, leaving more or less of the educational enterprise at the local, "grass-roots," level.

Federal Participation in Education

Many laymen, and many professional educators as well, are under the somewhat mistaken impression that the Federal government now plays no part in supporting or controlling the American school system. That attitude is often seen in the much debated question, "Should we have federal aid to education and can we

have federal aid without federal control?" The very question implies a lack of thorough knowledge of the part the Federal government now plays in education: we already have, for better or worse,
some federal aid and federal control in education, and we have had
this for many decades. The proper question is not *whether,* but
rather, how much and under what limitations? The Federal government is already a partner, sometimes unwilling and sometimes un-
welcome, with state and local authorities in education.

Changing Concept of Federal Role

It is doubtful whether the Federal government, in the early days
of our national history, was intended to have anything to do with
education. The question of whether education should be left solely
to the states was raised in the Constitutional Convention, and the
answer was definitely in the affirmative. Although Washington,
Adams, Jefferson, Franklin, Madison, and others of our great
political leaders all spoke in favor of the new nation's taking a
definite part in providing for the "general enlightenment of the
populace," the Constitution was actually silent on the question of
education. Gradually, however, the new government found itself
taking part in the educational enterprise, and in fairly recent years
the "general welfare" clause in the Constitution has been invoked
as a legal basis for increasing federal participation. This is not the
place to attempt to argue the vastly complex questions of constitutional law or of the intent of the framers of the Constitution; we
might as well recognize the *de facto* presence of the Federal government as a partner with the state and local governments in education.

Early Legislation

Even before the Constitution was framed and adopted, during
the period in which the new government was operating under the
Articles of Confederation, the national government began to support
education in spirit if not in fact. The famous Northwest Ordinances
of 1785 and 1787 indicate a recognition of the importance of public
schools. The first of these ordinances (1785) established the policy
of reserving every 16th section (square mile) out of each township
(36 square miles) for the benefit of public schools. (This grant was
later doubled, and still later redoubled, so that when the last of the

western states were admitted to the Union, four sections out of each township were set aside for school lands, to become the basis of state school funds.) Thus, under the provisions of this ordinance, one-thirty-sixth of all the public land to be opened for settlement was to be set aside as school land, the revenues therefrom to be used for the support and maintenance of a public school system. The second Northwest Ordinance (1787) in reaffirming this land-grant policy, added the historic statement: "Religion, morality, and knowledge being necessary to good government and the happiness of mankind, schools and the means of education shall be forever encouraged."

Now, this bold statement of national educational policy, coupled with the express provision for land grants, may seem at first glance like an extremely farsighted and generous bit of federal legislation to aid education. Actually, the ordinances did not at once establish or give financial aid to a single school; not until Ohio was admitted to the Union in 1803 was the land-grant policy really put into effect. Moreover, the motives of the lawmakers who phrased these ordinances were not primarily those of supporting or aiding education; these men were not so much interested in establishing schools as in encouraging settlers to migrate to the newly opened territories. Nevertheless, the Federal government was early committed to a favorable attitude toward education, and from the beginning of our national history did through these laws give a good deal of actual financial support to our public school system.

Perhaps even more important in the development of increasing federal concern with education were the Morrill Acts, the first of which was signed by President Lincoln in 1862. These Acts, the so-called Land-Grant College Acts, gave each state admitted after that time about 30,000 acres of public land per congressman, to be used for the founding and support of colleges of "agriculture and mechanic arts." Land-grant colleges continue to receive some special federal funds today.

Formalization of Federal Participation

In 1867, a federal Department of Education was established, headed by a Commissioner of Education appointed by the President, subject to confirmation by the Senate. This department, which later became the present United States Office of Education, has been something of an organizational stepchild. It has been shifted from one federal department to another, finally ending up in the Federal Security Agency in 1939. In 1953, the Office of Education became a part of the U.S. Department of Health, Education, and Welfare, thus coming closer to a long-cherished ideal of having the cause of public education directly represented at the Cabinet level. The U.S. Office has no direct control over education in the states, but in fulfilling its originally specified purpose of collecting and diffusing information about the progress of education nationally, it has grown to be an important force in American education. It has published and distributed countless important surveys and studies of educational problems and their solutions, directly administered many of the federal-aid programs mentioned in this chapter, and provided many consultative services to state departments of education.

Vocational Education and Guidance

Throughout the last several decades the Congress has continued to enact legislation increasing the scope and extent of federal participation in the educational program conducted in and through the 50 state school systems. Since we are interested at this point only in a broad view of how this movement toward increased federal aid has developed, we need not review in detail the various legislative enactments that have encouraged this trend. It is important here only to notice that there has been a long and growing development of increasing reliance by the states on the Federal government for funds for various types of educational programs, especially in the field of vocational education. The Smith-Hughes Act of 1917 was the first and perhaps most important of a series of legislative provisions for direct federal aid, through state boards of vocational education, to local school districts to help pay as much as fifty per cent of the instructional costs of high school programs in vocational agriculture, trades and industries, and vocational home economics. The George-Deen Act of 1936 increased the federal appropriations for these programs and added to the list of approved projects training in the distributive occupations—retail selling and related vocations. The George-Barden Act of 1946 further extended federal participation in these areas and again added to the scope of the program by including support for programs of educational and vocational guidance in the secondary schools. Today, thousands of schools (including some institutions of higher education which train teachers in these vocational areas) share these federal funds, generally on a dollar-for-dollar matching basis. Thus, the federal funds are not an outright grant, but quite literally a partial subsidy for state-level programs which come up to required federal specifications.

Depression Era Programs

During the Great Depression of the thirties the Federal government, operating, of course, through acts of Congress presumably expressive of the will of the people of the United States, extended further direct grants to schools for construction of school buildings and for adult-education programs. In addition, the Depression-born programs of the Civilian Conservation Corps and the National Youth Administration, together serving millions of youth and expending billions of dollars, were carried on for some ten years. While it is true that these programs were primarily "relief programs" in intent and nature, both of them provided direct educational experiences, vocational training, or part-time employment to permit the needy student to stay in school. Thus, the Federal government again became a participant and partner in the public schools of the states.

One of the most interesting and far-reaching of the federal programs affecting education is the school lunch program. As an emergency relief program, this was started during the period of the Great Depression, but with the passage of the National School Lunch Act of 1946 it became a regular part of federal participation in education. This act was designed "to safeguard the health and well-being of the Nation's children and to encourage the domestic consumption of nutritious agricultural commodities and other foods." Under this act the Federal government provides to the local schools, through the states, both direct grants of surplus commodities for use in school lunch rooms and money to facilitate the distribution and use of these food products. More than 14 million children and youth were participating in the school lunch program in 1962, with federal contributions to the program totalling nearly $280 million for that school year. Federal law requires that the states attempt to match these funds with local funds, according to the state's ability to pay. This enables local schools to provide federally subsidized, low-cost lunches to their students at an average cost of

27¢ per serving. It is quite significant that this federal aid is not designed primarily to help schools, but to help the farmers. Still, it is a direct form of federal aid to education.

The G.I. Bill of Rights

Nothing has yet been said of what is perhaps the greatest area, in terms of influence and cost, of federal participation in education. This is found in Public Law 16, and similar legislation passed during the Korean conflict; these laws are collectively and popularly known as the "G.I. Bill of Rights." In the peak year alone, 1948, nearly three billion dollars was spent in subsidizing programs of education for veterans. Incidentally, only very rarely was any charge raised of "government interference" in the educational programs of the schools, secondary or college level, which were involved in this "G.I." schooling.

National Defense Education Act

One of the most notable recent developments in federal legislation affecting the public school system was the enactment in 1958 (and subsequent renewal in 1961) of the National Defense Education Act. Although this was legalistically (and politically) speaking a *defense* rather than an *education* measure, the Act did for the first time in federal legislative history place the Federal government directly in the position of supporting somewhat *general* rather than specific and limited educational programs at the state and local levels. Included in the provisions for the action were monies for student loans, aid to teacher education candidates, purchase of science and foreign language equipment and facilities, and the expansion of guidance services. Although many educators felt that the NDEA was too greatly concerned with special curricular areas to education— science and mathematics, foreign language, and guidance—to the neglect of other equally important parts of the curriculum, and others were disappointed that no money was made available for school construction or teacher salaries, the Act was widely acclaimed as a first step toward federal participation in the general support of state systems of local schools.

Schools and Training Programs

Even a bare listing of some of the other areas in which the Federal government has participated in education may give some idea of the extent and importance of this participation. The government, through its various agencies, operates schools for the American Indians, schools for American dependents abroad, schools in territories, possessions, and protected and mandated areas; numerous schools and training agencies in such federal departments as Agriculture, Justice, Interior, and State; and the well-known service schools such as West Point and Annapolis.

Shall we have federal participation in education? The question is merely academic today. We have had it for a long time; we have increasing amounts of it. The question of how much and under what controls will be discussed in a later chapter.

Intermediate Levels of Educational Control

Although the three chief levels of educational control—local, state, and national—have been discussed above as though they were the only ones of importance, there are actually many other important levels and agencies of educational organization and control.

For example, in a good many of the states, the county level, intermediate between local and state, still has considerable educational function and importance. There is usually a politically-elected or politically-appointed county superintendent of schools, and often an elected or appointed county board of education. In some cases, such as in Maryland, Utah, or West Virginia, the county is the smallest unit of school organization; only in the larger cities, in these and other states employing the county-unit system, may be found a separate "local district," independent of the county unit. In other cases, the county unit is an intermediate administrative agency interposed between the state educational authority and the relatively independent local district, with some supervision over the smaller local units in educational matters. In still other cases, typically in the New England states, and in the state of Indiana in the Midwest, the town*ship,* rather than the county or the town, is the smallest operating unit of school control. Finally, in some areas, a mixture of the administrative units is found. For example, in one small city in a western state, there are three "superintendents of schools." One is the politically-elected county superintendent, who is charged with the supervision of the rural schools of the county. In the same town, the city school superintendent, appointed by a local school board, has charge of the city elementary and junior high schools. In another office a few blocks away there is an appointed superintendent of schools who has jurisdiction over the *county* high school system (including the local city high school) operated under a county high school committee elected from the boards of the various local districts in the county.

Confusing, isn't it? But it is worse than confusing; it is expensive, disorganized, and inefficient. There is widespread belief among educators and students of civil government that the county and township, once very logical and workable units of government, have through the development of good roads, through population shifts, and through economic changes become obsolescent governmental units, especially for the control of the schools. But the strong American belief in local control and in "leaving things the way they are" works against any change or improvement.

One possible solution to the problem of the county or other intermediate unit would be to use it as a basis for collection of school taxes and administration of school services that local districts could not afford individually, but to leave actual control of the schools at the local-district level. Thus, the county unit becomes a service unit, providing audio-visual, curricular, and special-education services—to name a few examples—on a broader and better-coordinated basis than the local level could afford.

Some Problems in Educational Control

The foregoing paragraphs point up some of the current unsolved problems of major importance in the American educational system.

Balance of Power

1. *What should be the balance among local, state, and national control of education?* We cherish as part of our most treasured American heritage the belief that the schools best serve the people

when they are controlled at the local, grass-roots level. It's the American Way! The schools remain responsive to the wishes of the people they serve, they are able to meet changes in local educational needs readily, and there is a minimum of bureaucratic dictation from "above." All of this is true, but it has become increasingly apparent, especially in the area of school finance, that educational problems are often not really "local," nor are their solutions within the power of local or even state educational authorities. For example, if a local district insists on hiring poorly qualified teachers in order to save money, should not the people of the state, acting through their legislative representative and state educational authority, insist that properly trained teachers be hired? Or, if a given state is unable or unwilling to provide schools that meet even minimum educational standards, does it not become a matter of *national* concern? These, and many similar questions, cannot be answered categorically, but the student of education must be alert to the problems involved.

Autonomy

2. *What autonomy should the local board of education have with respect to the other governmental units, such as the municipal government?* In some states, for example, the taxes levied for educational purposes, and hence the school budget, are matters for the local school board to determine, but before the action becomes effective the municipal administration or the county commissioners must give their approval. Is this merely one of our democratic checks and balances, or does it actually result in the school's being controlled, not by the elected educational representatives of the people, but by other governmental or political bodies? Would it be more efficient and economical if education were considered just another of the many services offered by the city, the township, or the county, like roads or police protection, and brought within the jurisdiction, fiscal and otherwise, of existing governmental units? Again, these questions cannot be answered categorically, though it is easy to understand why most educators favor greater, rather than decreased, autonomy for boards of educational control.

District Reorganization

3. *Should local school districts be reorganized and sharply reduced in number?* The local school district in the United States was

not the result of a planned, orderly development. Rather, as the older states increased in population and the newer states pushed the frontier westward, new districts were created to meet the current needs of the people for a workable and reasonable basis for school organization and support. Today, the district system, for all of its many virtues, is hopelessly outmoded. Better roads, improved means of transportation, shifts in population, and sharply diminished or increased wealth of an area have made the "little" district, with the one-room school in the center, within walking distance of all children in the district, something of an anachronism.

At the beginning of the school year 1961-62, there were still some 37,000 more or less autonomous school districts in the United States, far more than are desirable for economic efficiency or good management of the schools. Five states—Kansas, Minnesota, Nebraska, Pennsylvania, and South Dakota—still had more than 2,000 school districts each in 1961-62, altogether accounting for more than one-third of all of the districts in the nation.

Yet the number of districts is declining rapidly. Reorganization, redistricting, and consolidation have reduced the number of districts in a period of two decades from an almost incredible number of 108,579 to the present (1962) figure of less than one-third as many. The number of districts in a state still bears little relation to the population and varies greatly from state to state. Nebraska has the dubious distinction of leading all the rest of the states with 3,287 districts (down from 6,000 in 1954!). Maryland with 24, Delaware with 17, and Hawaii with one district represent the other end of the scale.

Fewer districts, of course, is not in itself a solution to all educational problems. As the number of districts is reduced, their geographic size is increased; the number of adult citizens directly involved with the schools as local board members is reduced; and the personalized local interest in the schools may waver. What can be done to reduce overlapping, inefficiency, and educational mismanagement so prevalent with the present excessive number of school districts, and still insure preservation of the local autonomy and local interest that the small district system has given?

Accreditation

4. *Have the so-called accrediting associations actually assumed an illegal or extra-legal control of the American public schools, in*

defiance of our national tradition and our national educational system of control? The regional accrediting associations, of which the North Central Association of Colleges and Secondary Schools is the largest, are groups of schools which have freely and voluntarily banded together to promote higher standards for public and private education, largely at the secondary and college level. Schools may belong to these associations only after they have satisfied the schools which are already members that they meet the relatively high educational standards adopted by the group as a whole.

In a sense, therefore, accrediting associations could reasonably be called educational "pressure groups" because they do as a group bring pressure to bear upon local schools to improve their academic standards and to bring their educational and administrative practices into conformity with association standards. Moreover, there is tremendous pressure from local citizens and especially from parents to have the local schools come into or maintain membership in the appropriate regional accrediting association. While membership is, as we have said, technically "voluntary" on the part of the local school, a school that does not choose to conform to the association standards loses the prestige that comes from accreditation and the privilege of having its academic credits accepted without question by other high schools and colleges. Thus, the real power of these associations lies in the fact that parents want their children to attend and be graduated from accredited schools whose prestige and credits will be universally recognized. Therefore, there is often an overwhelming pressure on the local school to belong, to be accredited—but the pressure comes from the people themselves.

In recent years, schools which could not attain membership, or which were dropped from membership because of failure to maintain educational standards and practices approved by the group, have charged these accrediting associations with becoming agencies of educational control operating "illegally," quite outside of and beyond the power of local, state, and national educational authorities. For example, one school in the Midwest which had applied for and received membership in the North Central Association, after promising to abide by the standards set up democratically by the total membership of the association, was dropped after several years of membership for its failure to maintain approved educational practices. The school board of the district involved thereupon threatened to bring suit against the NCA and to have the association investigated by the FBI. Furthermore, one member of the board charged that the association was "un-American," and hence, presumably, politically subversive; this board member also stated publicly that he would never allow any of his own children to attend a North Central school again!

It is surely true that the regional and other accrediting associations do now exercise a degree of control over education that is nowhere directly provided for by law. But that does not make the associations' control illegal. Since they are wholly voluntary groups, schools are perfectly free to remain outside the fold. If a school desires to join, or to continue to maintain membership already achieved, the school becomes obligated to maintain the standards set up by the group as a whole.

Professional Domination

5. *Have the "professional educators" taken over control of the public schools from the "common people" themselves?* As more and more of the specific tasks of public education have been entrusted to those professionally trained to do the job (the school administrators and the teachers) we hear more frequently that the schools have been taken away from the people and handed over to the "experts." These charges range from mild expressions of disapproval of the turn matters have taken to frantic and anguished charges that modern education has become a "racket." There is not space here to detail these charges and the replies, but the question raised is serious. A very brief, but substantially valid, rebuttal would be this: So long as the public schools in America operate solely under laws passed by the people, and so long as direct control of the schools is vested in board members chosen by the people—under these circumstances, if the American people are alert, no one group can ever control the schools. They will remain public schools in every sense: of, by, and for the American people and their children.

TWO: TOPICS FOR STUDY, REPORT, AND DISCUSSION

1. What are the functions of the state department of education in your own state? Through what organizational pattern are they carried out?
2. With your instructor's permission, invite some school board member to lead a class discussion on the duties and responsibilities of local school boards.

3. What are the chief arguments for and against more federal participation in the *control* of public education? (This would be a good topic for a panel discussion in class.)

4. Assume that you are trying to explain to an exchange student from a foreign country how the "American school system" is organized. Just what would you tell him, as briefly and clearly as possible?

5. Write a brief "letter to the editor" replying to the charge which has appeared on the editorial page of an imaginary local newspaper that the professional educators have "taken control of the schools away from the people."

TWO: BIBLIOGRAPHY

American Association of School Administrators, *School Boards in Action,* 24th Yearbook. Washington, D. C.: National Education Association, 1946. Readable, accurate account of how school boards work to improve the schools and to better their own competence in matters of educational planning and control.

Association for Supervision and Curriculum Development, *Forces Affecting American Education,* 1953 Yearbook. Washington, D. C.: National Education Association, 1953. Chap. 6 contains a forthright statement by Willard Goslin on the importance of maintaining ultimate *lay* control of the schools.

Carlson, Theodora E., and Catherine P. Williams, *Guide to the National Defense Education Act of 1958.* Washington, D. C.: U. S. Department of Health, Education, and Welfare, 1960. A useful analysis of an important current form of federal aid to education.

Chamberlin, Leo M., and Leslie W. Kindred, *The Teacher and School Organization,* 3d ed. Englewood Cliffs, N. J.: Prentice-Hall, Inc., 1958. Chaps. 2, 3, and 4 present with unusual clarity the complexities of the interrelationship of local-state-federal school controls.

De Young, Chris A., and Richard Wynn, *American Education,* 4th ed. New York: McGraw-Hill Book Co., Inc., 1960. A very complete description of educational control may be found in chaps. 1-4.

Grinnell, J. E., and Raymond J. Young, *The School and the Community.* New York: The Ronald Press Company, 1955. Chap. 5, "Unofficial Influences on the Schools," gives a good discussion of how the schools are affected and to what degree they are controlled by nongovernmental agencies.

Mort, Paul R., and William S. Vincent, *Introduction to American Education.* New York: McGraw-Hill Book Co., Inc., 1954. Chap. 4, "Control of Education," is a very authoritative summary of how schools are controlled at the various governmental levels. Interesting and readable.

NEA Research Division, *Estimates of School Statistics,* 1961-62. Washington, D. C.: National Education Association, 1962. The current version of this report, published annually, may be used for securing the very latest and most up-to-date statistics on schools and school populations.

Woodring, Paul, *Let's Talk Sense About Our Schools*. New York: Mc-Graw-Hill Book Co., Inc., 1953. Presents an interesting, fairly moderate view of contemporary American education. Some of his opinions and interpretations may well be questioned; that's what makes the book interesting.

Physical therapy program. *Is this a frill? Should fiscal support for such programs be solely a local-district responsibility?*

CHAPTER THREE

Finance: Everybody's Concern

The problems of public school finance, partly because they are so difficult, involved, and perplexing, are often assumed to concern only school administrators or government finance experts. Actually, they concern directly every teacher and every lay citizen. The teacher wants to know how he can get a better salary for his work, more money for books and materials needed in his classroom, and better buildings in which to teach. Moreover, teachers are often asked by parents for information about educational costs, school taxes, and bond issues needed to pay for new buildings. The average citizen, like the teacher, is interested in being able to provide a better education for the boys and girls of the city, state, or nation, but he is at the same time naturally concerned with keeping his tax bill down to a reasonable level—or even lower if possible!

The problems of school finance are somewhat like the perennial problems of personal finance that we all face: too much outgo and not enough income. The schools, like many private individuals today, are always on the verge of being "broke."

The question of sufficient money for the public school is not merely an economic one; it is an educational question as well, for two reasons. First, the kind of education we provide and the quality of our schools are directly dependent upon the amount of money we have for public education. Second, the heart of educational *control* is the power to *support*. The governmental agency or unit or level which pays for education has a powerful voice in how the schools will be run.

MONEY
FOR OUR SCHOOLS

Local and State Support

In keeping with the long American tradition, discussed in Chapter Two, of placing responsibility for operating the public schools primarily on the local district, local educational taxes still provide the major share of school support. For reasons which will be discussed later in this chapter, state and federal tax resources are being employed increasingly to supplement local school taxes, but the local taxpayer bears directly the largest percentage of the costs of education. In terms of national averages, local and county taxes provide approximately 56 per cent of school funds; state taxes provide 40 per cent; and federal tax sources yield nearly 4 per cent. These are national averages only; extreme variations in sources of school support are found among the 50 states, as may be observed in Table I.

It will be seen that the power to support—and hence control—our schools resides largely in the local district. From the time our earliest public schools were established, up until relatively recent times, the tendency has been for the state to delegate increasingly to the local districts, by legislative enactment, the power to support local schools. At first, the legislation was merely permissive: the local district could levy taxes for the support of the public school *if it wanted to*. Later, the power to support was made mandatory: the local district was *compelled* to raise money for the financing of its own schools.

In the last few decades, however, this local power to levy taxes for the support of local schools has been hedged about by many legislative restrictions. No community can impose any school tax in violation of the state laws or state constitution. Most states have very specific limits regarding the amount of tax a local district may levy, the limit of its bonded indebtedness (the extent to which it may sell bonds and go into debt for buildings and other educational expenses), and how the money raised may be spent. Mort and Vincent, recognized authorities on school finance, have stated the problem this way: "The local community has the power to do whatever it wants to do so long as it avoids doing that which the state specifically denies it the right to do." [1]

[1] By permission from *Introduction to American Education*, by Paul R. Mort and William S. Vincent. Copyright 1954. McGraw-Hill Book Company, Inc.

TABLE I

ESTIMATED PER CENT OF SCHOOL REVENUE
PROVIDED BY FEDERAL, STATE, AND LOCAL SOURCES
1961-62

State	Per cent of revenue receipts by source			State	Per cent of revenue receipts by source		
	Federal	State	Local and others		Federal	State	Local and others
50 States and DC	3.7%	40.2%	56.1%	Nevada	7.8%	54.6%	37.6%
				New Hampshire	5.7	6.0	88.3
Alabama	6.5	64.3	29.2	New Jersey	2.4	22.8	74.8
Alaska	25.6	54.5	19.9				
Arizona	7.9	39.5	52.6	New Mexico	12.5	74.9	12.6
				New York	1.7	41.4	56.9
Arkansas	8.1	46.0	45.9	North Carolina	4.3	71.0	24.7
California	3.2	38.6	58.2				
Colorado	5.3	20.6	74.1	North Dakota	3.5	25.2	71.3
				Ohio	3.0	28.5	68.5
Connecticut	2.6	35.8	61.6	Oklahoma	8.5	41.4	50.1
Delaware	1.8	81.2	17.0				
Florida	2.7	53.6	43.7	Oregon	4.4	31.0	64.6
				Pennsylvania	3.1	44.6	52.3
Georgia	5.3	66.9	27.8	Rhode Island	3.7	25.2	71.1
Hawaii	10.7	68.7	20.6				
Idaho	6.2	31.9	61.9	South Carolina	6.0	69.5	24.5
				South Dakota	7.5	11.9	80.6
Illinois	2.8	22.8	74.4	Tennessee	5.8	58.7	35.5
Indiana	3.7	31.4	64.9				
Iowa	3.9	13.0	83.1	Texas	3.9	55.3	40.8
				Utah	4.2	46.9	48.9
Kansas	4.4	20.5	75.1	Vermont	2.9	22.6	74.5
Kentucky	3.9	54.7	41.4				
Louisiana	2.4	71.5	26.1	Virginia	7.6	34.5	57.9
				Washington	5.0	61.6	33.4
Maine	5.8	21.7	72.5	West Virginia	5.5	54.2	40.3
Maryland	4.0	37.8	58.2				
Massachusetts	5.0	24.3	70.7	Wisconsin	2.8	24.9	72.3
				Wyoming	2.7	44.1	53.2
Michigan	2.6	42.4	55.0				
Minnesota	2.7	37.6	59.7				
Mississippi	6.5	66.5	27.0	District of Columbia	1.0	0.0	99.0
Missouri	2.5	35.7	61.8				
Montana	3.8	26.8	69.4				
Nebraska	4.4	6.1	89.5				

NEA Research Division. Reprinted by permission.

The Basic Questions of School Finance

Since schools are financed only so that an educational program can be carried out, the first question regarding any program of school finance is this: What educational services do the people want, and what order of priority should be attached to these services?

The second question is one of willingness: How much money are the people willing to pay for the services they say they want?

The third question is one of outside resources: What school support can be expected from state and federal sources?

The final question is the one that hurts: How much are we in this local district going to have to pay directly from our own pockets to support the local school program that we have decided we want?

The School Budget

Answers to all of the questions listed above are ultimately incorporated in the local school budget. The complete budget document is not just a list of income sources and anticipated expenses, though often this fiscal information is all that the taxpayer looks at. The complete budget document consists of two parts—the "budget message," containing a statement of the scope of the educational program that is to be financed, and the "budget summary," the fiscal details of anticipated income and expenses. Thus, it is both an expression of what the community wants to buy for its educational dollar and a realistic determination of what it proposes to spend for each item in the light of the money which will be available.

Preparation of the Budget

While there are in the 50 states and thousands of separate county and local districts almost innumerable variations in the method of preparing and approving the school budget, in general the following procedure is employed: several months before the beginning of the new school year the school board, acting on information provided by the superintendent, surveys the educational needs of the district for the coming year. Then (again relying heavily on the suggestions of the superintendent, who has prepared a suggested budget document with the help of his staff) the board sets up a fiscal plan which seems reasonable in the light of the amount of money which can be raised. Next, they establish, within the limits provided by law, the *rate of taxation* which will, when applied to all of the taxable wealth in the district, yield the amount of money they need.

Budgetary limitations. However, the procedure is not so simple as it seems. There are many limitations imposed by law on the taxing power of the school board. Limitations, as mentioned above, on amount of taxes that may be levied, limitations on bonded indebtedness, and provision for revision of the proposed budget through taxpayers' appeals to the state tax commission or the state department of education or through direct vote of the people in a special budget-approval election—all of these are ways in which state legislatures have provided that the board's exercising of the tax-levying power will not be extravagant or arbitrary. Strangely enough, experience has indicated that the *direct vote of the people themselves* on their school budget has provided more liberal support than when some higher governmental authority determines what shall be spent.

Actually, local willingness to raise money for public schools seems to be directly proportionate to how painless it is to pay. *Indirect* methods of school financing are much more popular than *direct* taxation. In the earliest history of our nation's schools, various methods of school support were tried before reliance was placed on taxing all of the people directly. For example, several New England states supported meager educational programs through reliance on private or church donation—the "charity" concept. Others quite commonly raised at least part of the money through a *pro rata* assessment on each parent who had children in school; one could escape this so-called "rate-bill" only by taking a pauper's oath, declaring publicly that his children had to be educated at the expense of the district because he himself had no money. Other early devices for school support included excise taxes on liquor and other commodities, state-sponsored lotteries (which were, of course, only a form of legalized gambling), and the sale or lease of public school lands awarded to the states by the Federal government.

Only after a long, bitter struggle was the present common method of supporting schools for *all* children through direct taxation of *all* available wealth adopted as common practice. For many decades it was argued that the policy of taxing one person for the education of someone else's children was both illegal and immoral. The famous Kalamazoo decision, handed down by the courts in 1874, finally settled the legality of using tax money to support public education. Yet even today, the editor of a widely circulated group of newspapers in the Southwest argues publicly and vehemently that the whole system of public schools is immoral, and in direct violation of the Ten Commandments, specifically the commandment, "Thou shalt not steal." The schools steal the children from their parents (compulsory education), and they steal one man's money to educate another man's child (principle of public support)! We can only hope that the absurdity of this editor's position is sufficiently obvious to his readers.

The fiscal details.   Assuming that the local district, through its elected representatives, and acting within the provisions of the law, has accepted a budget, the next questions are these: How much money can be raised, and where is the money coming from? Let us look at an actual typical small-town budget summary to see what the school money is to be spent for and the sources from which it comes.

This town of Midville (not its actual name) has an official annual budget for the local elementary school adopted by the board of education, summarized as follows:

ESTIMATED SCHOOL EXPENSES FOR NEXT YEAR

Account	Budget, 1960-61	Per cent of budget
Administration	$ 17,268	3.40
Instruction	343,027	67.60
Health Services	4,400	0.87
Pupil Transportation	22,740	4.50
Operation of Plant & Equipment	43,822	8.60
Maintenance of Plant & Equipment	14,405	2.83
Fixed Charges (Insurance, teachers' retirement, etc.)	23,831	4.70
Food Services	300	0.06
Student Body Activities	9,058	1.80
Capital Outlay (New buildings, sites, permanent equipment)	15,934	3.10
Outgoing Transfers (Tuitions to other districts)	800	0.16
Contingency Reserve	11,000	2.17
Community Services	1,050	0.21
	$507,635	100.00%

That is what the people of the local district, acting through their board of education, have agreed is needed, what they are willing to pay if they can raise the money. Now, where is the money coming from?

Estimated Income for Next Year

State aid (money appropriated by the state legislature for local schools)	$127,500
Federal funds (revenue from sale of lumber on national forests within the county, from lease of federally owned mineral lands, and direct payment for part of educational cost of children whose parents are employed on local federal projects)	8,000
Miscellaneous local funds (auto ownership tax credited to school accounts, tuition from other districts sending children to local schools, rental of buildings, etc.)	23,000
Balance from previous year	27,500
TOTAL estimated receipts	$186,000

There is $186,000 of the needed money, but the total budget is for over $500,000. The balance, the other sixty-plus per cent, must be made up by the local taxpayers, particularly the local property owners. So the school board levies enough local tax to make up the difference.

We can easily see that the money in this budget comes largely from local (including county) property taxes. A smaller amount comes from "state aid," which in turn is derived from various tax sources. A very small percentage comes from federal sources—again, ultimately from taxpayers.

There is no magic way to get school funds without taxes; the money always comes from the taxpayer, directly or indirectly. There are no "state" or "federal" funds which come as a gift. The people of America must pay for their own schools.

State Aid as "Equalization"

In the fairly typical local school budget summary presented above, it will be noted that the percentage of state aid was below the national average of 40 per cent. Extreme variations in practice of state school support exist primarily because the several states have each developed a somewhat unique theory of how state participation in the educational enterprise should be implemented. But in no state does state aid purport to pay all costs of public education; state aid is merely a more or less successful attempt to *equalize* the burden of education in the local districts by sharing in the costs.

It is for this reason that many of the state-aid programs are called *equalization* programs. They are also rather generally known as *foundation* programs, for they attempt to supply at least a foundation for a minimum education for all children of the state. Funds are provided from the state level for each local district on one or more of such bases as the number of pupils in the district, the Average Daily Attendance (known as "ADA"), a specified amount per classroom, or specified proportion of average instructional costs. States sometimes grant direct aid for certain educational programs or expenditures such as transportation of children, audio-visual programs, education of exceptional children, school health services, and the extra educational costs involved in sparsely settled districts.

The Obligation of Local Effort

But state aid cannot logically be given a local district unless the district taxes itself fairly—makes a reasonable effort to support its own schools according to its ability to pay. Taxes actually levied and paid represent one expression of local effort. However, both the degree of "effort" exerted and the actual "ability to pay" are very difficult to determine accurately. What might be a reasonable effort in one district would be unreasonable—too heavy or too light a tax burden—in another.

Suppose a local district has within its boundaries a total of ten million dollars worth of taxable property. The budget of the schools calls for an expenditure of $200,000 annually. If each taxpayer is taxed at the rate of 2¢ tax on every dollar's worth of property he owns (expressed in *mills,* as is common, this tax would be called a "20-mill" levy), the yield would be exactly enough to meet the school budget ($10,000,000 \times .020 = $200,000).

But, let us suppose that this is a much poorer district, in terms of taxable property, or "tax valuation" as it is called. Perhaps the district has a valuation of only five million dollars. A 20-mill levy would raise only half enough money to meet the school budget. If the district's valuation were, however, twenty instead of ten million dollars, then a 20-mill levy would raise twice as much as the budget calls for, while a mere ten mills would provide enough to meet budgetary demands.

Inequities of Valuation and Population

There are two other important aspects of this problem. In many, if not most, of the states the assessed valuation (valuation for tax purposes) is only a ridiculously low percentage of the true market value of the property. Moreover, such valuation or assessment rates vary tremendously from state to state, and in different counties of the state as well. For example, in one western state, a privately owned home worth $10,000 on the market might be assessed for as little as $1,500 for tax purposes in one county and at, say, $5,000 in an adjoining county. Using again our mythical 20-mill levy, the property would have a "tax yield" of $30 in the first county, and $100 in the next. Therefore, inequalities in assessed values (and hence, tax revenue obtained on the basis of these "values") only intensify the inequities in financial support of the schools from district to district.

Another problem is this: the children who need to be educated and the taxable wealth which is the source of revenue for education are not necessarily located in the same place. School districts may have many children and little wealth, or much wealth and few children. If a district with a ten-million-dollar valuation has, say, 1,000 children to educate, the "per-pupil valuation" is $10,000. But if this same district had 2,000 children to educate, the per-pupil valuation would be only $5,000.

In one western state, a large suburban school district whose taxable wealth consists largely of the small homes of low-income families is faced with this financial problem: the parents of the school children of this district work in the adjoining large city and contribute to the wealth of the city, but not to the wealth of the local district. The *city* gets a new ten-million-dollar industry; as a result, more workers move into the *suburban area,* bringing in a thousand more school children. The city gets the major benefits of increased valuation for tax purposes; the suburban area gets little increase in valuation, but a huge increase in number of children to be educated. Therefore, the city can reduce its levy for school purposes, but the suburban district must sharply increase its tax rate without any appreciable increase in taxable wealth. The per-pupil valuation is high where there are few children, very low where there are many children. Thus, already existing inequities between the districts are severely increased.

Need for Increasing Revenue Sources

The obvious answer to all of the inequities which are found among the districts of a single state in ability to pay for education would *seem* to be this: let the *state* supply a greater share of the funds, with less dependence upon local resources. But the difficulty is this: most state governments are short of money, too; income has not kept pace with the rising costs of government. State aid to education already, in some states at least, takes a fairly substantial slice of the budgetary pie. More commonly, the states have simply not faced up to their responsibility for supporting the state educational system and have kept taxes unreasonably low or diverted large sums of tax money to old age pensions, the building of roads, or other purposes. If the state cannot or will not supply more money, the next possible choice seems to be to secure more local revenue for schools. This may be done in three ways:

1. By imposing higher local tax rates
2. By broadening the base of taxation—taxing *more* property or *more* people
3. By increasing the assessed valuation of the local district through (a) increasing the *rate* of assessment or (b) increasing the actual wealth of the district through the building of new homes, developing of natural resources, or bringing in new industry and new payrolls

If more local revenue cannot be secured, however, then more state aid is necessary. Remember, state aid means taxes, and only the taxpayer can pay taxes; thus the money must come from the people in any case. Again the state can do three things: increase existing taxes, develop new sources of tax revenue, or set aside the income from certain taxes for the schools. State taxes which have been, in some states, "earmarked" for education specifically include income taxes, gasoline taxes, sales taxes, corporation taxes, and various utilities, business, and mining taxes, to name only a few.

Since it is becoming increasingly difficult for the local, county, or state governments to increase existing taxes or create new ones, a most workable suggestion seems to be to reorganize existing school districts into larger units to broaden the tax base and equalize the taxable wealth. The very poor and very rich districts existing side by side are mere accidents of geography anyway; there is no real logic in the present district organization. Therefore, most educators argue, we badly need *school district reorganization* to equalize the educational burden.

Federal Aid

One more major proposal has been made for equalizing the financial burden of education among the 50 states. Some of the poorer states, were they to make two or three times as much *effort* as the richer states, would still be unable to offer their children a fraction of the educational opportunities that children of the most fortunate states have as their apparent birthright. (See Figures I and II, pages 60 and 61.) But should the accident of place of birth or residence deprive any child anywhere the right to at least a minimum of education? Should the boy or girl born in Mississippi, say, have to be limited by an educational system which can spend yearly only about $220 per child, while the boy or girl in New York can expect to have the state spend $615 on his education? The mass movements of the American people, their ready migration from state to state, plus the fundamental interdependence of all peoples in a democratic society, make the educational poverty of one state the concern of all the other states.

Again, federal aid to education is no magic source of income for schools. Money still comes from the taxpayers, but federal aid may well be a means of *equalizing* both the burdens and the benefits of good education for all of our people.

Proposed Changes in School Finance

You can readily see that the problems of school finance are inherently complex, and that they are further complicated by the different financial abilities, legal restrictions and provisions, and public attitudes found in the 50 states and thousands of separate school districts. Out of this great confusion, however, have emerged several concrete, practical proposals for immediate steps that might be taken to give education better support and to equalize educational opportunities. Some of them have been suggested directly or indirectly above, but they are important enough to be repeated here:

1. Reorganize or combine many of the small school districts into larger districts to give a sound basis for school taxation.
2. Make assessed valuation of property uniform within each state, and raise the valuation to a realistic figure.
3. Put more of the educational burden on the state level; use the broader and more effective taxing power of the *state* to distribute educational funds more fairly.
4. Enact legislation to permit an even broader base for school taxation by using the taxing powers of the Federal government to equalize educational burdens and educational opportunities among the states.

FIGURE I

THE PRICE OF A YEAR'S SCHOOLING

Estimated Current Expenditure for Public Schools per Pupil in ADA, 1961-62

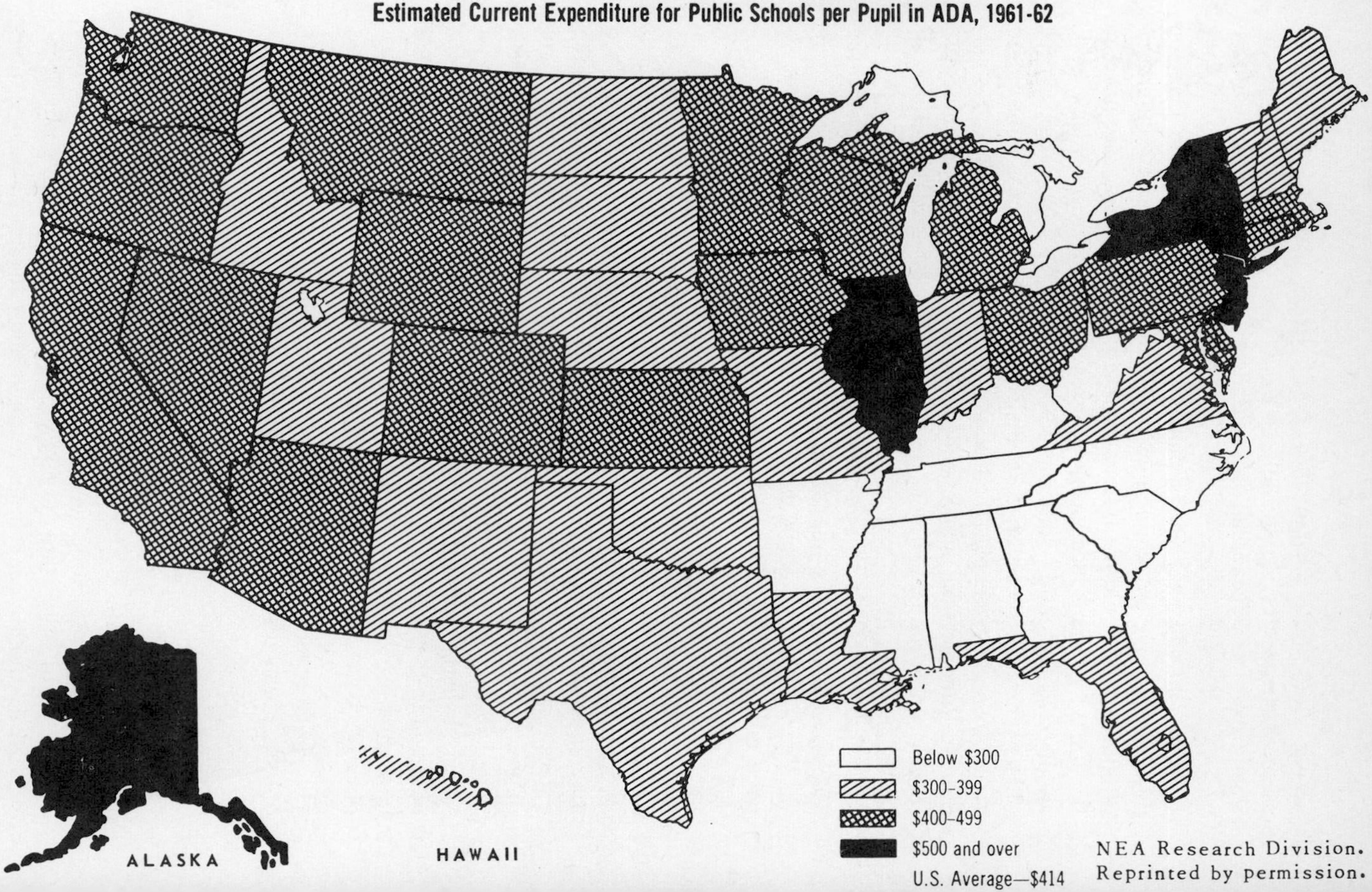
ALASKA
HAWAII
Below $300
$300–399
$400–499
$500 and over
U.S. Average—$414

NEA Research Division.
Reprinted by permission.

THE FINANCIAL EFFORT FOR PUBLIC-SCHOOL SUPPORT

Public-School Revenue from State and Local Sources, 1960-61, as Per cent of Personal Income, 1960

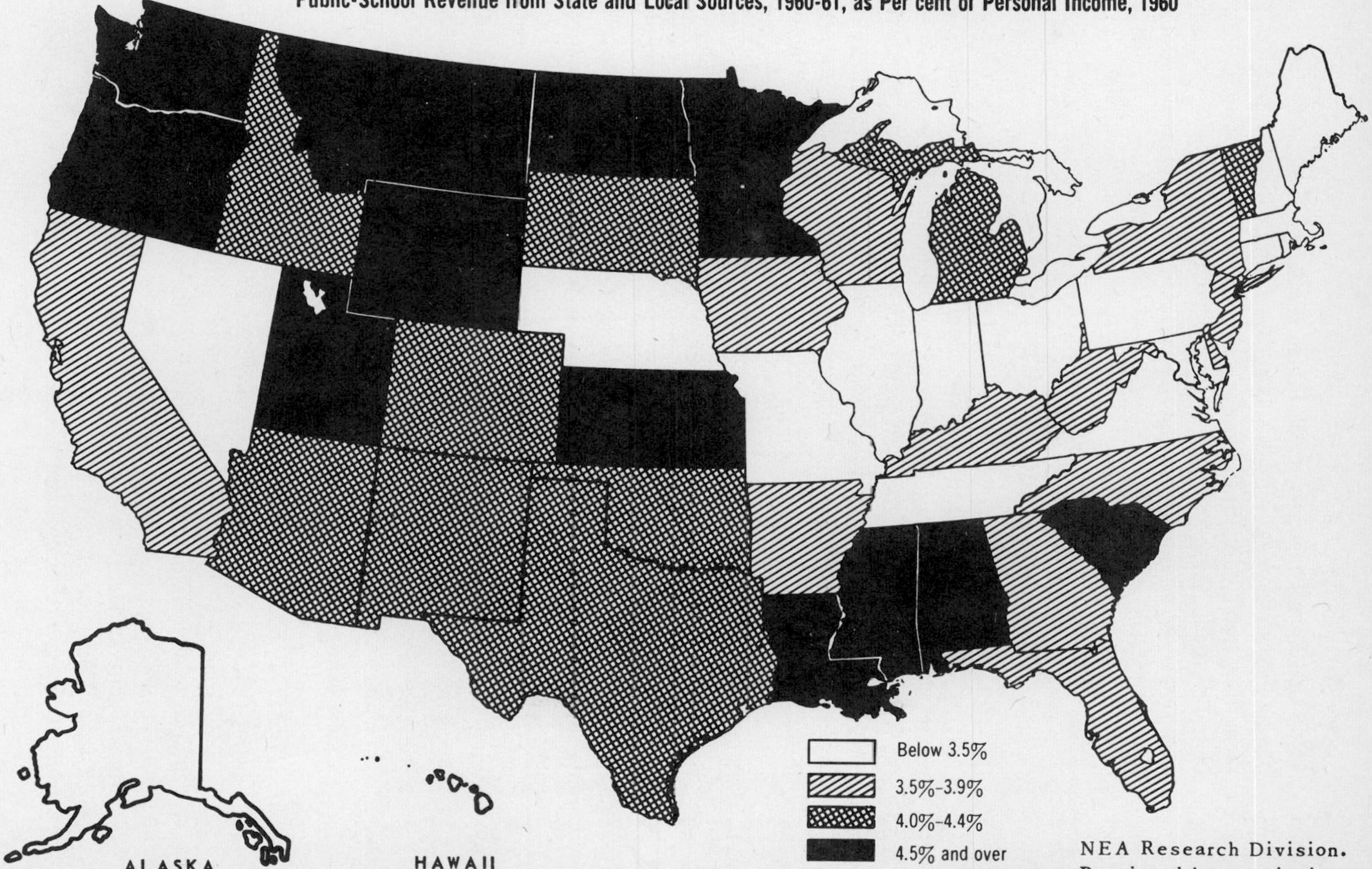

ALASKA
HAWAII
Below 3.5%
3.5%–3.9%
4.0%–4.4%
4.5% and over
U.S. Average—3.7%

NEA Research Division.
Reprinted by permission.

No one knows just how these things should be done; they are still very controversial issues in education. But nearly everyone is in agreement that good education is indispensable to our democratic form of government; good education is costly. One of the most realistic tests of just how great is our faith in education is this: are we willing to pay for it?

Why Does Education Cost So Much?

The Tax Committee of the local Chamber of Commerce is meeting with the school board and the superintendent to discuss the school budget for the next year, the budget that will result in setting a higher tax levy for school purposes. Mr. Hill, a member of the Tax Committee and a conservative, but by no means miserly, businessman, the father of three school-age children and an active worker in the school PTA, speaks up to voice a complaint so commonly heard nowadays, "Why can't we cut down somewhere on these school expenditures? Why does education have to cost so much?"

This is a good question, and the answer is not simple or always convincing. It would be unrealistic to maintain that there is no waste in school funds anywhere, that every budget item has been cut to the bone. With thousands of separate, independent school districts, and with hundreds of thousands of lay board members, there are bound to be some mistakes in judgment, some poor financial planning, some wasteful spending. But, when we look at the educational problems of the nation as a whole, it is fairly easy to see why school expenditures are soaring to unheard-of heights.

Sheer Growth

First, there is the tremendous physical growth of the schools, brought about by a tremendous increase in the number of children to be educated. With each new school year bringing an increase of well over a million new students into the public schools, more of *everything* is needed: more buildings, more teachers, more janitors, more school buses, more textbooks, more instructional materials. Even a fairly small city, with a projected enrollment increase of only a few score of children a year, finds that it must annually build and staff new classrooms and supply additional equipment.

Inflation

The "more of everything" costs more, too. Teachers' salaries are rising at an unprecedented rate, yet even so are barely keeping up with the increased cost of living. The cost per square foot of classroom space has more than doubled in many areas within the last decade; higher wages for workers in the building trades, higher cost of building materials, and higher costs of land acquisition for new buildings are all reflected in the sharply rising cost of providing new educational facilities. Everything the school buys—typewriters for the business department, library books, school buses, mimeograph paper, athletic equipment, basic readers, and even soap for the washrooms—costs more today. Inflation has struck the schools a heavy blow.

Curriculum Change

There are other, more subtle reasons for rising school costs. Changing practices and new developments in the educational process itself make the cost of schools soar. Whereas a single "reader" might have sufficed in the first grade a quarter of a century ago, today's method of teaching reading calls for a multiplicity of pre-primers, primers, readers, and supplementary reading materials. With much meaningless, repetitious busy-work and drill replaced by more modern, more effective methods, a greater variety of learning materials is a must. Attention to individual differences demands a broader curriculum, and with this comes increased school cost. If high school English classes are restricted in their assigned reading to the study of the older "classics," the school can buy thirty copies of *Silas Marner,* for example, and use them over and over; but if reading instruction for adolescents is to be made more meaningful, with reading both for pleasure and profit, constant additions must be made to the library holdings to keep them up to date.

New Programs and Services

And the public continually asks that the schools perform new educational tasks that cost more money. Parents of high-school-age youth want their sons and daughters to have driver education; it costs money. Society increasingly expects the schools to provide vocational training; this means more office machines, more bench saws, the latest kitchen appliances in the home economics room, and a new shop building for the boys taking vocational agriculture.

Other school services are constantly being added or expanded. The parents want a school lunch program, adequate health services, an expanded program of educational and vocational testing and guidance; there's another item or so in the budget. And very few parents will long remain satisfied with a staff of teachers scraped from the bottom of the barrel; if the salary schedule is so low that the local schools can hire and retain only those teachers who can't get jobs elsewhere, it will not be long before some of the parents and other community leaders will demand that the salaries be raised so that *their* school can have good, well-trained teachers too.

The extracurricular activities in most schools take up a substantial, but not necessarily excessive, portion of the budget, and there will be occasional demands from the public that these extras be cut out. But when it comes to cutting out something specific, like band or football or the school annual, a majority of the parents will rise up in arms against such heresy. The school administrator who proposes "cutting" one of the popular student activities may well succeed only in cutting his own professional throat.

Can We Afford the Cost?

Why does education cost so much? The answer, you see, is basically threefold: seam-splitting enrollments, higher prices for everything, and a constantly expanding educational program. School costs in the United States are expected to increase by at least $1 billion a year in the next decade; in this period we will spend more for our public schools than we have spent in the past 100 years!

Can we afford these high costs for education? There is no real reason to believe we cannot. At the present the people of the United States spend $18.1 billion for education, but this is only about 3.7 per cent of the total national income—less, percentagewise, than we spent in depression years. We, the American people, spend far more for minor pleasures and luxuries than we spend for our schools. The American people can well afford to pay for as much education as they really want.

THREE: TOPICS FOR STUDY, REPORT, AND DISCUSSION

1. Secure from the superintendent of the school system with which you are best acquainted, or from some other source suggested by your

instructor, a copy of the annual school budget. Try to determine the following:
   a) How much income does the school have?
   b) Where does the money come from?
   c) What percentage of the income is from local, county, state, and national sources?
   d) What percentage of the income is spent for actual instructional purposes?
   e) What are the "frills" that might be cut out of the budget?
2. With your instructor's permission (and help), ask some superintendent of schools in the area to explain to the class just how a district goes about floating a bond issue to build a new building.
3. From a county (or city) assessor's office in your home school district (or other source suggested by your instructor) secure a copy of the "abstract of levies" which gives the total tax levy for education and all other governmental purposes in the county. What is the total valuation of the school district? How much school tax is levied ("mill levy")? What relationship do school taxes bear to the total tax burden?
4. With other members of the class, prepare a panel discussion on the pros and cons of federal financial aid to education.

THREE: BIBLIOGRAPHY

Benson, Charles S., *The Economics of Public Education*. Boston: Houghton Mifflin Co., 1961. Far too comprehensive for the beginner in the field, but well worth sampling for a few insights into the magnitude and complexity of our system of financing public education.

Committee on Educational Finance, *What Everyone Should Know About Financing Our Schools*. Washington, D. C.: National Education Association, 1960. An extremely useful and understandable pamphlet prepared for lay distribution. Excellent charts and graphs picture some of the salient financial facts about our schools.

National Citizens Committee for the Public Schools, *How Do We Pay for Our Schools?* New York: National Citizens Committee for the Public Schools, 1954. One of a series of working guides for local citizens' committees concerned with school problems. Interesting, informal, nontechnical discussion of present and projected means for solving financial problems of the schools at the local level. Excellent checklists to be used in evaluating a local financial situation.

Special Project on School Finance, National Education Association of the United States, *Financing the Public Schools, 1960-1970*. Washington, D. C.: U.S.A., 1962. Rather technical, highly factual, but most interesting report and projection of the school problem in the current decade.

See also references at the close of Chapter Two. Most of the references cited there include discussions not only of school organization and control, but of school finance as well.

Biology laboratory. *Does the American public expect that secondary school biology will produce biologists, or what is the aim?*

South Mountain High School,
Phoenix, Arizona

Sallie Cone Elementary School,
Conway, Arkansas

Spanish class. *Why is there fundamental disagreement in our society about the necessity of foreign language study in the elementary grades?*

CHAPTER FOUR

The PTA meeting is drawing to a close when the discussion of new playground facilities is suddenly brought back to life by Mrs. Wilson, who has two children in the lower grades. "Now don't misunderstand me, Mr. Billings," she says to the elementary school principal who is leading the discussion, "I surely want our children to have adequate playground equipment, but it seems to me that perhaps they spend too much time on the playground now. At least, it seems that they aren't spending as much time as they ought to on their fundamentals—you know: reading and spelling and the multiplication tables."

Thus, with mild criticism, one mother speaks out to give her view of what she expects the school to do. A businessman asks his neighbor at the weekly luncheon-club meeting if he doesn't think that the schools ought to spend more time teaching about the advantages of the American system of free enterprise, and not so much about foreign "isms." A minister suggests from his pulpit that the schools should give more attention to moral and spiritual values. The Americanism committee of the local Legion post passes a resolution demanding that the schools teach more about the history of our own country and play down the importance of the United Nations. The

WHAT OUR SOCIETY EXPECTS OF ITS SCHOOLS

superintendent of schools listens attentively while a group of parents protests the dropping of Latin from the curriculum; tomorrow he will listen to another group of parents petitioning for more vocational subjects, not only in high school but down in the junior high, too.

The Cultural Bases of Educational Aims

Diversity of Opinion Inevitable

Such a diversity of public interests and expectations is a healthy influence on our American school system, and a sign of health within the system itself. For any good school system is an expression of the needs and desires of the society it serves; only as the members of that society feel free to say what they expect from their schools can the schools continue to be an expression of the popular will. Of course, there are obvious difficulties with this system of letting the general public decide what they want from their schools. Some individuals or groups are more outspoken than others, and what appears to be the "voice of the people" turns out to be nothing more than the clamor of a few; this results in undue educational influence by pressure groups. Moreover, the general public—the society which determines what its schools will be like—may often make educational mistakes; they may want something which is not educationally sound. Still, the American system of basing the work of the schools on the expectations and hopes of the public seems sounder than any system of centralized governmental control.

Expectations Have Changed with the Culture

The American people have always expected great things from their schools. Precisely *what* they have hoped the schools could do has changed from time to time, but the hopes have been high hopes —higher than the realizations. For faith in the power of education is part of the great American dream; good education is the key to our country's greatness. It would be naïve, of course, to maintain that the American people have always had an adequate grasp of what a really good educational system would be like; the ideas of education for all American youth, adequate support for schools, and other present-day educational goals were slow in developing in the public mind. But from the earliest days of our country's development, the American people have placed great faith in their schools.

Even the Old Deluder Satan, with all the infernal power he commanded, was no match for the strength of education—so ran the reasoning of the Massachusetts lawmakers in 1647 (see p. 7 above). Considering how strongly the Puritan legislators believed in the personal might of Satan, that early law was no small tribute to their belief in the efficacy of public education, even on so small a scale as this early legislation suggested. Later, in the passage of the Northwest Ordinance, the American people again affirmed their faith in education as being *necessary* to good government.

Even in those early days, however, there was considerable debate about precisely what education should attempt to do, what the schools should try to teach. Benjamin Franklin, in his outline of a proposal for an academy in Philadelphia in 1749, sensed the difficulty of getting everyone to agree on what they should expect this new school to teach, even though the faith in the power of education was generally accepted. His "Proposals Relating to the Education of Youth in Pennsylvania" read in part:

> The good Education of Youth has been esteemed by wise Men in all Ages, as the surest Foundation of the Happiness both of private Families and of Commonwealths. Almost all governments have therefore made it a principal Object of their Attention, to establish and endow with proper Revenues, such Seminaries of Learning, as might supply the succeeding Age with Men qualified to serve the Public, with Honour to themselves, and to their Country.[1]

After suggesting specific steps to be taken in establishing the Academy, Franklin tackled the problem of curriculum:

> As to their Studies, it would be well if they could be taught *everything* that is useful, and *everything* that is ornamental; But Art is long, and their Time is short. It is therefore propos'd that they learn those Things that are likely to be most useful and most ornamental. Regard being had to the several Professions for which they are intended.[2]

Franklin was expressing in this proposal a much more liberal view of education than was commonly held by the people of his time, but he was also giving voice to the opinion that was growing in

---

[1] For the full text, see Edgar W. Knight and Clifton L. Hall, *Readings in American Educational History* (New York: Appleton-Century-Crofts, Inc., 1951), pp. 74 ff. Reprinted by permission.
[2] *Ibid.*, pp. 76 f. Reprinted by permission.

popular acceptance: the schools were the "surest foundation" of the nation's welfare.

Thomas Jefferson, likewise, in his bill "For the More General Diffusion of Knowledge," introduced into the Legislature of Virginia in 1779, thirty years after Franklin's proposal, was far ahead of the popular belief in his specific proposals for universal education. Jefferson did not believe that everybody should have an unlimited right to as much education as he wanted; he proposed only that the state guarantee that everyone should have the opportunity for as much education as would be profitable to him *and society*. Thus, he proposed a broad-based "pyramid" system of public schools, with all children being provided a minimum schooling in the basic fundamentals; a limited number of the more successful of these students would be chosen for enrollment in the secondary schools; and only the most able of those completing this secondary level would be eligible for state-subsidized higher education. Jefferson's bill for a state supported educational system may seem quite limited in its outlook by today's standards, but he spoke for the growing faith of the American people in the power of education when he wrote in the preamble to this bill:

> Whereas it appeareth that however certain forms of government are better calculated than others to protect individuals in the free exercise of their natural rights, and are at the same time themselves better guarded against degeneracy, yet experience hath shewn that even under the best forms those intrusted with power have, in time and by slow operations, perverted it into tyranny; and it is believed that the most effectual means of preventing this would be to illuminate, as far as practicable, the minds of the people at large. . . .[3]

Jefferson's proposal for a "universal" educational system in Virginia was too radical for his time, and the law was never passed. But the law is still significant, not only as an early attempt to extend education to everyone "as far as practicable," but as an expression of the historic American faith that the very preservation of our democratic system from overthrow by tyrannical forces was dependent upon the illumination of the minds of the "people at large"—public education.

Long before the beginnings of our own American educational system, other people in other cultures and national settings had

[3] *Ibid.*, pp. 299 f. Reprinted by permission.

expressed, or had heard expressed by their leaders, great faith in the power of education. "Train up a child in the way he should go," said the Hebraic law, "and when he is old he will not depart from it." In the Middle Ages (1404), the Italian scholar Vergerius wrote:

> We call those studies liberal which are worthy of a free man; those studies by which we attain and practice virtue and wisdom; that education which calls forth, trains, and develops those highest gifts of body and mind which ennoble men and which are rightly judged to rank next in dignity to virtue only, for to a vulgar temper gain and pleasure are the one aim of existence, to a lofty nature, moral worth and fame.[4]

Of course, Vergerius was proposing a plan for the liberal education of only the wellborn and well-to-do, but the quotation shows how strongly he depended on education to make man what he ought to be. Similarly, John Locke (1632-1704), the noted English scholar and educational theorist, was interested largely in the education of the "gentleman," not the common man, but he expressed the growing belief in the efficacy of education when he wrote that men are, at least nine parts out of ten, formed by education rather than heredity.[5] Again, the English poet John Milton (1608-1674)—like the others mentioned, more interested in the education of the upper classes than in popular education—had expressed great faith in the power of education when he said, "I call, therefore, a complete and generous education, that which fits a man to perform justly, skillfully, and magnanimously all the offices, both private and public, of peace and war." [6]

Direct Antecedents of Present-Day Aims

The attempt to formulate the aims of education—or, put more directly, what we can expect education to do—has gone on for centuries, and the task will never be complete. What American society presently expects of its educational system, what it expects its schools

[4] Quoted in H. G. Good, *A History of Western Education* (New York: The Macmillan Co., 1949), p. 126. Reprinted by permission.
[5] *Ibid.,* p. 184. Reprinted by permission.
[6] Quoted in Frederick Eby, *The Development of Modern Education* (New York: Prentice-Hall, Inc., 1952). Second ed., pp. 209 f.

to do, is an indirect outgrowth of historical views, of cultural changes, and social forces; but two direct statements of educational aims, formulated within the last few decades, have considerably influenced our collective thinking.

One of these statements was found in Herbert Spencer's essay, "What Knowledge Is of Most Worth?" As an English scientist, Spencer (1820-1903) was greatly interested in the Darwinian concept of survival of the fittest. He believed that education must be judged by how well it would aid a society to survive, and arranged in order of importance these functions of education in society: "(1) those activities which directly minister to self-perservation; (2) those activities which, by securing the necessities of life, indirectly minister to self-preservation; (3) those activities which have for their end the rearing and discipline of offspring; (4) those activities which are involved in the maintenance of proper social and political relations; (5) those miscellaneous activities which fill up the leisure part of life, devoted to the gratification of the tastes and feelings." [7]

In the early years of this century, a committee of American educators, directly influenced by Spencer's listing of educational aims, published a set of principles for American education which have come to be known as the "Seven Cardinal Principles." They suggested that what the American people expect the secondary schools to teach should be this: (1) command of the fundamental processes, (2) health, (3) worthy home membership, (4) vocational efficiency, (5) civic participation, (6) worthy use of leisure time, (7) and ethical character.[8]

The difficulty with any lists of educational aims, objectives, or purposes such as those given above is twofold. First, they seem vague and general when we try to translate them into actual school practice. Second, they represent the deliberations and opinions of educational specialists, rather than the free and direct expression of the public who support our schools and send their children there to be educated. Perhaps we can list and discuss the present popularly accepted aims of education more meaningfully in the sections which follow.

[7] Quoted in John Brubacher, *A History of the Problems of Education* (New York: McGraw-Hill Book Co., Inc., 1947), p. 294. Reprinted by permission.
[8] National Education Association, Commission on the Reorganization of Secondary Education, *The Cardinal Principles of Secondary Education, U.S. Bureau of Education Bulletin 35,* 1918.

What the American Public Expects from Its Schools Today

Basis for Disagreements

There are three major problems, and several minor ones, in attempting to say just what the American people expect their schools to do. First, the current public expectations are often *paradoxical;* the public often wants two conflicting goals to be realized at the same time. Second, some of the educational expectations seem entirely *visionary;* they are long-range dreams rather than actual accomplishments. Third, many of these educational expectations are *disputed.* Some want this, some that; there seems to be no general agreement; often there is sharp and violent disagreement about what ought to go on in the schools.

The expectations of what our schools should do are further complicated by the scope of our educational ideals: we believe that everybody, regardless of his background, intelligence, social development, or general ability should be entitled to go to school and "get something out of" his education. Moreover, it is a common popular belief that everyone should be entitled to as *much* formal education as he wants.

Basic Agreements

Nevertheless, in spite of these complicating factors, there appear to be a number of things that the American people believe the schools should and must give to every child in the country. It is quite unanimously believed that the schools can reasonably be expected to:

1. teach basic skills—the "three R's";
2. impart basic knowledge—for example, of history, geography, literature;
3. teach civic competence—how to live in a democracy;
4. teach vocational competence—how to make a living;
5. offer unlimited educational horizons—no lack of opportunity to attend or continue in the "common schools" because of social class or economic condition;
6. inculcate a deep sense of moral values;
7. give training in social development—how to get along with people; and
8. afford protection of physical and mental health.

This list could certainly be shortened, lengthened, revised, or disputed. It is given here in this form only to get before us at least a working answer to the question, "What does America expect of its schools?" Now, let us look at each of these educational expectations in a little more detail. We will not attempt to say, at this point, whether the schools are doing all of the things that are expected of them, much less whether they are doing a good job in all of these areas. At the moment we are concerned with the real meaning of each of these educational aims and with some of the implications and complications found in them.

The three R's. Even though it is generally agreed that "reading and 'riting and 'rithmetic" are only a part of the general area of skills that the school must teach, the old phrase is still commonly used to describe the "fundamentals." Fortunately, there is no basic disagreement in American education on this point: these skills are necessary in our modern society. But there is much disagreement about whether the school today is actually doing a good job in teaching the fundamentals, or whether they are being neglected for other educational and social activities. We shall return to this particular aspect of the problem in later chapters; right now our task is to see just what kind of basic skills the American public thinks should be taught in its schools, and how, when, and to whom.

Reading, for example, is essential; only a literate populace can be trusted with the responsibilities of democracy. Reading contributes greatly not only to personal enjoyment but to vocational efficiency and economic and social progress. Many kinds of reading should be taught at the various levels—elementary, junior high school, secondary. Reading for information, reading for recreation, "skimming," and reading of pictures, maps, graphs, and movies—these are but a few of the many kinds of reading skills needed. Not all children are ready to read at the same time; there is as much difference in development of "reading readiness" as there is in development of readiness to walk, talk, or make adequate social adjustments. Furthermore, individual differences in intelligence and aptitude mean that some children will learn to read very readily and will read widely all through their lives; others will just barely learn to read very simple material, very slowly; and others may never learn to read at all. Moreover, newer methods of teaching reading have wholly or partially outmoded the methods by which we ourselves were taught; there are a variety of "successful" methods of teaching reading, and these will change as more experience and more evidence justify the superiority of the newly-developed methods. Teaching of reading goes on through all the years of school, even through college; the elementary teachers are not alone concerned—every teacher is a teacher of reading.

We need not continue the discussion of reading here, but every prospective teacher needs to know a great deal about this important, perplexing, and rewarding part of education. Despite all of the problems that reading entails, it is obvious that the American public rightly expects that every child who is capable of reading at all will be taught to develop that capacity to the utmost.

And so with arithmetic. Learning to use numbers effectively is a very complex skill, like learning to read, but every normal adult has some need, in many cases a very considerable need, for usable arithmetic skill. Again, the timing, the techniques, the content of arithmetic in elementary school or high school will vary with the needs of the children, the desires of the parents, and the competencies of the teacher. The modern school is more likely to use a problem-solving approach in arithmetic, rather than relying as heavily as earlier schools did on sheer repetition or rote memory. The modern high school is quite likely to offer general math or business arithmetic instead of, or in addition to, more algebra and geometry courses, and to add a college-level course for election by the more able and ambitious students. There are all sorts of possible variations, but still arithmetic is desired by the public; arithmetic is necessary; arithmetic will be taught.

Similarly, writing. Need for writing competence is a highly individual matter, but our verbalistic culture rightly places a high value on this skill for the ordinary citizen. Today, the modern school is likely to teach children first to print (manuscript writing) and later to write "connected" longhand (cursive writing); this change has disturbed some parents, but writing is definitely in the curriculum. In fact, instead of being taught as a separate subject, emphasized for a few minutes a day, writing is now a part of every subject; written expression is a necessary and legitimate part of almost all formal learning.

Knowledge. As with the three R's, there is no fundamental disagreement about the necessity of the school's teaching facts and information. There is—and probably this is a healthy situation— great disagreement about what information and what facts are really necessary and useful. Should the child's mind be considered a sort of storehouse, where the miscellaneous or related facts of geography, history, literature, and science are safely put away for later use? Or should knowledge be acquired only when it is needed in the solution of a problem or for the understanding of some next step in learning? This latter plan would eliminate from the curriculum much of the traditional "information" that the public school at every level has long been teaching. These and similar questions are beyond the scope of this section to explore and answer; remember, though, that they are serious and vital questions which teachers will be called upon to answer—if not directly, at least by implication—in their everyday teaching.

Civic competence.   This goal is one of the most universally accepted of all of the educational goals of the American school system. It is generally agreed that the very political and social system that makes American schools possible is dependent for its success upon a thoroughly alert and competent citizenry. There is even a great deal of agreement about the *content* of the materials for teaching civic competence—a knowledge and understanding of American history, American social, political and economic institutions, and whatever materials and teaching methods are needed to produce a body of citizens devoted to our democratic heritage. But here is the difficulty: Can we get this sense of "heritage" and "devotion" without developing at the same time a rampant nationalism, a blind acceptance of the mistakes of the past, and a placid willingness to "follow the leader"—so long as he tells us that *his* way is "true Americanism"?

Since democratic living is so obviously the one aim of the schools that is most closely related to our national life, the problem needs further exploration. Not just the *content* or the *method* of education for civic competence, but the organization and "spirit" of the school are involved. The school must be so designed and administered that the whole educational experience of the child will be conducive to democratic thinking and democratic living. That is not to say that each public school room can be a miniature democracy in every respect; we do not yet have the skill or the knowledge to operate our schools that way. It does mean that in each classroom we must try to develop that sense and practice of individual responsibility, coupled with the sense and practice of *social* responsibility, which is the best possible background for continued democratic living when children and youth later assume the responsibilities of adult citizenship.

For example, if the ordinary problems discussed in the classroom, even in the lower grades, are to have any real meaning and vitality, it is quite possible that they will include some controversial issues. Geography, history, science, and civics all involve basic social questions about which there is controversy—disagreement as to right and wrong, means and ends. It is not the job of the school to stir up controversy; the disagreements are already implicit in any honest facing of the questions that are legitimately studied in the classroom. Commitment to democratic living involves teaching children of any age or level of maturity to look at problems objectively, to get the facts, to assess the reliability of "authoritative" sources, to analyze propaganda, to respect differences of opinion, and to make judgments or to suspend judgment, as the case may require.

In all of these matters, the teacher's own civic competence is being tested. But not the teacher alone; the entire school system is on trial. Let's look at any school—pick one you are familiar with and answer these questions—to see whether the school itself is a good example of democracy in action.

Is the social life of the school democractic, or is it dominated wholly by the teachers and administrators, or run by small, selfish, snobbish cliques? Are the students "grouped" for class work according to abilities in such a way as to make some of the students feel personally and socially inferior? Are the college-bound students made to feel superior to those taking a vocational curriculum? Are racial and religious bigotries tolerated as being inevitable, or does the school have a definite program for improving inter-group feelings? Is the grading system so highly competitive that many children are made to feel like failures, even when they are doing their best, and others given a false sense of pride in achievement that does not represent their best work? All of these facets of school life, reflecting as they do the basic policies and practices of the school system, are indicative of how well the school is serving as a laboratory of democratic living.

Vocational competence. It is in our high schools that the problem of preparing youth to "make a living" seems most acute, inasmuch as for hundreds of thousands of young people secondary education is their last formal training prior to the time they graduate or drop out of school and go out to get a job. Actually, many vocational choices are already made during the junior high school years, and the attitudes and habits that are responsible for the degree of success of vocational adjustment are being formed throughout the child's entire school career.

The American public does not generally expect that the school will provide the specific technical skills most students will need in their full-time jobs, although the vocational curriculum is growing in many of our high schools. But the public that supports the schools does believe that the school must start each student on the road to better vocational competence by developing in him the work habits, the command of the fundamental processes (3 R's), and such actual experience with vocations as will enable him to make a wise and realistic vocational choice and a satisfying vocational adjustment. At the same time, the American public does not seem willing to abandon or alter extensively the college-preparatory curriculum which still makes up the bulk of the offerings of many high schools, especially the smaller ones.

Since one of the vocations which will attract nearly all of the graduates of the public schools is that of marriage, increasingly the school is being urged by the supporting public to give more attention to preparation for marriage and family life. Such courses, commonly miscalled by a name that represents only one facet of their content—"sex education"—are admitted only reluctantly to the curriculum of many schools, but the public expectation that the school will "do something about" the problem is increasingly evident.

Unlimited educational horizons. The people of the United States today have pretty thoroughly repudiated their earlier educational practice, imported directly from England and Europe by our earliest settlers, of a "dual" educational system. Instead, we have come to insist on the "single ladder" system as the right one for this country. By this we mean that there is no place in our concept of democracy for two educational systems, one for the rich or wellborn, and one for the less fortunate; one for the classes and one for the masses.

This dual system is quite common, even today, in other countries. France has had, for many generations, such a dual system; Germany has had throughout most of its history two kinds of education: the *volkschule* (or folk school), which extended only up through about ten grades, designed as a terminal school for the masses, and a *vorschule* (or preparatory school), designed for children of the upper classes and leading ultimately to the colleges and universities. Once started in the "wrong" branch of the system—and initial enrollment was determined largely by economic and social status—it was exceedingly difficult to transfer to the other branch leading to the higher institutions. In England, even though extensive modifications of the educational system have been made in recent years, there are still in actual practice two school systems, one terminating with a year or two of secondary or technical education after the elementary school is completed, and one which leads on up to university studies. Again, the student tends to remain in the system in which he started—one might almost say, the educational system into which he was born.

But the American schools have long operated on the principle of a *common* school, an elementary and secondary ladder open to all students, regardless of economic or social status, a ladder up which one may climb as far as his educational desires will carry him. Of course, economic and social status does play a part in determining how far the individual student can go with his education, and what schools he will actually attend, but the people of the United States are generally agreed that this discrimination simply represents an unsolved problem which can ultimately be worked out; it is not intended that we should have separate school systems for the classes and the masses.

This idea of universal education, open to all American youth and free to all (at least through high school and increasingly through junior college), has posed some real problems for American education. If just everybody is supposed to finish high school and nearly anybody to have an opportunity to attend college, how can cherished (though perhaps unrealistic) educational standards be maintained? The public will quite willingly bear the cost of high school education for everyone, but can the public purse afford to pay for college for anyone who wants to go? And if the traditional high school and college courses do not meet the needs of all students, shall we overhaul the curriculum? These remain unanswered questions, as yet. All we can be sure of is that the American people still expect the schools, in one way or another, to provide almost unlimited educational opportunities.

Moral and spiritual values. No greater instance of the faith the American people have in their schools can be found than is evidenced by the plea often heard today, "Why can't the schools *do* something about juvenile delinquency?" Writers in books and magazines, newspaper editors, and public speakers are prone to point out that juvenile delinquency, in all of its many forms, is a shocking, costly, and vexatious social problem. Without specifically blaming the school for what it may have done wrong or simply left undone in combatting delinquency, these spokesmen for the American public still seem to be sure that the schools *could* do something constructive if they really tried.

The people who support and control the public school system expect the schools to help "teach the kids some manners," teach them basic American virtues like industry, honesty, and thrift, and teach them to be good sports and to "play fair." Seldom, if ever, is the entire job of moral education consigned bodily to the schools; even the severest critics agree that the home and the church play an important part. The schools, however, are supposed and expected to do something about the manners and morals of the present generation, and do it now!

To complicate matters, the schools are supposed to create a fine sense of moral and spiritual values without calling on any religious faith or religious sanctions to undergird that morality, for by law and tradition the public school cannot teach religion.

The public school, then, in keeping with the spirit of this expectation of what the schools should be doing, tries in many ways to inculcate moral and spiritual values in the students without any hint of religious dogmatism or sectarian bias. The modern school encourages the development of morality by giving the student the opportunity to work out an acceptable and lasting set of social and moral values; to make many choices based on this value-system; to make his own decisions and abide by the consequences. This is moral training at its highest. The good school tries to exemplify the most meaningful of moral values by providing many opportunities for *social* interplay, and *social* development, at the same time prizing the *individual* as worthy in his own right. The guidance program now found in all really good schools (whether operated informally or officially designated as a "program"), with its attention to individual needs and individual differences *in a social context,* is part of the training in moral development. And the individual teacher's respect and affection for all boys and girls, even the least of them, can have moral and spiritual meaning.

Social development.   Much of what has just been said about moral and spiritual development could well be put under this heading. For when the American people say that they expect the school to provide for good *social* development, they are often thinking of this development in at least partially *moral* terms. But more plainly yet, they want children and youth to learn the answer to one of life's most important and challenging problems—how to get along with others.

Since democracy as a way of life relies on the ability of people of all different beliefs, backgrounds, and abilities to work harmoniously and effectively together, it is no wonder that education in a democracy is so vitally concerned with the question of the social development of the children it serves. But social development is not just "getting along"; it is a deeply significant problem of adjustment to both self and society, of achieving a balance between freedom and security.

Social development also includes the aim that was listed above in the Seven Cardinal Principles as "worthy use of leisure time." The school today is expected by most people to help children and youth learn to play together as well as work together, and yet at the same time to learn how to depend on their own resources—interests, hobbies, intellectual pursuits, or whatever—to use profitably the leisure time with which our modern technology has so generously provided them.

Physical and mental health. The American public expects its schools to keep school children in good health, physical and mental. Even more than that, really; the public school is expected not only to maintain the children's health, but to correct as many existing health deficiencies as possible. To that end the school operates publicly supported health services, including periodic general physical examinations, free inoculations and vaccinations, examinations of teeth, eyesight, and hearing, and provision for emergency nursing and infirmary facilities at school.

In addition, many schools now provide healthful lunches at low cost, often through the federally subsidized "hot lunch" program. Why, ask some critics of modern education, should the school go into the business of running a restaurant? Why not let the kids eat at home or downtown at a café, drugstore, or hamburger stand? Many teachers and administrators who have been involved in the fuss and bother of operating a school lunch program may sometimes be very privately inclined to agree with these critics. But the answer is clear. The school is involved in "feeding the kids" because the school lunch program helps to attain educational and social goals which have been set by public acceptance. All American children have a right to good nutrition, and no child is to be denied this right just because he happens to ride the school bus, or to come from a family that knows or cares little about the importance of good nutrition to good health and good learning, or is not able to afford an adequate diet.

There are critics who decry this concern of the school with the private eating habits of children as a step toward state control of family life, a step toward socialism, an un-American and subversive tendency. But the idea that the school is properly concerned with the total health of the child is not new, not one to be attributed to "newfangled progressive education." As early as the latter part of the seventeenth century, one of the most conservative of English educational writers, John Locke, had advocated somewhat grudgingly a meager school lunch program for "pauper children" in the "working schools" which he proposed. For, he said:

> What they have at home from their parents is seldom more than bread and water, and that, many of them, very scantily too. If therefore care be taken that they have each of them their bellyfull of bread daily at school, they will be in no danger of famishing, but, on the contrary, they will be healthier and stronger than those who are bred otherwise. Nor will this practice cost the overseers any trouble; for a baker may be agreed with to furnish and bring into the school house every day the allowance of bread necessary for all the scholars that are there. And to this may be added, also, without any trouble, in cold weather, if it be thought needful, a little warm water-gruel; for the same fire that warms the room may be made to boil a pot of it.[9]

Some concern for the total health of the child, therefore, is an old idea, but one which American schools today—at the insistence of the American public—are but slowly adopting as a common practice. Concern for the physical welfare of the students is found also in increased effort being made to make schoolrooms comfortable, sanitary, well-lighted and well-ventilated, and to provide well-fitting individual desks for each child.

The American public school has also been given the responsibility of furthering the mental health of school children. A good environment for learning includes provision for a healthy emotional setting. This need has long been recognized by competent educators. In the first part of the fifteenth century the Italian educator Vittorino da Feltra had established a school he called "La Casa Giocosa," or the Pleasant House, in the belief that children would learn best in a

---

[9] Quoted in Robert Ulich, *History of Educational Thought* (New York: American Book Co., 1950), p. 205.

happy and emotionally secure environment. A couple of centuries later, in 1628, the great teacher Comenius proposed that:

> The school itself should be a pleasant place, and attractive to the eye both within and without. Within, the room should be bright and clean, its walls ornamented with pictures, portraits of celebrated men, geographical maps, historical plans, or other ornaments. Without, there should be an open place to walk and play in, for this is absolutely necessary for children, as we shall show later, and there should also be a garden attached, into which the scholars may be allowed to go from time to time and where they may feast their eyes on trees, flowers, and plants. If this be done, boys will in all probability, go to school with as much pleasure as to fairs. . . .[10]

These earlier ideas of the school as a pleasant, happy place were in their time considered radical; today, there is almost universal acceptance of the belief that children and youth learn best in a setting that is both physically and emotionally satisfying and secure.

Conflicting Educational Beliefs

In the paragraphs above we have outlined briefly the common beliefs that the members of our democratic society have about what the public school ought to do. But it is obvious to anyone who has attended the public schools, who has observed them in action, and who has listened to or read discussions about our schools, that there is no complete agreement on the tasks of the school or the aims of education. It would be foolish and presumptuous to try to reconcile, just for the sake of simplification, these divergent beliefs, these different philosophies. We must recognize that perfectly intelligent, well-informed, and interested citizens will not always be in agreement about what is expected from the schools.

Conflicting philosophies of education—honest differences of opinion —involve matters extremely complex and technical, though also exceedingly interesting, and we could not do complete justice to them here. But a brief description of some of these different philosophies will help make clear why we find, sometimes, such sharp disagreement about what the schools *ought* to be doing.

One writer [11] has very helpfully classified the different philoso-

---

[10] Quoted in Good, *op. cit.,* p. 194. Reprinted by permission.
[11] Theodore Brameld, *Patterns of Educational Philosophy* (Yonkers-on-Hudson: World Book Co., 1950), *passim.*

phies of education current in America under the four headings often used to describe shades of political beliefs: the *regressive* position, the *conservative,* the *liberal,* and the *radical.* Notice that these terms do not in themselves imply any value-judgment about the philosophies; there is no "name-calling" or criticism intended in the description as used here. There is nothing morally bad about being a regressive, or spiritually ennobling in being a liberal. The terms, which are already familiar to us in their political usage, are merely convenient and reasonably accurate labels for the four major positions that are commonly found in educational thinking.

Regressive

The first, the regressive belief, is expressed by those who would like to see the schools react positively against modern social and educational trends, or go back to a past era or former culture-pattern for their goals and their educational program. Some educational thinkers who hold to this belief suggest that the schools would do well to go back to the political, social and religious theories and practices of the Medieval period or even of Greek civilization. Serious proponents of this regressive view are relatively few, and their concern is largely with higher education, rather than with the high school or elementary school. Those who adhere to this belief are convinced that the most fundamental truths are unchanging or perennial—hence the name "perennialist" is often applied to those holding this philosophy.

Conservative

The next, the conservative position, embodies perhaps the most widespread and popular beliefs about education. The conservative in education wants a school system which conserves or holds on to an already established, thoroughly tested set of social and educational values. He believes that our present social structure and economic system is quite satisfactory; our educational system, its practices and its aims, has likewise "stood the test of time." He wants to keep things as they have been, to stress order and discipline and the "essentials" in education. This group, thus, often label themselves "essentialists" in educational philosophy.

Liberal

Somewhat more forward looking than the conservative thinker, but by no means a radical, is the educational liberal. This view is perhaps best represented by the "progressive" in education. He wants to try new techniques and new aims, to experiment freely, to get new experiences. He has little patience with clutching at anything just because it has been satisfactory in the past, because the past is not the same as today. He does not believe that anything—in education, in politics, in economics, or in morals—can be considered to be definitely established, or already proved; the only test of truth is not "authority," but practicability and human satisfaction. If it "works," it is true; if it doesn't "work," it isn't true. He wants the school to keep right up to the minute, reflect quickly every change in the social order, and occasionally do a little discreet pushing to make society move along a little faster in "liberal" directions.

Radical

The fourth of the educational philosophies, the radical, is relatively new, having been developed only in the last two or three decades; it represents the firm belief of only a relatively small group of educators. The literal meaning of the word "radical" is "one who wants to *uproot*." The educational radical is sure that the very roots of our society and our educational system are decayed; he wants to tear them up and start over again. He is dissatisfied with our economic system, our moral traditions, and with the way our political system actually works—though he is a firm believer in democracy if it can be established on a new social and economic basis. His dissatisfaction with education and our school system is not so much for what it has done, but for what it hasn't. It is too complacent, too easily satisfied, not aggressive enough. The philosophic radical in education wants to use the school system to bring about immediate and revolutionary change in our way of life—to "reconstruct the social order," as he would say. Hence the label "reconstructionism," which he has given to his educational philosophy.

Even the amateur in the field of educational philosophy can at once see that these distinctions among the various theories of education are somewhat oversimplified here; many important, even basic, questions are not covered at all. What beliefs has each of these philosophies about the nature and meaning of God, of man, of human society? What does each believe about the real nature of truth—is it absolute, is it relative, can it be found out, how do we know truth when we see it? Is it possible to accept parts of two or more of these philosophies, or are the beliefs mutually exclusive? What about those people—educators and laymen alike—who don't seem to have any formal philosophy of education, any systematic pattern of beliefs? Will just plain "horse sense" do as well?

These questions cannot be answered adequately here, but the thorough study of educational philosophy is a challenging and rewarding pursuit for anyone who is seriously interested in American education. Our purpose here is to understand our schools, what is expected of them and what they are trying to do, without getting ourselves too deeply involved in philosophical discussion and philosophical terminology.

That purpose is best served by noting this: in spite of sharp and significant differences in the philosophies of education, a vast majority of the people of our country expect that our schools will do the things indicated earlier in this chapter—teach basic skills and impart knowledge; provide each student with civic and vocational competence; offer unlimited educational horizons; impart a high sense of moral values; give training in social development; and promote physical and mental health. The American people have a tremendous faith in their schools, and to their schools they assign tremendous tasks.

FOUR: TOPICS FOR STUDY, REPORT, AND DISCUSSION

1. Read some current criticism of the American public schools. (You can doubtless find one such in some popular magazine if you scan through a few issues.) What does the writer of this criticism expect of the American schools?
2. Are the "basic fundamentals" of education the same as they were in your parents' time? Explain and be ready to defend your answer.
3. With your instructor's permission, ask some businessman who has no direct connection with the public school system to talk to the class on what a businessman expects of the schools. Analyze what he says in the light of what society as a whole expects of its schools.
4. Which of the four general beliefs about education described in the latter part of this chapter most nearly expresses your own belief? Can you give a good, sound, logical justification for holding this particular belief?
5. With a full recognition that the list of the things our society expects of its schools, as given here, is by way of suggestion only, write out your own list of the things society wants our schools to do.

FOUR: BIBLIOGRAPHY

Cook, Lloyd Allen, and Elaine Forsyth Cook, *A Sociological Approach to Education,* 3d ed. New York: McGraw-Hill Book Co., Inc., 1960. The determination of educational aims according to community patterns is shown clearly in case studies of different communities (chaps. 3-7).

Gross, Carl H., Stanley P. Wronski, and John W. Hanson, *School and Society: Readings in the Social and Philosophical Foundations of Education.* Boston: D. C. Heath & Company, 1962. A comprehensive anthology of articles, often representing controversial and conflicting viewpoints, covering a wide range of ideas about the purposes and functions of American education.

Hughes, James Monroe, *Education in America.* Evanston, Ill.: Harper & Row, Publishers, 1960. Unit II shows clearly how contemporary American educational aims have been influenced by philosophical and social developments from previous historical eras.

NEA Research Division, "Ten Criticisms of Public Education," *Research Bulletin,* Vol. 35, No. 4 (December, 1957). Washington: National Education Association, 1957. Although this pamphlet is not recent, it contains one of the best available summaries of the conflicting arguments about educational aims in the American public schools.

President's Commission on National Goals, *Goals for Americans.* Englewood Cliffs, N. J.: Prentice-Hall, Inc., 1960. Although this book has as its concern the goals of education as only one facet of our national goals, it is well worth reading in its entirety to see how educational aims are related to large scale societal aims.

Scott, C. Winfield, Clyde M. Hill, and Hubert W. Burns, eds. *The Great Debate: Our Schools in Crisis.* Englewood Cliffs, N. J.: Prentice-Hall, Inc., 1959. A trenchant summary of the major issues which express the conflicting ideas about the functions of American education. Each of the positions espoused in the many selections reprinted represents a definite and controversial viewpoint.

Thomas, Lawrence G., Lucien B. Kinney, Arthur P. Coladarci, and Helen A. Fielstra, *Perspective on Teaching.* Englewood Cliffs, N. J.: Prentice-Hall, Inc., 1961. The determination of educational goals suitable for the "American way of life" is discussed perceptively in chaps. 10 and 11.

Wilson, Sloan, "Public Schools Are Better Than You Think," *Harper's Magazine,* Vol. 211, No. 1264 (September, 1955), 29-33. A penetrating analysis of what the American people expect of their schools and why they are so critical of them.

See also the bibliography for Chapter Fourteen, below, listing a number of books critical of American education.

PART TWO

THE WORK
OF THE SCHOOL

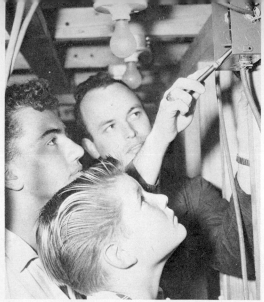

Electricity study unit. *What elements of a favorable learning environment are observable here?*

Mural project. *What basic human characteristics and needs are being recognized in such a school project as this?*

CHAPTER FIVE

Education Is for People

In the preceding chapters, we have emphasized the importance of our understanding the school as a *social force*. The school is a product of society, is controlled by society, is financed by society, has its aims determined by society. This is an important concept—the school as a social agency—but the daily life of the school and the daily work of the teacher cannot be satisfactorily described in such impersonal terms. Our schools are for *people;* the teacher works with *people*. Of course, the whole concern of public education is not just with people of school age; the school and the individual teacher work closely with the parents, too, with other adults like health officers and Boy Scout leaders who are working with children, and with other men and women in the community who are interested in the schools. Primarily, however, the work of the teacher is directly with the young folk who come daily to the classroom.

You may notice that we have used in this book a number of terms to identify those with whom the school works most closely—*students, pupils, children, boys and girls, youth*. It is very difficult to find a term that is wholly appropriate. We have tended to drop the

WORKING WITH
CHILDREN AND YOUTH

older term, "scholar," because it is both inaccurate and impersonal. "Student" has the same limitations. The coined expressions which have sometimes found usage in educational circles, "educand" and "pupil personnel," have a pseudoscientific, overly clinical sound. "Boys and girls" is often used because it describes quite accurately who these school folk are, but the compound term is cumbersome to repeat. "Children" is all right for those in the elementary grades, but "youth" is more appropriate for junior high and secondary levels. But whatever the term (and the terms are interchangeable in this discussion) we are always talking about people—not some educational statistic, not some impersonal "client," but real, live, important *people!*

Since the whole purpose of teaching is to help children and youth grow, develop, and learn, the importance of understanding these young folk cannot be overemphasized. It is the teacher's Number One Job; it is a long-term, even lifetime, professional responsibility and no brief chapter such as this can give more than a hint of all that is involved. Therefore, in preparing for teaching, you will need to study human growth and development, child psychology, adolescent psychology, mental hygiene, and the psychology of learning. More important, you will want to continue to study not only the formal subjects of psychology, but the children themselves throughout your teaching career.

We recognize, then, that this is but a brief introduction to the topic that is central to all understanding of education, but even though briefly considered, it is of supreme importance, for the child is the center of the school. Now, this does not mean that we have to adopt uncritically the term that became current during the heyday of progressive education, "the child-centered school." There are many teachers today who believe that this term, while it was originally useful in expressing an important point of view about education, has now become so overused and misunderstood that it really should be dropped from our educational vocabulary. To some teachers, the term came to mean that every activity of the entire educational program should be centered around the individual child, his momentary interests and his undirected "self-expression." The thoughtful educators and laymen came to believe that the term, however well intended, was resulting in an unwise orientation of the school program toward extreme individualism and away from the social needs of children and the needs of society. Some educators today have suggested that we should speak of the "society-centered" school to emphasize that the school is a *social* institution, set up and operated basically to meet the needs of society.

The debate over these terms continues in educational literature, but we can perhaps arrive at an acceptable concept for use here by suggesting that neither term—"child-centered" or "society-centered" —quite expresses what we really believe: that human personality is of supreme importance, more important than any institution or social agency, but that the worth of the individual is best developed and reaches its highest expression only in a social setting. The individual person is most important, that is, only as a member of a true community of other persons.

Some Basic Characteristics of Human Behavior

In popular terms, this subtopic might be called a discussion of "human nature" but this phrase is not really as descriptive as "human behavior." For whenever we think of human *nature* we think of something fixed, static, inherited, relatively unchangeable. Human *behavior* is a better term, for it suggests the human being in an active, dynamic pattern of doing, experiencing, living. And it is in this live framework of *behavior* in and out of school that we deal with children; education itself is a modification of behavior, and learning is the process by which we achieve specialized forms of behavior. Therefore, we as teachers need to know something about the basic principles that underlie all human behavior, especially that which is directly concerned with the schools. This is not the place to give a detailed outline of psychology, or to attempt to provide specific documentation for the ideas presented here, or to cite the many thoroughgoing scientific studies on which these conclusions are based. Rather, we need here to look briefly at some of the generally accepted principles of human behavior that have a direct bearing upon the educative process and upon the work of the teacher.

All Behavior Is Organismic

This statement means simply that a person—adult or school child —is a complete, unitary organism, not a chance combination of bits and pieces that can be separately understood or separately taught.

Rejection of older dualisms.   Much of the older psychology—from the time of the Greeks, down through the Middle Ages, and up until the beginning of the present century—was handicapped in its effort to understand and explain human behavior because of the persistent belief that man was explicable only in terms of separate parts or functions, unrelated and often working at cross purposes. Such "dualisms" are found in older educational writings which spoke of the "mind" and the "spirit" as separate entities, or the "body" and the "soul" as conflicting aspects of human nature. Today, most psychologists are convinced that the concept of the "wholeness" of the individual is more accurate than the earlier views.

"Faculty" psychology.   For example, it was common among educators up until the beginning of this century to think of the human mind as being made up of separate parts or faculties—like perception, memory, will, and reason—each existing in a separate part of the brain and each capable of being "trained" or disciplined without reference to any other. Specific school subjects were thought to be beneficial to certain special faculties of the mind—geometry was good for training the faculty of logic, Greek for developing the faculty of "form," and poetry for exercising the memory. Thus, school subjects were taught as tightly-compartmented areas, unrelated to each other or to real-life activities.

The mind, with its several faculties, was believed to be a complete entity in itself, wholly unrelated to the body; mental activity was thought to be of higher value than mere bodily activity because the latter was only an expression of the base, animal nature of man. Thus, in the older view, education was supposed to "train the mind," without any relation to the rest of the person who was being educated.[1] Any type of physical or vocational education was thought to be less worthy than pure "mental" training.

Organismic "wholeness."   Today, we often say somewhat glibly that "we educate the whole child." The statement is so general, so lacking in specificity, that it really does not mean much in and by itself, but it opens the way to an entirely new concept of education. Let us consider some specific examples. As you read this paragraph, you perhaps are trying to concentrate, to learn, to remember. But you are not just putting forth mental effort, not just exercising your power of concentration or memory. You are more deeply involved

---

[1] See John S. Brubacher, *A History of the Problems of Education* (New York: McGraw-Hill Book Co., Inc., 1947), Chapter VI, especially pp. 139 ff., for a further explanation of mind-body dualism "mental discipline" theories.

in the learning process than that. You are using your body—shifting your eyes from one group of words to another, perhaps tensing your larynx or even moving your lips silently, as many people do when they read. Your physical comfort or discomfort makes a difference in how effectively you are learning; if you are hungry or sleepy, or if you itch in the spot in the middle of your back that is so hard to scratch—these become factors in whether or not you learn as you read these sentences. Your emotions are involved, too. Maybe you are strongly motivated to get a good grade in the course; that has a bearing on how well you will learn. Or you may be emotionally upset at the moment—perhaps (in spite of what the advertisements say!) your best friend *did* tell you and you feel, at the moment, like a social outcast. These feelings, which would seem to have nothing at all to do with learning, as such, are affecting the learning process.

Perhaps now the meaning of the rather trite phrase, "We educate the whole child," is clearer to you. It is a general statement, all right, and sometimes blinds us to the very specific things that go on in the learning process, but it still expresses quite clearly what is meant by the psychological principle that all behavior is organismic.

All Behavior Is Caused

During the social studies period in Mrs. Pickett's fifth-grade room today, Frankie took careful aim and threw a small piece of chalk at his best friend, Tommy, catching him squarely on the ear. Mrs. Pickett saw the action out of that corner of her eye specifically reserved for such observation and called Frankie up to her desk. "Why did you throw that chalk?" "I dunno," Frankie says, "I guess I just wanted to." That, of course, is not the kind of answer that is very illuminating, nor is it one calculated to soften the feelings of the teacher, but it is nevertheless probably a very accurate one. Frankie honestly didn't know why he committed this comparatively minor infraction of the group rules; he just did it. Still, there *was* a reason.

Drives and motivations. We can't always understand human behavior, especially our own, but every bit of understanding we do have tends to confirm the belief of psychologists that all behavior is *caused* behavior. What we call "drives" or "motivations" in human behavior are very complex, and what we know about them is overshadowed by what we don't know. One thing is fairly certain: it is both inaccurate and futile to dismiss any act or attitude of either adult or child with the hopeless comment that "it's just human nature," or "that's just the way he is," or "there's just no explaining why he acts that way." Since there is every evidence that whatever a person *is* or *does* is the result of something else—background, environment, experience, psychological "drives"—the job of the teacher is to study the *causation* of behavior before attempting to judge it, alter it, or reward or punish it.

All Behavior Is Developmental

Most psychologists are agreed today that the real key to understanding and improving human behavior is a knowledge of the development and growth of children and youth. The "developmental" concept in psychology stresses especially three aspects of all behavior, including the specialized kind of behavior we call "learning."

1. Maturity affects behavior. At a given time (that is, level of maturity or stage of development) certain behavior patterns are likely to emerge.
2. Behavior is sequential. Certain kinds of behavior tend to follow or to precede other types of behavior in understandable order or sequence.
3. Past experiences strongly affect the development of behavior patterns at any given moment—previous learnings, for example, affect present and subsequent learnings.

If we know when to expect the appearance of certain types of behavior, the sequence of developmental stages of growth that is normal in most people, and the interrelationship of one type of behavior with another subsequent kind, then we are well on the road to understanding what people are like. This is especially important if we are trying to understand the learning process itself, which exemplifies very clearly what is meant by the developmental concept.

Readiness.   For example, the concept of readiness. We are very sure today that it is a mistake to expect all children to be ready to read at the same chronological age; reading readiness occurs in most normal children within somewhat the same age span, but it is still a highly individual matter. The child must develop physically, socially, and intellectually; he must develop a background of experiences and meanings before the printed page will really make sense to him. It is the job of the teacher to find out the present stage of development, the degree of readiness of the child to read, and then provide the right experiences at the right time to encourage that readiness and bring it into fruition as reading ability.

Development of interests. And so with other aspects of the developmental process. We cannot expect children of junior high school age to make valid and final vocational choices, but we do know that youth of this age are generally ready to be guided toward a serious look at vocations. Accordingly, in senior high school the development of the average boy or girl is such that matters of vocational choice will often be far more important than conventional academic subjects. Too, the high school student is at a stage of social development that makes boy-girl social relationships of supreme importance. We must plan our secondary school program with these developmental growth-stages in mind.

When we say, then, that we "start where the child is" in education, we are not merely mouthing a pious hope or a shibboleth of progressivism. We are stating a fact about learning: there is simply no other place to start in any stage of growth and development than the stage the child has already reached. To attempt anything else would be foolish and educationally ineffectual. This does not mean that we must sit back and wait for some desired developmental stage to be reached automatically; it does mean that we must know the developmental process in human beings very thoroughly, both the general rules and the individual differences, and plan our educational program in such a way that desired growth will be encouraged at the appropriate time. The child develops, but the teacher is an effective agent in guiding and encouraging that development.

Because this developmental concept is so important, the modern school is arranged to help bring about the development appropriate to each age group. The nursery school is keyed to the developmental needs of the three- and four-year-olds, the kindergarten to the "fives," the elementary school to the different needs of slightly older children, the junior high school to the pre-teens and early teens, and the secondary school to the developmental needs and tasks of the adolescent and the young adult.

One more problem. We know that physical and social and emotional growth is a slow, halting process, with unexpected spurts, occasional "backsliding," and disappointing "plateaus," where no progress is discernible. So it is with the learning process. Learning takes time. Teaching takes patience.

Some Basic Human Needs

Since teaching is largely working with people, it is important that we understand (or review) some of the basic needs of people, especially of children and youth, if we are to have a clear idea of the work of the teacher and the function of the school. As in the previous sections of this chapter, no attempt will be made to give a comprehensive treatment of this topic, but some of the important human *needs* as they relate to the classroom should be emphasized.

I. Physical Needs

Since all human beings need food, rest, and recreation, among their basic physical requirements, the modern school cannot afford to assume that the function of education is purely academic or intellectual. Not only does the child need certain physical things for the preservation and enjoyment of life itself, but the very success of the educational process, too, is dependent upon these physical needs being met adequately.

Consideration for the health and welfare of the child, simply as a matter of human decency, would compel the good school to be concerned with such mundane affairs as heating, lighting, ventilation, sanitation, comfortable seating, and proper rest and recreation for school children. But quite aside from such humanitarian considerations, these matters are of educational concern as well. A child can learn something if the light is poor in the classroom, with sharp glare and deep shadow, but he can learn more efficiently under better lighting conditions. A high-school boy can probably stay awake, just barely, if he gets less than his needed sleep, but his learning efficiency is at a very low level. The restless sixth-graders, wearied from long confinement in the classroom, can be told to "settle down and get to work," but their work will be more effective if a period of relaxation and recreation is provided. A well-nourished child is not only healthier and happier, he is a better learner—more alert, quicker, more efficient—than one who suffers from a poor diet.

The need for healthful school surroundings, then, is not just a physical need; it is absolutely and unequivocally an educational need as well. Academic excellence, a prime goal of the school, is best achieved when the physical conditions for learning are also excellent.

II. Personal and Social Needs

Human beings have certain needs that might broadly be called "psychological" which are just as basic as the more obvious physical needs. The modern school must be as deeply concerned with these needs as it is with the physical welfare of the child.

Affection. All people—and this is especially true of school-age children and youth—have as definite a need for *affection* as they have for food. It was the belief of some psychologists in the first quarter of this century that children were really better off if little or no affection were shown them. John B. Watson,[2] an eminent psychologist of this period, advocated that mothers and fathers should severely limit any display of affection toward the child. When the baby is first brought home from the hospital, he said, the parents should start right away to treat him in an impersonal fashion. Kiss the baby only once, lightly, on the forehead at bedtime, and shake hands with him when he awakes in the morning; that's enough outward display of affection. Thus, Watson said, the child very early becomes conditioned to impersonal treatment and will grow up to be less dependent, more sure of himself.

Today, most psychologists and most laymen who are not psychologists are convinced that the need for affection is deeply rooted in human behavior. It is obvious to even the casual observer that school children in the lower grades respond directly and favorably to an environment that is emotionally warm and satisfying, but it is just as true that the older child or youth in intermediate or secondary school needs to feel liked, wanted, appreciated, even though he may bitterly resent any overt display of affection.

Freedom. Closely related to the need for affection is the need for *freedom.* We are all aware from our own experience how we tighten up when we are met with constant restrictions of natural freedom, when we feel the weight of authority pressing too heavily upon us. Constant negatives—*no, you must not, don't, you can't, stop that*—are more than just annoying to the child (or the adult, for that matter); an atmosphere in the school that allows little or no freedom is disruptive of the learning process itself. The child soon learns that in a schoolroom devoid of freedom the safest thing is to do just what

[2] John B. Watson, *Psychological Care of Infant and Child* (New York: W. W. Norton & Co., Inc., 1928), pp. 81 f.

is required and nothing more. If you don't stick your neck out, the teacher isn't so likely to chop it off.

Security and order.   In trying to provide a maximum amount of freedom for the child, some schools have gone to extremes. They have confused freedom with license, liberty with anarchy. Boys and girls (and people of every age) need *security* and *order* just as much as they need freedom. Much has been written in recent years in praise of the "permissive" attitude in home and school, but permissiveness can easily become a fetish. Children need to know what is expected of them; this knowledge gives them security. You probably remember the well-worn story of the five-year-old in the ultraprogressive kindergarten who said plaintively to her teacher, "Miss Jones, do we *have* to do just what we *want* to again today?" Children, and older people too, need a sense of direction, a sense of security. Wordsworth sensed this basic human need for a balance between freedom and security when he wrote in his somewhat pompous *Ode to Duty,* "Me this uncharted freedom tires; I feel the weight of chance desires . . ." The school child whose every action and activity is left to "chance desire" is just as truly under a weight as one who is burdened by authoritarian demands imposed by adults.

Status, mastery, and recognition.   The modern school is coming to recognize and trying to provide for another group of basic human needs: the needs for *status, mastery, recognition.* The old proverb, "Nothing succeeds like success," is one way of stating this need. The current emphasis in education upon encouraging the child to do things that are within his present ability—letting him have a sense of accomplishment rather than a constant sense of frustration—is not, as some critics would have us believe, a lowering of the standards of the school. It is simple recognition of the importance of letting every child have his measure of success, or being "somebody" in his own eyes and the eyes of his fellow students.

The importance to the individual of his status in the group is hard to overemphasize. A third-grade boy will die a thousand deaths if his mother makes him wear wool pants to school when all the other boys are wearing blue jeans; he's not only miserably unhappy, he is literally so upset he can't do his school work. A junior-high girl who feels scorned socially by the group because she doesn't know how to dance is more than just an unhappy person; her disturbance will probably be reflected in her study habits and her learning. A high school senior might possibly ease up a bit on his class work if he finds his grades are too good to be quite respectable; he may be afraid of getting the unenviable reputation of being a "brain"; in many schools acquiring that designation is tantamount to social suicide.

Feeling and learning. It is not difficult to see how important human emotions are in the learning process. Most of the personal-social needs that have been briefly discussed in the paragraphs above are emotional needs—for affection, security, freedom, status, mastery, recognition. Some more conservative educators believe that the schools should stop being so concerned with how the children *feel* and concentrate on seeing that the children *learn*. But these two aspects of human behavior—feeling and learning—are not separate or opposed; they are deeply interwoven in human behavior, and any attempt to separate them is unrealistic. If the school is concerned with learning, as such, it must inevitably be concerned with the learner as a person—his personal, social, and emotional needs.

The Importance of Individual Differences

In any discussion of basic human behavior characteristics and basic human needs we are likely to become so aware of the common features of people that we may forget how much individual difference there is within the framework of our common humanity.

The Range of "Normal" Differences

A glance into any schoolroom—even an imaginary glance— would provide all the case material we would need for a lesson in individual differences. Let's look in a minute on Mrs. Payne's first-grade class. There's Timmy, normally bright, but so painfully shy and unsure of himself that, even after three months in this home-like first-grade room, he is still feeling homesick and lost. Right beside him is Billy, who is not plentifully endowed with academic intelligence, but who is so thoroughly sure of himself that he swaggers even when he is sitting down. And June, alert and eager, well-adjusted socially, but hampered by a defect in eyesight that hasn't yet been discovered. And Sarah, phlegmatic and almost sullen, seemingly withdrawn from all that goes on about her in the classroom. These one-sentence descriptions are of course not adequate, but even from these you will recognize types of people you have known. All so very different, yet each a normal person in his own right. Which one is most "normal"? All of them are normal, because normalcy embraces a very wide range of behavior characteristics and behavior patterns. All are normal, but each has special needs because of his individual differences.

Emotional Differences

The *emotional* differences of children require the teacher to have a thorough understanding of emotional problems and ways of dealing with emotionally disturbed children. The teacher must also be able to accept the fact that a wide range of emotional reactions is perfectly normal, and to remain imperturbable in the face of rather disquieting behavior. At the same time, the teacher must sense potentially dangerous behavior patterns in children, and see that these children get whatever psychological or psychiatric help is available.

Differences in Intelligence

The *intelligence* differences in children make it imperative that the teacher be able to provide a variety of learning experiences and a variety of learning paces adapted to the needs of the individual student, his strengths, or his limitations. To meet these needs the school must furnish a wealth of kinds of learning materials, a variety of curricular offerings that will provide some worthwhile educational opportunities for the very slow, the average, and the bright child.

The great number and marked degree of individual differences is an important and interesting topic for teachers, but it is beyond the scope of our discussion here. It should be clear even from this very brief treatment, however, that a recognition of the importance of individual differences creates new tasks for the school, necessitates a broader concept of curriculum and more materials for learning, and demands better-trained teachers.

Background and Home Environment

Not long ago in a midwestern city the daily newspaper carried a headlined story of delinquency involving two fourth-grade boys who played truant from school and spent the day in the city park. For no apparent reason, the little boys attacked two beautiful trumpeter swans on the park lake and bludgeoned them to death. On the newspaper's editorial page, the story was repeated with the stern editorial comment that there must be something wrong with a school system that couldn't teach these boys to refrain from destruction of public property and wanton cruelty to dumb animals. The school must be at fault.

Actually, the school was not involved in any direct way, though it was the boys' teacher who found out what the real difficulty was. One of the boys was in deep emotional turmoil because his mother had suddenly disappeared from home, without any warning and without any apparent reason. His whole world had dropped in on him; his personal security and status were suddenly upset in this terrible personal tragedy. Alone, lost, at loose ends emotionally, he had decided impulsively to skip school; persuading a friend to accompany him, he had set out rather aimlessly for the park. The brutal and senseless killing of the swans was likewise impulsive, but the swans were not the object of his unreasoning anger; he was striking back blindly at a world which had struck him a crippling emotional blow.

When this boy returned to school after several days of detention by juvenile authorities, the job of his teacher was extremely difficult and important. He must be protected from the taunting insults of his schoolmates who knew of the episode from the newspaper stories; he must be helped to adjust quickly to the daily tasks of school; but most of all he needed to get in school some of the affection, security, and feeling of assurance that were completely missing now in his own home life.

Educational Significance of Home Background

The background and home environment of each child needs to be known to the teacher in as complete detail as possible. As someone has said, the boy or girl who comes to school is not "born anew on the steps of the school"; the student brings his home background with him. The joys and troubles at home, the attitudes of the parents, the security or insecurity the child feels—all of these come to school with him. Two children with identical intelligence quotients, identical scores on achievement tests, and identical grade placement may be as different as night and day because of different home environments.

A home that is racked by domestic strife and bickering leaves its mark on the child. Economic insecurity in the home is translated into a feeling of personal and social insecurity in school. The child who comes from the wrong side of the tracks, from a racial or religious group against which there is community prejudice, or from a family that lacks respect in the community can be severely handicapped in school. Other children are extremely conscious of the social approval or social stigma attached to one's "position" in the community, and from the earliest grades on up through high school—and often especially in high school—existing community cleavages are sharpened by the class-consciousness of the students. The school has not only to know about these differences in individual backgrounds, but to engage in a positive effort to break down such artificial social and economic barriers as may invade the school itself.

Relationships of the school child to his parents are extremely important educationally as well as from the standpoint of his personal happiness. The child who has been rejected, openly or subtly, by one or both of his parents, is not only an unhappy child; he is often handicapped in reading and other educational experiences closely associated with emotional security. Likewise, the child who is the victim of parental overprotection often fails to adjust to the work of the school, both socially and educationally. If the teacher knows what difficulties the child faces at home, adjustments can be made at school which will help compensate for the handicaps imposed by the home life.

How well the school child gets along with his brothers and sisters, if any, can have an important bearing on his success in school. If the "sibling relationships" at home are reasonably harmonious, there is a much better chance that the child's social adjustments at school will be pleasant. This is true not only of the younger child, but of the teen-ager as well. Many cases of painful social withdrawal or overaggressiveness can be understood and helped if the teacher knows more about the status of the child in his own family.

A Favorable Environment for Learning

We have been concerned so far in this chapter with some of the knowledge about human behavior, human needs, individual differences, and home backgrounds that is necessary if we are to understand the children and youth with whom the teacher works and for whom the school exists. Now, let us see more specifically how this knowledge can be put to use by teachers and the schools to create a more favorable environment for learning.

The term "learning" as we use it here has an inclusive meaning. Some teachers and some schools would restrict the meaning of learning to intellectual and academic development, the acquisition of knowledge and the attainment of skills. Others would emphasize more the personal and social development that is also implied by the term "learning"—cultivation of the personality, learning to get along with oneself and with others. Neither of these emphases—the intellectual and academic, or the personal and social—seems alone adequate as a definition of learning. Both points of view are included in the broad concept of the responsibility of the modern school for promoting the learning of its students.

As a prospective teacher, you will doubtless study a great deal about the psychology of learning in other professional courses. We will not attempt here any systematic outline of educational psychology, learning theory, or the steps in the learning process. Rather, let us look at how the school can create an environment favorable to good learning, learning that is efficient, permanent, meaningful. Such learning is *good* learning.

1. Learning Takes Place Best in a School Environment That Is Attractive, Happy, Pleasant, Free ~

The school strives for such an environment not just because it is pleasant, but because it is effective. First-graders learn to read better in such a setting, and high-school seniors learn more chemistry. For every age-level in school this holds true: An emotionally satisfying, free but stable school environment advances the educational work of the school. An unattractive, tense atmosphere is not only emotionally upsetting; it is educationally unproductive as well.

2. Learning Takes Place Most Effectively When Students Are Interested

The modern school tries to keep its environment and its activities interesting because interest results in better learning, not just because interest keeps the children happy and contented. Common sense tells us, and psychological research verifies this, that the boy or girl who is interested in what he is doing—who is strongly motivated to achieve, to find out, to get more information, to solve a problem—

comes out of the experience with more understanding, more knowledge, and a longer retention of what he has learned. The opposite is also true; bored, apathetic students in a dull environment are relatively poor learners, and the results of what effort they do put forth are meager.

Being interested is not the same as being entertained or amused. Real interest springs from motivations deep within human nature and the individual; real interest drives the student to put forth more than routine effort; real interest generally continues over a substantial period of time. Of course, we know that the interest-span of small children is very short, and grows longer only as they mature and develop intellectually and emotionally. We know also that what appears to be interest may be only trivial curiosity; but with good teaching methods, interest can and should be made more selective, more effective in producing educational results, and more enduring.

3. *Learning Is Most Effective When It Is* Directed Toward Achievable Goals

Goals or aims can, of course, be detrimental to learning if they are imposed solely by the authority of the teacher rather than developed out of the need of the student, or if they are rigid or inflexible, yielding slowly to changed conditions and unresponsive to the student's real needs. With such criticisms of educational goals in mind, some of the early proponents of progressive education decried the importance or validity of *any* goals in education and suggested that there should be no set aim or even direction in learning, save the growth of the child.

It has become increasingly apparent, as psychologists have done further research on the patterns and motivations of human behavior, that people need to have goals in order to lead happy and useful lives. Just as we said above that a child needs to know what is expected of him by his parents, his teachers, and his peers, so a child— or an adult—needs to know what to expect of himself. He needs to have a sense of direction, a sense of purpose; this is best achieved if he has some reasonable, some achievable goals.

This is especially true in school work. Reading is not very efficient or effective unless the child is reading for some purpose appropriate to his maturity level—to see what the pictures are about, to find out what happens in the story, to get information he needs for some other activity or task. Likewise, the seventh-grade boy can enjoy and profit from required physical education classes if the required activities help him achieve his own goal of developing his muscles or gaining popular acclaim for his athletic abilities. The fifth-grade girl will practice her clarinet very reluctantly if all she has to look forward to is next week's music lesson, but if achieving a certain degree of proficiency on the instrument will make her eligible for the elementary-school band, then she really goes to work.

Children naturally want to learn; anyone who has spent any time around small children (think of your younger brother or sister!) knows that spontaneous curiosity regarding the world, and the things and people in the world, is natural in the child. In some sad fashion, many of our schools manage to kill this spontaneous desire to learn, not by any sudden act of educational violence, but by a slow process of attrition and suffocation. It is not at all unusual to find a child who has been alert and eager in the first three grades gradually developing an attitude of infinite boredom toward school when he gets into the middle grades and junior high. What has happened? Many things, perhaps, but almost surely one of the causes for this intellectual apathy has been the failure of the school to help the child set and achieve his own goals.

4. Learning Is Most Effective In a Rich Environment

This does not mean at all that a school must be wealthy or completely supplied with a great variety of costly materials for learning. It does mean that children and youth learn best in an environment rich in learning activities, experiences, meaningful books and other materials, and human and natural resources. This is especially true because learning itself is a special kind of experience, an active experience directly connected with ideas and materials and people. The best learning is active learning, the kind in which the student is actively involved in doing something important within his own environment.

Personal involvement.   Unfortunately, this concept of learning as an active process was misconstrued by many teachers who sought to follow the principles of the "new education" in the first decades of this century; they were of the mistaken belief that learning would take place only when the child was physically active. Hence, the term "activity school" was sometimes applied to schools where nothing much was going on except physical activity. Actually, the principle of learning as an active process means only that the child must directly and purposefully be *involved* in the experience if it is to have maximum benefit. Sometimes this involvement is primarily physical, sometimes it is chiefly creative, sometimes it is simply studious or contemplative. But the environment that provides as many kinds of activities and experiences as possible is the most effective in bringing about good learning.

Association of ideas and experiences. Since most psychologists believe that a fundamental part of the learning process is learning by *association,* it is imperative that there be in the school the kinds of things and activities and experiences that will let the child associate what he already knows with what is next to be learned. Since the new, in other words, is learned in terms of the old, and since each new experience becomes the basis for still other learning, the modern school must provide for the associations that are conducive to this kind of learning.

Problem-solving. Much of learning, also, can be described as problem-solving. This does not mean that every learning situation can be set up in the form of a problem; some things that need to be learned just do not lend themselves to the formal "problem" approach. That is, not every bit of reading that the student will do throughout elementary school and high school can be designed to answer some formally stated problem, and not every social studies lesson can be phrased directly as a problem to be solved. It is still true, however, that insofar as students can be helped to formulate what they want to know and need to know in terms of problems to be solved, the more meaningful will their learning be. For both the *process* and the *result* of the problem-solving approach are valuable; the process of defining the question, getting the facts, experimenting to determine the results, and drawing conclusions from the study— these are all educationally valuable in themselves. And if the solution to the problem is correct—valid and usable—then the learning cycle is complete.

Shared learning. Out of a rich environment for learning comes another kind of experience that is good and satisfying for the student because it both meets his personal needs and results in effective, permanent learning. This experience comes through what we may call "shared learning." When the boy or girl learns something not just as an individual achievement or a bit of information to be stored away in his "memory," but learns something as a result of the shared work-and-study experience of the student group, then that learning is more meaningful. For example, it is quite possible to require a third-grader to memorize some simple facts about the science of weather. But when the third-grade study of weather is planned jointly by students and their teacher, when the observations and discussion and simple experiments and reports are all the result of students working together, then the very "sharing" of the learning makes it both more pleasant and more profitable.

Studying Children

When we see how important it is to know something about the nature of the people with whom the teacher works, it becomes apparent that part of the job of the teacher is to study children, both in their home environment and in their school life. Some people shy away from this concept of "studying" boys and girls because it seems to imply a clinical, cold-blooded approach, or a snooping into private affairs. Actually it is neither. It is simply a process of becoming better acquainted with the young folk you are working with, the people for whom the school exists.

Only briefly here can we indicate some of the effective ways we may learn more about the children and youth in our schools. One is through formal college courses, preferably the kind that involve direct work with the age group you expect to teach, both in their school and their out-of-school environments. Another is continued formal study of human behavior through additional college work taken as in service training after you begin teaching.

However, most of your study of children will be through actually working with them in a classroom setting. Through careful, systematic but sympathetic observation of the individual alone and in groups, in class and on the playground, the teacher can gain much valuable insight. Visits in the homes and informal conferences with the parents when they visit the school or attend special school functions help give background understanding of the individual student and his relations with his family. A careful and continuous study of existing school records—attendance records, health records, guidance and counseling reports, and the results of achievement and intelligence tests—is another invaluable source of helpful information about the students with whom you work.

FIVE: TOPICS FOR STUDY, REPORT, AND DISCUSSION

1. Was the elementary school you attended "child-centered"? Describe the school sufficiently to justify your answer.
2. Did you study any subjects in high school for their alleged value as "mental discipline"? If so, what is your appraisal of the success of the studies in "disciplining" your mind?
3. If possible, arrange to observe a group of children or youth at school, at play, or engaged in some other group activity such as club work. Without presuming that you can thoroughly analyze individual or group behavior, try to see if you can observe the *behavior characteristics* mentioned in this chapter actually "in operation" as the children work or play together.
4. Write a brief, autobiographical sketch of the year in school (elementary or high school) that you remember best. Indicate how the school and the teacher(s) did or did not succeed in providing for your personal and social needs. Be as objective as possible!
5. How did your home background and family environment help or hinder you in school? Could the school have done anything to make the home-school adjustment easier for you?
6. Ask permission to visit some school, elementary or secondary, with which you are acquainted, or one in the town or city where you are attending college. After the visit, list the provisions the school is making for a rich environment for learning.

FIVE: BIBLIOGRAPHY

Baller, Warren R., and Don C. Charles, *The Psychology of Human Growth and Development.* New York: Holt, Rinehart & Winston, Inc., 1961. The effect of background on behavior is well portrayed in chap. 8, "Social-Cultural Basis of Behavior."

Bernard, Harold W., *Human Development in Western Culture.* Boston: Allyn and Bacon, Inc., 1962. The influence of family in the development of the learner is expertly described in chap. 12.

Frandsen, Arden N., *Educational Psychology: The Principles of Learning in Teaching.* McGraw-Hill Book Co., Inc., 1961. Many penetrating insights into the nature of the learner are found in Part II, "The Children We Teach."

Haskew, Laurence D., and Jonathon C. McLendon, *This Is Teaching,* 2d ed. Chicago: Scott, Foresman & Company, 1962. Ways of studying and understanding learners are illustrated and discussed perceptively in chap. 3.

Havinghurst, Robert J., and Bernice L. Neugarten, *Society and Education,* 2d ed. Boston: Allyn and Bacon, Inc., 1962. A distinguished analysis of social forces operating upon school youth. See especially Part Two, "The Child's Social Environment."

Hymes, James L., Jr., *A Child Development Point of View*. Englewood Cliffs, N. J.: Prentice-Hall, Inc., 1955. Simply written, but very illuminating explanation of how children develop in school. Brief, and specifically for teachers.

Jenkins, Gladys Gardner, *Helping Children Reach Their Potential*. Chicago: Scott, Foresman & Company, 1961. A brief handbook containing a large number of useful suggestions for dealing with the learner individually and as a group member. Sympathetic but not maudlin.

Lane, Howard, and Mary Beauchamp, *Human Relations in Teaching*. Englewood Cliffs, N. J.: Prentice-Hall, Inc., 1955. Informal, but very informative study of the needs of children in the modern school. Enlivened by many cartoons. See especially Part III.

Martin, William, "Gee, I'm Glad We're All Different," *NEA Journal*, Vol. 43, No. 4 (April, 1954), 219 f. Fine suggestions for capitalizing on individual differences in the classroom.

Morse, William C., and G. Max Wingo, *Psychology and Teaching*, 2d ed. Chicago: Scott, Foresman & Company, 1962. The youth with whom the schools are concerned are sympathetically but realistically described in chap. 6, "The Teen-ager."

Mouly, George J., *Psychology for Effective Teaching*. New York: Holt, Rinehart & Winston, Inc., 1960. The range and significance of individual differences is clearly explained in chap. 15.

Woolf, Leonard, "Adolescents Are Here to Stay," *Educational Leadership*, Vol. XII, No. 3 (December, 1954), 142-147. Healthfully optimistic suggestion that we need not consider this a "problem age" if we really understand what adolescents are like.

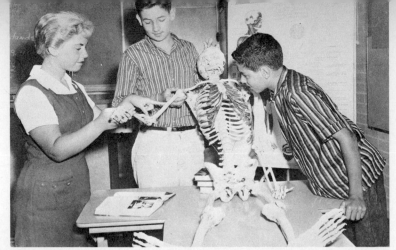

Torrance (California) Unified
School District

Science class. *What kinds of curriculum organization are evidenced here?*

American School and University Yearbook,
Norman (Oklahoma) High School,
Caudill, Rowlett & Scott; Perkins & Will
—architects. Hedrich-Blessing Photo

Between classes. *What curricular values may come from such noncurricula
activities as lounging and visiting?*

CHAPTER SIX

Along in November of each new school year, the American public schools give a special invitation to parents to visit their schools as a part of the observation of American Education Week. During this week, and on other less formal occasions during the year, thousands of parents will enter the classrooms where their sons and daughters are "going to school" and look about to see just what is going on.

The Curriculum at Work

In a good school—or almost any school, for that matter—the parents will find many things going on: children in the kindergarten, for example, playing games; primary-grade children reading a story about Dick and Jane and their dog Spot; fourth-graders reading silently in their social studies books; junior-high-school girls cooking in the home economics laboratory; high-school seniors carrying on a perhaps desultory discussion in a world history class. There are a lot of things happening, the parents observe—children engaged in all sorts of traditional school tasks, and maybe doing some "new" things;

THE MODERN SCHOOL CURRICULUM

teachers helping groups and individuals to learn new facts and see new relationships and develop new skills; students and teachers both using a wide variety of books and other learning materials.

The parents observe, and are pleased, and nod approvingly, but they still wonder: just what is the school teaching? What are my children learning? What kind of an education are they getting? The visitors are perhaps too diffident or too polite to ask these questions aloud, but they need not be; many teachers ask themselves much the same questions, and educators everywhere are concerned with these same problems. The questions and problems may be stated in many ways, and answered in almost as many more, but the central topic is always the same: the modern curriculum.

Definitions Are Elusive

"Curriculum" is a rather technical term, used more often by professional educators than by laymen, and often grossly misused by both. In more traditional schools, curriculum usually means "subject matter," the list of topics and books studied, the course of study, the formal materials "taught" by the teacher and "learned" by the student. In this context, the curriculum is thought of as a body of materials rather than a group of interrelated experiences; or as a fixed list of facts and skills that are passed on to each new generation of students through a one-way teacher-to-pupil transmission process.

In the extreme progressive school, however, the curriculum has quite a different meaning. In such a school it is often said that the curriculum is "as broad as life itself"—it is literally everything that happens to the student, every experience, every aspect of living. Under this definition, a school dance is just as much a part of the curriculum as a class in American history, and the garter snake brought to school by the third-grader is as truly subject matter as the third-grade arithmetic book.

Certainly, each of these definitions of the curriculum of the school —extremely narrow or extremely broad—represents a real and reasonably tenable view of what education means; these contrasting definitions may be overstated here to make the distinction clear, but the contrasts are not caricatured. Some teachers, schools, and parents actually do believe quite sincerely that the curriculum is solely book-learning and subject matter; others believe quite as sincerely that all experiences, in school and out, are rightly included in the concept of "curriculum."

Somewhere in between these two extremes, however, will be found the viewpoint of most teachers and laymen: the curriculum of the modern school is neither so narrow as to be just formal subject matter, nor so broad as to include everything, all of life itself. To put it positively, the curriculum today is generally thought of as the whole body of human learnings and experiences, planned and organized under the control of the school, which can be used for carrying out the purposes of the school.

Definition by Illustration

Any attempt to *define* the curriculum, however, leads (as you can see in the above paragraph) to involvement in ambiguous or confusing statements. Let us, then, try to see what the modern curriculum includes, what it consists of; a workable definition may emerge from this list.

Generally speaking, the curriculum at any school level includes these things:

1. Knowledge, information, facts—the "subject matter" that was so often the whole of the older curriculum and is still of great importance in the modern curriculum
2. Generalizations and relationships—the wider understandings that come from personal involvement and direct experience with subject matter
3. Applications—the actual use of content or subject matter in real and meaningful "life situations"—or ones as nearly life-like as the school can manage
4. Skills—being able to do, to perform, to make and use (ranging all the way from reading to woodturning, from spelling to maintaining good posture)
5. Creative expression—in written or oral communication, perhaps, or in one of the fine or practical arts
6. Attitudes, ideals, interests, and tastes—outlooks and emotional reactions taught directly or indirectly by the school

Even such a list as this, of course, does not tell very clearly what is actually taught in the modern school, what is actually presented, studied, and discussed. Part of the difficulty of getting a clear concept of the curriculum arises from the variety of learnings, subject matter, or activities which may be included in the typical school curriculum at the various levels. Moreover, there are many different curriculums (technically, curricula) in common use in the schools of America, and many different names attached to these various curricular concepts or viewpoints.

Curriculum Viewpoints

Experience Curriculum

In some present-day schools the whole organized learning activity of the school is spoken of as an experience curriculum, or as an experience-centered curriculum. This term comes from an assertion that learning is itself a kind of experience and that the most meaningful materials for learning are those which derive directly from human experience. Knowledge of facts, ability to make generalizations and applications, and the development of skills and creative abilities— all of these mean something only as they are related to the child's experience, or to the larger scope of human experience that we call society.

The idea of the experience curriculum is eminently sound, both psychologically and socially; it relates education directly to the learning process as it actually takes place, and grounds the work of the school in the nature of the society which the school serves. Nevertheless, this curriculum concept has some weaknesses. First, it has often been contrasted, in the thinking and writing of educational specialists and laymen alike, directly with what was called the subject-centered curriculum, as though the two terms represented true opposites; you had to accept one unreservedly and reject the other completely. Actually, traditional school subjects can be taught in direct relation to individual or group experiences, and these same experiences can in turn be directly related to the "courses" that are taught in school. It is not a matter of absolute choice; the good school curriculum deals with both subjects and experiences.

Another difficulty with the concept of the experience curriculum has been the undiscriminating assumption that all experiences are of equal worth or effectiveness educationally. This has led some schools and some teachers to a rather smug belief that any experience the student has is good education; if the students are having a lot of experiences, regardless of quality, a full and rich curriculum is being provided. Under this misconceived plan, excessive and fruitless "class discussion" is sometimes encouraged because "it gives the children experience in expressing themselves and sharing points of view," and time-wasting construction activities are permitted on the ground that "the boys and girls are getting a lot of new experiences."

Still another difficulty with the experience-centered curriculum has been found in the uncritical acceptance of the idea that all experiences must be direct, firsthand—that nothing could be learned unless the child had the whole experience, from beginning to end, all by himself. This viewpoint tended to discount the importance of books, for example, because they represented the experience of the writer of the book, not that of the child himself.

It is easy to see that all of these misuses and overstatements of the experience-centered curriculum came about from an attempt to make education less bookish, less academic and to make it more meaningful, more closely related to life itself. Moreover, these extreme views represented the first halting and imperfect attempts to put into effect the new theories of learning that resulted in the first decades of this century from a better, more precise, scientific understanding of the psychology of human behavior. The errors of the experience-centered concept of the curriculum have been serious, but the lasting results of this concept have been beneficial.

Activity Curriculum

Closely related to the concept of the experience curriculum has been that of the activity curriculum, which has developed in the past few decades, sometimes under the broader name of the activity school. Again, the viewpoint is essentially sound: all the learnings that we want children to have are active, not passive learnings; the materials which are used to aid in bringing about this type of learning must be actively used by the student, not passively accepted or memorized or assimilated. Learning is by its very nature an active process; facts have meaning when they are applied to real-life activities of the student, and skills are not really "learned" until they are put to active use.

The activity-curriculum concept, however, was subject to much the same errors of overstatement and misuse of good psychological principles as was the "experience curriculum" viewpoint. Some teachers thought that the student must be physically and even vocally active for any learning to take place, and hence deprecated the use of more formal learning situations and learning materials. Some educators felt that every activity was intrinsically good and educationally valuable; the only important thing was to keep the students engaged in activities, and learning would automatically take place. These educators seemed to forget that good learning requires periods of quiet study as well as more overt activity, and that learning through activity, while natural, is not always spontaneous or automatic, but must be planned and directed.

Needs Curriculum

Another attempt to summarize a curriculum viewpoint in a single term and to plan an entire curriculum from a single approach has been seen in the so-called needs curriculum, based on the needs of the individual (personal-needs approach) or the needs of society (social-demands approach) or a combination of the two. As before, the idea underlying this viewpoint was quite sound. The school exists to serve the individual as a member of a society, and the school should teach what the individual needs as a social being. This is perhaps the most tenable of the positions that we have discussed so far. The school, as we have pointed out in earlier chapters, is a social institution, a product of a society or culture, and it exists primarily to fulfill the wishes of that society. And what society expects of the school is expressed (see Chapter Four) in terms of what is good for the individual as a member of that society—basic intellectual competencies, social and civic and vocational training, moral sensibility, and physical and mental health. The list is of course incomplete, but these are examples of what would be taught in a school that subscribes to the needs concept of curriculum building.

The limitations of this view have been almost entirely those of overemphasis on one or the other of its two aspects: some schools emphasized the *personal* needs of the student without regard for the fact that he was also a member of a society of individuals, and others did just the opposite and buried the individual and his individuality under a welter of subjects or courses that could be justified because "society expects it."

Curriculum Organization

Since there is no universal agreement about just what the modern public school curriculum should be or should include, it is not surprising that there is also disagreement about how the curriculum should be organized. That it should be organized in some fashion is beyond any question, for the good, effective curriculum is planned, sequential, purposeful.

Separate-Subjects Organization

Most teachers today do agree, in theory anyway, that the least desirable and effective method of curriculum organization is found in the traditional arrangement of material-to-be-learned as separate and unrelated "subjects." This type of curriculum organization violates several sound principles underlying effective education. It tends to treat children as though they were all just exactly alike, each needing the same dosage of the same required material; it makes little provision for individual differences. The separate-subjects organization gives little recognition to the level of maturity, the degree of advancement, and the individual needs and interests of the student. It fosters a view of learning as the acquisition of specific facts and knowledge without any understanding of the interrelationships of the various "subjects." It puts the major emphasis upon the subject matter itself, not on the needs of the student as a member of an interdependent society.

Despite these fairly serious and obvious faults, the separate-subjects approach is still the most common method of curriculum organization. It is relatively clear-cut, is fairly easy to teach, and follows a traditional pattern that is understood by most parents and teachers because it is just what they studied when they were in school. For these reasons, perhaps, it is just as well that the separate-subjects organization, with some modifications, should be continued in many schools until we have attained these goals: (a) a public ready to accept and support some of the newer types of curriculum organization, (b) teachers adequately trained to teach under the more complex (but more effective) newer curricular patterns, and (c) instructional materials and classrooms provided which facilitate the less "bookish" approaches to instruction.

Problems Approach

Some schools, particularly those which have become most deeply involved in progressive educational practices, have tried to organize the curriculum around the everyday problems of individuals and societies. These problems may range from fairly uncomplicated questions in elementary school science ("What Makes Changes in the Weather?") to very complex topics in high-school social studies ("How Can We Secure World Peace?"). This approach has many worthwhile features: it captures the student's interest, it motivates effective effort, it provides rich opportunity for teacher-pupil planning, it encourages reading and research, it ties various traditional subject matters together—the list of good features is not complete. This "problems" approach appears now to be one of the most promising ways of organizing some, but not all, of the curriculum of the school. It is fairly obvious that not all learnings lend themselves to this approach, that not all desirable learnings can be included in a single problem, and that certain fundamental learnings and skills could easily be overlooked while searching for the answer to the problem posed. Too, the problems can be merely traditional, unrelated subject matters disguised by a thin layer of sugar-coating calculated to arouse at least a semblance of student interest. Furthermore, the authoritarian or egocentric teacher could easily make the problem a one-man show, completely leaving out effective student participation and activity. Still, the problems approach to curricular organization seems to be a step in the right direction.

Unified Approaches

The problems of curriculum organization are extremely complex, and the beginning teacher can become involved in—even be the cause of—a great deal of misunderstanding among both professional educators and lay people by bandying about such terms as "integration," "correlation," "fusion," and the "core curriculum." We will not attempt here to examine all the ramifications of these terms, but even the teacher just starting on his professional study should have a nodding acquaintance with the trends in curriculum organization to which these words refer.

All of these terms are descriptions of a movement in curriculum organization that seeks to adapt the subjects and materials of a fairly traditional curriculum to the newer concepts of education as an active process, effected through meaningful experiences, involving the child as a unitary organism (the whole-child concept) living and learning in a social setting.

Correlation. The least radical of these unified curricular approaches is *correlation,* which preserves the idea of separate subjects but relates them in the teaching and learning process. For example, in the elementary school, spelling may be taught as a separate subject, but the spelling words studied will be taken from concurrent work in, say, science or social-studies classes. In high school, American literature will be correlated with the same period in American history, both studied at the same time but in separate classes and under separate teachers.

Fusion. A slightly bolder approach to the unification of the curricular material is found in the *fusion* ("broad fields") type of organization, in which some of the individual subjects lose their separate identities. For example, reading and spelling and penmanship may be fused into a broader field, the "language arts," giving the students a longer block of time for the study of related areas and emphasizing the natural interrelationships of the once separate subjects. Or, at the secondary level, separate courses in history, civics, geography, and government may be replaced by a large block of studies known collectively as the social studies.

Integration. The most striking of the innovations in curriculum organization is the *integrated* curriculum, in which all or nearly all of the subjects completely lose their separate identities, and no systematic attempt is made to teach traditional "subject matter" as such. The experience-centered and activity curricula are, in varying degrees, examples of this latter type of the completely unified or integrated curriculum.

Other unified patterns. There are many other variations of these patterns of curriculum organization. In some schools, especially at the junior high school level, two or more subjects have been combined into a *core curriculum.* English and social studies, for example, are taught as a single core, covering a large block of time daily (perhaps the whole morning) and utilizing the full-time services of a single core teacher, assisted by other teacher-consultants as the need arises. Still another pattern of curriculum organization is the life-adjustment education emphasis, found sometimes in senior high schools. This plan (a) retains some of the traditional courses as separate subjects, (b) fuses others into larger units of work, and (c) introduces many important but somewhat unusual courses such as personal and social development, family-life education, and education for economic competence.

Choosing the appropriate curricular organization. The choice of pattern for curricular organization, it will be seen, should not be made in any school system on the basis of an inflexible conviction that any single organizational pattern is inherently the best. Rather, certain areas of the curriculum, as indicated in the previous paragraphs, lend themselves quite naturally to certain approaches.

The experience approach, for example, is often nicely suited to such a curricular area as the social studies; the activity approach is especially appropriate to art and music; the needs curriculum fits in well with many courses in the practical arts and creational studies; and the problems curriculum is ideal for many of the topics studied in science and mathematics.

This is not to suggest that each curricular area can properly lay exclusive claim to a given curricular approach. Nevertheless, the special purpose and activities of each of the areas of the school curriculum are often best achieved through emphasis on the organizational pattern especially suited to that area.

No one can say which is the *right* way of organizing the curriculum; even in the improbable event that agreement of all competent educators and lay persons could be secured, changing conditions would still bring about need for reorganization and readjustment. It is to this problem of curriculum change that we now turn our attention.

Curriculum Change

"Things ain't like they used to be, and they never was," one of our American humorists once said. This is particularly true of the curriculum. When the middle-aged parent today expresses the wish that the schools might return to the good old days, go back to the fundamentals, teach what they used to teach—when he asks for this return to the school which exists only in his nostalgic memories, he is asking for what can never be, and probably never was.

Because—despite the charges we hear today that the public schools are too progressive, too modern, are moving too fast—the schools have *always* been changing; they have never really been static. It may be true that the older schools took longer to effect some of the changes, but even the relatively inflexible schools that we have had in certain periods of our national history were changing schools, adapting slowly but surely to the changes in the society which supported and sustained them.

Teachers and other school officials today are often asked such questions as these: "What has become of geography in the grade school; why don't they teach it any more?" "Why aren't children taught to read in the first grade?" "Don't they study civics any more?" "Why isn't my daughter taught the classics in high-school English?" "Don't you require algebra for high-school graduation?" "Why don't they teach the kids to write? We used to have penmanship three times a week!"

Well, the answers are not easy to give in a few words, and such answers as can be given do not necessarily satisfy the questioner. Geography is taught more intensively and effectively than ever in most elementary schools, but it is a part of a unified or "broad fields" course called "social studies." The students studying geography to-day are not very likely to learn the names of all of the counties in their state, or the capitals of the countries of South America, or a list of the principal exports of Brazil. These things *may* be learned, formally or informally, but it is almost a sure bet that the elementary school student will learn more than his parents did about local and state history and American culture; about other peoples of the earth, and how the climate and topography of their country affects their way of life; and about how the economic and political interdependence of the nations of the earth affects life in our own country. This knowledge may not come from a geography book as such—some of it will be studied in "units" on the Dutch, on Alaska, on Indians, or other unit topics; some of it will come from studying science; some of the learning will come from reading the weekly newspapers prepared especially for children at each grade level; some of the knowledge will come from movies seen, field trips taken, or exhibits prepared by the student. There is still much room for improvement, but geography is definitely in the curriculum. The content, the context, the method, the materials, the emphasis—these may all have changed, but important curricular areas are still covered in the work of the school.

The changed place or form of geography in the curriculum, described very briefly above, is merely illustrative of the many curricular changes that are continually taking place. Since what is happening to the curriculum is of direct concern to the teacher (even the beginning teacher must work with a changing curriculum, and be able to discuss these changes intelligently with parents), let us look briefly at some of the reasons for these changes and the forces which bring them about.

Factors Influencing Curriculum Changes

Social factors. If the school is really, as we have said, an expression of the society which it serves, then the curriculum of the school must be in a constant state of change and growth just to keep up with changes in society. "New occasions teach new duties; time makes ancient good uncouth," wrote an American poet a century ago, and while the statement, of course, was not intended to describe the reasons for changes in the curriculum, it serves well to summarize the idea that as society changes, so the curriculum must follow.

For example, more children go to school and stay in school longer; the curriculum, especially at the junior high school and secondary level, must be broad enough to include materials and experiences that will have meaning and worth and interest for a large, unselected, often poorly motivated group, not just for a selected group of academically able students. More vocational training is needed for more students, since actual on-the-job training is now delayed until a somewhat later period in life and the formal apprenticeship system is declining in importance. New kinds of jobs are constantly being developed by the employment of new inventions and a new technology; half of all adult workers today are employed in jobs which did not even exist fifty years ago. The school is expected to give the preliminary vocational training and background for these new jobs. A few years ago the importance of typing as a subject in the high school curriculum was just beginning to be realized; now, typing is a common subject, and training in the use of other business machines widely used in commerce and industry is coming to be of equal importance.

The reading habits of the present generation are being altered by the introduction of new media of mass communication; reading is not today less important, but more important in a society where so much depends on the citizenry's being able to make sense of the tremendous amount of printed material that is poured forth in books, magazines, and newspapers. But training in the communication skills today must also include some study of the moving picture, radio, and television if the average person is to understand and make good use of these newer marvels of mass communication.

Social studies instruction today is not complete if all the student studies is the *history* of ancient and modern nations. The complexities of modern society require that each citizen understand something of the perplexing relationships of one nation to another—he must study (though not necessarily as separate subjects) about economics, political science, sociology, psychology, and such distinctly new topics as the United Nations, UNESCO, and nuclear fission.

Science is a dynamic, not a static, part of the school curriculum; vast and challenging new frontiers of scientific knowledge are almost daily being discovered and explored. Understanding of these new frontiers of science—especially the significance of atomic energy as a means of increasing peace and economic prosperity and the exciting new vistas of the world of outer space—must of necessity be made a part of the modern curriculum. With a tremendous increase in world population, coupled with a prodigious waste of our irreplaceable natural resources, problems of conservation education cannot safely be ignored in the schools.

"Where Children Live Affects the Curriculum" is the title of a challenging report by the U.S. Office of Education on how schools in the various parts of the country are adapting the life and work of the school to the geographic *area* as well as the social *era* in which the children live. Obviously, a standardized elementary or high school curriculum for all parts of the United States would be an educational monstrosity; if the curriculum is related to life, then it must be related to the kind of life the student actually leads. Some of the basic learnings will be much the same in any section of the country, but the problems, the illustrations, the methods, the activities, and the books and other learning materials used will vary widely in different states and even in different sections of the same state.

Psychological factors.   With our constantly expanding knowledge (based on research and experimentation) of patterns of human growth and development and the psychology of learning, it would be impossible to justify an unchanging curriculum based on old beliefs about human nature that are no longer tenable. If we know beyond the shadow of a doubt that children develop reading skills and reading readiness at different chronological ages, depending on a number of differences in individual abilities and rates of growth, it would be patently foolish to insist on retaining a curriculum in reading that called for all children to read the same books at the same time with the same degree of understanding. Since we know that handwriting is a complex skill that involves muscular coordination, proper motivation, and learning by "wholes" rather than parts, it is not conceivable that the modern school could persist in teaching penmanship in the traditional fashion: unmotivated drill in the mechanics of writing (actually, drawing) the isolated parts of letters—the old

"Palmer method" that critics of the schools today often suggest should be restored to the curriculum of the elementary school.

We realize today that skill in the use of the English language is not developed most easily and effectively by memorizing parts of speech, locating and listing subjects and predicates, and learning verbatim the "rules" of grammar. All of these activities may have some part in developing communications skills, but a far more fruitful approach to this problem lies in giving the student guided experiences in actual communication, written and oral. When the boy or girl has something to say, something to communicate to others, something to talk or write about, then he can much better be "taught" communication skills through the actual process of communicating, rather than by just studying *about* language.

Since the findings of modern psychology indicate quite clearly that people "think" when they are puzzled, when they have problems, it seems far more practical today to help the students learn to think clearly and effectively by giving them real problems to work with, rather than by forcing them to study subjects that will "train their minds." It used to be argued that geometry should be included in the high school curriculum required of all students because this was a subject of superior worth in training the student to think logically. Geometry is still included as an elective in the modern curriculum, and rightly so, but it is not prescribed for everybody as a "think tonic." Students will learn to think logically much more easily and effectively if they are given a chance to study arithmetical, scientific, and social problems that have a direct bearing on their daily lives.

We sometimes hear the complaint that the modern school neglects the teaching of civics and chronologically organized American history as such; hence, say the critics, the school is not teaching American citizenship. We know now, however, that good citizenship and deep pride in our country's rich heritage are not gained through study of specific subject matters alone; these studies may aid in the desired development, but they are not enough. Far better than a routine course in civics is a planned sequence of experiences and learning activities that lead to direct participation in the life and government of the school, a firsthand understanding of the responsibilities for voting and making other important choices, and a personal involvement in living democratically with other people. This we know, because our better understanding today of the psychology of human behavior indicates clearly that good citizenship is a combination of knowledge, experience, and motivation—not just the acquiring and remembering of isolated facts about our governmental system and our national history.

Changes in the school itself. Some curriculum change comes almost automatically from changed conditions within the school itself. We have already pointed out the influence of the school's greater educational responsibility—more children staying in school longer, needing to learn more things—on the school curriculum. What society expects of the school, as we have suggested earlier, is reflected directly in curricular changes. And the kind of school society provides also makes a difference in the curriculum.

Many schools today are overcrowded, seriously overcrowded. Double sessions (or more accurately, half-day sessions) are found in thousands of schools. Certain of the offerings of a good, modern curriculum must be severely curtailed. If the woodworking shop has to be used for an extra classroom, shop courses must be dropped. If there are too many students for the available laboratory space in general science, direct laboratory experiences for the students must be temporarily replaced by lectures or routine filling in the blanks in laboratory workbooks from material supplied by the instructor. If there is overcrowding in the lower grades in the elementary school, individual instruction or small-group instruction in reading will be replaced by the older device of having all children reading from the same book at the same time. When the overcrowding creates a serious teacher overload—as it often does—laboratory-type experiments and projects involving the planned *use* of arithmetic will be dropped in favor of seat-work assignments like "Now do the first fifteen problems on page 64 in your arithmetic book."

On the other hand, as new schools are built and more space and facilities become available, curricular changes that most educators believe are distinct improvements will be seen. If the classroom is large enough, much more emphasis can be placed on relatively independent work in small groups—research projects, sharing of information, preparing material to be given as a class report, constructing maps or charts or graphs that will both record what the student has learned and make the material available to the rest of the members of the class. As the public expresses its faith in the work of the school by providing more space and more materials and more money, the offerings in art, music, physical education, and vocational subjects can be expanded. More use can be made of the newer audio-visual methods and materials. Other favorable curricular changes will be seen as the school itself changes in response to changed public attitudes regarding the importance and scope of modern education.

Planned Curricular Change

So far in this chapter we have considered curriculum change as though it were largely inevitable, a natural evolutional occurrence rather than a planned program. But it is both; the good school changes its curriculum in part because it must, in part because it wants to. The school must not, of course, submit to every social or cultural pressure; nor must it subscribe to every new idea, or run after each educational fad. It is neither hidebound nor spineless.

But, as the authors of one book about the American school system have put it,

> The good school is the *adaptable* school. The good school recognizes its place in society and adapts its purposes and its curriculum to changes which have occurred in the society it serves. The good school takes advantage of new scientific insight and adapts its methods accordingly. The good school adapts its program to the new procedures and provisions which have been tested and proven by other good schools, and itself possesses an inventive staff able to create and test improved methods.[1]

This last sentence, especially, should interest us here. It is the "inventive staff," the capable and informed teachers and administrators, who are very largely responsible for deliberate curricular change, for planned curriculum reorganization.

The curriculum is changed in the classroom.   In the older schools (and in some still today) where the curriculum was thought to be wholly embodied in a list of subjects to be taught, in a course of study worked out by higher authority, the teacher had relatively little curricular responsibility aside from teaching just what he had been told he should teach. Today, with a broader concept of the curriculum as all of the learning experiences planned and carried out under the auspices of the school, the teacher has a central part in working constantly to make the curriculum in his own classes a good and effective group of learning experiences for the children he teaches. The teacher selects the range and variety of experiences to be used, the sequence to be generally followed, the books and other materials

---

[1] By permission from *Introduction to American Education,* by Paul R. Mort and William S. Vincent. Copyright, 1954. McGraw-Hill Book Company, Inc.

to be studied, and what is perhaps most important, the atmosphere in which the learning will be carried on.

For example, two high-school biology teachers following the same stated "curriculum" would teach entirely different courses, actually, if one of them emphasized laboratory experimentation, use of slides, filmstrips, and motion pictures, and gave frequent opportunities for well-planned field trips; while the other taught the same "subject matter" through the use of formal lectures, strict adherence to the textbook, and heavy reliance on workbooks filled in (all exactly alike) by the students and carefully checked for compliance with the basic text.

Likewise, two elementary teachers could both be teaching the sixth grade, but the actual curriculum would be quite different in their two rooms (even though the same subjects were taught) if one encouraged a relatively informal atmosphere, with much opportunity for individual and small-group work and for teacher-pupil planning, and the other taught the material straight from the textbooks in a heavy-handed, authoritarian manner. Actually, in both the biology classes and the sixth-grade rooms, the academic learning (as measured by standardized tests, at least) might be very similar for the two groups studying the same material, but the *curriculum* would be very different. For the curriculum is the actual *learning experiences*—the *how* of the learning as well as the *what*—and each teacher to a large degree develops and organizes his own curriculum.

Committee activity. But the teacher does not work alone in curriculum development and organization. Committees of teachers and administrators, in every good modern school, are constantly working on various phases of curriculum improvement. In most good schools, specific help and guidance is also sought from parents and other laymen interested in what the school is teaching. It will not suffice just to have a general invitation issued by the school, welcoming any suggestions at any time about the curriculum. No, to get real and effective lay participation in curriculum improvement, a definite, planned schedule of lay-professional working conferences must be set up.

The students' part. The students of the modern school are involved in planned curriculum reorganization, too. What the students themselves want and need finds concrete expression in curricular change, sometimes directly, through formal representation of the student body on curriculum committees, but much more often indirectly, as the ordinary classwork proceeds. In a good school, students have a voice in selecting activities, projects, materials, group and individual reports, and the other learning experiences that actually constitute the curriculum.

The teacher's responsibility.   Still, even though many persons working together help build and change the modern school curriculum, the real responsibility lies with the classroom teacher. The very life of the school depends on what you do as a teacher; and your work is felt not only in your own classroom, but throughout the whole school. Therefore it is a real necessity that each teacher understand in some detail the whole curriculum of the school—not just his own grade level or special subject matter. Every teacher, for example, is a teacher of reading no matter what subject or grade he teaches. We as teachers need to know about the reading development program as a whole, as a continuous process throughout all the school years, if we are to do the very best job possible of teaching our own students to read. And so with social studies. The first-grade teacher needs to have some knowledge of the whole pattern of the social studies, kindergarten through twelfth grade, in order to make the maximum contribution to the child's understanding and development as a first-grader. And the high school teacher whose major interest and major teaching field is American history has a real need to know how younger children develop expanding concepts of the society in which they live in order that he may effectively teach his own specialty to high-school seniors.

While it is perfectly legitimate and necessary for the teacher preparing for work in the elementary school to give major attention to the elementary curriculum, and the secondary school teacher to do likewise for the high school subjects he expects to teach, teachers at all levels can well afford to spend a considerable amount of time and effort studying "how the other half lives"!

The "Extracurriculum"

There are a number of activities in most present-day schools which occupy a "betwixt and between" status; theoretically we would like to see them be considered a part of the regular curriculum, but practically and in the eyes of the general public they are still outside the fold. These have been called "extracurricular," "extra-class," "co-curricular," and simply "student activities." Each of these terms has been an attempt (in varying degrees) to indicate that these activities are to be thought of as closely related to the regular curriculum, if not actually a part of it. Ideally, as Professor Fretwell said many years ago, "The extracurricular activities should grow out of the curricular activities and return to them to enrich them." [2] They may thus be considered as an adjunct to the broadened curriculum of the modern school, if not yet a part of the curriculum itself.

Why are these extras necessary, you may ask. If these activities have real educational value, why not put them right into the curriculum of the school, rather than giving them a peripheral status? If they don't have real educational value, why does the school concern itself with them at all? The answer is basically this: individual differences! The purpose of the entire school program is to meet the needs of children and youth as members of a society of people. Some of these needs can be met by the "common learnings" areas of the regular curriculum; some may be met by provision for "elective" courses or subjects. But there are still other needs that we have as yet found no way to meet within the framework of either required or elective courses. The extracurricular part of the school program tries to meet these needs.

The extracurricular program, as compared with the regular school curriculum, has several distinguishing features that make it serve a special purpose in the school:

(a) It is less formal, both in organization and operation, than the regular curriculum.

(b) It is more readily adaptable to the changing interests and enthusiasms of the students.

(c) It lends itself to a greater amount of student planning.

(d) It provides greater opportunities for social development.

(e) It involves types of expenditure of money that could not, in many communities, be supported out of public school funds.

Maybe none of these reasons for having the separate activities program is very convincing; maybe the school *should* ultimately organize the regular curriculum so that it could do all of the things the activity curriculum does, and do them better. But the fact remains that, at the present, the activity program definitely serves the needs that are not met by the regular program of more formal classroom instruction.

[2] Elbert K. Fretwell, *Extra-Curricular Activities in Secondary Schools* (Boston: Houghton Mifflin Co., 1931), p. 2.

The extracurricular activities, however, are still part of the work of the typical classroom teacher. That is why you, as a prospective teacher, should have some understanding of your part in the program. It is not just a program for the secondary schools; good elementary schools also have an extra-class activities program. Thus, every teacher at every level is or should be personally involved in some part of the program.

Although some phases of certain of the student activities are found also in regular classroom work, several distinct kinds of activities are usually scheduled as "extras." Included in this list of extracurricular activities in most schools would be the athletic program (as distinct from the regular classes in physical education), art and music activities not taught as regular classes, home room programs, student government and student council activities, out-of-class drama and speech programs, club work, school publications, and social activities. In certain schools several of these will be considered strictly curricular but, generally speaking, they have an "extra" status.

None of these activities can be justified unless it has sufficient educational value to warrant the student's and the teacher's spending the required time. On the other hand, none of the activities has to be justified for its specifically academic or intellectual value or content. That is not their purpose. If they arouse the interest and enthusiasm of the student to the extent of inducing worthwhile effort and achievement, if they serve to relieve some of the boredom students often experience in regular classroom work, if they teach new skills and new appreciations, if they encourage development of new interests, if they teach students how to get along with others and work with others toward a definite goal, and if they help create good public attitude toward the work of the school—if any of these outcomes can be found in the extracurricular program, the activities may be educationally justifiable.

On the other hand, if the programs take a disproportionate amount of the student's time, or cost too much money, or teach attitudes (such as poor sportsmanship or social cliquishness) that are contrary to the basic purposes of the school, or sacrifice the welfare of the majority to the aggrandizement of the few—if these are the outcomes, the activities program deserves the public censure it sometimes receives. It is unfortunate that one of the most popular and worthwhile of the student activities—the athletic program—is often the worst offender, and that the obvious abuses in high school athletics have tended to give all extracurricular activities a bad name.

Prospective teachers, while still in college, would do well to get as much experience as possible in extracurricular activities as preparation for taking their part as teachers in the school activity program. Sound, thorough knowledge and experience, we mean, not just the superficial acquaintance that comes with joining a lot of organizations or with halfhearted participation in every activity that presents an opportunity. The best possible educational values will come from these programs in the public schools, and the most common abuses avoided, if the classroom teacher has had firsthand experience with the activities himself, and is able to make the benefits of this experience available to his own students.

The Out-of-School Curriculum

Although the curriculum has been discussed here not as something as broad as life itself, but rather as those learning activities specifically planned by and under the direct control of the school, the school cannot afford to ignore the out-of-school curriculum, the environment that affects every boy and girl in his school work. As one writer has said,

> . . . each child brings to school with him the total impact of his out-of-school living. He comes to school permeated with the special social milieu in which he is daily immersed. And so of necessity every aspect of the child's living outside of school becomes a part of curriculum.[3]

The high school freshman may study something about the problems of economics, the elements of labor-management disputes in his classroom work in social studies, but he is exposed to another economics curriculum at home when his father is out on strike and there is little money for shoes or groceries. The first-grader is learning to read from the books his teacher gives him, but his ability to grasp concepts, to understand even the simple phrases he is reading, is conditioned by the "curriculum" of experiences he has had and is having at home and at play. Literature of varying degrees of worth and interest may be studied in courses taken by the teen-ager, but the formal curriculum in school is in constant competition with the "course of study" provided by comic books, movies, and television.

[3] Julia Weber, "Child Development Implications for Curriculum Building," *Educational Leadership*, XI, No. 6 (March, 1954), p. 343. Reprinted by permission.

This is not to say that the curriculum of the school is the right one, and that of out-of-school living, wrong or inferior. Simply, we need to realize that the two curricula must both be fully understood, so that one may be used to complement and supplement the other. Where the two are at odds, the conflicts that result must somehow be resolved, so that the student does not suffer from the strain of trying to adjust to two different worlds, school and out-of-school.

Finally, the best curriculum is the most adaptable curriculum, the one that "fits" the individual in his social setting, the one that has real meat and meaning, the one that makes sense to the student. That is, the best curriculum is the one most closely related to the life of the student, of the school, and of the community; not a curriculum "as broad as life itself," but a selected, organized, flexible arrangement of learning experiences that is *educationally* better than ordinary "life itself," specifically because it is designed for maximum educational effectiveness.

SIX: TOPICS FOR STUDY, REPORT, AND DISCUSSION

1. What special training or experience would a teacher need to be qualified to teach a problems approach curriculum?
2. What topics, areas, or subjects are now decreasing in importance in the general field in which you expect to teach? What ones are increasing in importance? What is the reason for these changes in emphasis?
3. Secure a copy of the state course of study or the curriculum outline for some school system and see if you can determine what type of curriculum *organization* is employed therein.
4. What subject matters and learning experiences would be included in a "unit of study" in the area or grade level at which you expect to teach?
5. Besides those mentioned in this chapter, what other forces are operating to bring about curriculum change?
6. Prepare a brief report on how the out-of-school curriculum affected your own learnings and development during your elementary and high school years.
7. A critic of present-day education has said that modern school practices have resulted in "the enrichment of the curriculum and the impoverishment of the students." Defend or criticize his position.

SIX: BIBLIOGRAPHY

Alberty, Harold B., *Reorganizing the High School Curriculum,* 3d ed. New York: The Macmillan Co., 1962. A broad and comprehensive— often quite technical—explanation of the design of the present high school curriculum, with many direct suggestions for its improvement.

Association for Supervision and Curriculum Development, *Curriculum Materials—1962*. Washington, D. C.: National Education Association, 1962. A selective listing of first-rate curriculum materials and guides from leading school systems throughout the nation. Not to be read, as such, but extremely useful for discovering where current curriculum materials can be obtained.

Bathurst, Effie, *Where Children Live Affects the Curriculum*, Bulletin No. 5. Washington, D. C.: U. S. Office of Education, 1949. Descriptions of how schools throughout the country have adapted their curricula to the local area and its needs. Not a recent publication, but very useful.

"Curriculum Improvement: Who Participates?" *Educational Leadership*, XI, No. 6, March, 1954. A symposium, with excellent articles by several writers, on securing good parent-teacher-student cooperation in curriculum planning and improvement.

Frederick, Robert W., *The Third Curriculum: Student Activities in American Education*. New York: Appleton-Century-Crofts, Inc., 1959. An excellent explanation and appraisal of the curricular importance to be found in the extracurricular activities program.

Gwynn, J. Minor, *Curriculum Principles and Social Trends*, 3d ed. New York: The Macmillan Co., 1960. Part I, "New Factors in Curriculum Development," and Part V, "Other Influences on Curriculum Change," give especially detailed treatments of social forces influencing the curriculum.

Hollingshead, August B., *Elmtown's Youth*. New York: John Wiley & Sons, Inc., 1949. The effect on school children of the out-of-school curriculum embodied in the life and culture of a typical American community is thoroughly analyzed by an eminent sociologist. An older reference, but a classic in the field.

Pounds, Ralph L., and Robert L. Garretson, *Principles of Modern Education*. New York: The Macmillan Co., 1962. An expanded discussion of some of the more technical facets of curriculum organization, treated only briefly in the chapter above, can be found in chap. 9 of this reference.

Pritzhan, Philo T., *Dynamics of Curriculum Improvement*. Englewood Cliffs, N. J.: Prentice-Hall, Inc., 1959. A rather technical book, but chap. 8, "How Environment Can Help Learning," is a valuable reference for those interested in the social bases of curriculum development.

Ragan, William B., *Teaching America's Children*. New York: Holt, Rinehart & Winston, Inc., 1961. A very good discussion of the elementary curriculum, with many concrete illustrations, is given in chaps. 5-10.

Storen, Helen F., *Laymen Help Plan the Curriculum*. Washington, D. C.: National Education Association, 1946. Not very recent, but an excellent statement of problems and good practices in promoting lay participation in curriculum making.

VanTil, William, "Curriculum Frontiers of the 1960's," *Baltimore Bulletin of Education*, Vol. 39, No. 2 (1961-62), 9-12. A brief, but very thought-provoking set of questions which should guide curriculum revision in the present decade.

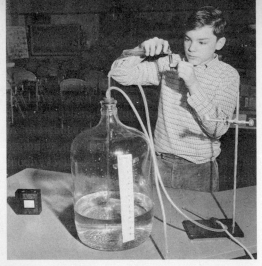

Individual learning. *What part does the teacher play in learning such as this?*

Small study group. *What functions does the teacher have in this learning situation?*

CHAPTER SEVEN

What do teachers actually do, day by day and week by week, in the ordinary school classroom? What will you actually be doing when you are teaching? The answer to these questions is given in part in earlier chapters of this book, where we focused our attention on such topics as the place of the school in our society, the problems and pleasures of working with children and youth, and the special educational framework for living and learning that we call the curriculum. But we need to know much more specifically just what the teacher *does* in his or her job.

It is very difficult to be specific about the job of teaching. We speak sometimes of regular classroom teaching, but regularity and uniformity are not the distinguishing features of good teaching. More-

IT HAPPENS
IN THE CLASSROOM

over, teaching as a job differs at various grade levels, in different kinds of schools, and with teachers holding different educational views. Without considering such variables as these mentioned, teaching is still a complicated process in its own right, almost impossible to describe *exactly*. Nothing that we can say, then, about the job of teaching will be wholly applicable to you, or tell you precisely what your job of teaching will involve. No description can substitute for direct, firsthand observation and experience in the classroom; you are urged to visit good schools at work, systematically and frequently, as an integral part of your preparation for teaching. Both to supplement and to prepare for such observation of teachers at work, however, we ought to look critically at the job of teaching *generally,* to get some understanding of what teaching is actually about.

Some Variables That Affect Teaching

Grade Level

Even to the casual observer, the work of the teacher is not the same in first grade as in sixth grade, or in junior high school as in junior college. What the teacher actually does is quite different: books, assignments, lesson plans, tests, and the students themselves— all of these differ at the different grade levels, and the work of the teacher is affected accordingly. So, you may ask yourself, why shouldn't I as a prospective teacher just stick to learning my own business—second grade, or junior high science, or high school English? Why should I concern myself with levels and subjects that I don't teach? The answer to this common query is twofold: first, really good teaching involves many of the same duties and responsibilities at any grade level; and second, only by knowing what the teacher does in teaching other grade levels than our own can we understand our individual teaching assignment most fully.

Or, put it this way. As you read in this chapter or elsewhere about teaching problems and practices applicable to grade levels in which you are not particularly interested, don't dismiss such information as unimportant to you. Rather, if you are preparing to teach in high school, try to see how an understanding of the problems of the elementary school can help you in your work. And the situation is reversed for the elementary teacher. You can learn something from good teaching practice anywhere, wherever you see it going on or hear it described.

Kind of School

The job of the teacher varies, of course, with the kind of school in which the teaching is done. The attitudes of the community toward the school will affect the daily work of the classroom. The school curriculum adopted in a given community may preclude the use of certain methods and materials the teacher would like to use. The kind of students the community sends to the school will also tend to determine just what the work of the teacher will be.

If the community, for example, takes the attitude that the job of the school is to cram the students with facts, keep them from playing around in school, and train them to follow orders, then the work of the teacher is quite different than it would be in another, more liberal community. If the curriculum of the school includes a wide variety of activities, experiences, and learning situations, the day-by-day task of the teacher is quite different from that of the teacher in the school with a strict follow-the-state-course-of-study curriculum. If the children of the community come from homes where they are generally well cared for, treated with reasonable firmness and affection, and given necessary security and freedom, then the teacher will do many different things in the classroom than would be necessary with children from less favorable home environments.

Prospective teachers, noticing that some of the teaching practices and methods advocated in the education courses they take and the professional books they study would not seem applicable to the schools that they know best, sometimes become impatient with this "stuff that won't work." Again, it is important to remember that the best teacher is one who understands and is thoroughly familiar with a great variety of classroom practices such as might be found in many kinds of schools. Then, with this prior knowledge, the teacher can later select those which will be most appropriate in his own school—those that will work where he is actually teaching.

The Teacher's Own View of Education

The last of these major variables in the work of the teacher is the teacher's own ideas about education: what the purpose of education is, how learning does take place, what children and youth really are like and what they really need. The teacher's ideas on these important educational matters will inevitably be translated into a conception of the function of the teacher in the school, and hence into actual classroom practice.

As with the other variables mentioned above, so with conflicting views of education: the prospective teacher is likely to be confused or impatient or both. "That isn't what I believe," he will say to himself as he reads about some recommended classroom practice. "It may have worked for her class, but it isn't what I'd do with mine."

You can readily see that it is very difficult to describe what happens in the typical classroom, what ordinary classroom teaching is, what the teacher really does day by day—it is difficult if not impossible to do all of this in a way that would be acceptable to all readers. So remember, what follows in this chapter is an attempt to give you an understanding about classroom teaching as it is carried on in the ordinary school, not to present, necessarily, an idea of what is ultimately right or what ought to be.

The descriptions of practices will not, therefore, necessarily fit in with your own thinking of what ought to be, nor will they be slanted toward a "conservative" or a "radical" viewpoint. These practices represent what good, modern, adaptable schools are doing; if there is a bias in the descriptions, it is that of a moderate progressivism.

Some Misconceptions About Teaching

The work of the teacher in the classroom is often badly misunderstood. Ask a businessman downtown what he thinks the job of the teacher is, and he will quite possibly think back to his own boyhood as he answers, "Well, the main thing is for the teacher to keep order; you've got to let the kids know who's boss." And the father standing by, listening to your conversation, will comment, "I think the teacher ought to drill the pupils on the fundamentals; see to it that they learn the things everybody ought to know." And another bystander will add, "Well, I believe the teacher is somebody who knows her stuff and gives it to the students in a way they'll remember."

Others will take a more liberal view, one they fondly believe is "progressive." "The teacher is a guide," they will say. "The teacher guides learning." Some even more extreme progressives have suggested that the teacher is just another person in the classroom, just "one of the boys," a member of the group who sits back and watches the children develop naturally.

What is your own recollection of what the teacher did in your own elementary and high school classes? The teacher was one who made assignments, perhaps, required classwork and homework, demanded class recitation, asked questions and corrected your answers, dispensed information and gave tests to see if you could "put it down on paper."

All of these beliefs about the work of the teacher have some merit; all are more or less accurate depending on the kind of school and the kind of curriculum. But none of them is wholly correct, and some of the views are grossly out of keeping with present-day ideas of what teaching should be. The teacher as a taskmaster, a disciplinarian, one who tells, assigns, requires, hears recitations, gives grades—all of these are limited, obsolescent views. No more accurate are the mistakenly "progressive," hopelessly vague and general concepts of the teacher as merely a group member, a guide, or a spineless nonentity who gracefully presides over the anarchy of undirected, wholly spontaneous "activity" of boys and girls.

No, these views of the job of classroom teaching are not very useful. Even if they were correct, they are too introverted. They focus our attention too exclusively on what the *teacher* does, and not enough on what the students are doing. Let's try another approach: what are the students doing in the typical modern classroom, and what does the teacher do to make *their* activities more worthwhile, more pleasant, more productive? In brief, what does the teacher do to help the students learn?

A Laboratory for Learning

Any school can be thought of today as a kind of laboratory for learning. The modern, progressive school is very accurately described as such a laboratory, and is clearly seen as such. Within the more traditional patterns of the conventional school, however, we are increasingly seeing signs that even these schools are taking a "laboratory" approach. So we are not restricted to just one kind of school when we try to generalize an answer to the question, "What are children doing in today's schools?" In and out of the classroom, but still mostly *in,* the boys and girls in American schools are daily doing these things:

1. They are learning specific things systematically, by reading, writing, talking, listening, figuring, practicing, reviewing.
2. They are setting up and solving problems.
3. They are creating and expressing.
4. They are living together as a group.
5. They are developing individually.
6. They are being examined, judged, evaluated.
7. They are developing and modifying attitudes.

This list could be criticized on several counts. To some, it would seem to emphasize a too-traditional, too-academic approach to education. To others, some of the activities mentioned would seem inconsequential, trivial, not "intellectual" enough. The list might be criticized as giving too much emphasis to what happens in the elementary school; others would see it as largely a list of high school learning activities. These criticisms doubtless all have some justification, but as a brief summary of what actually goes on in the ordinary school, it will do for our purpose.

1. Specific Learnings

Parents want their children to learn; they send them to school to learn. The job of teachers is to help children learn. A natural desire of boys and girls, psychologists tell us (and common experience confirms this) is to learn new things. Everybody, apparently, is in agreement that the school's main concern should be with learning. But just what is learning; what does it mean to learn?

The meaning of the term "learning" is one of the most complicated of psychological problems, and we would doubtless only confuse the major purpose of this chapter—finding out what the teacher does in the classroom—by getting too deeply involved in definition. Our own individual experiences with learning will perhaps give us sufficient answer.

Learning to read. How did you learn to read? It's difficult after so many years to remember exactly, but you know that reading was a "developmental" process; you didn't learn to read all at once, but *developed* the skill gradually. You had to have some previous experiences into which to fit the new "book" words. "C-A-T" doesn't really *mean* "cat" to a child who has never seen the animal. You had to learn to grasp whole ideas when you read, but you also had to recognize minute similarities and differences in letters. You had to have words explained, you had to be told specifically how to "attack" new and unfamiliar words, you had to be corrected when you were wrong, and encouraged when you were right. You had to learn to read along with the group and to read independently. You had to learn to pick up clues to new words and groups of words by looking at the pictures in the book, and by noting the familiar prefixes and suffixes as a key to unlocking new words. When you were finally able to read for meaning, and get and enjoy the meaning—when reading became a way of finding out and a way of having fun—then you had "learned" to read. As an adult, now, you recognize that this learning is not finished, completed; you are still *learning* to read—or should be!

You will notice that the preceding paragraph is not very orderly; it is that way on purpose. Although the learning process is a developmental process—one step or stage after another—and although good teaching is systematic teaching, the process of learning is not standardized for all children. There is no one step-by-step plan, no one pattern, no one systematic sequence in learning. That is what makes teaching so difficult—and so challenging and rewarding.

Learning as adjustment, growth, development.   Learning may be described in many ways, each of them partly accurate but none of them complete. Learning is a process of *adjustment* to oneself and one's environment, but the teacher obviously doesn't go around "adjusting" students, like a mechanic tinkering with a car. Learning is *growth,* and teaching is "guiding growth," but this concept is useful only as a general framework; it is tremendously important, but again not specific enough. Learning is *development,* but the teacher can't be very sure of his classroom practice if all he can say is that in some mysterious way he is seeing to the development of his students.

No, if education means, in part, that children are learning specific things systematically, the teacher's task is both specific and systematic—still, of course, within a broad, comprehensive view of learning as *adjustment, growth,* and *development.* What are some of the specific and systematic things the teacher does to aid learning?

The teacher's part.   The teacher in the ordinary classroom—even in such less formal subjects as music, art, physical education, and industrial arts—does a lot of lesson planning. But this is not a solo job; in almost every school, no matter how traditional, and no matter how immature the students, there can be a degree of genuine pupil-teacher planning. How great the degree of this shared planning at any given stage in the development of the student is not so important; it is imperative that whatever there is of pupil-teacher planning be completely honest and genuine—not just a make-believe.

The teacher develops units of work—long-range and short-range objectives, materials to be used, actual instructional steps to be followed, student experiences to be undergone, definite outcomes expected, and plans for evaluation of the unit. The teacher, then, in any subject and at any grade level helps students learn specific things by working directly with them in making plans, giving assignments, explaining unfamiliar words and materials, providing for direct experiences out of which meanings develop, and providing for necessary drill and practice.

Because two of these suggestions of what the teacher will be doing to help students learn seem, perhaps, rather old-fashioned—giving assignments and providing for drill—a little more might well be said about how those activities fit into the work of the modern school. The direct assignment has been condemned by some educators on the grounds that it is a teacher-oriented practice, rather than student-oriented. This is not necessarily so. If the assignment is a specific set of things that must be done, thought up by the teacher, ordered by the teacher, directed and evaluated by the teacher, it is a poor teaching method. If the assignment is given without explanation or discussion ("Read pages 334–345 tomorrow and be ready for a test over those pages!"), if it is not related to the purposes of the course and the interests of the class, if it does not provide for a continuity of learning experience by tying what is already learned into what is yet to be learned—under those circumstances, the assignment is no real aid to learning.

And so with drill. Drill and practice have been utterly abandoned by some schools and some teachers on the grounds that they are ineffective teaching media. Support is given to this position by citing the vast amount of educational theory and psychological research which seem to discredit these methods. This complete abandonment of drill is a mistake; there are some learnings which cannot be attained efficiently by any other method than drill, some things which can never be learned except by practice. The real contribution of the newer theories regarding practice and drill is this: unmotivated, meaningless drill or dully repetitious and often punitive practice is *not* favorable to good learning. Used very carefully, very wisely, with a thorough understanding on the part of the teacher of the whole learning process, these teaching techniques can be extremely useful.

What does the teacher do, then, to aid his students in learning specific things systematically? He

—provides a learning environment rich in materials and experiences;
—helps students relate these experiences to new experiences;
—makes lesson plans and develops units of work with the students;
—uses when appropriate the more traditional methods of assignment, drill, and practice;
—sees that the students are productively busy—reading, writing, listening, speaking, experimenting, computing, remembering, using, doing; and
—provides through these activities a framework for learning as adjustment, growth, development.

2. Setting Up and Solving Problems

In any grade and any subject in a good, up-to-date school, children and youth are meeting and solving problems. Some of these problems seem to emerge naturally. The boy in woodworking shop learns to file a saw so he can have a sharp instrument for cutting the boards he needs; the little girl in the third grade checks with her teacher on punctuation so her note inviting her mother to the class party will be clear and correct; Jim, in the sixth grade, learns how to measure an acre so his class can claim the land a neighboring farmer has offered them for their school garden project. Other problems are frankly "contrived"—finding out how the story comes out in a Shakespearean play that has been made assigned reading, or figuring out the answers to the questions at the close of the chapter in the arithmetic book.

Problem-solving is a very effective kind of learning; it is perhaps the most normal of all learning situations. A person wants something, wants to know something, wants to go somewhere; in achieving his objective, he solves his problem; he learns in the process. But not all of the things that need to be learned in school come in neatly-packaged problem form. The teacher's task is not only to put as many learning situations as possible in problem form, but to teach the student to recognize the problem, to get partial understanding that will give clues to the next step to be taken, to understand why he takes each step, and to check his final solution or results.

Since many of the "problems" in school do not, at least initially, appear real to the student, one of the jobs of the teacher is to motivate the student, to arouse his interest, to make him want to attack the problem. Rewards, punishments, cutthroat competition—all of these are motivating devices of a sort, but the good teacher learns how to use a wealth of other motivational techniques that have far more value for the learner.

Real, significant problems cannot exist in a vacuum. One of the jobs of the teacher is to provide ample materials with which the students can work. Problems in science that stress *finding out* and understanding can be real and meaningful only if there are materials for experimentation. Even in the traditional school, limited by its narrower educational outlook and the sparsity of laboratory equipment, the good teacher can improvise, with the help of the students, much useful material for problem-solving activities. Likewise, if geography is to be more than a memorization of routine, unrelated facts about the countries of the earth, many resource books, working materials (books, reference works, moving pictures, materials for making maps), and opportunities for such activities as field trips are necessary or highly desirable. Problem-solving as a learning device needs special materials and equipment; it is a primary job of the teacher to make these available at the right time.

3. Creating and Expressing

The teacher who is doing a more than routine job of classroom teaching is often referred to as a "creative" teacher. But the creative atmosphere in learning is not found in the work of the teacher alone, but in the work of the students also, and in the entire life of the school.

To some, the word "creative" conjures up visions of a starry-eyed, somewhat mystical, self-consciously "arty" atmosphere, rather than a real schoolroom. This is not what is meant at all. Simply, children and youth are by nature creative; they want and need to express themselves in a variety of ways. This, in turn, does not mean that the classroom must be the scene of constant, unbridled "self-expression" that some overeager extremists in education have advocated. Rather, children in a healthy, normal learning environment should not only be permitted but actively encouraged to create, to express; that is one important way they learn.

That is why so much emphasis is placed, in the modern school (secondary as well as elementary), on providing opportunities for ceative self-expression both within and without the bounds of the regular curriculum. Children in the lower elementary grades acting out a story, playing store, dramatizing a unit in healthful living are not just "playing around"; they are learning in one of the most normal and effective ways possible. This same sort of creative activity is much harder to introduce into the junior high school, and even more so into the senior high school. The greater sophistication of the students, the more stringent demands of the traditional curriculum, and the reluctance of teachers to depart from familiar methods of teaching—these all work to stifle creative expression in the upper grades of school. Even at these more difficult levels, however, the able and inventive teacher can find ways to encourage such expression through use of dramatic activities, writing that expresses individual feelings and insights, assignments that allow the individual student to do work that is personally rewarding, and group and class activities that permit each student to be a recognized contributor to genuinely creative learning experiences.

4. Living Together as a Group

Although farsighted educators down through the centuries of educational history have emphasized the importance of the school as an experience in group living, it has been largely in the last half-century that the schools of America have given serious attention to this function of the schools. We have but to notice what children themselves consider most important in school to understand the educational significance of the group.

The students' value system.   High school students, for example, frequently put far higher on their scale of values "belonging to the crowd" than they do academic excellence or outstanding scholarship. We are not arguing that this is right; it is simply true. Many a high school girl would willingly trade her *A* in English for an invitation to an exclusive social affair. More than one student has eased up on his school work for fear of being called a "brain." To a high school freshman, pimples are more important than Pythagoras. In the lower elementary grades, the boys and girls usually struggle harder to obtain social approval and inclusion in playground groups than they do to get their arithmetic lesson just right. If we have enough sympathy, insight, and understanding to recognize how important group living is to our students, we will make the improvement of group attitude and action a matter of highest educational priority in our teaching.

Children at every age need to learn how to work together harmoniously and effectively—to use group action to get things done. They are not born with this knowledge; they do not learn it automatically. They are *taught* the techniques of group action; they *learn* them through directed experiences.

Committee work. For this reason, the competent teacher makes a great deal of use of committees for setting up projects and units, for dividing responsibility for individual and group research, for determining and carrying out the group rules for behavior in the classroom and on the playground, for assembling and preparing materials for class work, for making reports to the class, for evaluating the work of the unit. This use of committees is not, as a few teachers have found out to their sorrow, a way for the teacher to get out of work, or an easy way to "cover ground" in the course of study. It is difficult, time-consuming, and often a sore trial to the patience of the teacher. On the other hand, it is not just a pipe-dream theory, beautiful but unworkable. Organizing the whole class on a working-group basis, and then breaking the group down further into subgroups or committees is difficult—but workable and effective. Not only are the social learnings and social developments enhanced, but the more formal academic outcomes are more successful—if the teacher knows what he is doing.

Development of leadership. Group action develops positive leadership, not just the routine leadership that allots tasks, vetoes suggestions, and generally "runs things." Even children in the lower elementary grades can come to see that their elected group leader is something more than one who just bosses the other kids. Group action as a classroom teaching device develops not only the responsibility of leadership but the responsibility of group membership— good followers and cooperative workers as well as strong leaders. Students learn to share materials and ideas and leadership roles; they learn the importance of recognizing and meeting differences of opinion; they learn the significance both of consensus and of honest disagreement.

Group work and academic learning.   But, you may well say, while all this is going on do they learn anything else—reading or arithmetic or journalism or economics? There is not space to document the answer here, but the reply is definitely *yes.* The social learnings and social developments are not something extraneous introduced into the curriculum of the school; they are part of the normal activities and experiences of children and youth. They contribute to, rather than detract from, the so-called academic learnings. It is the job of the teacher to devise ways in which the normal group living can be made to contribute in the maximum degree to *both* the social and the academic development of his students.

One of the things the teacher will do, then, is to make as conscientious a study of group relationships as he does of the more formal learning experiences. He will know his students thoroughly, and advance that knowledge through such scientific devices as the use of the sociogram and other means which are used to measure objectively how each student feels about his own place in the group, and how other people react to him. The good teacher will be as concerned about how the students can help themselves to learn as he is about what he may do as a teacher to help them learn.

Discipline.   All very well, you say again, but what about discipline —order, behavior, good conduct. You can't have a good classroom learning experience without discipline! That is entirely true; only in slapstick caricatures of the "progressive" school is discipline lacking. No good school was ever conducted without discipline, and no teacher can escape the responsibility of being a disciplinarian.

But our view of what constitutes good discipline or classroom order has changed a great deal in the past few decades. Good discipline has traditionally been thought of as order, quiet, good behavior, obedience to authority. All of these are only partial descriptions, and when taken collectively as a complete explanation of what we mean by classroom discipline, they are very misleading.

Discipline is not an end in itself, but a means to an end. Discipline is always associated with a goal.[1] If the type of discipline that obtains

---

[1] See Cecil V. Millard, *Child Growth and Development in the Elementary School Years* (Boston: D. C. Heath & Co., 1951); his chapter on "Discipline and the Growth Process" has served as the source of many of the viewpoints in this section.

in the classroom is a means of achieving the goals that the students themselves have understood and accepted, then there is an excellent chance that good discipline will be achieved.

Self-discipline is the ultimate goal of both the school and our society. A person is well-disciplined when the control comes from within, not from without. But self-discipline (like any other learning) is not automatic; at some stages of maturation a child simply cannot be allowed to do whatever he wants in the hope that he will naturally and ultimately develop self-discipline. Even though we do not really like to accept—or impose—any discipline that is not directed toward understood and accepted goals, that does not come from within, we sometimes must. Domination in discipline is not a pleasant concept, but, as Millard has said:

> . . . the consequences of self-expression and other evidences of lack of discipline are even more dangerous and threatening to the development of children. In this respect it can even be said that the traditionalists are justified in the emphasis which they place on discipline. Order, restraint, and frustration are less undesirable than self-will and its accompanying conflict with group will.[2]

But that does not mean that the teacher must self-righteously choose the harsher disciplinary methods because the students "aren't mature enough to discipline themselves." Many improvements can be effected right now in the American educational program which will sharply reduce the incidence of "disciplinary" problems.

Some of the most common causes of these problems in school, as Millard has pointed out, are an uninspiring curriculum, material that is too difficult or too easy for the student, teaching methods that are so poor that they bore or frustrate the child, and a monotonous, unbroken school program that results in undue fatigue for both student and teacher. Furthermore, there are often personal, home, and emotional problems that may be disturbing the student and causing socially unacceptable behavior. No one of these problems has any complete and easy solution, but all of them represent areas in which the ordinary teacher, provided he is intelligent, sympathetic, and understanding, can make so many improvements over ordinary school practice that a vast proportion of the so-called discipline problems could be alleviated.

[2] Millard, *op. cit.*, p. 442. Reprinted by permission.

5. Developing Individually

At the same time the students in the typical classroom are learning to live together, they are also developing as individuals. No one can state the relative importance of individual and social development to the child; both take place at the same time; both are essential.

Since individual development is going on all the time in the classroom (and is itself of course a form of learning), promoting desirable development becomes one of the jobs of the classroom teacher. As with some of our previous subtopics in this chapter, we must say again that this is not the place for an extended discussion, but we can say this—the teacher who is ordinarily competent can arrange the learning experiences favorable for this individual growth. How? Imaginative, differentiated assignments; a wide variety of learning experiences and a rich supply of the materials for learning; opportunities for much genuine teacher-pupil planning; and group work that encourages rather than stifles individuality—these are but some of the ways that ordinary classroom routine can be arranged to contribute to individual development.

6. Being Examined, Judged, Evaluated

In school, every day is a day of judgment! That is really not quite so ominous as it sounds; we mean that whatever the children and youth are doing in their daily school life, judgments and evaluations are being made. Unfortunately, the more mechanical part of this evaluation program—the formal tests used for grading purposes, the standardized examinations given at regular intervals, the report cards that are sent home—these are the aspects of the evaluation program that occupy first place in the minds of the students and the work of the teacher.

Probably of more real importance in the long run is the self-evaluation that a student makes of himself, and the evaluation made of him by his classmates. The student who learns to judge his own learnings, his own progress, his own weaknesses and strengths, is well along the road to becoming an educated person. Likewise, the boy or girl who can measure up favorably in the eyes of his peers has made a long step in the direction of attaining maturity.

Formal evaluation. Nevertheless, the teacher's chief concern is often with the more formal evaluative devices—tests, examinations, grades, and report cards. (This field of measurement and evaluation is rightly considered one of the most important special areas in teacher education, and you will doubtless study it in another course.) Briefly, here are some of the important tasks this problem of testing and grading creates for the classroom teacher. The teacher must make out tests covering specific learnings and specific units of work; even more important is devising other evaluative devices so that judgment of work occurs not sporadically, only when tests are given, but as a part of each day's work. Especially important are the pre-tests and diagnostic tests, used to discover what has been learned before the unit of work is begun and to disclose any specific academic weakness, or any deficiencies in skill or knowledge the individual student may have. Use of such devices makes it possible to differentiate assignments and other learning experiences on a sound basis of real individual need. The teacher must use grades as a description of the child's achievement in terms of his own ability, not in terms of some general averages or norms. The reports to the parents should ideally be used "as an instrument of child guidance, rather than a means of pressure or of discipline." [3]

This list of evaluative activities is, of course, not complete, but since the children in the active life of the ordinary school are constantly being examined, judged, evaluated, and reported on to the school and the parents, the job of the teacher always includes these duties—and they can never be considered merely "routine."

7. Developing Attitudes

Included all along the line in the previous sections have been overtones of this final area at which we must look briefly if we are to see with any clarity what happens in the classroom, and what thus affects the work of the teacher. "Attitudes" is an unfortunately stuffy, pompous term; it always seems to carry with it the unctuous tone of the college assembly speaker who talked for a whole hour on the importance of developing what he called "a great, big, fine attitude!"

Nevertheless, as we look back on our own elementary-school and high-school experiences, we will probably observe that some of the things we learned best, the things that have stuck with us and have

[3] Ruth Haas, "An Experiment in Changing Reporting Practices," *Educational Leadership*, XI, No. 8 (May, 1954), p. 492. Reprinted by permission.

been most important to us, were not the formal academic learnings at all, but the *attitudes* that affect everything we do.

There is no doubt that these attitudes are being built in all children and youth throughout their school years: attitudes about honesty, industry, doing an assigned job as well as possible, respecting or despising people of other races or religions, appreciation or dislike of music and art, beliefs about religious and moral values, attitudes toward earning a living, and that particularly important attitude toward one's own country and fellow citizens that we call patriotism. These attitudes, beliefs, value systems are being developed day by day; what does this mean to the teacher's task?

Attitudes and the culture.   First, the teacher has to work with the children and youth within the framework of *existing* attitudes—those developed already at home and in natural social groupings of neighborhood and playground, those influenced by religious organizations and by youth groups such as the Boy Scouts, and those which are the effects of magazines, movies, and television. Second, the teacher is working with attitudes that are constantly *changing;* it is never accurate to assume that because a student now has an attitude he will keep it.

Attitudes and the classroom.   Important social attitudes—like respect for others and acceptance (not mere tolerance) of differences in race, nationality, religious faith, and cultural patterns—can be taught quite specifically in many regular school classes. The teaching here, like other good teaching we have discussed, is not primarily *telling* or *explaining* or *requiring,* something done *by* the teacher *to* or *for* the students. Rather, it is providing systematic, cooperatively-planned individual and group experiences in living together, finding out about each other, understanding why the people of a society or of a world differ, and finding concrete examples of the contributions that different kinds of people have made and are making to our modern life. Fairly traditional courses in history, geography, civics, American government, and social problems can be used to help build the attitudes we believe are necessary to successful living in a democracy. But other types of classroom work can also be directed to this end: the group organization of the class itself, the reading materials that are supplied throughout the curriculum, the films and field trips and other audio-visual approaches to learning that the class experiences, and the quality of relationships that the school develops with different segments of the community—all of these are definite contributors to specific development of good attitudes.

Attitudes that are traditionally considered to be primarily the concern of formal agencies for moral instruction—the churches and Sunday schools—are perhaps the most difficult to build and develop in the ordinary school classroom. Honesty as a personal and social virtue may, with some positive success, be developed in children by direct religious appeal: the Ten Commandments forbid stealing; if you lie you will go to Hell. We do not mean in any sense to mock or deprecate such religious teachings, but two comments must be made: first, they are really not as effective ways of teaching moral values as we have sometimes thought; and, second, regardless of their effectiveness, they cannot very well be used in the secular and nonsectarian public school.

Other appeals, other reasoning, other approaches than direct didactic instruction must be used by the public school teacher in developing a favorable attitude toward honesty. Here is where modern psychology and modern education can be definitely allied on the side of traditional religious values. Without calling on the sanctions of the teaching of the churches for support, we can state definitely that honesty is an individual and social imperative—a definite good to be sought. But a favorable *attitude* about honesty (and again, the argument here is psychological rather than specifically religious) is not enough; the attitude means something only in practice, only when the person *lives* honestly. Therefore the school can provide, throughout all the grades, direct experiences in social living that will guide and develop working concepts of honesty. The teacher's own honesty, the attitude of the other children, the practices of the school itself, and the child's personal striving for acceptance by the group and his own growing sensitivity to the rights of others and the need for fair play—these all can be used to teach honesty as a way of life.

One more example. Most people in our culture believe that the school should help develop a favorable attitude toward work: respect for work well done, for the value of industrious effort, for the worthwhileness of all honest labor. The school can definitely do this; if children and youth are developing attitudes anyway, it becomes part of the work of the teacher to help them in this part of their growth. The teacher who adjusts the work-load to the ability of each child, so that he gets the habit of success rather than the habit of failure, is helping the child develop a favorable attitude toward good work. The teacher who helps the child to set reasonably high goals

for himself—goals of industry, neatness, accuracy, productive effort—
is helping the child to become a good worker in his adult life. And
the school that believes and teaches that work is a privilege—not a
biblical curse laid upon man in some far-off past, but an opportunity
for each individual to do something worthwhile and rewarding with
his life—is contributing to the formation of a lifelong attitude toward
work that our society will heartily approve.

Routine Work in Teaching

The National Education Association has made several ex-
haustive (and, as you read them, somewhat exhausting!) studies of
the amount of work that the ordinary classroom teacher does, the
amount of time he puts in on school work in a typical week. One of
these studies indicates that the average teacher in the elementary
school has a work-week of 47 hours, 50 minutes, and the secondary
school teacher 47 hours, 58 minutes. Of this time, about 59% is
spent in actual class instruction by the elementary teacher, and 48%
by the secondary teacher. This means, roughly speaking, that about
half of the teacher's time is devoted to non-instructional duties, work
that is often called "routine."

The Range of Activities

These extra duties are many and varied; the "average" amount
of time spent on them is not necessarily indicative of what you would
personally spend in your own teaching situation, so no attempt will
be made here to indicate just what proportion of your time each of
these duties may be expected to take. But somewhere in the neighborhood of half of your work-week will be taken up with

> —correcting papers
> —preparing outlines, units, and lesson plans
> —getting materials ready for your class
> —helping students individually
> —talking with parents
> —monitorial duties (study halls, playgrounds and lunchroom
>   supervision
> —sponsoring clubs and activities
> —preparing report cards and school records
> —staff meetings and committee work with other teachers.

The Educational Significance of "Routine"

At first glance, it might seem that it is a shame to waste the time and training of a professionally prepared teacher doing so much relatively routine work, leaving so little time for actual classroom teaching. More careful analysis of these duties, however, will reveal that many of them cannot be performed adequately by anyone other than the teacher who is in direct, daily contact with children in the classroom and who understands their group and individual problems.

No one else, for example, could prepare your lessons for you, unless we were willing to revert to the former practice of having each teacher follow the state course of study slavishly, teaching one topic after another in the prescribed sequence without variation or imagination. Or if we were willing to do straight textbook teaching, or go back to the old assignment-recitation-examination routine, we could probably relieve the teacher of much of the necessity of individual daily preparation. Likewise, if we were satisfied to stick to the course outline and the textbook, we could do away with the necessity of getting other learning materials ready for the class—supplementary reading materials, moving pictures, laboratory equipment, related art and music materials, and pictures.

Working with individual students could be eliminated if we were content to consider each boy and girl as just another occupant of a certain seat in the classroom, just another statistic in our average daily attendance. No time would need to be set aside for conferences with parents if we were really not concerned with the individual backgrounds, problems, and needs of each student as a person.

"Outside" activities such as sponsoring, supervising, and counseling students in their club activities, class organizations, home rooms, social affairs sponsored by the school, and similar extracurricular enterprises could easily be done away with if we wanted to retreat to the older notion of school as just a place for formal studying of material in the school books. Furthermore, we could relieve the teacher of much of the responsibility for recording and reporting student progress and achievement if we could look on grading as a purely mechanical process, and the report to the parent as merely an arithmetic average of scores obtained on classroom tests.

There is one more extra-instructional duty we could dispense with: staff meetings and committee work, especially the committees of teachers who work on revision of the curriculum, improving the continuity of learning experiences from one grade to another, and setting up an adequate system of school records and reports. We could do this, that is, if we were willing to have a school system entirely dominated by the superintendent and principals, and to reduce the estate of teaching to the mere carrying out of orders issued by higher authority.

The trouble, you see, is that the so-called routine work of teaching is for the most part not routine at all; it is an integral part of the kind of teaching and the kind of education that most of us believe is a vast improvement over more traditional methods and systems. If teachers are to become increasingly important in the educational enterprise, if education is to be made more useful to the students and more meaningful to society, if individual differences are to be recognized and provision made for them in the educational program—if this is what we want, then many of these out-of-class duties must be expected to take even more time than they now do in the average work-week of the teacher.

Freeing Teacher Time

But there is another way to look at this problem. Many teachers are unnecessarily burdened with duties that *are* routine and sub-professional in nature: janitorial work, routine clerical operations like recording test scores and cutting stencils, supervision of halls, lunchrooms and playgrounds that could be a shared responsibility with older students (and often, in a good school, with younger students as well). We need to make changes in our school program that will take these time-consuming duties off the shoulders of the already overburdened teacher.

Moreover, if we are constantly expecting more of teachers outside of the regular classroom teaching, provision needs to be made (as it is in a growing number of schools today) for more free time, more periods during the school day with no scheduled classes. Freed at certain hours from the pressure of regular classroom duties, the teacher will have time to do committee work, to prepare lessons, to get materials ready, and (goodness knows it is needed!) just to rest and relax before the next class.

The increasing scope of what is expected of the teacher argues well for another innovation: putting all teachers on a twelve-months' salary, with regular teaching assignments for the usual nine months, a full month's vacation, and the balance of the time to be spent in tasks such as extended committee work on the curriculum, preparation of materials for teaching, working in school-sponsored summer recreational and camping programs, and other professional duties that would fully justify a twelve-month contract.

The Classroom of Tomorrow

The discussion of what happens in the classroom has been phrased largely in terms of the typical classroom today, where each teacher is given and accepts an individual, almost autonomous, responsibility for instruction in a single grade at the elementary level or a single subject or group of related subjects at the secondary level. Two important changes are taking place in the organization of the educational program that promise to alter markedly the traditional concepts of teaching described above. One of these innovations is the ungraded or multigrade elementary school; the other is the concept of team teaching.

The Ungraded School

An increasing number of elementary schools today have abandoned the traditional concept of dividing the elementary school into definite and separate grades, one to a room with a fourth-grade teacher, say, teaching a fourth-grade class.

Both common sense and experience make it amply clear that the typical grade division doesn't really make very good sense, either descriptively or operationally. In the first place, a fourth-grade class isn't really a group of children all studying and achieving at a single level. Second, because they may be working at levels ranging from the second grade (for some students in some curricular areas) to the sixth grade (for other "fourth-graders" in other subjects), they cannot practically be taught as though they were all the same: fourth-graders studying fourth-grade subjects.

The ungraded or multigrade concept simply recognizes the situation as it is—that individual children are working and learning not by *grade* but by *level.* So, a typical ungraded elementary school will abandon all reference to the traditional grades and group students in perhaps ten levels of achievement, encompassing the work of the first four primary grades, let us say.

This permits each child to work at his own level—along with other boys and girls of similar level of achievement—in each curricular area and to advance to the next level as his rate of learning permits. Thus, Jane might be at level three in arithmetic, level four in reading, and level five in social studies—all at the same time, in the same room, and under the same teacher.

You can readily see that this is a complicated problem, one too involved for lengthy discussion here. The adoption of such a program—and schools of this sort are found today in small and economically poor as well as in large and wealthy school districts—poses many challenges for the teacher, making his work at once more complicated (preparing assignments and activities and materials for several levels at once) and simpler (by not forcing all children in the room to be working at a single assumed "grade-level," really appropriate for no single one of the students). In any case, the ungraded plan profoundly alters the simple assumption that an elementary teacher can describe his job as simply a teacher of first or third or fifth grade.

Team Teaching

Teaching has been described largely in this chapter as what is done by a single teacher taking actually sole responsibility for the operation of a single classroom. The concept of team teaching, so far applied almost exclusively at the secondary (junior and senior high) level, provides an entirely new dimension to the idea of what teaching means.

In order to utilize the special skills of individual teachers more effectively, many secondary schools are now organizing their teaching staffs into teams in certain subject-area fields. This team will work together to provide learning activities for a large number of students at the same time that this organizational pattern for the instructional staff gives even better provision for individualized instruction.

The typical teaching team will consist of a master teacher, especially equipped by training and experience to direct the planning of the course, to supervise the other members of the team, and typically to give the major lectures or presentations to the class. He will be assisted by one or two other teachers, professionally prepared but less experienced, who will take part in some of the presentations before the whole class but will work mostly with smaller groups or individuals. The team is completed by the assignment of a full-time or part-time subprofessional worker—a person with only minimal professional training whose main responsibility is preparation of teaching materials and grading of papers.

This system of team teaching has several advantages. It allows certain materials to be presented to large groups (up to 150 students) by the most expert teacher available, using well-rehearsed techniques often involving television, overhead projection of transparency materials, or other audio-visual aids. Thus, the team teacher or master teacher could present to a large group once a week a single top-notch illustrated lecture, instead of having to teach this same material to several small classes as part of a crowded daily schedule. With the time of the teacher freed from multiple and repetitious presentations, the quality of teaching can be improved.

Furthermore, while one member of the team is giving a general presentation, other members of the team are free to make plans for working with smaller groups of students or for directing individual study programs. Time and staff are thus made available also for much more systematic and effective preparation of teaching materials for the class.

Under such a plan, the individual student might spend some forty per cent of his time as a member of a large (50-150) group with one teacher, another forty per cent as a member of a small (15-20) discussion-study-activity group with another teacher, and the remaining twenty per cent of his time in directed individual study and research.

Whatever specific plan of team teaching may be employed, and for whatever educational reasons, this growing practice of reorganizing the time and special skills of teachers, and the consequent reorganization of the schedule and activities of secondary school students, will have a marked effect on the traditional concepts of what it means to be a teacher.

SEVEN: TOPICS FOR STUDY, REPORT, AND DISCUSSION

1. With your instructor's permission, arrange to visit a classroom of the grade level or the subject-matter field in which you expect to teach. Bring back to the class a report of what actually happens in the classroom.

2. Borrow from your college curriculum laboratory or other source suggested by your instructor a unit of work, or a unit plan, actually used in the grade or subject you expect to teach. Study it to see how well the kinds of learnings emphasized in this chapter are actually carried out.

3. Design a problem approach to one of the learnings appropriate to the grade or subject-matter field you expect to teach, and write out clearly the part you as the teacher would play in the problem-solving process.

4. What do you believe about the nature and conditions of good classroom discipline—that is, what is discipline and how would you achieve it in your own classroom?

5. Secure from your college curriculum laboratory or test files copies of some of the tests of various kinds (intelligence, achievement, personality, adjustment, etc.) actually used in schools. Study them to find out just what is being tested—what evaluation is being made of the students.

6. With your instructor's permission, invite some successful classroom teacher to discuss with the class the actual day-by-day "routine" of teaching.

7. What can be done to relieve teachers of much of the routine and subprofessional work that teaching now entails? (You might well read about some of the experiments designed to accomplish this purpose now being carried on in several schools under grants from the Ford Foundation and as individual experiments.)

SEVEN: BIBLIOGRAPHY

Brembeck, Cole S., *The Discovery of Teaching*. Englewood Cliffs, N. J.: Prentice-Hall, Inc., 1962. Parts 2 and 5 give a particularly refreshing and down-to-earth description of the day-to-day work of the classroom teacher.

Brubacher, John S., *A History of the Problems of Education*. New York: McGraw-Hill Book Co., Inc., 1947. Chaps. 7 and 8 contain an unusually interesting account of classroom methods used in various historical periods, from earliest times to the present.

Dale, Edgar, "To Choose Wisely Is to Live Well," *NEA Journal,* Vol. 43, No. 3 (March, 1954), 146 f. Discusses how school may help students learn to make wise choices, and hence achieve growth in one of the most important but least tangible dimensions of education—developing aesthetic and ethical values.

Educational Policies Commission, *Moral and Spiritual Values in the Public Schools.* Washington, D. C.: National Education Association, 1951. Describes in excellent fashion what values the school affirms and how it tries to teach them.

Goodlad, John I., and Robert H. Anderson, *The Ungraded Elementary School.* New York: Harcourt, Brace & World, Inc., 1959. A comprehensive discussion of the operation of ungraded and nongraded schools.

Haskew, Laurence D., and Jonathon C. McLendon, *This Is Teaching,* 2d ed. Chicago: Scott, Foresman & Company, 1962. "What Learners Do in School" (chap. 5) and "What Teachers Do in School" (chap. 6) are clearly described in the chapters noted.

Hymes, James L., Jr., *Behavior and Misbehavior.* Englewood Cliffs, N. J.: Prentice-Hall, Inc., 1955. Very brief and to-the-point discussion of modern concepts of discipline and their application in the classroom.

Rothney, John W. M., *Evaluating and Reporting Pupil Progress.* Washington, D. C.: Department of Classroom Teachers, NEA, 1955. One of the best brief treatments of the problem of grading and reporting, based on the most pertinent research findings.

Strang, Ruth, *How to Report Pupil Progress.* Chicago: Science Research Associates, 1955. Very worthwhile suggestions, in brief form, for reporting to parents. Contains some interesting and unusual points of view.

Thomas, Lawrence G., Lucien B. Kinney, Arthur P. Coladarci, and Helen A. Fielstra, *Perspective on Teaching.* Englewood Cliffs, N. J.: Prentice-Hall, Inc., 1961. Contrasting views of the teaching process are clearly presented in chap. 7.

Trethaway, Edwin H., "Don't Just Turn Them Loose," *NEA Journal,* Vol. 43, No. 4 (April, 1954), 214 f. Interesting and workable suggestions for carrying on one of teacher's "routine" duties—playground supervision.

Trump, J. Lloyd, and Dorsey Baynham, *Focus on Change—Guide to Better Schools.* New York: Rand, McNally, 1961. Suggests far-reaching plans for reorganizing the physical plant, the curriculum, and the teaching methods of the present secondary schools, with emphasis on small-group and individual study and team teaching.

Van Dalen, Deobold B., and Robert W. Brittell, *Looking Ahead to Teaching.* Boston: Allyn and Bacon, Inc., 1959. The daily work of the teacher is described with insight and precision in chap. 15, "The Teacher at Work."

Wiles, Kimball, *Teaching for Better Schools*. Englewood Cliffs, N. J.: Prentice-Hall, Inc., 1959. The role of the teacher is presented effectively in chap. 2; subsequent chapters detail ways of improving classroom teaching from the standpoint of the learner's activities.

Special facilities for partially sighted. *What other special school services might be required for this learner?*

School planetarium. *Is this facet of education one belonging to the school or to some other educational agency?*

CHAPTER EIGHT

Change Brings Expansion

In a dynamic culture that is constantly changing and expanding, in a growing country that is experiencing a tremendous rise in population, standard of living and national income, and in international importance as a world power, it is apparent that the school system too must change and expand. In previous chapters we have studied some of the effects of cultural change in our American school system: expansion of the schools in terms of numbers served, increasing time spent in school, increasing amount of money needed to support the public school system. We have also noted the expanding range and coverage of the school curriculum—the introduction of new courses, the increase of vocational offerings, the addition of such specialized subjects as driver education, the inclusion of more extra-

EXPANDING
EDUCATIONAL SERVICES

curricular activities. Together with these changes we have noted the expansion of the concept of education to include concern for personal and social development of the students, inculcation of a sense of moral and aesthetic values, and provision for the maintaining and improving of physical and mental health.

A Two-Way Expansion

These changes in the concept of education and in the actual operation of the educational system represent a two-way extension of educational services, vertical and horizontal. The vertical (up and down) extension of education is seen largely in the lengthening of the years of the common school to include preschool, kindergarten, junior college, and adult education, in addition to the more traditional elementary and high school work. The horizontal expansion of education is found in the broadening of the curriculum to include new courses, new areas of student activity, and new school services.

Criticisms of Expansion

These new tasks which have been undertaken by our educational system have not met with universal public support and approval. There are some critics of modern education who feel that the schools are "power-hungry," that they are trying to "take over" in areas which would best be left to other agencies—the home, the church, business and industrial concerns, or existing governmental units other than the school. These critics would have the schools give up some of their present educational duties and prerogatives (which they believe the schools have selfishly arrogated to themselves) and return them to the "appropriate" group or agency outside the school system. Moral development would be the sole responsibility of the home and the church, vocational training would be provided by business and industrial concerns, and all health problems of children would be the concern of the individual family.

Other critics of modern education do not accuse the schools specifically of grabbing for power over the minds and lives of children, or of trying to usurp the proper functions of other institutions and agencies; these critics merely feel that the schools are attempting to do a job that is too big to handle. Schools are criticized for trying to offer a curriculum that will meet the needs and interests of all children and youth; they are criticized for trying to extend the years of school attendance for the average youth through high school or even junior college; they are criticized for trying, with limited finances and personnel, to provide such "extras" as kindergarten, guidance services, and a full range of extracurricular activities.

We must assume for the purposes of our discussion here that these critics are honest and reasonably well informed; there would be no point at all in considering dishonest or stupid criticism. Under the assumption that these criticisms have at least some merit, then, we will not attempt any argument or refutation; rather, let us look at this phenomenon of the expansion of educational services as a fact to be understood and studied. A reasonably adequate grasp of the reasons underlying this extension of education both horizontally and vertically, and of the direction this trend is presently taking, will give us a more realistic knowledge of the nature of the American school system and the meaning of the term "education" in our culture. Moreover, the better we understand what the school is trying to do, the better will we know what teaching is about. These relatively new expansions of education have created many educational vocations that are now open to persons who have training and experience as teachers. You will do well to keep in mind the interesting vocational possibilities that some of these new areas of school service may afford you as a prospective teacher. As education has extended in many new directions, the vocations related to teaching have likewise developed new dimensions.

Nursery School and Kindergarten

Slow Acceptance of Early-Childhood Education

The belief that the public school should provide for educational experiences for younger children is relatively new in this country, and like most new concepts in education, is far from being universally accepted. The very terms used to describe this area of early childhood education are themselves somewhat unfortunate. The generic term "preschool" sometimes used for both nursery and kindergarten implies that these educational enterprises are not really a part of school at all, but just some kind of preliminary to *real* school. The term "nursery school," used generally to designate the educational activities and experiences provided for the three- and four-year-olds has an unfortunate connotation of baby-sitting—a place where the children are "kept" as a sort of custodial service while the mothers are working. Even the term "kindergarten"—an ingenious and delightful term American schools borrowed verbatim from the founder of the movement in Germany, Friedrich Froebel (1782–1852)—has certain limitations. "Child's garden" is an appropriate enough name for a part of the school where a child is encouraged to grow and develop naturally, as might a flower in a pleasant garden, but it doesn't sound enough like *real* school to satisfy some critics. (Perhaps, though, we should be grateful for Froebel's final choice of a term for this school; he started to call it "school based upon the active instincts of children." Think how *that* would sound in German!)

We would probably do well not to quarrel further with the terminology, but it is unfortunate that these terms have all had overtones of something that didn't quite deserve the name of school, a kind of education that did not really merit public approval and public financial support. Perhaps the newness of the early childhood education movement and the lack of widespread support from laymen are chiefly responsible for the relatively small place nursery schools and kindergartens still have in our public school system. The first public kindergarten in the United States was established in St. Louis in 1873, less than a quarter of a century after Froebel had developed the term for this school in Germany. The kindergarten movement has grown slowly and steadily in this country, except during the years of the Great Depression. Both the number of children in public school kindergartens and the percentage of the total school enrollment represented in the kindergarten have nearly doubled in the last ten years, but even today only about a third as many children attend kindergarten as attend first grade. Since all but a few nursery schools are operated privately, rather than by the public school systems, an accurate estimate of the total enrollment in these schools is difficult to obtain.

Rationale for Nursery School and Kindergarten

Despite the difficulty of securing adequate public interest and support for this downward extension of public education, many very sound and realistic reasons can be advanced for the operation of both nursery schools and kindergartens. As psychological research and experimentation give us more adequate knowledge of the development of human behavior and learning patterns, the importance of the early childhood years becomes more apparent. It is in the years before the child enters first grade that he develops many of the behavior patterns that will affect his entire life. Since we know that all human behavior is developmental—that it proceeds from one step to the next in relatively orderly fashion, that one learning experience affects in turn each subsequent learning—could any period of the child's life lend itself better to planned guidance of this natural development than those early years?

What can we expect of nursery school and kindergarten education? Very little formal learning, certainly; one of the first mistakes that was made in the early childhood education movement (largely as a result of parental pressure) was that of setting up a junior-grade "curriculum," patterned quite closely after the learnings that could be reasonably expected of older children. No, the child will not learn to read or to write or to work arithmetic problems in kindergarten, but he will, with proper instruction and under good environmental conditions, develop more reading readiness, better number sense, more systematic work habits, longer interest span, more ability to respond without tension to adult leadership, and any number of other abilities that will make his personal and family life more pleasant, help him to get along with other children, and facilitate his later adjustment to formal school. The nursery school is, of course, even less concerned with "formal" learnings than is the kindergarten, but both of them would be fully justified as parts of the total public school system if they did nothing more than help the child to develop individual abilities and social skills, and to grow out of immature behavior patterns that would hinder later learning and adjustment to the requirements of the first grade.

Many school systems have dropped (or considered dropping) existing early childhood education services in times of financial difficulty; these services have often been considered "frills" which might be easily dispensed with. Nursery schools in particular have had an uncertain status in this country. Many such schools were operated with the help of federal funds during the Great Depression as a means of providing jobs for teachers and other workers, and federal funds were again used to establish nurseries for children of mothers working in defense industries during World War II. These were frankly emergency measures; a sounder basis for these programs seems likely in the future. The general lay public is coming to see these schools as something more than a frill, more than a means of providing work for the unemployed or "sitter" service for working mothers. As a regular part of the public school system, both the nursery school and the kindergarten seem to be finding a more secure place in American education.

Extension of the Schools Upward

Growth of the High School

At the same time that schooling for the younger child has been slowly developing as a common feature of American education, upward extension of education has had a phenomenal growth. Whereas at the beginning of this century the "common school" that everyone was supposed to attend was generally assumed to extend only through the eighth grade, today it is assumed as a matter of course that the "common schools" include high school as well. In 1889–90, only 7 per cent of high-school-age youth (14-17 years) were enrolled in secondary schools; this percentage has increased year by year until in 1959 over 90 per cent of all youth of normal high school age were attending the secondary schools. There is every indication that this trend toward more nearly universal high school attendance will continue, and that its effect will be felt increasingly by the colleges as well. For as the "common school" concept comes to include high school attendance, so much more will it become a matter of course that students will go on to college.

Formal Higher Education

In 1900, only about 4 per cent of college-age persons were enrolled in college; just before World War II the figure had risen to 16 per cent; by 1953, the number in college represented 28 per cent of the total college-age population.[1] As of 1962, the 3.4 million students enrolled in institutions of higher learning represented 37 per cent of the college-age population. Because the general population of the country is increasing so swiftly and so steadily, even this relatively modest increase in terms of percentage would mean approxi-

[1] Francis H. Horn, "Our Expanding College Enrolments," *NEA Journal,* Vol. 43, No. 4 (April, 1954), p. 217. Reprinted by permission.

mately a doubling of present college enrollments by 1970. Colleges are, like high schools, rapidly becoming a part of the common school system.

Conflicting viewpoints.   Whether or not this increase in college enrollment is wholly desirable is another question, often raised by critics of public education. Should college education be reserved for the relatively small percentage of our population most able to profit from college, or should we open the gates and admit everyone to college who aspires to a post-high-school education? If not, how can we be sure that the "right" people go on to a higher education? At the present, fewer than half of the *most able* students academically (those in the upper quarter of their high school graduating classes) go on to college; the rest of this group who would appear to be able to profit most effectively from college training are either unable to afford a college education, are more interested in getting a job and starting to make money, or are otherwise insufficiently motivated even to attempt college. Furthermore, we have no real evidence that those in the lower brackets of the high school graduating classes, say the next 25 per cent or even 50 per cent, could not profit from at least a part of a full college education.

Reasons for growth of college enrollments.   Two conflicting points of view are evident. Some say that too many of our American youth are encouraged and allowed to attend college, to attempt an educational program that they cannot profitably pursue and complete; other critics of higher education maintain that we are somehow failing the youth of this nation in not making it financially possible for more of our most able students to attend college, or in not making college education meaningful enough and attractive enough to motivate at least the abler students to undertake a college career.

However this debate may be decided (and it is a critical problem of top-level national importance) it is still obvious that college education is gradually becoming a part of the common school system. It is also apparent that there are strong forces at work in our culture to make college education even more attractive to many than it is now, and to cause an even more substantial increase in college enrollment than we now anticipate. As one college president has put it,

> No other nation in the world attaches as much importance to education as does the United States. Our democratic tradition holds that education is a means to individual social and economic advancement.

Surely the motivation that in 50 years [1900-1950] has increased the percent of college-age population in college from 4 to 28 will continue to influence more and more young people to seek a college education.

This seems especially true in the light of the social and economic pressures operating to enforce this belief in the power of education. It is made increasingly apparent to young people that ours is primarily a technological civilization, and that technical and specialized training is needed to get ahead in this world.[2]

This same writer goes on to suggest that factors other than our national tradition of respect for higher education and the increasing requirements for college-trained people in business and industry will also work to increase college enrollments. High schools are offering broader curricula which contain introductions to fields of academic interest that may strike a spark of intellectual curiosity sufficient to spur the student to go on to college. Junior colleges, in many cities and states as "free" as high schools (or nearly so), are making it possible for thousands of high school graduates to get a taste of college, a taste that may encourage continuation of formal education. Many very able students (and some very indifferent ones) have been encouraged to attend college under the financial support offered by the G.I. Bill of Rights. Moreover, the opportunities offered in business and industry for immediate employment upon graduation from high school are diminishing in number and financial attractiveness; this tends to help the student decide that he might just as well go on to college—not a very high motivation for college work, to be sure, but a reasonably effective one.

All of these factors, then—some of them educationally sound and some not so sound—tend to emphasize the importance of formal higher education in our country: the American people's historic faith in education (the more the better!), the demands of our economy for college-trained workers, the desire of parents that their children should have the same (or better) educational opportunities as they themselves enjoyed, and the increasing availability of higher education subsidized at least in part from public funds.

The junior college. But there are less formal and less extended programs of post-high-school education than those found in the regular four-year colleges. The growing importance of the junior college movement has been mentioned. The junior college in many

[2] *Ibid.,* pp. 217 ff. Reprinted by permission.

areas is already considered as a logical and normal extension of
high school education, and there is a growing belief among many
educators and laymen that the time is not far off when many, if not
most, of the average class of high school graduates will continue
their work in the junior college as a matter of course. The President's
Commission on National Goals has recommended (1960) that[3]

> . . . there should be roughly within commuting distance of
> every high school graduate (except in sparsely settled regions)
> an institution that performs the following functions:
>
>   (a) offers two-year terminal programs for students not going
>   on to a four-year college career.
>   (b) offers transfer programs for students who do wish to
>   complete a four-year program.
>   (c) serves as a technical institute for the community, serv-
>   ing local needs for vocational and subprofessional edu-
>   cation.
>   (d) offers continuing education to adults.

Adult education. There are now in operation a growing variety
of adult education programs, many of which are not intended as a
sequential continuation of regular secondary education, but are designed for any adult who is interested, regardless of his educational
background. Some of these may be conducted by the regular public
school staff, others by the junior college, and others under the
auspices of four-year colleges and universities. It has been estimated
that some 30 million adults are now partaking of formal or informal
educational programs conducted by various educational agencies.
Evening classes of "subject-matter" or hobby or interest-group type
are now widely offered by both public schools and colleges. The agricultural extension services of various land-grant colleges and other
public and governmental agencies provide continuation education for
hundreds of thousands of rural people. Libraries often conduct study-
discussion groups for adults. Scores of colleges and universities offer
countless extension and correspondence courses designed specifically
to meet the needs of the adult population. Educational radio and
television programs are growing in importance (and improving in
quality) as media for adult education. This brief mention of forms
of adult education is but indicative of some of the ways in which
provision for the upward expansion of education from the traditional

[3] President's Commitee on National Goals, *Goals for Americans*
(Englewood Cliffs, N. J.: Prentice-Hall, Inc., 1960), p. 91.

eight-year or twelve-year program is offering new educational horizons for the people of America.

The problem of illiteracy. There are still some critics who view this upward extension of public education as an unwarranted expenditure of public funds and of educational effort. "Why not leave good enough alone," say these critics, in effect. "If we provide free education through the twelfth grade, isn't that enough?" There are many answers that might be given to this objection to adult education, but perhaps one will be sufficient. For all our boasting of being an educated nation, a nation which provides universal and compulsory education for all of its citizens, the cold fact remains that we still have a shocking degree of illiteracy in the United States. Complete illiteracy, total inability to read and write, is not a particularly serious problem in this country. But *functional* illiterates (defined by the Bureau of the Census as those with less than five years of schooling) constitute a problem of grave national importance. One study published by the United States Office of Education indicates that there are today some 10 million adults in our country—2.2 per cent of the adult population—who are "functionally illiterate." Fortunately, most of this group of illiterates is found in the older portion of our population; the younger generation is so much better educated, on the whole, that the problem of illiteracy may—literally—die out before too many years. Yet perhaps a few of the older illiterates can still be helped.

Nevertheless, illiteracy is a serious matter, and failure of many of our youth to complete their formal education (even though they go beyond the fifth grade and thus escape the stigma of being technically "illiterate") is even more serious. Nearly one-third of the students who enter our American high schools drop out before graduation. When we realize that about 600,000 men were rejected during World War II because they were not even literate enough to be used for the most routine of military assignments, we can see what a serious problem illiteracy is in terms of our national security.

Strengthening of our national security, however, is only one of the many reasons for advocating the extension of education upward, for increasing opportunities for adult education. Our social, economic, and technological progress as a nation depends upon not only a literate, but a truly enlightened, populace. In terms of human happiness and human values alone, the extension of educational opportunity upward is a worthy aim of American education.

The Education of Exceptional Children

Up to this point we have been concerned largely with what we have called the vertical expansion of education—extension of educational opportunities downward to the children below the first grade, and upward to youth beyond high school age and to adults who have "finished" school. As was indicated earlier in this chapter, however, public school education in the United States has been expanding horizontally as well—broadening its offerings, its coverage, its services to include areas which have been neglected in the more traditional schools of the past.

One of the most devastating criticisms that has been made of the traditional American public school is that it is so concerned with the average student that it neglects the un-average. Some critics have phrased this criticism by saying that our schools are too democratic, too much concerned with the common man, and this at a time when what we need to develop is the uncommon man. It is certainly true that democracy in education has all too often meant mediocrity, though this is a fault not of democracy, but of the way our schools have actually been operated.

For example, there is no honest way to refute the statement that our public schools have all too often neglected the bright and gifted children in order to provide a program for the just-average student. We have wasted one of our most precious human resources—intellectual ability—in our attempt to pitch our educational offerings at a level suited to the majority. At the same time, we have been guilty of gross educational malpractice in neglecting the dull or mentally retarded child, letting him sit out his years of school alternately frustrated by having to attempt assigned tasks too difficult for him to accomplish, or bored by having nothing to do because the teacher has given him up as hopeless.

The Bright and Gifted

Only a relatively few children are naturally endowed with superior mental ability. The bright—I.Q.'s of 120 to 140—and the gifted— I.Q.'s above 140—represent only a very small fraction of the total group of children with whom the school works, but they have been

quite accurately described as "America's underprivileged children."
What happens to the exceptionally able child in the average schoolroom? He sits. Normal assignments do not tax his ability or take
much of his time. He has, typically, a reading skill several years in
advance of his grade level; a bright fifth-grader may read as well or
better than the average high school sophomore. Since he has already
learned what the rest of the class is struggling with, he is often bored
by the hourly routine of the classroom. He may become withdrawn,
given to excessive daydreaming; his work habits and his attention to
what he reads and hears may deteriorate so sharply that his actual
school achievement is poor, and his grades low. Or, becoming bored
with what *isn't* happening in class, he may become a disturbing influence just for the sheer fun of having something to do. In all prob-
ability, however, he will continue to do good work, to get along well
with his teachers, and to be well adjusted to the social grouping of
his class. For the exceptionally able child, contrary to popular opinion,
has not been equipped with this special intellectual ability at the
expense of other skills and abilities. The bright or gifted child is more
than likely to be healthy, well adjusted socially, and endowed with
the normal range of interests common to his contemporaries.

Promising practices.   The modern school is making a conscious
effort, in most cases, to extend its program in ways that will mean a
better education for the exceptionally able child. One technique used
to help such children is simple grade acceleration; push the child a
grade or two ahead so the work will be more challenging. This sometimes works out well, depending on the individual child, but more
often it is a less-than-satisfactory solution to the problem. The child
may find the work of the higher grade more suited to his ability, but
the rich and worthwhile experiences of living and working and playing and growing up with his own age-group are lost. Another positive
step that the school may take to help create an adequate school
experience for the bright or gifted child is to provide special rooms
or special teachers. In the more challenging and appropriate environment that such special rooms or special teachers offer, the child may
find intellectual satisfaction, but again he is cut off from the kind of
normal school life he needs. Perhaps the most promising of the
newer practices in dealing with this special group of children is
enrichment—provision (in the normal classroom environment and
at the normal grade placement) for a variety of reading materials,
laboratory experiences, opportunities to construct and experiment

and create that will actually *enrich* the learning situation to a satisfying and challenging degree for even the brightest student.

The Slow Learner

Each public school has a share of the children endowed with less than normal intelligence, ranging downward from the dull-normal to the literally hopeless mental incompetent. Fortunately, there are not really as many of these dull students as we used to assume; many students whose academic achievement and schoolroom attitude would have once marked them as mentally deficient we find now are suffering from reading difficulties, emotional upsets, or physical disabilities rather than from any serious lack of intellectual ability. The truly dull student, however, is not at all well provided for by the normal classroom procedures or environment. He is, typically, retarded in reading, that basic skill without which he cannot hope to begin to keep up with the class. He doesn't understand what he tries to read, he can't make sense out of the arithmetic problems, he is not articulate in oral or written expression, and his understanding of such intellectual subtleties as logical conclusions or cause-and-effect relationships is very inadequate. So what happens to the dull? Often he lives in a constant state of tension and frustration; he slows down the class, he makes the work of the teacher extremely difficult, but most important of all, he feels useless and hopeless. Things are always moving too fast for him; he is always behind. The emotional upsets which accompany his feeling of failure and inadequacy tend to prevent even the slow learning which for him would be normal.

Promising practices. As we noted in discussing the problems faced by the exceptionally bright child, the typical school is not yet equipped in terms of staff, money, or materials to do the best possible job that could be done with the slow learner, the dull or retarded child. But at least the modern school is recognizing this as a problem, and is expanding its educational services for this group by providing special teachers and special rooms and special books for the slow learner. Most important of all, the modern school is trying to give the slow-learning child a needed sense of personal worth, and a chance to achieve at his own level of competence. This means adjustments in the curriculum, in the teaching methods, in the grading system and— what seems so horrendous to some critics of modern education—a modification of the "standards" of the school itself.

The Emotionally Disturbed

Another type of exceptional student that the modern school tries to help is the emotionally disturbed student, the one with the beginnings of what might later develop into true mental illness. This concern of the school for the psychological well-being of its students has necessitated another expansion of traditional educational services. Good schools have always been concerned with their students as people, but the modern school has a special interest in the *personal* problems of its children and youth.

Prevalence of mental ill-health. Mental illness is probably no more prevalent today than in earlier times, but we know more about it, particularly in its early stages, and have more accurate bases for recognizing and treating its various manifestations. Still, it is quite startling to review some of the facts about mental illness which have been summarized by the National Association for Mental Health:

> One out of every twelve children will at some time suffer from mental illness severe enough to require hospitalization.
> Almost half of the hospital space in the United States is taken up by patients suffering from mental illness.
> A quarter of a million new patients are admitted to mental hospitals each year.
> Nearly half of all persons who seek medical treatment have illnesses associated with emotional disturbances.[4]

The schools of today cannot conscientiously afford to ignore a problem of such magnitude. Every classroom has its "cases": Johnny seems constantly withdrawn from the world of reality, spending excessive amounts of time daydreaming; Mike is always extremely belligerent; Sally breaks out into frequent temper tantrums, even though she is a senior in high school; Paula is pathologically weary, fatigued, and despondent. These are not unusual instances; persons like these can be found in almost any school. Are these but minor quirks of personality, individual differences that must merely be accepted? Possibly; more probably not. They are more like signs of emotional disturbance that could become very serious, incipient mental illness that may ultimately be disabling.

The school's concern. What can the school do? Unfortunately, very few schools are equipped with adequately trained personnel in

---

[4] *12 Facts about Mental Illness* (New York: National Association for Mental Health, 1951).

sufficient numbers to embark upon any real program of treating mental illness, and certainly the average classroom teacher should hesitate to rush in where even psychiatrists fear to tread. But the good school today can try to spot cases of incipient mental illness as early as possible and make referrals to existing mental health and child-guidance clinics. The good school can try to make the school environment favorable to the development and maintenance of sound mental health by offering a realistic curriculum geared to the needs and capabilities of each student and a program of school living that will foster good mental health.

For although the problems of mental health and mental illness are often extremely complex, challenging the best understanding and deepest insights of even the most expert psychologists and psychiatrists, the basic concept of mental health is well within the understanding of every classroom teacher. The National Association for Mental Health has given a simple, understandable listing of some of the characteristics of people with good mental health, as follows:

1. *They feel comfortable about themselves:*
    They are not bowled over by their own emotions—by their fears, anger, love, jealousy, guilt or worries.
    They can take life's disappointments in their stride.
    They have a tolerant, easy-going attitude towards themselves as well as others; they can laugh at themselves.
    They neither underestimate nor overestimate their abilities.
    They can accept their own shortcomings.
    They have self-respect.
    They feel able to deal with most situations that come their way.
    They get satisfaction from the simple, everyday pleasures.

2. *They feel right about other people:*
    They are able to give love and to consider the interests of others.
    They have personal relationships that are satisfying and lasting.
    They expect to like and trust others, and take it for granted that others will like and trust them.
    They respect the many differences they find in people.
    They do not push people around, nor do they allow themselves to be pushed around.
    They can feel they are part of a group.
    They feel a sense of responsibility to their neighbors and fellow men.

3. *They are able to meet the demands of life:*
    They do something about their problems as they arise.

> They accept their responsibilities.
> They shape their environment whenever possible; they adjust to it whenever necessary.
> They plan ahead but do not fear the future.
> They welcome new experiences and new ideas.
> They make use of their natural capacities.
> They set realistic goals for themselves.
> They are able to think for themselves and make their own decisions.
> They put their best effort into what they do, and get satisfaction out of doing it.[5]

There is no teacher or school that could not do a better job than is now generally being done in fostering the kind of mental health described above, as a distinct part of everyday classroom "living and learning."

The Physically Handicapped

Another extension of educational service that is quite widespread today is better provision for the physically handicapped student. This is nothing new; for a long time schools have recognized their responsibility for the "whole child," not just for his intellectual or academic development. This concern has been, however, largely humanitarian; common human decency demands that the school make special provisions for the handicapped child. But there has today been added another reason for the school's concern with such children: it is very evident now that the purely "educational" or "academic" work of the school cannot be successful unless the student with a physical handicap is given special treatment. And even from a purely economic standpoint, it costs less to educate them than to neglect them!

Competent medical authorities have estimated that approximately 12 per cent of all school children have visual handicaps; 5 per cent, hearing difficulties; and lesser but substantial numbers suffer from speech defects, impaired motor abilities, and other chronic disabilities and illnesses. Diseased tonsils, faulty heart action, malnutrition—these and many other physical weaknesses are found quite commonly among school children.

A positive approach.   Yet, these children are basically like other children: they have the same rights, the same needs, the same sensi-

[5] *MENTAL HEALTH IS . . . 1, 2, 3,* published by the National Association for Mental Health, 1790 Broadway, New York 19, N. Y. Reprinted by permission.

bilities, the same emotions, and often the same potentialities. We should think of the visually handicapped student not as the "blind child," but as the *normal child who can't see*. Better yet, we need to put our educational emphasis on the inherent strengths, not the chance limitations, of the "exceptional" child; to emphasize not what he can't do, but what he can. We should treat these children as normally as possible—give them special help, special educational programs, special teaching, but keep them with normal children as much as we can. And in no case should our concern with special educational treatment of handicapped children lead to such overemphasis of *their* needs that we diminish or impair our educational program for the normal children.

The present-day school has no desire to compete with existing agencies concerned with individual and community health, or to try to duplicate the work of private physicians and hospitals. From both a humanitarian and an educational point of view, however, the school seems obligated to expand its traditional educational services for all children to include a broad and continuing health program. Adequate health records, regular physical examinations, and provision for nursing and infirmary service are the bases of a minimum program. Much more far-reaching, and of particular importance to the handicapped, are such practices as special instruction for the students with poor eyesight or poor hearing, special remedial health programs for those with other handicaps, and provision for special teachers to visit the "homebound" students and bring the school right into their homes. To some critics this last program seems beyond the proper scope of the school, but an American school system that boasts of being free and universal cannot blandly condemn to educational oblivion the child who is so unfortunate as to be physically unable to attend school in a regular classroom.

Guidance Services

"I don't want any teacher guiding *my* child!" This was the instant reaction of one college professor recently when the proposal for a guidance course for teachers was brought up for discussion in the college Curriculum Committee. Such misunderstanding of the guidance concept, even on the part of otherwise well-educated and well-informed people, is not at all uncommon. Another teacher, this time a public school elementary teacher in a large and progressive city school system, told the writer not long ago that she believed the present system of keeping cumulative personnel records for each school child—a practice found in a majority of school systems today —was all a part of a subversive plot to overthrow the American way of life. When questioned further about the reasons for her belief, she explained that some foreign power was secretly encouraging the keeping of these records showing cultural background, health status, family economic status, and the achievement of the school child so that, when the "revolution" finally came, these records could be seized by the new government and used as a basis for liquidation of reactionary families and the assignment of political undesirables to forced labor camps!

The School Guidance Concept

Informal guidance is as old as education itself, but the more formal guidance programs and guidance services are relatively new developments. Partly because they are new and partly because guidance connotes to some people the dispensing of advice or the handing out of ready-made solutions, these programs and services which the school has undertaken are often suspected or misunderstood.

Guidance in either the elementary school or the secondary school is a systematic, sympathetic, informed way of helping students solve their own problems. It is not concerned primarily with the so-called problem child; it is not basically a disciplinary function. Guidance is for *all* children and youth; every normal person has some problems which he can solve more quickly, more easily, with more lasting satisfaction if he has some help.

The field of guidance is sometimes divided into separate component areas, such as "vocational guidance," "educational guidance," and "personal guidance." This division into areas is useful in pointing up certain facets of the guidance program which require special attention or special training for the teacher, but it is wrong to assume that each of these areas is separate, unrelated to the others. Guidance is concerned with the whole person. How can you separate vocational choice and vocational fitness from problems of educational achievement and personal adjustment?

There are several reasons for the expanding concern of today's school with guidance programs and services. One is the modern concept of education as a sequence of real experiences, and of learning as a change in behavior occurring as a result of these educational experiences. If we believe that concept of education to be true, then a substantial part of the work of the teacher becomes that of guiding the learner's growth and development so that he may gain maximum benefits from these learning experiences.

Another reason for the growing participation of the school in guidance lies in the development of a modern psychology which gives us more knowledge of human behavior. Now that we have more accurate psychological knowledge, better-trained teachers, and better instruments for measuring individual differences in intelligence, aptitude, personality traits, and interests, the modern school is better equipped to engage in systematic guidance programs.

Changes in the public educational system itself argue for the devotion of more school time to guidance services and activities. For example, thousands of children come today from homes and communities lacking in adequate provisions for normal social development, opportunities to make meaningful choices, chances to live surrounded by the love and affection that begets a feeling of personal security. Now that education has become almost universal—nearly every child of school age continues through elementary school at least—the number and variety of the problems the school has to deal with are multipled. Moreover, the general public expects more of the school today, expects the school to help the child not only in formal academic learning experiences, but in individual, social, vocational, aesthetic, and moral development as well.

As the need for school guidance services has expanded, the need for trained guidance personnel has grown, too. Specialists trained in various aspects of guidance—vocational guidance and occupational-aptitude testing, for example—are needed in the public school system, but the main reliance for getting the guidance work done must still be placed upon the ordinary classroom teacher. For it is the classroom teacher who is in daily, personal contact with the children and youth, and it is the curriculum, the methods, the materials, and above all the spirit that pervades the individual classroom that serve best as effective instruments of guidance.

The Testing Program

One aspect of school guidance services that has received considerable emphasis in recent years is the formal testing program. If we are really to do a good job in helping children learn and grow and adjust, we must know more about them. Diagnostic achievement tests, which show not only the amount and extent of knowledge "possessed," but disclose the specific academic strengths and weaknesses of each student, are an integral part of any testing program. Equally necessary are intelligence tests, used not so much to determine the standard measure of innate mental ability or I.Q. as to find out specific intellectual strengths and limitations of each student so that he may be aided in capitalizing upon those strengths and helped in overcoming those limitations. Social development or personality tests, still not really perfected nor wholly accurate, are—despite their limitations—another instrument for finding out more about the individual student so that the teacher can better aid him in attaining satisfactory emotional and social adjustment and maturity. Specific vocational interest and aptitude tests, like the others mentioned, are by no means infallible; the results of a single test or a battery of tests give the teacher no safe grounds for telling the student what his vocation should be. They provide, however, valuable objective background information that can wisely be used by the teacher in helping the student to arrive at a relatively firm vocational choice.

The testing program provides no magic key to unlock all the inner recesses of the mind and spirit of the child, nor does it provide any ready-made solutions for individual problems. It serves, and intends to serve, only the purpose of helping the child to help himself.

Recreation and School Camping

Each of the areas under our general topic—the expanding educational services of the modern school—must be approached, it seems, on a somewhat defensive note. Each area is introduced as though it first had to be justified, then explained. Perhaps the reason for this seemingly apologetic approach is simply this: most of the expansions of school services that have appeared in the past few decades have been subject to severe and heated public controversy. Each has had to fight to win recognition and support, both from the general public and often, as well, from conservative educators representing somewhat vested academic interests.

So, again we must prepare to meet the inevitable question: "Why does the school have to get involved in organized recreation and school camping programs? Isn't the school overburdened as it is with a constantly expanding program of a more distinctly educational nature?" After-school, weekend, and summer recreation programs and outdoor camping may seem, at first glance, unjustifiable extensions of the public school educational services, but convincing reasons can be advanced for their introduction, continuation, and expansion.

The Obligation of the School

Most professional educators and laymen are in agreement that any sound concept of the task of the public school must view education as a lifelong matter, not just something that happens to the child for a few years between the hours of nine and four, nine or ten months out of the year. If this belief is correct, it becomes a special concern of the school to provide for the out-of-school hours, days, and months, and for the post-school years—to provide, not just more of the traditional academic program, but something that the children and youth definitely need, something they will not get otherwise. This means quite simply that in those communities where out-of-school leisure-time activities are already provided informally by the culture pattern or more formally by other agencies, the school will in no way try to duplicate adequate existing services and programs. But in places where existing programs of nonacademic educational experiences are not available, the school must, within the limits set by public desire and public financial support, seek to provide such worthwhile experiences.

In many cities and towns, and in some rural areas, opportunities for wholesome, constructive leisure-time activities are extremely limited; readily available in the place of these desirable activities for children and youth (and many adults as well) are much less desirable, many vicious, harmful, physically and morally debilitating "things to do." With no opportunity for good leisure-time pursuits, the young folk are faced only with a choice among the undesirable activities. Is it not only reasonable, then, that the school should solicit public support for a program that would make it possible to keep the school playground open under competent supervision after school hours, on weekends, and in the summer, rather than condemn the children to play in hazardous streets, to find their recreation in the "asphalt jungle" of the modern city? Is it not also reasonable that school officials and teachers should try to work out plans for opening the woodworking and metalworking shops, the art rooms, the home-making laboratories during out-of-school hours so that young folk and adults alike could have a place to pursue constructive leisure-time activities under helpful supervision?

These off-hours, whole-year programs have justifications beyond the purely recreational or leisure-time values. They may contribute directly to better academic work, to better classroom spirit and discipline, to the development of important individual growth and social interplay, and to the enlargement of interests and the enrichment of experience.

School Camping

Of all of the "extras" mentioned in the preceding paragraphs, school camping is the most radical and least understood of these new proposals for expanding the services of the schools; it deserves special mention and explanation. This is a pioneer movement; only a handful of schools, relatively speaking, have made even a beginning in providing school-sponsored camps and camping trips for their students. No one would recommend that this should become a regular part of the program of all schools: many rural, town, and small-city areas can provide a sufficient number of the same experiences that camping would bring by using the ordinary school and community setting. Many schools, however, are located in areas that provide no suitable and easily accessible camping facilities. Many other schools simply do not have the money (or any foreseeable chance of getting the money) that it would take to operate such a program.

School camping means, basically, providing opportunities for children and youth to "go to school" for a period of time in a special outdoor environment conducive to good learning and happy group living. A group of boys and girls, usually a given grade or class as a whole, is taken out to a camp (owned by the school or rented from some private or public agency) and given a week or so of guided experience in outdoor living. The child's own family, in keeping with American custom and culture patterns, provides the cost of food and perhaps a nominal "room" fee, but the school bears all of the expense of transportation and instruction—this is real school, not just a recreational outing. The regular teachers are used, their services supplemented by special counselors or resource persons who can help enrich the educational experiences provided.

Educational justification. A school camping program is quite in keeping with the best of modern educational theory and practice: it provides learning by direct experience, enrichment of the traditional curriculum, opportunity for individual growth and experiences of working with a group, and occasions for the development of worthy attitudes toward work, conservation of natural resources, and protection of the rights of others. The camping experience provides plenty of opportunity for formal and informal learning activities. One state which has pioneered in the development of the school camp program has listed these among the activities that could be carried on:

> physical improvement of the camp site and surrounding area
> study of elementary forest management, wildlife management, and fish management
> fire fighting and prevention
> study and practice of soil conservation
> gathering and recording of useful data (weather records, stream-flow records, etc.) [6]

The above list is given in terms of general activities. If we further refine and expand this list, it will be seen that such activities as those mentioned, and others that might be suggested, can be closely related to the regular classroom curriculum at both elementary and high school levels. A partial list of the distinctly and directly educational experiences that the campers might have could include these:

> —*Science*—study and identification of plants and animals; study of geology; gathering science specimens for school laboratory or museum.
> —*Social science*—history of the region; study of local industries; study of maps.
> —*Language arts*—writing reports, records, journals; pre- and post-planning in oral and written form.
> —*Mathematics*—figuring costs of food and supplies; operating camp store; mathematics applied to logging, building of dams, soil conservation practices; measuring land areas.

This is, of course, only a partial list of what might be done and what

---

[6] Lee M. Thurston, *Community School Camping* (Lansing, Michigan: Superintendent of Public Instruction, n.d.), pp. 12 ff.

might be learned. You could probably suggest many other possible educational experiences that camping could bring to the students.

School camping is new, and will probably grow rather slowly; it is, however, an extension of educational services that the school can legitimately undertake, because it is in keeping with the most convincing educational theory and the best educational practice, and because it fits in well with the regular work of the school in meeting the needs of individual students, of school groups, and of our society.

Limitations on the Expanding Role of the School

This chapter has dealt with the areas in which the public school is now expanding its educational services or adding new services. The field of possible further expansion in the future may seem practically unlimited, but certain specific limiting factors should be noted. The first is public sentiment; each school system is a direct expression of what the public feels is most important educationally, and each school tends to teach those things the public wants it to teach. Public sentiment is powerful, and rightly so in a democratic society, but sentiment is in turn influenced by financial considerations. There are many things which the general public would be perfectly willing for the school to do if it didn't cost any money.

The Pioneering Role of the Private School

Because public sentiment favorable to worthwhile educational ventures into new and unfamiliar fields is often slow in developing, and because public financial support for such ventures is often lacking, it is well that we have in our democracy a private school system as well as a public one. For the private schools are in a position to do many things that the public school is prohibited by law from doing, financially unable to do, or limited in doing by tradition or public sentiment.

Since this book is concerned with the American *public* school system, little attention is given herein to private schools, even though they enroll more than 4¼ million elementary and secondary students. But it is only fair to note in passing that many of the extensions of educational services mentioned in this chapter—as well as many commonly accepted educational practices now found in public school classrooms—were first pioneered by private schools of one sort or another. Much of the first experimentation with the new progressive education championed by John Dewey and other educators in the first decades of this century was carried on in the private schools of America. These schools had the courage and opportunity to make many of the first experiments and many of the most egregious mistakes with progressive education—and the public schools are the beneficiaries today of these early private-school efforts.

There are limits, then, to how far public educational services will expand during any given era, and many notable experiments will have to be carried on by private schools and other nonschool agencies before the "new" becomes the "common" in the public school system. Every indication, however, points to a continued, orderly, yet exciting expansion of the role of the public school in American culture.

EIGHT: TOPICS FOR STUDY, REPORT, AND DISCUSSION

1. With your instructor's permission and help, arrange to visit (as individuals or in very small groups) a good nursery school or kindergarten. After the visit, record what kinds of "learning" you saw in process, and discuss the value of considering early childhood education as a "real" part of the public school system.
2. With the permission of your instructor, select a committee to interview the director of adult education in your college, and bring back to the class a firsthand description of the program, problems, and future of adult education in the area the college or university serves.
3. What would be your reply to the criticism that our schools are too democratic, too much concerned with the common man?
4. How do you personally measure up to the yardstick of good mental health given in this chapter? What possible weaknesses do you detect in yourself that might hinder you as a teacher?
5. Find out what your state is doing in the area of education of exceptional children. How is the program organized and supported? Is it adequate to meet the needs of all of the exceptional children for whom the school must feel a legitimate concern?
6. Assume that you are a teacher who has been chosen to explain briefly to the PTA why the school is instituting a formal program of guidance services. What would you say to the parents?
7. Would school camping be practical in the public school system with which you are best acquainted? Give reasons for your answer.
8. Arrange, with the help of your instructor, for a panel discussion of the place of the private school in American education. It would be well to have on the panel one or more persons who are directly identified with the work of private or parochial schools.

EIGHT: BIBLIOGRAPHY

Association for Supervision and Curriculum Development, *Guidance in the Curriculum,* 1955 Yearbook. Washington, D. C.: National Education Association, 1955. "Treats primarily one aspect of Guidance— that part which can and should be done by *teachers* on all school levels and in all their contacts with children."

Christianson, Helen M., Mary M. Rogers, and Blanche A. Ludlum, *The Nursery School: Adventure in Living and Learning.* Boston: Houghton Mifflin Co., 1961. Chap. 7 does an especially good job of explaining the educational bases for the downward extension of early-childhood education.

DeHaan, Robert F., and Robert J. Havinghurst, *Educating Gifted Children,* rev. ed. Chicago: The University of Chicago Press, 1961. An excellent general survey of this facet of the expanding role of the public school.

De Young, Chris A., and Richard Wynn, *American Education,* 4th ed. New York: McGraw-Hill Book Co., Inc., 1960. The horizontal expansion of education is described in detail in chaps. 5 and 8, and the expansion of education into the co-curricular areas, in chap. 14.

Frandsen, Arden N., *Educational Psychology: The Principles of Learning in Teaching.* New York: McGraw-Hill Book Co., Inc., 1961. The school's concern for mental health is examined in detail in chaps. 12-14.

Gilliland, John W., *School Camping: A Frontier of Curriculum Improvement.* Washington, D. C.: Association for Supervision and Curriculum Development, NEA, 1954. Describes existing programs in school camping to show educational values, possible difficulties, and great future promise of such programs.

Heely, Allan V., *Why the Private School?* New York: Harper & Row, Publishers, 1951. A private school official makes a good case (from one point of view only, of course) for the maintenance of the private school in America.

Hoppock, Anne, *What Are Kindergartens For?* Washington, D. C.: Association for Childhood Education International, 1959. This brief pamphlet contains an excellent rationale for the publicly-supported kindergarten.

National Education Association, *Testing, Testing, Testing.* Washington, D. C.: National Education Association, 1962. A brief, very well written pamphlet on the "burgeoning testing movement" in our school system, with cautions and specific recommendations regarding the use of standardized evaluative instruments.

Research Division, National Education Association, "College Attendance and Youth," *NEA Research Bulletin,* Vol. 40, No. 1 (February, 1962), 18-21. Examines briefly but succinctly the reasons for college attendance and nonattendance of the nation's youth.

Wilson, C. C., ed., *School Health Services*. Washington, D. C.: National Education Association, 1953. Produced by a joint committee of the NEA and the American Medical Association, this is primarily a handbook for school health workers, but is also a good overview of the school's function in health education and services.

A high school science class. *Does the greater maturity of high school students imply a lesser need for nonbook materials than is found in the elementary school?*

A good learning environment. *What educational outlook does this classroom appear to illustrate and implement?*

CHAPTER NINE

If you were to ask a teacher at the end of a long, hard day, "What did you work with today?" he would probably reply "Thirty-five sixth-graders," or "Five science classes." The reply would be substantially correct; teachers work primarily with children and youth, individually, in groups, and in classes. But teachers also work with the "tools of the trade," for education—like every other trade, job, occupation, or profession—has certain occupational instruments used in getting the job done.

These tools of teaching, these materials used in the learning process, are of interest to teachers first of all because they make teaching more efficient and more enjoyable. Furthermore, the teacher needs to become familiar with these materials and tools of teaching just to be able to keep up with the changing developments in the field. And finally, the teacher today has more of a voice than did his predecessors in the selection and use of teaching-learning materials; he needs to know about these materials in order to participate intelligently in decisions about what the school should purchase and how these materials should be utilized for maximum effectiveness.

THE TOOLS
OF TEACHING

The Educational Setting

The school building and the classrooms in the building would not seem to be, at first glance, properly included under the general heading of "Tools for Teaching." The building is—well, just a schoolhouse, built by the community; the teacher merely teaches there, and the children go to school there. And the individual classroom—well, it's just the room where Miss Spring teaches or where the history class meets.

Educational Importance of the School Building

This view of the educational setting—the school building with its play yard, classrooms, corridors, shops, and service facilities—as just a place where "school happens" was quite justifiable in earlier times. As long as educators persisted in the old view of a mind-body dualism, any concern for the physical conditions under which learning was to take place seemed ridiculous. If education consists in training the mind, then any concern with the body or the emotions is superfluous and any attempt to make the school surroundings actually pleasant would be looked on by many as downright sinful. Of course, throughout the ages of educational history, some especially wise and forward-looking teachers realized the importance of the educational setting, but those who did so were in a distinct minority.

Today, most educators and an increasing number of laymen tend to view the school plant as something which exists to implement the work of the school, an educational instrument designed with educational objectives in mind. As such, the educational setting becomes in reality one of the chief tools for teaching; it is one of the most important of the pieces of equipment we provide for teachers.

The teacher's concern.   The teacher, then, is legitimately interested in the school building and the rest of the educational surroundings because the teacher's work is directly affected thereby. Some teachers feel, however, that building problems and problems of space utilization and classroom equipment, however educationally important they may be, are really the proper concern of the school board and the administrative staff only. Surely, they are important, they say, but these problems lie quite outside the sphere of the teacher's responsibility.

The tendency for teachers to leave building problems to others on the school staff perhaps reflects a commendable desire not to meddle with affairs outside of the teacher's jurisdiction, but it does not represent a defensible viewpoint today. For today the teacher is often called upon to consult with committees responsible for planning new buildings or remodeling of old structures for better educational efficiency. What the teacher proposes to do in her classroom and what the teacher believes the educational needs of the children to be are often determining factors in the planning. The teacher, also, is in part responsible for the educational planning that goes into the furnishing and equipping of classrooms, libraries, shops, and playground facilities; these also are tools for teaching, and the teacher is in a better position than almost anyone else to make constructive and practical suggestions for equipment needs and arrangements. The school board and the school administrator must, by virtue of the responsibilities inherent in their positions, make many of the final decisions—subject, of course, to the will of the general public which supports the school— but the teacher cannot escape the responsibility for knowing how the educational plant can best be arranged as an instrument for teaching and for the education of the children. If the teacher has adequate knowledge and understanding of building problems, this should be shared with the board and the administration.

A Good Learning Environment

Common sense and successful experience both support the findings of the educational and psychological research which says that children and youth are happier in an environment that is pleasant, healthy, aesthetically pleasing, and which combines an atmosphere both stimulating and restful. Teachers like to work in such a setting, parents want their children to attend school in pleasant surroundings, and community pride in the schools is enhanced by having "nice" schools for the children of the community. But it is not just the happiness of the students, the satisfaction of the teachers, or the pride of parents and the general public that dictates the kind of school buildings we should have; the real reason for better buildings is that children *learn* better in a good school environment. Since the schools exist solely to advance the cause of learning (in a broad, not just a narrowly academic, sense), then anything that can be done to the educational setting to make learning more effective is wholly justifiable. Let us see some of the steps that are being taken to improve the school environment.

New Schools and the "New" Education

There are many features of modern education that are of such relatively recent development that we may speak of education today as the "New" education. We do not mean necessarily the type of education that has often been designated "Progressive," with a capital "P"; certainly the Progressive Education movement of this century—excluding the rare excesses and occasional unmitigated chicanery which unfortunately destroy part of the good of any new movement before it really gets under way—played an important part in bringing about the type of education we can call "Modern." We mean here to speak of the liberal, scientific, humanitarian tendencies in present-day education which have escaped the extremes and excesses of much that passed for "progressivism," and which have given us the kind of education quite generally accepted by a majority of laymen, parents, and professional educators. This "New" education has developed certain principles, practices, and ideals that have quite markedly altered our public school system; and in changing the schools, these newer ideas in education have changed the school buildings as well.

Learning as an Environmental Outcome

For example, most people today believe that environment is a tremendously important factor in the growth and development of children and youth. We lay much stress upon the relationship of the physical and emotional environment of the home to the present and future development of the child. We say that a good community environment can make all the difference between success and failure for the younger generation; a great portion of our civic effort and our tax money goes toward creating good community environment for our youth. Our schools, too, are coming to recognize the importance of environment as an educational factor. A dark, dingy, uncared-for building, a crowded classroom, an unsightly play space—these are all recognized as unhealthy environmental factors. As we recognize the importance of environment in modern education, we must make provisions for bettering that environment in the modern school plant.

Learning as an Active Process

There is quite general agreement in modern education that learning is an active process; long rows of fixed seats, virtually unadjustable and immovable, are certainly not conducive to active learning. Nor does a building which provides no space for activities such as drama, music, shop, laboratory experiments, and directed play lend itself to the support of the "activity principle" in education. Most educators today believe that children and youth must be *free* to learn; not just have "freedom to learn," but have a measure of physical, personal, and social freedom while learning is going on. Again, the physical and educational facilities provided by the older schools usually restricted and intimidated the student; any freedom that was enjoyed came about in spite of, rather than because of, the building itself.

Learning as an Organismic Growth

We believe today that the whole child is involved in the learning process—the principle of organismic behavior discussed in Chapter Five. This belief, too, necessitates a change in the traditional school building and traditional classroom. You cannot provide for the social growth of the student, for example, in a room so equipped and arranged that it precludes or forbids any real group work or group living. Likewise, if we really believe that education is growth, the school environment must be conducive to growth. How can the child grow intellectually or academically to the fullest degree in a classroom that offers no space for supplementary reading materials, no adequate place to display examples of individual and group work, no facilities for carrying on independent research and experiment? How can youth of high school age experience the fullness of emotional and social development in a school that restricts its offerings to a barren academic curriculum because there isn't room for social clubs, a school newspaper, musical organizations, or shops and laboratories for vocational training and work experiences?

Learning as an Expression of Individual Differences

Very few persons today would deny the modern educational concept of the presence and significance of individual differences among students, and of our need to make real provision in the school program for these differences. But many school buildings and classrooms

still in use today are a *structural* and *functional* denial of the existence
of individual differences. Standardized desks in standardized rows; no
provision for individual study tables or study corners; no place in
the room for the materials needed for carrying out differentiated assignments of reading, research, experimentation, construction, or creative effort; no place in the school plant designed to meet the needs
of the slow-learning child, the visually handicapped, or the hard of
hearing! Individual differences are of supreme importance in the
modern educational program, but the very buildings and classrooms
make it difficult for even the well-trained and conscientious teacher to
differentiate assignments, activities, and teaching methods to care for
the individual needs of students.

Methodology Hampered by Facilities

The modern concept of education puts much less emphasis on such
time-honored methods as extensive blackboard drill, formal study
halls, whole-class participation in a uniform reading lesson—each
child in the room taking his turn at reading a sentence or two from
the book while the rest listen. These and many other somewhat
obsolescent teaching methods, however, are still found in many classrooms just because the physical arrangement and equipment make
it difficult to use any other. Education has progressed, but the environment for learning has not yet been made a fit instrument to
implement these newer educational practices and to help bring about
the realization of the newer educational goals.

Provisions for Physical Well-Being

We have said earlier in this chapter that the physical well-being
and comfort of the student cannot be separated, actually, from his
educational well-being any more than the mind can be thought of
as unrelated to the body. What contributes to physical health, safety,
and welfare also contributes to educational and social growth and development. But since the most obvious changes in the buildings, classrooms, and other educational facilities in the modern school have
been those directly concerned with physical comfort and health, these
should be discussed separately from the changes effected primarily
for more expressly educational reasons.

Lighting.   One of the changes in school buildings most noticeable today is the trend toward better lighting of classrooms and other work areas. Greatly increased window areas in the outside walls, more use of clerestory and skylight windows, and the construction of many walls and partitions utilizing the new directional glass brick (which throws the light up to the ceiling to be reflected down into the room) —all of these are examples of the better use of natural daylight. These innovations make the modern school building seem, to some people, disturbingly open—almost naked; not a bit like the grim-faced, monolithic structures that used to be built to shelter the students from the sights and distractions of the outside world. "Won't the children be looking outdoors with so many windows in the classroom?" ask some troubled parents when they first see such "open" construction used. The answer is affirmative; the students *will* look out at the world around them! Is that so bad? The school is not an island unto itself; it is a part of the world, and the surrounding view can be made a part of the regular curriculum, a part of the learning experience. If the students should spend an inordinate amount of time gazing out of the window, the trouble lies not in too much window space, but in poor study habits, emotional disturbance, or a classroom situation lacking in interest and proper motivation.

But of course the primary reason for the use of more outdoor light in the classroom is not to minimize the boundary between indoors and outdoors; it is to provide better light for better sight. More efficient artificial illumination has the same purpose. Someone has said that in the modern school we learn by seeing; certainly the school today requires more reading, more looking, more observing, more use of the eyes than ever. Most classrooms, with the exception of those built or modernized in very recent years, do not come anywhere close to providing enough bright but glareless light for all students, all the time, for whatever task they are doing. Good classroom lighting is one of our best assurances that the children's eyesight (now often severely damaged during school years by bright glare or insufficient light) will be safeguarded; at the same time, good lighting is one of the best assurances that each child will have a fair opportunity to make normal advancement in academic achievement.

But the mere introduction of sufficient light is not enough; many dark, drab, dismal classrooms are so devoid of light-reflecting surfaces that whatever light is introduced naturally or artificially is almost wholly soaked up by the dark surfaces. Unless you attended a fairly up-to-date elementary or high school, you probably remember very well the dark floors ("won't show the dirt"), dark desks ("won't show pencil marks"), and dark walls ("don't have to be cleaned so often") that have for generations characterized the American schoolroom. These light-absorbing surfaces, plus high, dingy ceilings and a blackboard running the entire length of two or three sides of the room did a marvelously efficient job in one respect: it would be hard to conceive of any more thorough provision for soaking up what little light there was!

The modern school provides one of the best tools for teaching we could ask for: LIGHT—lots of it, controlled, adjustable, engineered for maximum "seeability" in the classroom. Is this a provision for the health and physical welfare of the children, or is it a provision for better learning conditions? Foolish question—the two are inseparable. But one more question (this time from the sincere and troubled taxpayer), "Doesn't it cost more money to equip rooms with good light?" Yes, of course it does, but not as much as one might think. New construction methods have made it almost as economical to build window-walls as to build conventional ones; simple, single-pitch roofs have made possible the introduction of lighting in the far side of the room through clerestory windows; light-colored walls, floors, ceilings and furniture, if properly finished with modern materials, are no more difficult to maintain—often easier—than the conventional dark surfaces. Modern lighting fixtures do not take a great deal more current; they are merely engineered to use that current more effectively.

In a small rural school, tucked up in an isolated mountain valley in one of the western states, the school board finally let itself be persuaded to install modern lighting fixtures in the two classrooms. The bill for the new fixtures was paid somewhat grudgingly, but parental pressure on the board for the new lighting system had been very persistent. Then came the first electricity bill: almost ten dollars for one month! In pious horror the board ordered the large bulbs in the brand-new fixtures replaced with small sixty-watt bulbs. They could stand to pay for the fixtures, but blamed if they were going to waste taxpayers' money on all that electricity. You may shake your head in disbelief, or say it must be a made-up story! But it actually happened very recently. It is still almost unbelievable how parsimonious some school districts are in providing adequate physical facilities, even when the health and learning of children are clearly at stake.

We must not be surprised, therefore, if some of the advances that are described here are not by any means to be found universally in American public schools. Do not for a minute believe that the extremely poor physical condition of school plants is found only in isolated rural areas; go to the effort to see for yourself how incredibly bad the conditions are in some of the older school buildings of many towns, cities, and large metropolitan centers.

Other physical improvements. Advances in school lighting have been paralleled by improvements in heating, ventilation, sound control, and classroom seating—each of these is a separate topic of interest to teachers, but too complicated and space-consuming to be discussed here. In fact, it is almost impossible to find a school building in America built since materials became more plentiful following the close of World War II which does not incorporate some or a good many of these desirable advances in better facilities for the comfort, safety, and health of the school child. Modern equipment and materials for adequate schoolroom lighting, heating, ventilation, and seating are now so universally available on the market that it has been said that it is today virtually impossible for school boards to buy the older, obsolescent "junk" at all. Moreover, good school architects are available in all sections of the United States, even the most isolated or remote, and experienced contractors who have built and know how to build good school buildings can be found in every state. Too, boards of education are generally alert to at least some of the trends in school building methods and materials and planning; the general public has seen these newer buildings in adjoining towns, perhaps, and they will insist that their local school be "just as good and up-to-date as Riverton's."

The teacher's concern. "Well," you may say, "if all these forces are uniting to give us school buildings designed for better physical comfort and better learning, why does the classroom teacher have to be concerned? They'll give us a good building!" But it is not that simple. The teacher still has three very major concerns with the school-building provisions for pupil comfort, safety, and well-being: first, the teacher may be called on to work in committees with the architect in planning new buildings or remodeling old ones. Second, the teacher must know how to make use of the newer physical facilities—you can easily destroy the light balance of the room by poor adjustment of window shades, or upset the electronic temperature control by improper adjustment. Third, the teacher may have to teach in a classroom which is almost hopelessly outmoded in physical equipment—you must know how to arrange an existing room for the best possible lighting, ventilation, and sound control.

Design for Learning

So far we have been concerned largely with the school plant in its relation to the health and comfort of the students from a physical standpoint. But the very design of the building, its relation to the building site, the number and arrangement of the classrooms, its inclusion of multipurpose rooms, its furnishings and equipment, and the range of educational facilities provided—all of these are part of a "design for learning" that goes much further than mere provision for physical comfort and well-being.

Site

"School sites," according to the authors of one book on modern school plants, "can be more vulnerable to obsolescence than the school buildings themselves." [1] The basic trouble with many of the newer school sites is simply that they are too small for today's educational program. They are usually large enough for the building itself, with a fair amount of room around them for play space. They may be well-located, easily accessible to the majority of students, well out of the range of unusual traffic hazards, and set away from unsightly or undesirable surroundings. That is better than can be said of many schools built just a few years ago, and much better than can be said of many schools presently being constructed in very crowded urban centers. But what would once have been considered an adequate—even a nearly ideal—site may be simply not good enough for the kind of school we want today.

Space-consuming buildings.   For example, today's "spread-out," one-story buildings take up more space than did the "stacked" buildings that were commonly constructed to house both elementary and high schools just a generation ago. But why must the building be this new shape? A more traditional multistoried building takes up less space, calls for only one foundation and one roof, and often results

[1] Lawrence B. Perkins and Walter D. Cocking, *Schools* (New York: Reinhold Publishing Corporation), p. 19. Reprinted by permission.

in substantial economies in plumbing and heating costs. Why change?

The answer is fairly simple. The spread-out building makes it possible to do away with stairways and most of the interior corridors, two of the most dangerous features of traditional buildings from the standpoint of fire safety, and two of the features most conducive to noise and disturbance within the building. Too, the one-story building lets each classroom (in all but the most severe climates) have direct access to its own "outdoor living room," a provision which encourages flexibility in the school program and adaptation of the day's activities to the educational and emotional needs of the children. No longer, for example, must the recess for an elementary school grade come at a certain predetermined time, ready or not; it can come when a natural break occurs in the classroom work, or whenever the lagging interest and decreasing alertness of the children signals the experienced teacher that it's time for a "break." In the secondary school, the one-story plan makes it possible to isolate the noisy activities—large bands and vocal groups, shopwork and the like—from the school activities which require a quieter atmosphere.

With a spread-out building, then, the school site must almost inevitably be larger, but more room on the school ground serves in other ways. More room for playgrounds encourages a more flexible, varied physical education and recreation program, suited to different interests, abilities, and age levels. A low, comfortable building on a site of suitable size is more emotionally and aesthetically pleasing, less formidable, more homelike, than the crenelated or becolumned institution of yesteryear that literally frightened the children (especially the little ones) with its awesome monumentality. But what is most important, the school grounds, if they are large enough and suitably arranged for the purpose, can become a real outdoor classroom, an extension of educational facilities into a new dimension.

The outdoor classroom.   The outdoor classroom concept has been slow in developing; it is new, even radical; it is expensive, in terms of land values; and it requires training and imagination that relatively few teachers yet possess. An outstanding example of the use of the school site for educational purposes has been observed at the Twin Lakes Elementary School in Tampa, Florida. There, on a thirty-two acre school campus which includes a five-acre forest left in its unspoiled natural state, a program of functional landscaping has been developed to take educational advantage of this unusual site. The landscaping and planting is a continuing work project for the students and teachers together, a continuous education in science and wildlife study, conservation practices, and appreciation of nature. Various types of wildlife native to the area have been introduced to the school campus, and the caring for these animals and birds provides a valuable experience for the children. A school garden gives direct, firsthand experiences of a kind that bring interest and meaning to much classroom work of a more traditional nature. An outdoor classroom, complete with shrubbery walls and equipped with movable tables and chairs, encourages classes to meet occasionally right out on the school campus.

The Twin Lakes School campus is indeed unusual, but it indicates the direction in which some modern schools are moving; if school is to be related to real life, get the school itself as close to real living as possible. And since it is estimated that school children spend from 10 to 15 per cent of their school time out on the school grounds—before school, at noon, at recess, in the evening before going home—why not utilize the school site itself for educational purposes?

The Self-contained Classroom

Another part of the "design for learning" that is literally built into many modern schools at the elementary level is the "self-contained" classroom. This is an attempt to build a school in keeping with the principle that learning at its best is a series of closely-related, integrative experiences—that the more "wholeness" we can bring into education, especially for the younger child, the more effective that education will be.

So, many primary-grade classrooms are built so that all of the facilities called for by the educational program and the needs of the children are right in one room: a work center with tables, benches, sink, and tools; an art center with easels, tables, and equipment; a science center with perhaps an aquarium and exhibit space; a music corner, with appropriate records and music equipment; a news center or area, with space and facilities for writing and recording and displaying; a drinking fountain; access to adjoining outdoor play space; and often adjoining individual toilets. Thus, the room becomes a sort of second home—an important consideration for younger children making the sudden and often upsetting transition from the sheltered environment of their own homes. More important, a classroom like this allows for and encourages continuity in the learning process at the same time that it permits significant provision for individual differences. No interruption of the work to leave the room or get a drink, no mass exodus down long corridors to a remote play yard, no shifting of the entire class to another room for music or art work; in short, no unnecessary break in the continuity of the living-and-learning environment that the good school should provide.

While the self-contained classroom is, of course, particularly valuable for and adaptable to the elementary school program at levels from kindergarten through grade three, many of the features of homelike atmosphere, inclusion of varied types of learnings in a single room (so that individuals may learn to work independently in small groups and alone), and other advantages that are to be found in this type of classroom can well be adapted, in part, to the upper grades and to the secondary school.

Multipurpose Rooms

Another "design" change in the school plant brought about by an expanded concept of the role of the school in modern life is the multipurpose room. Many schools which cannot financially afford to build a separate room for each worthwhile class or school activity, but which are not satisfied with a program which limits "school" to what goes on regularly within the four walls of the classrooms, have included in the school building a room designed for many different activities. This room, ordinarily much larger (2,400 to 6,000 square feet) than the regular classroom, often contains equipment and space for large musical groups (such as band and chorus), a stage for small informal or semiformal dramatic presentations, a place for indoor play, lunchroom or cafeteria facilities, seating provisions for assembly programs, areas for club meetings and work groups, and comfortable quarters for meetings of parents and other out-of-school groups. Not all at once, of course! But such a room provides needed space and equipment for a variety of programs that the good modern school will want to carry on.

When the construction of a new school plant is planned, one of the first proposals often made by the administrative staff and teachers is for such a multipurpose room; it not only contributes to the scope of a good school program, but makes possible many activities that the school might otherwise have to relegate to unsatisfactory quarters or just omit altogether. But as soon as the cost of the proposed building is calculated, tax-conscious citizens usually suggest the multipurpose room as one of the first of the extras to be cut out of the building plans. They will agree that all of the uses proposed for the room are admirable, but their own school experience has simply not given them sufficient background to see how important such a room could be to the real work of the school. Here again we can see the gap that exists between public recognition of what constitutes a good school program and public willingness to accept and pay for a school plant adequate in size and design to implement that program. The newer tools of teaching have not yet achieved complete acceptance by the general public.

Furniture and Equipment

What the school building really *is,* functionally, is determined in a large degree by how well it is equipped and furnished. The modern educational program makes demands for types and quantities of relatively expensive equipment that was virtually unheard of in schools of a generation or two ago. As long as education was thought of as a process of teacher-to-pupil transmission of knowledge, conducted under conditions conducive to maximum disciplined order and quiet, the typical classroom needed little by way of furnishings and equipment other than a desk for the teacher and fixed seats for the students.

But today (as we have said so often before) we believe education to be a more active process; real learning comes from what the student *does* as well as from what he hears or reads. Real learning takes place when the curriculum and school program are flexible enough to meet the needs of individuals and groups. Movable furniture helps the teacher and the students to arrange the learning environment for maximum effectiveness. Tables provide space conducive to individual and group work, study, and construction projects. Chairs can be grouped for reading and discussion; other furniture can be moved about to suit the needs of a specific project. Working space for construction or creative work, individual and group, is provided. The great variety of materials for learning that are needed in the modern school program require significantly more storage space *right in the classroom;* supplementary reading materials lose some of their immediate value, and science equipment often goes unused, if the teacher must journey down the hall to an inaccessible locked closet or look up the principal or custodian to get such materials just when they are most needed.

The audio-visual equipment (which will be discussed in greater detail below) needs to be stored near the classroom, much of it—such as maps, charts, globes, equipment for demonstration and dramatization—preferably right in the classroom; and electrical outlets, darkening shades, and other physical provisions for the use of some of this equipment should ideally be built right into the classroom itself. One of the most important devices for visual education has for many years been the blackboard; it is still used widely, but not nearly so extensively by the students for routine work as it once was. The chalkboard (as it is more appropriately called now, since black is neither the universal nor the preferred color) is used as a means of demonstration, illustration, and display; the wall space it formerly consumed must be shared with other media for the same purposes—bulletin boards and other space for displays and illustrations. So the modern classroom is *built* differently, *equipped* differently, for optimum usage of the newer instructional techniques and materials.

The changes in furniture and equipment in the classroom described briefly in the foregoing paragraphs are now found most typically in the newer elementary classrooms, and more rarely in secondary schools. The reason for this is not that these innovations are applicable to the elementary school only, but rather that the majority of the new buildings constructed in the past few years have been designed to care for the rising tide of elementary enrollment. Furthermore, both the curriculum and the general educational climate of the secondary school tends to be much more traditional than that of the elementary school in most sections of the United States. The changes that the new educational program have brought about in the design, furnishing, and equipping of the classrooms at the elementary level will soon be seen much more generally in junior high school and high school buildings as well.

Facilities for Expanded Programs

In the new design for learning that is coming to characterize the present-day school plant, no more important instructional tool can be found than that provided by the inclusion of facilities for areas of education that were formerly neglected or relegated to the educational background. A good teacher can teach acceptably even under the most adverse conditions, but the better the tools and facilities we provide our teachers, the better the instructional *program* is likely to be.

Today in many schools, elementary and secondary both, there have been built into the building special provisions, by way of space and rooms, for teaching many subjects or activities once thought to be within the range of possibility for only the larger schools. Art rooms, music rooms, a wide variety of shops and laboratories (for industrial arts, vocational agriculture, homemaking, business education, distributive education, diversified occupations programs, and every phase of science) and other space-facilities for activities of a distinctly curricular nature are now quite commonly provided. In addition, it is becoming increasingly common to find school buildings equipped with complete health-service units, lunchrooms and cafeterias, and indoor play space in addition to the regular gymnasiums designed for physical education classes and athletic contests.

Now, it must be agreed that none of this is entirely new; many schools have had these facilities here designated as new for quite a good many years. What is new today is their inclusion in even relatively small buildings, in ordinary-sized schools, and not as "frills," either, but as legitimate and necessary provisions for the regular educational program of the school.

Of particular importance to teachers (though perhaps of admittedly minor interest to the students) is the growing practice of including in new buildings adequate, pleasant, and relaxing teachers' rooms—not just a private lavatory or a hole-in-the-wall closet with a broken down couch where the teacher can flop down in those rare moments when complete exhaustion happens to coincide with the time when the music teacher, say, "takes over" the class for a few minutes. No, these "teachers' rooms" are designed and equipped for the regular use of teachers during their planned free periods—for rest and relaxation, a quiet cup of coffee, or an opportunity to do advance planning for classroom activities. At last we have discovered that provision of special rooms for *teachers* pays off educationally, too.

Tomorrow's School Plants

What will our school plants be like in the next few years? It is apparent that the new type of school being built today is not just an educational or architectural fad. Buildings will continue to be designed as educational tools, instruments for bringing about better education of our children and youth. There is every evidence that school buildings will continue to be built, as someone has phrased it, "from the inside out"; that is, the building will take shape around the central core of the educational program. But additional changes and improvements are also very likely.

More provision will probably be made for special rooms and facilities for the exceptional child—the one with reading difficulties, the partially blind, the hard of hearing, and those with other physical or educational handicaps. As the educational program becomes more flexible and individualized, so will the building and classroom arrangement be designed for flexibility. It is likely that increased emphasis upon preliminary vocational training will result in the multiplication of shop facilities of all kinds—and those not limited to the senior high school exclusively. The growing importance attached in many communities to post-high-school education will call for buildings designed to house a junior college of the community college type, both for formal higher education and for short courses and terminal vocational courses.

Of especial importance in predicting the design and arrangement of future educational plants is the rapidly expanding community use of the school building. Playgrounds, shops, and meeting rooms designed for after-school and summer-months use by both children and adults of the community are sure to become increasingly popular. The school building is well on the way to becoming a true community center.

Materials for Teaching and Learning

Historical Reluctance of Public to Supply Learning Material

In the American schools of early times, books and other teaching and learning aids were virtually unknown, except for such texts as the teacher himself might possess. Separate books for each child were an unheard-of luxury, and such simple materials as blackboards, chalk, writing paper, and pencils were rare or nonexistent. For many generations the situation improved only slowly; the introduction of such primitive texts as the *New England Primer,* and—much later—Noah Webster's famous blueback speller and the McGuffey Readers were real landmarks in educational history. The transition from crude slates or equally crude quill pens to more adequate writing instruments took many, many decades. Even as the most elementary of the materials needed for teaching and learning became commonly available, there was no acceptance of a sense of public responsibility for providing these materials out of school funds; the growing concept of free education as a right of every child did not include so radical a proposal as paying for learning materials too.

The history of the development, acceptance, and furnishing of learning materials in our public schools is a long and interesting one which we do not have space to recount chronologically here. If we should skip in our discussion from the earliest American schools up to the beginning of the present century, we would still find at this later date very poor provision (by today's standards) for learning materials in most schools. At the beginning of the twentieth century, all except the most advanced of our public schools still offered very few learning aids beyond a single textbook in each subject, a case of wall maps and perhaps a globe, a blackboard, a small amount of basic science equipment (with of course somewhat better provision for high school science courses), and a limited number of reference works.

Good learning and good teaching did, of course, take place in these earlier schools, even though the instructional equipment was very meager. This has led some of our older and more conservative school patrons and taxpayers to say, in effect, "What was good enough for me is good enough for my children; I went to school and got a good education without all these fancy gadgets, and they can too." Few adults, to be sure, would phrase their objection to the newer learning materials and devices quite that crudely, but the idea that the schools don't really *have* to change is implicit in much modern criticism of education.

But the schools *do* have to change if they are to reflect accurately the viewpoints of a changing culture, and if they are to teach the things society wants taught. And as education has changed, the materials used in the educative process must change too.

Instructional Materials and the "New" Education

Let us review briefly some of the improvements in modern educational practices and ideas that we have discussed in connection with changes in school buildings and classroom facilities; we can see clearly how instructional materials will differ in number and variety and use under the influence of the "New" education.

We believe today that the schools must provide a rich and varied learning environment, with opportunity for a variety of experiences and activities. Provision must be made in the instructional program for individual differences—not just because this sounds progressive or up-to-date, but because it is the only way we know to make education meaningful and effective in the lives of the children and youth entrusted to the care of the school. Provision must be made for a balance of individual and group work in the curriculum at every school level, kindergarten through high school; children need space and facilities to pursue *individual* learning projects, but they also need opportunities to learn *together* in small and large groups. Modern education calls for a maximum of real—not halfhearted or synthetic—pupil-teacher planning; this takes a different kind of equipment for learning and teaching than is found in the school where the teacher just dishes out to the student the facts recorded in the textbook or prescribed by the state course of study.

The modern school at every level—when it operates according to the soundest of educational principles—is a laboratory for learning, a place for study, research, experimentation, testing of hypotheses, verifying results, finding out new things and putting these new facts and ideas to use. Learning in today's school often is approached through study of integrated units or problems, a plan which necessitates having available in the classroom a large variety of suitable, related learning materials and opportunities for participating in a wide range of related learning activities.

Modern psychological research and experimentation have given us a fairly good grasp of the concept of maturation, an understanding of the successive interrelated stages of human growth and development, and of the needs of children and youth at each of the developmental periods. Learning isn't the same thing for a first-grader as it is for a high school junior, and uniform textbooks and maps and art equipment (even though "graded" in terms of intellectual difficulty) cannot possibly satisfy the needs of the students at different levels of mental and emotional and social maturity—in the same grade or in different grades.

Printed Materials

The most widely used of all instructional materials are those which appear in printed form—most notably, textbooks. But, one text for each child in each subject is not enough and "textbook teaching" is inadequate. Does this mean, as some of the more radical "progressives" suggested in the early 1920's, that we should completely discard the textbook in our teaching? Not at all; throwing out the textbooks was one of the most grievous educational errors committed by the overenthusiastic proponents of extreme progressivism. We need more, not fewer, texts for good teaching and good learning. We need more, not less, printed material. Fortunately, the school today has access to a wide variety of books, texts, pamphlets, reference works, bulletins, magazines, and newspapers specifically designed for the modern classroom. Better printed format, better subject-matter organization, more interesting presentation, more profuse and more appropriate illustrations, and closer attention to a graded vocabulary—all of these characterize the printed material available for school use today.

But the availability of these better printed materials does not insure their correct use, or even that they will be used at all. The teacher of any subject or at any grade level can still, if he wishes, base all assignments and learning activities on the narrow range of material presented in the basic text. He can still use supplementary materials for routine or even punitive assignments: "Since you talked out loud during the study period, John, you must look up this topic in the encyclopedia after school today and hand in a written report." There is no guarantee that this rich offering of printed materials will be used efficiently or used at all—no guarantee except that which comes through the interest, ingenuity, and competence of the well-trained teacher.

Audio-Visual Materials

One of the fastest-growing, most interesting, and potentially most effective of all the kinds of teaching materials are those commonly designated as "audio-visual." Included under this broad designation are usually such materials, devices, and techniques as these:

the motion picture	models, specimens, objects
slide (projected transparency)	school museums and exhibits
filmstrip	demonstrations
radio, phonograph, tape recorder	dramatic representations
television	school journeys (field trips)
opaque projector	blackboard, bulletin board, felt-board
unprojected (flat) pictures	
charts, maps, graphs, globes	

Misnomers, confusions, and criticisms. You will notice that some of these audio-visual aids to learning are mechanical devices, others are materials, and still others are activities. The confusion of "kinds of things" arises from the rather loose use of the generic term, "audio-visual," which is in itself something of a misnomer. For really, these aids to learning and teaching should be called "multisensory"—they utilize not only the senses of hearing and sight, but all of the sensory avenues through which learnings may come.

Furthermore, the term "audio-visual education" is inaccurate in that this is not a special type of education, a new or different kind of teaching. The whole range of multisensory devices, techniques, and materials is simply a tremendous *aid* to good teaching and to more pleasant and efficient learning. These materials, all of them, must be *taught;* you can't just show a moving picture, display a chart, hang a map on the wall, or "take" a field trip. Each of these must involve directly both conscious *teaching* and planned *learning.*

These relatively new teaching and learning aids have already had a great impact on the modern school, and further development of the aids themselves and the methods of using them promises to bring about even greater advances in curriculum and method. They are good tools for teaching, properly used, but they have often been misunderstood and misused. The result has been a negative reaction on the part of many teachers, parents, and even students; a justifiable suspicion against the whole audio-visual field has been built up in some schools.

Some critics suggest that these devices and techniques (for example, the moving picture) are being used to replace the teacher. This is ridiculous—as teachers who have tried to take the easy way out by just "showing a movie" have discovered. None of these audio-visual aids can substitute for the teacher, make a poor teacher good, or make teaching easy. Effective use of these aids requires better teachers and better teaching skills. More careful planning of the entire activities of the class, for example, must precede use of a filmstrip, the giving of a demonstration, or the taking of a field trip than would be necessary in more routine teaching. Otherwise, if the class is not ready for the experience, it will not have any real meaning; and if the class is not encouraged to follow up the filmstrip or the demonstration or the trip with further learnings there will be no continuity in the educative process.

Effective use of "AV."   Good use of audio-visual aids, then, demands that the teacher have a thorough understanding of the learning process: the factors involved in preparation for and readiness for certain learning experiences; how meanings develop out of experiences and activities; the part played by emotion in learning (a motion picture or still picture may have heightened *emotional* quality that would be lacking in verbal presentation of an idea, for example); and many similar understandings. The teacher must know that "memory" cannot be trained effectively apart from the whole of the learning experience. The student remembers those concepts, ideas, and facts which have for him a sense of importance and relevance, those which he really understands and sees clearly, those which he can put to actual use in other learning situations or in daily life. Think how excellently films, field trips, demonstrations, models, diagrams and the other audio-visual devices and techniques can contribute to helping the student *remember* what he has learned—provided the teacher understands the principles of learning well enough to use the teaching aids effectively.

As we have seen it to be true of the other materials used in teaching and learning, so it is for the audio-visual aids: they are good tools only in the hands of the competent workman. Used wisely and well, they can *motivate* study, *clarify* difficult concepts, and *stimulate* further learning in ways often superior to more traditional approaches like textbooks, library assignments, and formal recitations. The more traditional ways of teaching, and the more traditional materials for learning, are not abandoned in the modern classroom, but others are added. And the additions include not just the now almost standard equipment like the motion picture projector, the phonograph, and supplies of maps, charts, and models, but still other types of equipment and facilities: rhythm band toys for the lower grades, a wide variety of materials for artistic and creative expression, a schoolroom store for teaching arithmetic and social studies, a school bank, a small garden, and opportunities for out-of-school work experiences and participation in worthwhile and educationally valuable community service projects. All of these, too, are multisensory aids to learning, tools for teaching. But they are good tools only when they become not ends in themselves, but means to desirable ends within the range of the work of the school: providing for individual development and adjustment to the group, making everyday learning meaningful, broadening the range of student experience and knowledge, motivating necessary practice and drill, and teaching the facts, concepts, and skills of the basic subject matters.

Educational Television

Although television has been listed above under the generic grouping of audio-visual devices, the use of television programming specifically designed for and geared to the educational setting raises so many questions and engenders so much controversy that the topic deserves specific and separate consideration.

Educational television, while still in its experimental stages, is no longer just a theory or a dream; it exists in one form or another in hundreds of schools. Educational TV may be programmed for general broadcast by a commercial station or a special educational TV station for reception in the immediate receiving vicinity; it may originate in the school itself through use of a closed-circuit system; or it may, as in the Midwest Airborne Television experiment, be beamed directly to classrooms in a several-state radius from an airplane far aloft in the skies. It may be received by the students in a central viewing room at school, in a regular classroom, or on a set at home.

The use of educational TV suggests many advantages. The very best teachers, provided with ample time to prepare lessons and equipped with every conceivable device for presenting ideas clearly, can be brought at relatively low cost to the individual school and individual classroom. The presentations can be expected to have much the same emotional impact and to produce the same absorbed attention that is the strength (and often fatal weakness!) of commercial television. Educational TV can widen enormously the range of experiences available to students and bring the outside world almost directly into the classroom.

With such promised advantages, why has educational TV still experienced a relatively slow development? For one thing, it may suggest to some the dire threat of eliminating the classroom teacher or even the conventional classroom itself. For another, it provides generally only a one-way transmission of ideas—you can't talk back to the glowing screen. And finally, it has often been promoted as an educational panacea by those who did not understand its educational implications and limitations and were only interested in the prospect of educating vast numbers of students at a lower cost than would be found in conventional instruction.

How then can we properly assess the value of this new instructional medium? Perhaps as informed and unbiased an approval as it is now possible to make is contained in a report from the Subcommittee on Television of the North Central Association of Colleges and Secondary Schools, which summarizes an extensive study of the problem with the following pertinent comments:

> Television has no magic. No matter how complex its electronic processes may be, television is simply another medium of communication, like a book or a human voice. Communication be-

gins with intelligible transmission and ends with intelligent reception; any medium of communication is but a middle link between two or more minds. . . .

. . . Television is a new medium of communication, not a new method of teaching and learning. It permits many variations in the teaching-and-learning process, but its effective use is based upon the same fundamental psychological principles which apply to all successful processes of learning. The attitudes of the learner and the results of teaching are as certain to be affected by the quality of instruction and its adaptation to the needs and motivations of the learner in televised as in conventional instruction. . . .

. . . Television is not a self-contained educational entity, but an instrument which is significant only in the particular educational context in which it is employed.[2]

Teaching Machines

Another of the newer and most widely discussed of the tools of teaching is the teaching machine. It is perhaps unfortunate that the term teaching machine ever came into common use, for it is patently a misnomer—no machine can teach, though it may facilitate learning. As a matter of fact, the so-called machines are not, strictly speaking, machines at all, but mechanical devices that display in sequence certain instructional materials previously arranged or programmed by some expert or group of experts.

Thus, a better term to use for this new family of devices commonly called teaching machines is the more descriptive and accurate term, programmed instructional materials. Just what are these and what can—and can't—they do to facilitate teaching and learning?

They are nothing really new, except for certain mechanical refinements. A primary-school flashcard sequence is programmed learning of a sort; so is a conventional textbook or workbook. For in each of these instances, certain material is arranged in sequential, step-by-step order, and subsequent learnings (responses) of students are determined in part by what has been presented before.

The chief feature of both the devices more commonly denominated teaching machines and the consciously programmed textbooks, however, is what might be called "interlock." That is, one bit of information is interlocked with another so that the student cannot or should not get one until he has revealed, by his response, that he has learned

[2] Subcommittee on Television, North Central Association, *The Uses of Television* (Chicago: North Central Association, 1961), pp. 7, 10. Reprinted by permission.

what has preceded. In the machine, the student's response determines whether he can unlock the machine to go on to the next step. In the programmed book, the student is told whether or not he should proceed, and if so to what subsequent page or lesson.

The chief advantages of the programming of instructional materials are these:

1. The learner receives immediate "reinforcement" of his learning after successful completion of each sequential step; he finds out whether he has responded correctly without the usual long-term process of hearing a lecture or explanation, reading an assignment, handing in written work, and taking an examination and waiting for the results.
2. The learner engages in relatively "error-less" learning; he cannot easily make a mistake that is compounded into other subsequent mistakes, for the program tells him his errors at once and virtually forces him to delay further progress until he has successfully completed the task at hand.
3. The successful use of programmed material requires active student commitment. By requiring continual responding, the material or devices prevent the student from inactive and noncontributing class-sitting. When he stops working, he knows it, and the teacher knows it too.
4. The student can progress at his individual pace—the machine or the programmed book will never get impatient with him.[3]

Obviously, programmed instruction, like educational television, is a newer instructional medium of great potential, but not a panacea for all instructional problems. Its success depends largely on good programming and appropriate use. The conference summary cited above makes this final observation:

> The programmer asks the educator, "Define what you want the student to *do* with your subject matter. Do you want him to manipulate things, solve problems, and develop insights? Do you want him to produce original proofs in mathematics?" Then the challenge to the programmer is to help the student achieve this objective. In some cases, this may be possible through a program only, but it will probably also require classroom discussion,

[3] Annice L. Mills, *Programmed Learning and the Educational Process.* (Stanford, California: The Center for Advanced Study in the Behavioral Studies, 1961), p. 7.

laboratory work, and other activities to achieve the total objective. Although these other learning experiences may always be needed, the programmer will try to take the student by means of the program as far as possible toward the desired behavior.

Thus, the effective use of programmed material must always rest in the hands of those who determine specific educational objectives for specific students—the teachers in the classroom.[4]

Too Little, Too Late

We may hope that you have followed this description of some of the newer tools for teaching with interest and appreciation, for every teacher has a natural concern with the kind of building he will teach in and the equipment and materials he will have for classroom use. At the same time, you may feel that it is unrealistic to expect—certainly during the early years of your work in the profession—anything like the ideal teaching conditions that have been described as existing in the best of modern schools.

It is certainly true that we know far more about what constitutes good education than we have been able to put into practice; our knowledge of teaching and the learning process has outstripped our current provisions for a good educational environment. Hundreds of buildings are obsolete or obsolescent for a modern school program, thousands of classrooms substandard in heating, lighting, ventilation, and equipment. Tens of thousands of teachers find their plans for good learning activities hampered by lack of adequate books, supplementary reference materials, and available audio-visual aids.

"Too little and too late" quite accurately describes the current situation in adequacy and availability of good materials for teaching and learning in many schools, but there is really no reason for despair. The intelligent, resourceful teacher, well educated and well prepared for the job of teaching, can do wonders with even the most meager equipment and surroundings. Such a teacher can spur the repainting of dingy classrooms, the refinishing of dark, unsightly desks, the beautification of the school grounds and the rearrangement of the classroom furnishings. Much instructional material designed for classroom use is available for the asking—free motion picture films, filmstrips, booklets and pamphlets on a variety of subjects, maps from travel agencies, models from business and industrial concerns, pictures from innumerable sources—there is practically no end to the list. Teacher and students working together can create or construct many

[4] Mills, *op. cit.,* p. 14.

devices for use in studying mathematics, science, geography, and other standard school subjects.

Most important of all in making the best of a currently unsatisfactory educational environment is the part the teacher can play in helping develop favorable community sentiment for school improvement. If good teaching and good learning are going on day by day in the classroom, the students carry home an enthusiasm for school that is "catching" in the homes and in the community. A poor educational program is almost always supported grudgingly, but a superior one is likely to create a degree of community interest and pride that will result in more generous support for new buildings, new equipment, new materials for classroom use.

And finally, with either the poorest or the best of tools for teaching, the teacher still has a job that is his responsibility alone: that of *organizing* the whole learning environment, all of the experiences designed to teach, in such a way that the community's investment—in buildings, supplies, equipment, and, most of all, children—yields a maximum educational return.

NINE: TOPICS FOR STUDY, REPORT, AND DISCUSSION

1. Recalling the high school you attended, write a brief report on how that educational plant did or did not contribute to effective learning.
2. Look through several recent issues of *The American School Board Journal, Overview,* or a similar professional periodical, and report on the most interesting innovations in school buildings and equipment that are suggested in the advertisements and articles.
3. How would you like to have your own teaching room arranged? Propose a hypothetical teaching situation in which you might find yourself, and make a rough sketch of how you would like to have the room arranged—and tell why!
4. Assume that the board of education where you are teaching has invited the teachers in your school to help plan a new building. With a committee chosen from your class, prepare a report for the rest of the class that would tell the board, the administrative officials, and the architect just what the teachers wanted in the new building.
5. With your instructor's permission and assistance, arrange a field trip to some modern school buildings for firsthand observation of the newer instructional materials in actual classroom use.
6. What audio-visual materials were used by your teachers in elementary and secondary school? Were they effective? Why or why not?
7. Borrow from the professional library, curriculum laboratory, or the school used for demonstration and student teaching in or near your college (a) some of the textbooks used in your proposed teaching field and (b) some of the other printed materials in actual school use.

How can these materials be used to promote good teaching and good learning?
8. Arrange for a demonstration of a teaching machine in your class, and evaluate its strengths and weaknesses.

NINE: BIBLIOGRAPHY

Association for Supervision and Curriculum Development, *Creating a Good Environment for Learning,* 1954 Yearbook. Washington, D. C.: National Education Association, 1954. Narrative case-study examples of just how the ordinary school can create a good learning environment. See especially chap. 8 on physical resources (but you can profitably read the entire volume in just a few hours!).

————, *Using Free Materials in the Classroom.* Washington, D. C.: NEA, 1953. Shows sources and uses of free materials available to teachers.

Deterline, William A., *An Introduction to Programmed Instruction.* Englewood Cliffs, N. J.: Prentice-Hall, 1962. An excellent, balanced, nontechnical explanation of new development in "auto-instruction." Contains useful bibliography and an appendix illustrating one sample of programming.

Haskew, Laurence D., and Jonathon C. McLendon, *This Is Teaching,* 2d ed. Chicago: Scott, Foresman & Company, 1962. Chap. 9, "Resources for the Teacher," contains many illuminating ideas and suggestions.

Herrick, John H., Ralph D. McLeary, Wilfred F. Clapp, and Walter F. Bogner, *From School Program to School Plant.* New York: Holt, Rinehart & Winston, Inc., 1956. As the title indicates, the concern of this book is with devising school plants to accommodate specific educational programs. See especially chap. 11, "The School Program as the Key to School-Plant Design."

The Institute for Communication Research, *Educational Television the Next Ten Years.* Stanford, California: Stanford University, 1962. An extremely thorough analysis of the future of educational TV; not for the casual reader, but very worthwhile for those especially interested in the problem.

Lisonbee, Lorenzo, "It Looks Easy," *NEA Journal,* Vol. 43, No. 6 (September, 1954), 358 f. Excellent cautions on using the newer materials of instruction (especially the audio-visual materials) as supplements of good teaching, rather than as an easy way of getting out of work.

National Education Association, *And TV Too!* Washington, D. C.: NEA, 1961. An excellent discussion by the Department of Classroom Teachers and the Department of Audio-Visual Instruction of the NEA regarding the proper use of educational television. Brief and balanced.

————, *Magazines in the Classroom.* Washington, D. C.: NEA, 1960. Useful guidelines to the employment of current periodicals as a tool of teaching.

"New Schools, Economy Too," *Life,* Vol. 36, No. 5 (February 1, 1954), 74 f. Excellent pictorial suggestions for new, low-cost schools making better use of space than traditional buildings do.

Nulton, Lucy, "A Classroom for Living," *Educational Leadership,* Vol. XI, No. 5 (February, 1954), 291-295. Describes teacher's part in effecting inexpensive changes in the classroom to create a better environment.

Perkins, Lawrence B., *Work Place for Learning.* New York: Reinhold Publishing Corp., 1957. A profusely and beautifully illustrated book on modern school design, with explanations of the educational reasoning which underlies such design.

Rogers, Virgil M., "Textbooks Under Fire," *The Atlantic Monthly,* Vol. 195, No. 2 (February, 1955), 42-48. An eminent educator discusses the widespread and often vicious attacks by uninformed critics on the suitability of public school textbooks.

Thomas, R. Murray, and Sherwin G. Swartout, *Integrated Teaching Materials.* New York: Longmans, Green and Co., Inc., 1960. An extensive presentation of the problems of classroom use of a wide range of the materials of teaching and learning. Useful as a preview of later courses the prospective teacher will doubtless take in this field.

A field trip. *What learning possibilities are there that couldn't be achieved
in the regular classroom?*

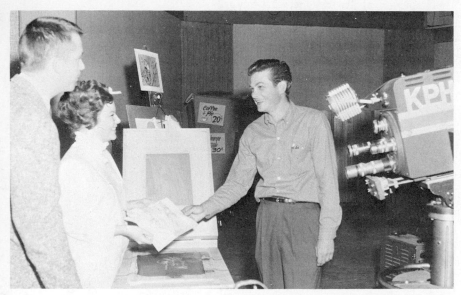

Central High School Phoenix, Arizona

Art demonstration on TV. *How do
programs such as these, produced by
high school students, help develop
closer school-community relations?*

CHAPTER TEN

The Gradual Cultural Schism Between
School and Community

The school as a formal educational agency has perhaps never had complete identity of interest and purpose with all of the other agencies and institutions of the community it serves, but schools of an earlier age were in many ways closer to their communities than they are today.

Unity of School and Community in Primitive Cultures

In preliterate, primitive societies, for example, the curriculum (if it could be called such) consisted of everyday activities of the tribe or culture, passed on from one generation to the next by the wisest and most skilled members of the group. There was no separate class of teachers; the teaching staff was made up of regular members of the community group. Bow-making was taught by fathers who were skilled in making bows; the rudiments of primitive agriculture were taught to the daughters as they worked with their mothers in the

THE SCHOOL
IN THE COMMUNITY

fields; and the lore of the tribe was passed on to the younger generation in impressive initiation ceremonies conducted by the sages and
priests who lived right in the village. There was no distinction between
school and life; hunting was learned by hunting, art by drawing on the
cave wall, architecture by constructing rude shelters, and history by
listening as the ancient stories of the tribe were recounted by the village campfires or re-enacted in ceremonial dances. There was no
school building as such; the communal camp or village, with its surrounding fields and forests and rivers was the "educational plant" in
primitive societies.

Increasing Formalization

As the functions of education became more formalized, special
teachers, curricula, and buildings came to be set apart for the carrying
out of this important social function: the preservation of the cultural
heritage and the group way of life by indoctrination and training of
the young. Gradually, education became synonymous with schooling,
and the school grew apart from the community it served. Sometimes
education became sharply and consciously divorced from the life
of the community—witness the Spartan custom of taking male children from the home at a very early age and putting them in state-
operated barracks for a military type of instruction until the years of
early manhood; or the medieval practice of conducting formal education of youth in an other-worldly environment of monastery, cathedral,
or feudal court. In other eras and other cultures, education drifted
more gradually and imperceptibly away from the everyday life of the
community.

The Transitional American School

Religious unity.   In the early period of the history of our own
American school system, for example, formal education was in a
transitional status with respect to the community it served—by no
means as closely related as in primitive societies, but more closely
identified with community life than is education today. The Puritan
schools were, almost without exception, local schools controlled by
local village and/or church officials, supported by local charity and
assessments levied against the parents of children in school, taught

by a teacher certified and hired by local officials, and serving a group of students who lived within walking distance. The Puritan curriculum in the common schools (and the Latin Grammar schools and the colleges as well) seems formal and stilted to us today, but in many respects it reflected quite closely the community interests and cultural values of the contemporary society. Reading was centered on biblical and theological materials, but so was much of Puritan life. Latin was still the language of learned men; anyone who presumed to aspire to secondary or higher education might be expected to learn the ancient tongue as a matter of course. Puritan discipline was harsh, often cruel, and Puritan schoolrooms reflected a Spartan simplicity. Life was like that in those days.

Physical closeness.   Even as recently as the period from 1890 to 1920, when the curriculum of the American schools was becoming so obviously unrelated to everyday life that a tremendous reform movement (now generally called "Progressive Education") was being launched—even as recently as this, the public school in our country was closer to the community than it is today. This closeness, we must grant, was largely physical; the district school was close to home—in the prairie states you might even see it from the kitchen window of the farmhouse. And, except in the larger towns and cities, most children could walk to school and back easily, and even come home for lunch. School districts, accordingly, were comparatively small; school-board members were your neighbors, and if you didn't like the way these "trustees" were running the school, you voiced your complaints over the pasture fence, in the post office, or on the party line. Most of the rural school houses (and many of those in the smaller towns) were community meeting places—political groups, the Ladies' Aid, and the Grange all met at the school. The close attachment which many folk of a generation ago felt for their schools can be seen in the tremendous emotional uproar that was aroused when consolidation of districts was first proposed. Nothing was too good for the kids, of course, but we can't give up OUR school! The support for the local school, to be sure, was often more emotional than financial, but it was nonetheless genuine.

The neighborhood spirit.   All of the children knew each other; they were neighbors, and, likely as not, their parents had gone together to school and lived on adjoining farms or within easy visiting radius. And the teacher knew the families—she didn't have to look up family data in the cumulative records; perhaps she even "boarded around" with the various families, or lived with her parents on the "home place."

Impact of Urbanization

The school-community situation just described cannot be associated exclusively with any given period in American cultural history; it disappeared in the cities long ago, yet still exists today in some rural areas. But now there is evidence that a rift is developing between school and community that did not generally exist fifty or a hundred years ago. The urbanization of our population has brought millions of people together into our great metropolitan centers, and tens of thousands into our cities and towns; the older concept of "neighborhood" has in many places virtually disappeared. The children are strangers to each other, their families are not acquainted, the teacher is in many cases just another hired professional worker (conscientious and devoted to her work, of course), perhaps here today and gone tomorrow—not a local resident who went away to the "normal" for a couple of years and returned home to teach. Rural schools have been abandoned or consolidated; schools are more centralized, generally much larger; they serve not a community or a neighborhood in the older sense of the terms, but a geographic area circumscribed only by the distance which a school bus can travel. The school district may be very large, covering perhaps a whole county or parts of several counties; the school board members see each other only at board meetings, and never see many of their constituents at all.

Changes in the School

And the school itself has changed. The curriculum is not the same as it was in the parents' time; fathers and mothers are often a bit intimidated by the new education. They don't understand what is going on, and they hesitate to ask. Besides, both of them, often, are employed at places far removed from the school—when could they ever visit their child's classroom? New methods and new materials of teaching have been developed and put into common practice since the older generation attended school; the parents speak truly when they complain that they "just don't understand what the schools are trying to do." Jimmy doesn't learn his alphabet as soon as he begins the first grade; Sally learns to do long division by a strange method;

high school geometry is now optional, so Bob takes a new-fangled course named "shop math," and Mary hasn't studied European history but is taking something called "Social Problems," where she learns how to get along with boys and discusses such dangerous issues as socialized medicine! No wonder the parents don't feel that the school is familiar; no wonder that they feel there is a great chasm between the life of the school and the life of the community.

Fundamental Changes in the Culture

Both school and community have changed, and it sometimes seems that they have perversely changed in opposite directions, moved farther and farther away from each other every year. For example, the typical school, caught in the cross fire of denominational bickerings or attacks by antireligious groups, has today pretty much divorced itself (by law and tradition) from the teaching of formal religion; the school building rarely serves as the meeting place for religious groups in the community. As this has been happening to the school, the community itself has undergone changes in patterns of formal religious membership and observances; old denominational groups have declined, new ones have sprung up, and many families no longer profess any church membership at all. So the religious tie between school and community, formerly a very strong one in many areas, has been all but completely severed.

Other culture patterns have changed, too. Shifting populations, the decline of the old semifeudal agrarian patterns of life, the inmigration of foreign-born persons or those from other sections of the country, the decline of the family as an independent economic unit, the questioning of firmly established moral and social values—these are but a few of the changes that have affected the closeness of school-community relations. The school can no longer expect, to the degree it once could, that all of the children and youth will share a reasonably common background or that because they attend the same school they all are members of the same "community." Almost any public school classroom will have in it children and youth representing an almost complete diversification of cultural patterns, races and nationalities, previous schools attended, economic status and standard of living, religious affiliations, and value systems. How can we develop in these students a sense of "community" within the school when the communities from which they come seem to be so different? How can we regain that lost sense of close school-community relationship which now appears to be disintegrating year by year?

Closing the Gap

We must note that for every present-day tendency that seems to be pulling school and community farther apart there is also one which promises a stronger bond than ever before between the two. For the "good old days" of school and community oneness never really existed. Through the years past, the schools have been in some ways closer to their communities than they are today, but, in other ways, the gap is closing rather than widening. The growth of suburban living, for example, has created new common-interest communities, sometimes more rural than metropolitan in their interests, possessed of strong school-community spirit which may be expressed in a lively and effective PTA.

Much of the alleged unity of feeling and purpose that cemented school-community relations in years past is but a nostalgic memory of a time when the pace of our culture was less hectic; when there was time and inclination for a more simple neighborliness, a more "folksy" feeling in most communities. So as we consider today the problem of school-community relationships, we are not trying to recreate the pace or pattern or feeling of a passing era; we are not trying to recapture that cozy, warm, folksy, all-one-big-family feeling that (perhaps) existed a generation ago. What we do need to do is to examine the present trends and practices that are now bringing school and community closer together, not primarily in terms of the better "feeling" they create, but in terms of their educational importance.

The Educational Significance of Closer School-Community Relationships

Better Educational Opportunity

A school that reflects the needs, interests, and highest educational and social ideals of its own immediate community (and the larger state, national, and world communities of which it is a part) provides a better education, academically and socially, than the school that stands apart. A public school is simply not doing an effective job unless the life of the school is integrated with the life of the community. Brief reference to a few of the basic principles of learning and curriculum construction, discussed earlier in this book, will make this clear.

Academic learnings. Children learn best, we have said, when they are *interested* in what they are doing; what better wellspring of interest can we find than the life and activities and environment in which the child himself lives? Learning is most effective when there is a chance to experiment and find out and verify facts, individually and in groups; what better laboratory for identifying and solving problems than the community itself? We must start in the learning process, we have said, "where the learner is now," building on his past experiences and devising new learning experiences; how can we know where he is now unless we know the environmental and experiential background the community has given each learner? We must teach the "whole child," most of us would agree; how is this anything but an easy platitude to which we give meaningless lip service, unless we can know the whole child in the light of his whole background? The good modern school, it has been pointed out, is the adaptable school; how can the school adapt to changes in the life of society unless the school is constantly being made sensitive and responsive to what goes on in the community? And finally (though this list of applicable principles could be extended much further), most educators and laymen are agreed that the ultimate test of education is this: Is it useful? Can it be applied? What better place than in the everyday life of the community to make and test applications of what is learned in school?

Vocational learnings. In one community of a western state, the small local high school continued for years to offer only a straight college-preparatory curriculum even though relatively few of its graduates went on to college. At the same time, the school made no effort to offer any vocational subjects which would give training in those areas really needed by the students in that community—vocational agriculture, home economics, and business education. Their educational program, no matter how excellently designed and taught, was just not adequate for the community the high school served.

In another secondary school in the same area, the superintendent, persuaded by an overenthusiastic but inexperienced teacher of business subjects, convinced the board that the school should sell most of its regular typewriters and invest in a very expensive electric typewriter so the students could have the most modern equipment available. It was not until after the change-over had been made, at very considerable loss to the school, that someone thought to make a survey of what kind of typewriters were actually in use in the local offices in which the graduates of the high school were usually employed. Only then was it found that not a single office in the area served by this school had or even contemplated buying an electric typewriter!

Personal and social development. These illustrations, which are actual but perhaps extreme, serve to show how easily a school can fail to adapt its curricular program to community needs, and to the needs of the children and youth it serves. But other features of the school program than curriculum may also operate to divide the school from its community. The school must be alert to the social, emotional, recreational, and health needs of the children and youth the community sends them, and must build a program to meet these needs. For example, in many poorer rural areas and in the blighted sections of towns and cities, actual malnutrition of school children is not uncommon; the good school makes special effort to teach concepts and habits of good nutritional practice and—more directly—to better the school lunch program. In new housing developments where from dozens to hundreds of families have recently moved in, and where there are few community traditions, little community social life, little sense of belonging, the school needs to step up its social and recreational program on a community basis. In a community torn by racial intolerance and religious bigotry, the school cannot meet its educational obligations to the children if it avoids all but "safe" topics and steers clear of any direct teaching of respect and appreciation for all sorts and conditions of men out of fear that the issues involved are "too controversial."

The community must decide its educational goals. But what if the community doesn't want its schools to be adaptable, to take an active part in community life, to alter in any way the academic traditionalism that isolates them from the real life of the community? In short, what if the needs of the community and its children and youth aren't recognized by the community itself and any proposed alteration in the school program is opposed by the parents and denied administrative or financial support by the board of education? Shouldn't the professional educators—teachers, principals, and superintendents—insist on a good program and go ahead with it anyway?

The answer to this question is a somewhat reluctant but otherwise unqualified "No."

It is a responsibility for professional educators to work honestly and courageously and intelligently for the kind of education they believe to be best, but the final decisions on plan and program must rest with the community—the public that supports and controls the school. The educator has the same citizenship rights as any other citizen, but his professional rights are only accorded or loaned to him as the general public sees fit. As Willard Goslin (himself a teacher and administrator who has pioneered in developing community acceptance of many new educational ideas) has said, in discussing the rights of teachers, "The teaching profession may develop the core curriculum, for instance, but the people have the right to throw it out on its ear or on any part of its academic anatomy." [1]

Contributions of the School to Life of Community

Improvement of the quality of community life. In the preceding paragraphs we have suggested that the closer relationship of school and community will be felt directly in a better educational program as such. But this closer relationship contributes also to the community as a whole. Good schools make better communities. An alert, informed body of citizens can work together to create a lively, interesting, satisfying community life. The higher the level of educational opportunity, the higher the economic level of the group. Well-educated and appropriately educated people make the best citizens; they study and understand community issues and problems; they are politically active; they read more intelligently and more widely; they vote more courageously and more consistently; they support such community programs as movements for better civic government, better roads, improved soil conservation practices, and community health services. In every way, the community that has good schools is a better community.

Direct leadership assistance. The school that is closely integrated with the life and work of the community serves its supporting public even more directly. In almost any city, town, village, or rural area,

---

[1] Willard E. Goslin, "The People and Their Schools," *Forces Affecting American Education,* 1953 Yearbook of The Association for Supervision and Curriculum Development (Washington, D.C.: National Education Association, 1953), p. 147. Reprinted by permission.

if you were to take away the teachers who are leaders in the professional tasks of the school, you would also deprive the *community* of some of its most diligent and effective community workers. Good teachers strengthen the community and contribute directly to its welfare, quite outside of their regular school work, by sponsoring and directing youth group activities, teaching Sunday school classes, working for civic betterment projects, maintaining active membership in service clubs, and personally leading drives such as Community Chest, Red Cross, and the March of Dimes. Sometimes teachers representing a school that has a well-developed sense of responsibility for meeting community needs are actually exploited by the community, called upon to make contributions of time and effort far beyond the normal call of duty. But even this exploitation is preferable to having an educational system so far withdrawn into the halls of ivy that community life affects neither the school nor its teachers.

Direct service to the community.   The good community school serves its area directly through the work of the students, too. Again, some communities have exploited the students, expecting them to be on call to help out in every worthwhile civic project, from conducting clean-up day to collecting scrap iron and selling tickets to the Fireman's Ball or soliciting donations on the downtown streets on every one of the numerous "tag days" which raise money for worthy enterprises. This danger of exploitation must not be minimized, but the school can avoid much of the difficulty by having its own program of student service to the community which will be recognized as sufficient contribution.

The list of possible community service projects which can be performed by students is almost limitless. High school students particularly, because of their greater maturity and capacity for independent work, have in various communities undertaken such projects as the following as part of regular classwork or as special "extra-class" activities:

> —clean-up and beautification of school grounds or other civic properties
> —planting of shrubs, grass, trees, and flowers in selected areas; conservation work (flood control measures, reseeding, etc.) in town, city, or state parks or on national forests
> —surveys of community needs (health, sanitation, recreation, etc.)
> —get-out-the-vote campaigns
> —safety surveys and safety patrol work

—contribution of personal services in playground supervision, recreation programs, health and child-care centers, neighborhood branch libraries, and working with younger groups of children in clubs such as Blue Birds, Brownies, and Cub Scouts

—conducting campaigns (through actual work and through community education) against such health hazards as flies, mosquitoes, rodents, and other dangers to personal and community health

Elementary school children can also make contributions to community life and welfare through such work-service projects, many of them centering around their own homes or the school building and grounds. What these younger children lack in maturity and experience is often compensated for by their great enthusiasm and willingness to work.

Work experience programs. Another form of service that the community school can render through its students is found in the work experience programs in high schools. In connection usually with the regular vocational and academic courses of the school, students are urged and helped to get "real" jobs which will (a) give them direct, firsthand experiences with adult work, (b) help them apply on the job what they learn in school, (c) yield in most cases a small income, and (d) at the same time provide valuable community service.

As an example, one high school helps students in the principles-of-business class to get afternoon, after-school, or week-end jobs in stores, filling stations, printing offices, light manufacturing industries, and similar business enterprises. The work they do is educationally useful, productive of some spending money, emotionally satisfying, and a real service to the businessmen. What is perhaps most important from the standpoint of community relations, it indicates the willingness of the school to make its program useful and practical, to adapt it to local needs, and to make it possible for the businessmen down on Main Street to see just what is actually being taught and what kind of students the school is "turning out."

The School as a Community Center

Father looks up with interest from his after-dinner newspaper as Mother, dressed in a house dress and last winter's coat, starts out the door. "Oh," he says without surprise, "this is the night you go to school." In many homes in many communities there is today a matter-of-fact acceptance that some of the adult members will attend informal "school" quite regularly. Tonight Mother is going over to the junior high school to attend a furniture-refinishing course conducted by the shop teacher. Next month Father will go up to the high school to help some of his neighbors install new library shelves. The week after next both of the parents will attend the monthly PTA meeting.

It is not at all unusual today to find the community-minded school serving as a community center and meeting place to a far greater degree than was usual even in the "good old days" when life seemed to center around the little red schoolhouse. It doesn't have to be a fancy, modern school with lots of meeting rooms and good equipment. One rural teacher in an isolated elementary school in a mining community far up in the Rocky Mountains reports how her school ("our school," she quite naturally calls it) serves as a regular community meeting place even though it is only an old log blacksmith shop left over from the days of the early prospectors and converted ultimately into a rude schoolhouse. It is only 11½ by 20 feet in size, unfinished on the interior, the rough board floor covered by linoleum (bought by the teacher from her own small salary), and furnished with cheap, movable chairs and tables (again bought by the teacher) which can be grouped around the coal stove in the middle of the room on the 30-below winter nights. Still, it is the largest (the only) public building within a radius of thirty miles, and serves constantly as a meeting and working place for the whole community.

Whatever the physical facilities available, the community school can serve the adult population in many ways. In rural areas, villages, towns, or cities, it can become a place of meetings of all kinds, the center of the entertainment and "cultural" life of the community (through school-sponsored musical, athletic, dramatic, and recreational programs, or such activities conducted by the adults themselves); if properly equipped, it can be a general activity center as well. Many schools today use the home-economics facilities for serving banquets and dinners for nonschool agencies and groups; a small charge for use of the building must be made, of course, but the results in terms of community service and community interest are well worth the effort. In rural areas, especially, these same facilities may be used for conducting adult classes in cooking, dressmaking, home furnishing and decoration, and other projects for the mothers. Especially in the rural South, forward-looking community schools have set up canning centers to help the parents better their economic and nutritional standards.

Shop facilities are often used for hobby and craft centers; one school has reported the use of its vocational agriculture shop and laboratories for free evening adult classes where farmers from the surrounding areas may come in and make or repair farm equipment, using the metal and woodworking machinery and the blacksmith and welding facilities. Testing of seed, soils, milk, and other agricultural products can be done in the school laboratories, either directly by the adults themselves, or as a service of laboratory classes to community welfare.

In addition to formal and informal classes and work groups, the school serves in many communities as the recreational center, with its playing fields, gyms, sports equipment, and other recreational facilities open to public use under competent supervision, at a nominal charge or no charge at all. The library can be opened at specified times for community use, and small meeting rooms or the auditorium and stage made available to the public that supports the schools.

There are problems, of course. Some wear and tear on the building and equipment is inevitable, as well as some disturbance of regular school work. Lights and water and heat must be provided; janitorial services are necessary. Supervision of some of the activities by school personnel is often advisable. The actual instruction of adult classes must usually be conducted by regular teachers, many of them already underpaid or overworked. But these problems are not insurmountable; costs can be prorated and teacher loads adjusted. The results in better community living, improved educational and economic conditions, and, best of all, an increased feeling of respect and support for the school program are well worth the effort involved.

The school that serves the adult groups of the community effectively becomes more than a building open from eight to five, Monday through Friday, more than a strange and unfamiliar place that the average parent visits only to see a basketball game, the Junior Class play, or the principal when Freddy throws a rock through the shop window or has failed arithmetic again. It becomes more than the locale of an impersonal education system, noticed by the general public only when the football team wins the conference championship, the marching band parades down Main Street, American Education Week is observed, or the property tax is raised. It becomes not *the* school, but *our* school. When that happens to the maximum degree possible, it is a community school in the fullest sense of the word.

Making Use of Community Resources

We have said that the school becomes a community-minded school when it adapts its regular instructional and activity program to the needs of the children and youth in the community; when it serves the community by contributing direct educational values, the services of the teaching staff, the work of its students to worthwhile community projects; and when it serves as a community social, recreational, and educational center for the adults of the area. But one further major feature of the good community school is that it *gets* as well as *gives;* it asks the community for help (other than tax support) in its program and makes use of community resources.

Every Community Has Resources

Some schools seem to believe that they exist in a sort of educational and social vacuum; they admit somewhat reluctantly that they would like to utilize the resources of the community, "but," they say, "we don't have any." Not many years ago, the writer visited a small secondary school as a member of a committee seeking to establish the acceptability of this school for approval by one of the accrediting agencies. The school officials and teachers had been asked, as is customary in such cases, to fill in a series of self-evaluation blanks, on which they recorded their own strengths and weaknesses as they saw them. One of the questions was this: "How well do you use the resources of your own community in your educational program?" Instead of rating this use on the sliding scale provided, the school staff had written in this statement: "This question does not apply to ———— High School. We have no community resources!"

Of course, this peculiar notation reflected in part a misunderstanding of the question asked, but it also revealed the thinking of the school staff. Because the community was small, located in a rather poor, sparsely settled rural area, and isolated by mountain roads from larger communities around it, the immediate assumption was that the school existed in a community devoid of any resources of educational value. Actually, every school has many potential community resources, no matter how impoverished or isolated the area it serves. As a nation we are richly blessed with all sorts of resources that can contribute to education—physical, material, cultural, and human resources. "Large Was Our Bounty," says the title of a booklet published by one of the divisions of the NEA in describing the necessity for conservation practices in our society. "Large *is* our bounty!" we might say by way of paraphrase. The resources of our communities upon which the school may call for help in its educational program have been tapped only to a slight degree by most American public schools.

Human Resources

There are numerous people outside of the school in nearly every community who could contribute to the activities and life of the classroom and the school as a whole. "But the most able people—the ones we want—are too busy! You can't ask *them* to help." Yes, you can; and they *will!* This fact has been documented by the experience of hundreds of good schools; only a few examples can be given here. The Metropolitan School Study Council [2] records the experience of one school system that surveyed the human resources of the community and found, as the title of the report puts it, *Fifty Teachers to a Classroom*. The school system of Alice, Texas, annually compiles, through the joint efforts of the staff, the students, and the adult members of the community, a detailed list of persons in the area served by the school who are ready to offer their free services and unique talents and abilities to further the educational program.

Classroom visitors from the community. Resource persons can be asked to come into the classroom to talk to the students on specific topics, to answer questions, to give prepared lectures, to conduct demonstrations, to recount their firsthand experiences. The banker will be willing to explain to the business-practices class some of the elements of banking procedures, and perhaps later conduct the group in a field trip through the bank itself. A parent who runs a creamery station can perform a milk-testing demonstration for the sixth-grade science class. A cabinetmaker may be willing to help the class with some of the fine points of a classroom construction project. A local housewife who has just completed a tour of Europe will be eager to bring her colored slides and show them to the social-studies class as part of a study unit.

Help from governmental personnel. Many representatives of civic and governmental agencies will, upon invitation, come into class-

[2] Metropolitan School Study Council, *Fifty Teachers to a Classroom* (New York: The Macmillan Co., 1950).

rooms or school assemblies and present, very competently, interesting programs of real educational value. Some of these visitors will be trained educational experts in their fields—conservation education specialists from the State Fish and Game Department, traffic safety officers supplied by the State Highway Patrol, visiting nurses from the state or county health department, forest rangers or trappers of predatory animals, representatives of the state or national park services—men and women especially trained in presenting an interesting lecture-demonstration before a group of school children. Others of the resource persons will have had no special training in educational work, but their interest in and knowledge of their own work will often make up for the lack of formal training in how to teach. The local policeman can help present safety rules, a post-office worker can talk about what happens to a letter after it is mailed, a member of the fire department can discuss fire safety with the class. Nor will all of these, or any of them by necessity, just "give a lecture." They may use all sorts of audio-visual aids, perform demonstrations, stimulate discussion, and answer questions.

Nonclassroom use of resource persons.   Moreover, resource persons need not actually come into the classroom at all; they may be interviewed by the class as part of a field trip, or interviewed by small groups or individual students in connection with special learning projects. A newspaper editor can be visited in his office by a group trying to find out more about the public press; the county agent can be called upon by a committee engaged in writing a report for a science or social-studies unit; an old-timer in the community can be interviewed for firsthand information about the life of the area in the early days as he experienced it himself.

Not only as "teachers" are these resource persons available for work in the program of the school. Selected adults in the community (they need not, and in many cases should not, be parents with children in school) can be invited to serve in other ways. (Let's be realistic; people being what they are, the "invitation" is sometimes a polite term for more stringent persuasive methods!) They will often be willing, after a period of initial self-deprecation ("Oh, *I* couldn't do *that!*"), pleading "no time to spare," or suggesting others who have more time or could do it better—after this initial refusal, such persons can be persuaded to act as assistant sponsors or advisors for clubs, classes, hobby groups, youth organizations; assitants on school journeys; hosts and hostesses (often just a euphemism for chaperones) for parties or other social affairs; assistants in the planning and operating of the lunchroom program; assistants in the school library; and in similar capacities.

Members of the community—and again they will probably be parents, but need not be—can be used as resource persons in school *planning* activities as well as regular classroom work. Many schools invite in adults in the community to help plan new buildings, to make suggestions on the annual school budget, to work with committees planning curricula and courses of study, to assist in planning the formal program of public relations, to offer suggestions for improving the reporting practices of the school, and for other similar purposes. This is not done as a sop thrown to the parents—a make-believe way of getting the parents to think that the school is seeking advice and counsel which they don't expect to use. Unless such ventures are real, honest cooperative effort, they become so much meaningless busywork for the parents and the school alike.

Using Physical Resources of the Community

If we mean what we say when we declare that the curriculum is something more than the books, assignments, classwork, and course of study—if we really mean that we want to broaden and enrich the life and activities of the public school—then we must make better use of the physical resources of the community. These resources are almost innumerable in every community, and are seldom exhausted, much less even utilized extensively.

Wealth of resources available.   Every community has much to offer to the sort of school which promotes a variety of kinds of learning activities through the use of field trips, investigations, community studies, making collections and displays, and similar uses of the physical resources that the community offers. Nor are such activities limited to a few fields; they can be used successfully by the well-trained and alert teacher and the interested students in almost any class or subject. Studying various aspects of community life is obviously possible in such subject-matter fields as history, art, music, science, conservation, health, civics, journalism, and geography, to name only a few.

The field trip.   The field trip offers opportunity for perhaps the most obvious use of the physical resources of the community. One teacher in a small two-teacher rural school, located far away from any city, in an area completely devoid of the usual places of interest and information often found in even the smallest towns and villages, has reported how she and the other teacher took a well-planned walking trip with their children (representing all eight grades) right in the environs immediately surrounding the school. A road construction project was in progress nearby. The whole student body went on a three-hour trip that took them from the school to the construction work and back. Included in the activities surrounding this trip were these:

a. Writing preliminary letters to parents, seeking their approval for the excursion
b. Inviting two or three of the mothers to go along, and thanking them later, by letter, for their help
c. Studying both pedestrian and automobile safety practices and safety signs and laws
d. Collecting data for use in arithmetic problems of all sorts, and later solving these problems
e. Studying the effect of road-building on erosion and other conservation problems
f. Studying the natural phenomena—animals, birds, insects—seen along the route of the journey, and collecting specimens to take back to the classroom

They even sat down on the railroad track (the teacher reported this with rare lack of appreciation of the safety rules she was trying to teach!) and each student had his art "lesson" made more meaningful by being encouraged to make a rough sketch of some aspect of the construction work, to be used as a basis for further learning activities upon the return to the classroom.

The list of activities given above is not complete, but you can see that in even this simple, cost-free walking trip there were many opportunities to use the resources of the community directly in connection with the activities of the regular class work. No community is completely lacking in interesting places to visit, though the list may vary from place to place. Museums, stores, factories, plants, fire and police stations, city and county offices, post offices, creameries, bakeries, places of historical interest, unusual geographical features, farms, parks, woodlands, newspapers, offices, exhibits provided by business and industry, concert halls, areas where "foreign" culture patterns may be found—this list is incomplete, only suggestive of the rich physical resources that are so near the school and so easily available for study. And yet they are often completely overlooked; many students have doubtless had an experience similar to that which one college student related to the writer—of living all his life in a community rich in historical, geological, and industrial resources (including a world-famous molybdenum mine that attracted visitors from every country) and never taking a single field trip anywhere under the sponsorship of the school!

Nonschool Educative Agencies in the Community

The Unique Function of the School

The influence of the out-of-school educative agencies in the community is important, inevitable, in many cases very beneficial—but not always desirable. In any case, these nonschool agencies which do teach—which change in one way or another the behavior patterns of children and youth—must be understood by the school and its teachers, and utilized in every possible way to improve education, formal and informal. Many of these agencies and institutions may be equipped (in terms of purpose, staff, and financial resources) to do even a better job of education in certain areas than the school itself. Health services, psychiatric counseling, preparation for the responsibilities of homemaking, and religious instruction are but a few of the educational tasks for which the school is only imperfectly equipped, compared with other agencies. But the primary interest of all these other educative agencies is not education of children and youth in the usual sense of the word. The home is primarily interested in providing physical care and emotional security; the church has for its chief interest the inculcation of specific religious beliefs; the public press is chiefly a medium for dissemination of news (or, less idealistically, a business venture which makes its money from advertising); and the motion picture, radio, and television are primarily media of entertainment-for-pay. The school remains in our society as the *one* agency which has as its sole aim the education of children and youth, but in this task it has many partners—and some competitors.

The Home

The effectiveness, for better or for worse, of the home as an agency of education is too well understood to necessitate more than a brief consideration here. The home provides (or sometimes fails to provide) for the child his first six years of basic training—a familial "boot camp," we might say. Laura enters the first grade already "educated" in many ways: she is healthy or sickly; she adjusts well to unfamiliar situations or hangs back from new experiences; she has a start on good work habits or is sloppy and indifferent; she feels secure and wanted, or she is troubled and worried about her status; she acts her age or reverts to infantile behavior. All of these "learnings," and many more, directly reflect the efficacy of the home as an educational agency. Nor does the influence of the home on the child stop when he starts school; it continues throughout life. So the high school sophomore, Jerry, reflects his "bringing up" in the way he responds to new ideas, his acceptance of persons of different religions and races, the experience-background he brings to new studies in school, his study habits, and his physical vitality.

Since the home is so obviously important to the school, understanding—not just sentimental eulogy—of the home as an educative agency is very necessary. We who teach must be as thoroughly acquainted as time and circumstances permit with the homes of the community where we teach; we must understand their influence, their strengths, their possible shortcomings. We must know the parents' viewpoints and use the parents as senior copartners in the education of their children. And again, this means not just a warmhearted, sentimental feeling about the parent-child-school relationship, important as sentiment and warmheartedness are. It means a positive program of cooperation between school and home in starting the child in kindergarten or first grade (sometimes a severe traumatic emotional experience for both parent and child), in safeguarding and improving the child's physical and mental health, in using and explaining the school guidance services, and in getting mutual understanding between home and school on such apparently routine matters as how and when homework should be done. All of this means neither *telling* the parents nor *asking* the parents; like any effective joint effort, this requires *cooperation* in the plainest sense of the word.

Religious Groups

The growing secularization of our culture in general, the loss, or at least alteration, of habits of family worship and family attendance at church services, the disappointing results of scientific investigations which tend to reveal that we are a "faithless generation," and the over-all decline in moral standards which many people think characterizes our present generation—all of these factors, and others you can probably think of yourself, have led some critics of modern society to suggest that formal religion no longer has any particular place and value in our modern American culture.

But there is contrary evidence that in hundreds of thousands of families formal religious groupings and agencies still provide a profound out-of-school educative influence. Even though the public school cannot—and should not—teach religion as such, or even venture into cooperative religious-education enterprises which might give the school a taint of denominationalism or sectarianism, the work of modern education cannot be well integrated with community life and needs, if the significance of religious groups on the life of the community and its children is overlooked.

In some communities the schools will have to face the problem of bitter, even vicious, opposition from certain religious groups; in other communities the school may be overwhelmed by excessively generous offers from some denominations to provide speakers, reading materials, and films that would promote in the school a particular sectarian view. In any case, the public school must take into account the effect of these religious agencies on the lives of the children who attend school; and educators must make such decisions and engage in such practices that the educative influence of religious agencies is constructive.

Tolerance and acceptance of religious differences may be taught by the school; basic moral values acceptable in and necessary to democratic living are well within the scope of the learnings that the school may seek to teach, reinforcing the teaching of the religious groups themselves. There is no easy answer to the problem of the relationship between organized religious agencies and the public school (see Chapter Fifteen below), but one thing is sure: the school must recognize the churches as an agency of education having often profound effect on community life and the growth and development of school children and youth.

Mass Media of Information and Entertainment

If you should listen (without being noticed) to the casual, spontaneous, unsupervised play and conversation of children and young folk of any age level, you would be reminded again of what you probably know already—how much of their conversation, their vocabulary, their concepts, their understandings and misunderstandings, their emotional attitudes, and their prejudices is a product of the newspaper, the comic book, the radio, the moving picture, and, increasingly, television.

Many studies have been made of the educational impact (using education in its most general and generous sense) of these mass media of information and entertainment on the lives and actions of children, youth, and adults. We need not review the scientific or near-scientific evidence here; common sense and common experience tell us that school children are often more thoroughly educated (in the sense of changed behavior patterns) by these out-of-school experiences than by what the school itself offers. This is no place to decry the influence of these media for their obvious weaknesses and undesirable effects. We all know the inaccuracy of many newspapers, the cheapness of many of the pulp magazines, the downright vileness of some of the stuff that passes as "comic books," the vapidity of many radio programs, and the immaturity (a very charitable word!) of many of the current television programs that the child of school age soaks up by the hour.

There's no use in just dismissing media of such *potential* educational value as so much trash, or pretending that the school can ignore the problem just because it isn't up to "our" level. The school must be concerned with these influences in the community it serves; this concern must be translated into positive action. Just understanding the tremendous impact, say, of crime "comics," gangster movies, sexy pulps, and yellow journalism in the daily tabloids—understanding the impact of these on the child or youth of school age helps the teacher understand why children act the way they do, where they get some of their culture patterns and their value judgments, and why they sometimes behave undesirably in the school environment.

These mass media of "information" and "entertainment" are teaching our children in their own way; we must try using these potentially fine educative devices to teach toward more effective goals. If nothing else, the modern school must try to use such means as newspapers, radio, movies, and television to teach worthwhile and interesting things in school, borrowing from these media such good features as strong emotional impact, interest-creating approaches to the learner, and the quality of producing *lasting* learnings. Moreover, the school can and must teach better discrimination and finer appreciations to the students who will be under the influence of these mass media no matter what we say in school; and at the same time teach those skills on which a democracy depends for its existence—skill in evaluating facts, in discerning what is behind emotional appeals, and in analyzing propaganda techniques and motives.

Clubs and Societies

Among the out-of-school educative agencies that the school must inevitably work with (or else find itself competing against) are the clubs and societies that are a part of the community life everywhere in this nation. Even a bare listing of the most common of these would fill a page or more of this volume; they are almost literally innumerable.

For example, there are the "youth-serving" clubs or groups: Boy Scouts, Girl Scouts, Hi-Y, Rainbow Girls, DeMolay, 4-H, and church-sponsored youth organizations, to name only a few. There are also adult groups with varying purposes and memberships, but all trying in some way to change or promulgate certain behavior patterns—in a word, to educate. These adult clubs have a tremendous range of importance and influence: the service clubs like Rotary, Kiwanis, Lions; the fraternal-social-philanthropic groups such as the Elks and Masons and Knights of Columbus; patriotic clubs like the American Legion and the Daughters of the American Revolution; social clubs of every sort; and study groups ranging from the League of Women Voters to the Tuesday Afternooon Metaphysical Club ("Ladies who pursue Culture in bands," as the novelist Edith Wharton put it, "as though it were dangerous to meet alone").[3]

Whatever may have been our experience personally with such groups, or whatever we have heard or found out about them that we like or do not like, one fact is clear: they exist as nonschool educative agencies in every community. The community school recognizes them as potential partners in the work of education at every level— child, youth, adult—and seeks to give support to (and seeks the support of) those whose program is in keeping with the educational ideals of the school.

There are difficulties, of course. Some of the youth-serving groups will occasionally request more of the students' time than the school can afford to give; some of the civic clubs may ask for an indefensible amount of assistance of the school in money-raising projects; some of

[3] Edith Wharton, *Xingu* (New York: Charles Scribner's Sons, 1916). Reprinted by permission.

the superpatriotic groups may want to censor the school textbooks; and, unfortunately, some of the groups still try to perpetuate racial and religious bigotries. But they are all part of the community life, and the community-minded school must at least be aware of their programs.

Other Agencies and Institutions Which Educate

Organized labor.   Labor organizations have long been favorable to the cause of public education. In some communities labor unions are extremely potent forces in organizing community opinion, and the effect of prolabor or antilabor sentiment is seen in the attitudes of children in the classroom. The public school is sometimes found in the troubled position of seeming to take sides in labor-management disputes for the simple reason that controversial issues are and must be discussed in the classroom—especially those issues that affect the welfare of the community and determine the economic status of the children and their families.

Business groups.   Commerce and industry as organized forces have had a somewhat less consistent record of support of public education than have labor groups, but in recent years some of the finest educational publicity has come from these business groups. The National Association of Manufacturers and the Chamber of Commerce, both quite conservative groups economically, and both of them groups which have often opposed any changes in the schools or any addition of school services which would raise school taxes, often lend support to public education at local, state, and national levels.

Political parties.   Organized political parties, likewise, have had a somewhat spotty record in their support of public education, but a review of their education platforms (and what is more important, their performance in matters affecting good educational legislation) gives most heartening evidence of influence for better community support and increased public sentiment in favor of a strong educational system. Some critics of the political parties take the cynical view that all of the statements these powerful groups make in favor of education are only pious platitudes, mere campaign talk designed to sway voters. But a review of the records of state legislatures and of Congress indicates a decided shift toward effective support for education by both major political parties—a support made manifest in sound educational legislation.

In every American community there are other out-of-school agencies which influence education in one way or another; a complete study or even a complete listing of them would be impossible here. The important point is this: the modern school is not an isolated social agency or educational influence; it has many partners in the educational enterprise (and some enemies) whose influence on the life of school youngsters, older youth, parents, and the total life of the community must be taken into account by any school which would become really community-minded.

School Public Relations

The Real Meaning of Public Relations

If the thesis of this chapter is correct—that the good school is an integral part of the community it serves—then one of the major tasks of the school is to engage in a program of effective public relations. Now, the term "public relations" has a somewhat unfortunate and unsavory connotation in the minds of many people; it suggests "selling the public" on their schools, "putting over" a new idea or a new program, or "influencing favorable opinion," or even "putting your best foot forward," and (by implication) concealing from the public the limitations, failures, or mistakes of the school system they patronize and support.

Really, school public relations—often abbreviated simply to "PR" —means none of these things; it means establishing better *working* relations with the public; it means working together with the general public for better schools and a better educational program.

The recent wave of attacks and criticism of modern public education have made many schools more conscious of a job they have sometimes neglected: finding out what the public expects of its schools, keeping the public informed about what is happening or is about to happen in their educational system, and soliciting public help in joint planning for ways to improve the schools.

Parents and Public Relations

The obvious place in the community to concentrate the cooperative effort of school public relations work is with the parents. Parents have no special *right* to make criticism or suggestions regarding the schools, any more than does the rest of the citizenry, but they have a very special *interest:* their children. One of the best tests of the degree to which a school is a true community school is this: how closely does it work with the parents? For although the school sometimes tends to make the assumption that the ultimate responsibility and authority for the children and youth have been given into its care, the legal and moral responsibility of the school is well expressed in the old Latin phrase which says that the school and its teachers stand *"in loco parentis."* They *serve* in place of the parent; they do not *take the place of* the parent.

Recognizing parental humanness.   As we have said throughout this volume that children are important people, so we must say too that parents are important people. They are much more important than teachers, really; they make our job possible! And parents are human beings, though we sometimes seem to forget this. Like any other human beings, they follow normal patterns of human behavior; much of what we said about human behavior in Chapter Five is true also here. Parents, as people, are individually different; they learn and react by "wholes," they have previous concepts and experiences on which further growth must be built, they need a sense of security and status, they learn through active involvement in an experience or problem, their learning is conditioned by emotional feelings. "Except you become as little children . . ." Well, parents are like children or any other human beings; in a very real sense, we must treat them as well and wisely as we treat their children.

Reporting to parents.   Parents are supremely interested in their own offspring; that interest becomes, at once, the opening wedge and the focal point of any good program of school public relations. What the parents know and hear about the school is what happened to their own child today or last week. The value of pleasant, interesting, meaningful learning experiences for children and youth that can be reported at home should encourage the school to develop good public relations by developing good educational programs. And not only are the word-of-mouth or other casual reports the children may bring home important; of equal value in a good school public relations program are the regular written reports or report cards. No one has yet discovered the ideal system for reporting pupil growth, learning, and progress to parents, but several features of a more desirable system have been suggested by one writer as follows:

> (a) any change in the reporting system should be introduced gradually—for parents are accustomed to the kind of report cards they took home when they were schoolchildren

(b) any new system should be worked out in cooperation between the school and the parents

(c) all reports should probably be both in terms of class standings (using norms of one sort or another) and in terms of the child's own ability

(d) and the reports should be instruments of child guidance rather than being used for "pressure" or disciplinary purposes [4]

Direct contacts with the schools. Parents can be approached through their children, then, but they may also be brought directly into the life of the school. The use of parents as resource persons and leaders in school activities, the development of a strong parent-teacher organization, the sponsoring of child-study groups under the auspices of the school, parent-teacher conferences, home visitation, a vigorous plan of encouraging classroom visitation—these are all effective ways of getting a better working relationship between parents and the school. Special school-visitation weeks and parent's nights are good public relations techniques, but far more effective is a continuous, not just a "one-shot," program.

Parental visitation in the school may be encouraged by preparing special programs to which they are invited; many parents will come to see Johnny dressed up as Billy Goat Gruff in the classroom or assembly program who would not think of just dropping by the school for a visit. Some communities have built up such a strong tradition of encouraging parental visitation that business houses and industrial plants allow parents a certain number of hours off from work with no loss of pay to encourage their visiting the schools. Schools can provide and circulate among parents a wide range of pamphlets and books describing the meaning of the newer educational program, giving information on problems of child growth and development, or furnishing the parents criteria they may use in judging the schools which their children attend.

Communicating with the community. But the school which seeks to develop good working relations with all of the members of the community must not concentrate on the parents alone. Every adult in the community may have a better opportunity to become informed about the schools if every possible effort is made to secure adequate coverage of school affairs and problems in the local newspaper, over radio and television, and through wide distribution of interestingly

[4] See Ruth Haas, "An Experiment in Changing Reporting Practices," *Educational Leadership,* Vol. XI, No. 8 (May, 1954), pp. 491-494. Reprinted by permission.

written school reports and newspapers and the presentation of programs and displays which will be seen by the "downtown" folk. Best of all, there will develop a natural and effective intercommunication between school and community if the former is doing an effective job of serving the total educational needs of the community and its children. The community-minded school already has a head start on the road to good public relations just because of the kind of school it is and the richness of the program it offers the community.

Trends and Frontiers in School-Community Relations

A Revival of Public Interest

In the past quarter-century or so there has been a definite revival of public interest in schools and educational problems. Part of this great revival can be seen—in a grim sort of way—in the great rash of attacks and criticisms which the public schools have had to face recently, especially in the years since World War II. Some of the criticisms of schools, educational aims, teaching methods, new instructional materials, the cost of education, and even the loyalty of the American teachers have certainly had some merit—nobody's perfect and everybody makes mistakes—but many more of them have reflected ignorance, selfish disregard for the rights of others, bigotry, and downright demagoguery. But there is one encouraging sign (two, in fact)—people are beginning to notice the schools, to think they are really important in our society; and the public, by a substantial majority, has risen up in vigorous defense of our public school system and its teachers. This is evidence of a widespread increase in public interest, and, generally speaking, public approval of American education.

The schools are getting more publicity—good and bad—than ever before. In one very recent year, over 200 articles about public education and its problems appeared in the nonprofessional magazines with wide general readership—*Reader's Digest, McCall's, Saturday Evening Post, The Atlantic Monthly, Saturday Review, Life, Look, Time, Ladies' Home Journal,* and the like. Some of them were extremely critical, even unfair, but many of them gave constructive accounts of what American schools are doing. All of this publicity helps to take the school and its work out of the limited academic environment that has so often stultified American education; it helps to build community understanding, awareness, and appreciation of our schools. Even the bitterly critical attacks should be read with interest, for they often contain valid, though overstated criticisms of present school practice; and the most unfair articles at least identify for us the sources of some common public misinformation.

Citizen Participation

There has developed in recent years a rebirth of active public interest in the schools of local communities. Perhaps this interest is best seen in the rapidly growing number of Citizens' Committees, independently organized in each community and functioning in ways unique to the community of their origin, but many of them drawing upon the National Citizens Commission for the Public Schools for advice, suggestions, leadership, and research facilities. These local committees, and other groups set up as lay advisory committees to boards of education, together with lay-professional committees operating within a single school—all are a convincing answer to those critics who say that the schools have been taken away from the people and are being run exclusively by and for the professional educators. Because each of these citizens' groups is local in origin, control, and purpose, they represent what almost might be called a renaissance of public concern with the public schools. They provide a wonderful opportunity for the schools to call upon community folk to advise with and help the school in such matters as planning new buildings, suggesting budgetary allocations, working for more financial support of the schools, bringing about more efficient consolidation and operation of the schools, and working with the professional staff on such matters as curriculum, report cards, and an enriched school activity program.

The greater the cooperation of citizens with their community schools, the better chance we have that the decisions of the whole group will be more valuable, more valid, and better defended against unwarranted attack by those who would destroy or cripple our public school system. If the adults in the community have helped develop the school program, they will feel competent to defend—even obligated to defend—what they think of not as *the* school, but as *their* school.

Schools Study Their Communities

In addition to more publicity for the problems of education and more citizen participation in the affairs of the school, there are other signs that the schools of America are today successfully bridging the gap that has existed between school and community. One is that schools are constantly studying (in a more or less scientific fashion, according to the needs and practices of the particular school) to find out what the community is really like and how education can serve it better.

Much highly technical work has been done in the field of community analysis and the identification of community characteristics; [5] all of this sociological and economic analysis of community structure is valuable to the specialist, but of little present use to us here. We do not even have to pause for a technical description, in sociological or anthropological language, of just what the term "community" means. It is enough to suggest that the wide-awake school will study the area from which it draws its students and its support, and the area and culture group which it serves educationally. The good school and its professional personnel will know (or find out) a great deal about the physical setting of the community, the kind of people that make the community their home (their occupations, economic problems, educational background, their social life, their intergroup relationships), the social organizations and existing institutions (formal and informal groupings, business and industrial concerns, governmental agencies, churches and clubs), and above all, the concepts the community has about itself and its members—status concepts, hopes, fears, aspirations, and ideals.

The Community School

In the same way (and for the same reasons) that we have not attempted a technical description or definition of the concept of community, whe have not yet tried to define exactly the term "community school." By way of summary, however, we may use Olsen's description of the good community school as one which (a) improves the quality of living here and now; (b) uses the community as a laboratory for learning; (c) makes the school plant a community center;

---

[5] See Edward G. Olsen, *School and Community,* 2d ed. (Englewood Cliffs, N. J.: Prentice-Hall, Inc., 1954).

(d) organizes the curriculum around the fundamental process and problems of living; (e) includes lay people in school policy and program making; (f) leads in community coordination; and (g) practices and promotes democracy in all human relationships.[6]

Can the modern school in the modern community do all of these things and still carry out its other primary obligations to society? Enough schools have so fitted their entire programs to community needs and interests that it appears to be a not impossible task. Basically, what the school needs to do is *adapt* and *lead*. For example, if a shifting and growing community population brings elements of unrest and disturbance into ordered community life, the school must be ready to make some quick adjustments. New families, for example, may bring to the community new problems, but they also introduce new and untapped community resources on which the school may draw.

As American culture and society and our various communities find themselves faced with new problems, we can have two reasons for a feeling of assurance about the future. First, the United States is a dynamic, not static, country—we cannot and will not stand still —and the presence of problems is a sign of healthy growth. Second, we have built in America a school system which, with all of its many faults, thrives on problems and difficulties; it is the kind of flexible and adaptable enterprise that grows as it faces new challenges. As our culture and our communities change, the school that is sensitive to its obligations to the community that gives it life and meaning as an educational institution will change too—and both school and community will become stronger in the growth process.

TEN: TOPICS FOR STUDY, REPORT, AND DISCUSSION

1. Ask your parents or some other adult in your community to describe what the schools were like a generation ago. Note the changes that have taken place, and see how many of the educational changes are attributable to changes in the community itself.
2. Did the high school you attended offer the kind of educational opportunities really appropriate to the needs of secondary-school youth in that community? Try to list the strengths and weaknesses of the high school you attended as measured by its adaptation to the community it served.

[6] *Ibid.*, p. 14 ff. First published in the *North Central Association Quarterly*, Vol. 26, No. 2 (October, 1951), pp. 174-80. Reprinted by permission.

3. Justify and explain the statement in the text, "Good schools make better communities."

4. What are some of the kinds of community service projects that would be appropriate for the *elementary* school to undertake? (The high-school ones aren't so hard to figure out!)

5. Recall the educational programs of the elementary school and the high school which you attended (or the ones you attended for the longest periods of time). In what ways did these schools make good use of community resources, both physical and human?

6. As a class project, make a detailed list of the possible "community resources" that might be used for educational purposes in an ordinary community. (You might use the community in which your college or university is located as an example, though such communities are not wholly typical.)

7. Interview very informally some elementary school or high school student to see if you can find out some of the out-of-school educational agencies that are affecting his or her learning in school. Is the effect good or bad? In what ways?

8. With the help of your instructor, get hold of some of the formal "public relations" statements of representative elementary schools and high schools (annual reports, news releases, policy statements, forms used in reporting pupil progress to parents, brochures used to create favorable sentiment for a bond issue, etc.). Study these to determine the kind of "public relations" that these printed materials seek to promote.

TEN: BIBLIOGRAPHY

Association for Supervision and Curriculum Development, *Creating a Good Environment for Learning,* 1954 Yearbook. Washington, D. C.: National Education Association, 1954. Chap. 6 suggests many ways in which a secondary school can provide direct community services through its students.

Bathurst, Effie G., *How Children Use the Community for Learning.* Washington: U. S. Department of Health, Education and Welfare, Bulletin 1953, No. 6, rev. 1955. Though not a very recent publication, this is an excellent source of ideas for school utilization of community resources.

Chamberlin, Leo M., and Leslie W. Kindred, *The Teacher and School Organization,* 3rd ed. Englewood Cliffs, N. J.: Prentice-Hall, Inc., 1958. Chap. 20 gives many thoughtful suggestions for using the school to improve community life; chap. 21 indicates ways in which the teacher can serve as an agent for good school public relations.

Cook, Lloyd Allen, and Elaine Forsyth Cook, *A Sociological Approach to Education,* 3rd ed. New York: McGraw-Hill Book Co., Inc., 1960. The social dynamics of school-community relationships, in a relatively technical discussion, are forcibly shown in chaps. 14-16.

Cox, Philip W. L., and Blaine E. Mercer, *Education in Democracy: Social Foundations of Education.* New York: McGraw-Hill Book

Co., Inc., 1961. Chaps. 19-21 give an especially thorough analysis of the sociology of school-community relationships.

Havinghurst, Robert J., and Bernice L. Neugarten, *Society and Education,* 2nd ed. Boston: Allyn and Bacon, Inc., 1962. Part Four of this book discusses some of the more complex sociological relationships between schools and various kinds of communities and community groupings. Scholarly and most interesting.

Hymes, James L. Jr., *Effective Home School Relations.* Englewood Cliffs, N. J.: Prentice-Hall, Inc., 1953. Simple, direct appeal to parents and educational workers for more effective cooperation, with many narrative case-studies of good practices actually in use.

Kindred, Leslie, *How to Tell the School Story.* Englewood Cliffs, N. J.: Prentice-Hall, Inc., 1962. Although designed primarily as a how-to-do-it book in school public relations, this handbook illustrates clearly many of the subtle and important relationships between school and community.

Menge, J. Wilmer, and Roland C. Faunce, *Working Together for Better Schools.* New York: American Book Co., 1953. "A handbook for school-community planning," based on actual experiences in typical communities. Includes good discussion of how to deal with attacks on the schools. Entire book can be read in a very few hours.

National Society for the Study of Education, *Citizen Cooperation for Better Public Schools,* 53rd Yearbook, Part I. Chicago: University of Chicago Press, 1954. Symposium (read a sampling of the many articles) showing how effective use may be made of lay citizens in bringing about better public schools. Many accounts of actual practices that have been successful.

Olsen, Edward G., ed., *The Modern Community School.* New York: Appleton-Century-Crofts, Inc., 1953. Sponsored by the ASCD, a division of the NEA, this is a cooperatively written case-study book reporting good school-community programs in actual use. Good illustrated definitions of "community school."

Van Dalen, Deobold B., and Robert W. Brittell, *Looking Ahead to Teaching.* Boston: Allyn and Bacon, Inc., 1959. Chap. 17, "The Community and the Teacher," contains an especially good discussion of school-community relationships.

Woody, Thomas, *Life and Education in Early Societies.* New York: The Macmillan Co., 1949. Chap. 2 contains a very readable account of education in primitive and preliterate societies; this will help give you a new slant on the meaning of "community" as related to education.

PROBLEMS
FOR TEACHERS

A teacher at work. *What professional competencies are needed to teach such a class as this?*

CHAPTER ELEVEN

The problems of the teaching profession (and here we use this convenient term to mean the entire organized and unorganized body of teachers; later we will consider whether the designation of "profession" is justified) are sometimes erroneously thought to interest only those who have already definitely chosen teaching as their life work and who are already firmly established in the job. Naturally, the person who is most deeply involved in teaching, who has had several years of experience, and who expects to continue in the work may be expected to be more thoroughly profession-minded than the beginner in teaching. But the beginner, too, usually has a real desire to know about and become involved in the "professional" aspects of teaching.

What You Need as a Beginning Teacher

Let us approach the problems of the teaching profession from the standpoint of the needs of the beginning teacher. Put it more personally: what will your needs be as you start teaching? The answer can be given first in brief statements, but these will need some elaboration later in the chapter. In teaching, the beginner needs

1. to be assured of reasonably adequate salary, protection against losing his job, and provision for the future (retirement);
2. to know he is doing a worthwhile and satisfying job, and doing it well;
3. to feel the security of belonging to a group that is recognized and appreciated by our society and is bound together by group ties; and
4. to be able to grow in his job, and to get adequate help in achieving this professional growth.

THE TEACHER
AND THE PROFESSION

You will perhaps notice that these needs—real, live problems to the teacher—are the same needs described in Chapter Five above as those of human beings everywhere, the psychological needs for *security, mastery, status,* and *growth.*

Therefore, the beginning teacher not only desires but *needs* to know more about his profession, occupation, job—whatever we call it. Since there is so much confusion in the nomenclature of the work of teaching—is it really a profession?—perhaps we should attack that problem first.

Is Teaching a Profession?

There has been, among teachers at least, so much labored and sometimes frantic argument over this question that it seems almost heretical to suggest that it really doesn't matter! That is, it doesn't matter what we are called as long as we do a job of professional caliber. But the question of public recognition and acceptance of teaching as a profession is certainly an interesting and important if not a crucial one.

Definition of "Profession"

In certain respects teaching has the same characteristics as the commonly recognized professions such as law, medicine, theology, and engineering. The National Education Association has listed these criteria for a profession as a yardstick against which we may measure the professional status of teaching. A profession

1. Involves activities essentially intellectual;
2. Commands a body of specialized knowledge;
3. Requires extended professional preparation;
4. Demands continuous in-service growth;
5. Affords a life career and permanent membership;
6. Sets up its own standards;
7. Exalts service above personal gain; and
8. Has a strong, closely knit professional organization.[1]

Does Teaching Meet Professional Criteria?

You can readily see that teaching measures up well in some ways and very poorly in others. For example, teaching is quite strong with

[1] Quoted by T. M. Stinnett, *The Teacher and Professional Organizations* (Washington, D.C.: National Education Association, 1953), p. 4. Reprinted by permission.

respect to criteria numbers 1 and 2 (intellectual activities and specialized knowledge) but relatively weak in meeting criterion number 3, extended professional preparation. Teaching is certainly more professionalized in its standards, occupational outlooks, and recognition by the general public than it was a decade or a half-century ago—progress in this direction has been both steady and substantial —but it is now in the process of establishing itself as an *emerging* profession, rather than one generally accorded full professional status.

The Road to Professionalism

The futility of imitation.   Teaching cannot expect to become a profession just by trying to be like the other professions. We cannot attain professional status by imitation or emulation of the other professional groups.

A leading "professional" magazine for teachers carries an advertisement for a license plate insigne, picturing the lamp of learning, which teachers are urged to buy and display as an evidence of their professional status. The assumption is that since doctors display the familiar caduceus by *their* license plates and are known thereby as members of a profession, what we teachers must do to be recognized as professionals is to display the lamp of learning by *our* licenses! This seems ridiculous, of course, but it represents one of the mistaken ways we have tried to achieve professional status—the "me too" attitude. If we could only *do* like the recognized professions we would *be* professional too!

The authors of a widely used introductory text in teacher education suggest, with evident sincerity, that we will never become professional until we substitute the name "educator" for "teacher." That is like trying to make street cleaners professional by calling them "sanitary engineers." A change in nomenclature is not enough.

Organizations don't make professionals.   The suggestion is sometimes made that teachers should join their professional organizations and thereby automatically become identified as professional. A professional teacher should hold active membership in his professional organizations, for reasons which will be discussed below. But mere membership as such in any group confers no instant accrual of professional status. As teachers we often think somewhat wistfully that if we could only achieve public recognition of our professional status our problems would be solved. Really, it is the other way around: if we could first solve the problems of our occupational group, we would then become a true profession. We cannot become a profession by trying to accumulate the privileges or accrue the prestige of the recognized professional groups. Professional status comes from doing a professional job; recognition comes from the public itself. We cannot arrogate to ourselves this professional status; it will come when we deserve it.

First things first. Perhaps even more significantly, we really ought to be concerning ourselves not with professional status—a fixed and ego-centered goal—but with professional *stature*. What must we seek first as a step toward professional stature? For increased professional recognition, with all of the advantages that would bring, teaching needs

1. More discriminatory recruitment and initial selection of teachers;
2. More adequate training of teachers;
3. More effective teacher-certification laws;
4. More demanding requirements for in-service growth;
5. More continuity in teacher-service—less casual dropping in and out of the profession;
6. A much higher level of teacher competence;
7. Improved economic conditions for teachers; and
8. Better public response to public education and to those who carry out its work.

Let us look at each one of these problems and its possible solutions. The presence and seriousness of these problems is today well recognized by most members of the teaching profession as a whole, and promising solutions are already being experimented with. Professional organizations of teachers are playing a very large and very effective part in bringing about the necessary changes for the better.

Recruitment and Selection

Since the time of the founding of our first schools in the United States, and much earlier than that in other countries abroad, there has been a persistent popular notion that anybody can teach. Benjamin Franklin, in his proposal for the founding of an academy, suggested that certain students "of the lesser sort" might be trained as teachers! Jefferson, with his far-sighted proposals for universal education, remarked casually that there should be "annually raked from the rubbish" some who could become teachers. Today, we realize that effective teaching calls for the very best people that can be found. Many lists of the desirable qualities to be sought in prospective teachers have been formulated and can be found in almost any book about teaching. We need not repeat these lists here. Just think of the very best teachers *you* had in elementary and high school: those are the kind of people that should enter teaching.

Effective Recruitment

Through careful guidance, counseling, and testing we need to discover and interest these prospective teachers very early, quite possibly as early as in junior high school, when many initial and at least some permanent vocational choices are commonly made. Teachers already in service, who are in daily contact with boys and girls, young men and women, who are constantly formulating and reformulating vocational choices, are in an ideal position to influence able people to choose teaching as a career. But it should be noted that many teachers actually have the opposite effect on their students; by self-deprecating remarks, constant complaining, and a generally negative attitude, they discourage many of their students from even considering teaching.

Through such organizations as the Future Teachers of America, the student NEA, and other preteaching clubs in high school and college, many good prospective teachers have an opportunity to learn about the work of teaching and even to get some opportunity to serve as "helping teachers" or "teachers' aides."

Continuous Screening

The selection process continues throughout the years of college training, and in nearly every institution which prepares teachers, a continuous screening process takes place. Through wise application of guidance techniques and the use of various intelligence, achievement, personality, and aptitude tests, students who are not qualified or adapted for the rigorous demands of the work of teaching are screened out and guided into other work. Some totally unfit persons still enter teaching, but the selective processes that have been set up are operating to bring into teaching a much more able group of people, as a whole, than generally entered teaching in decades past.

Who Does Enter Teaching?

The charge is frequently made that we still don't get the best and most promising students into teacher education programs—that teaching may attract better students than in the past, but that the average prospective teacher represents the dregs in the academic chalice!

In particular, critics like to note that on the Selective Service tests used for college deferment in the 1950's, education majors ranked near the bottom in total score. There were two reasons for this. In the first place, the tests were primarily designed to identify potential science and mathematics students, and thus were heavily weighted in favor of certain aptitudes possessed in greatest measure by prospective engineers—who naturally scored high. In the second place, undergraduates who list themselves as "education majors" often include many persons of limited academic potential who have no particular vocational orientation and think vaguely that they "might teach sometime." They are usually screened out in the lower-division years, and rarely enter teaching.

Actually, persons who are admitted to the teacher education programs of most accredited colleges and universities represent a very fair cross-section of college students. This, however, should not blind us to the plain fact that not *enough* of the most highly qualified students yet choose teaching as a career.

Teacher Training Education

Common Criticisms

There is a common belief today, expressed quite often by some members of the faculties of our colleges and universities and rather frequently by self-appointed spokesmen for the general public, that teacher education is a pretty sorry affair. Even among students who are engaged in taking such a program, or teachers who have completed it, it is not uncommon to hear complaints about the dullness, overlapping, repetitiousness, and impractical approach of education courses. The professors of education and the textbooks in education are subject to the same criticisms.

Basis for Criticisms

Painful though such an admission must be, the writer must acknowledge the truth of some of the charges. Professional courses in education at the college level are a relatively new venture; only for the last half-century has the field of professional education been in a process of development. Like any new field, education has suffered from the lack of definition of aims and content, lack of a respected academic tradition to fall back on, lack of a well-developed body of professional literature and research, and lack of trained instructors.

Recent Improvements

These growing pains have not all been relieved, but even a casual review of the newer, more readable, more literate books in education which have been published, say, within the last ten years, and a careful comparison of the content of professional education courses with those of ten or twenty years ago will indicate how great is the progress being made. More thorough training of the teachers of college-level courses and better use of the newer materials and techniques of instruction have also improved the quality of preservice training.

Furthermore, there has been a vast improvement in the over-all educational pattern for prospective teachers. You will sometimes hear it said that prospective teachers get almost nothing but education courses in college, and mostly narrow methods courses at that. This was certainly true when, in the early part of this century, it was common for public school teachers at both secondary and elementary levels (though especially the latter) to have little or no college education beyond their strictly professional courses. In a brief six-weeks teacher's institute, or in a year or two of normal-school training, there was very little opportunity for a broad liberal education.

Now, however, there are very few colleges which attempt to prepare teachers with less than four years of college work. This means that the typical prospective teacher gets as much "general education" or "liberal arts education" as the typical college graduate anywhere.

Balance in the program.   In no respectable teacher-education program, as a matter of fact, can a student even enter the professional sequence until he has completed the entire basic general education courses prescribed for all freshmen and sophomores. On the average, students preparing for secondary-school teaching spend fewer than one-sixth of their college hours in professional education courses, and only a portion of these hours are in specific "methods" courses. Even prospective elementary teachers, who must take courses in the teaching of the entire range of subjects—reading, language, arts, science, arithmetic, social studies, etc.—normally devote only one-third of their college hours to education courses.

Are education courses necessary?   Even though the fraction of total college time devoted to strictly professional courses is relatively small, you as a prospective teacher may sometimes resent "taking so much time" for courses in education and psychology. When you look at the problems of education and the duties of teachers realistically, however, it is difficult to see how anyone would want to go out and start teaching unless he knew something about these matters:

—How children grow, develop, and learn
—How to carry on actual classroom teaching
—Working with students outside of the classroom
—Using effectively the books and other materials of teaching
—Judging and reporting school achievement—testing and grading
—Working with parents and the community

To help you know these things that every teacher ought to know, you may be required to take certain specified courses in such areas as educational psychology, human growth and development, methods of teaching various subject matters, audio-visual materials, educational measurements, and student teaching. Such courses are basic to a sound preparation for teaching, and are taken as a complement to, rather than a substitute for, other courses in major and minor academic fields and basic general education courses required of all college students.

The Influence of Professional Groups

There is still, however, a great deal of improvement to be effected in the education of teachers. One of the strongest influences for better teacher education has been felt in the work of the professional groups at state, local, and national levels, which have constantly worked with the colleges and universities to make the preparation of teachers more intensive and extensive, practical and functional. These groups are of several sorts—scholarly associations, such as the American Association for the Advancement of Science and the American Historical Association; professional organizations, such as the NEA and the 50 state education associations; and accrediting groups, such as the North Central Association and the National Commission on the Accreditation of Teacher Education. These and other groups have met frequently and conscientiously in large and small working conferences in the past few years in an attempt to resolve the conflicts of opinion among those seriously interested in teacher education.

A notable example of professional concern with improvement of teacher education is to be seen in the "New Horizons" project of the National Committee on Teacher Education and Professional Standards (TEPS Commission) of the NEA. This forthright statement of the policy of the profession with respect to teacher education includes the following unequivocal pronouncement: [2]

> *The Profession's Responsibility for Ensuring Competent Professional Personnel Through Standards of Preparation.* The beginning and the end products of teacher education are persons—individuals who achieve as educators chiefly because of the persons they are. Arrangements for teacher education, therefore, must be arrangements for affecting persons.
>
> Focusing education on a person in his role as a citizen-teacher requires *a sharp new emphasis on the acquisition and control of knowledge.* Preparation for all teachers, and for leadership personnel, must be based on purposefully planned programs in which:
>
> 1. *Content is selected to provide:*
>
> Continuing *liberal education* that actually liberates a person. This means content selected with reference to problems and issues—general education that effects syntheses of knowledge.
>
> *Specialization* required by the scholar-teacher—a person who possesses and continues to acquire the knowledge of his teaching field important for his work and who has a genuine and contagious interest in knowledge. This means content that deals pertinently with the teaching field. Further, it means penetration that provides understanding of how the various elements of the subject are ordered and related and that gives command of the logical procedures by which facts, concepts, propositions, and arguments are analyzed and evaluated.
>
> Study of *educational theory and practice* essential to a successful beginning in the profession of teaching. This means content to provide adequate initial ability and a grasp of possibilities of the teaching role sufficient to enable the teacher to see and seize the opportunities presented to him. It means closing the gap between courses in theory and those designed to develop skill in the practice of teaching.
>
> 2. *Mastery of content includes:*
>
> *Control of knowledge* that goes beyond understanding to appropriate use of knowledge in varied situations. This means going beyond knowledge to action and requires immersion in the stuff of which decisions are compounded—familiarity with choices which are possible and ceaseless practice in testing the

[2] National Commission on Teacher Education and Professional Standards, *New Horizons in Teacher Education and Professional Standards* (Washington, D.C.: National Education Association, 1960), pp. 12 f. Reprinted by permission.

pronouncements of authority and tradition. Professional competence must be tested in the laboratory situation with children and youth.

Understanding by the individual of the "why" underlying his behavior. This means basing action on a tested set of personal and professional values.

Current Preparation Standards for Teachers

In spite of the progress being made in teacher education, teachers are still the most poorly educated of all the professional groups. Most of the recognized professions require from five to seven years of college training for minimum acceptance in the profession, but this is not true of teaching. Even with the remarkable gains that have been made in recent years in increasing the levels of preparation for teaching, several states still require less than the four-year baccalaureate degree for teachers—25 per cent of all elementary school teachers now in service have less than four years of preparation. Fortunately, nearly all secondary school teachers—except for those on some sort of emergency or temporary certification—have at least a B.A. degree, and 13 per cent of elementary and 44 per cent of secondary teachers have preparation at the M.A. or higher level. The table below shows the level of preparation required by states for initial regular certification as of 1961.

TABLE II

SUMMARY OF MINIMUM PREPARATION REQUIRED BY STATES FOR
LOWEST REGULAR INITIAL CERTIFICATES
AS OF JULY 1, 1961

College years of preparation required	Number of states requiring	
	Elementary school teachers	High school teachers
5 years	0	3
4 years	44	48
3 but less than 4	1	0
2 but less than 3	6	1
1 but less than 2	1	0
Less than 1 year	0	0
Total	52	52

W. Earl Armstrong and T. M. Stinnett, A Manual on Certification Requirements for School Personnel in the United States (Washington, D. C.: NEA, 1962), p. 7. Reprinted by permission.

Fifth-year programs. It will be noted from the above table that while three states require a fifth year of preparation for full initial certification for secondary school teachers, no state has yet made this a requirement for elementary teachers, although several states have enacted legislation which will require the M.A. or its equivalent for all teachers after a specified date in the future. Yet there is every reason to believe that within the next decade a fifth-year preservice requirement for all teachers will become as common as is the baccalaureate degree requirement today.

In the present situation of a continuing teacher shortage, the fifth year of preparation has often been introduced in teacher-education programs primarily as a means of encouraging liberal arts graduates who had no work in professional education to return for an intensive course at the graduate level leading to certification. This has often brought many excellent persons into teaching and has helped alleviate the teacher shortage. But the real purpose of the fifth year of preparation is coming to be an extension of the total educational background of every teacher, not just a means of getting late-comers into the profession.

Certification

One basic reason for the relatively low level of college preparation of teachers in the United States is found in the minimum requirements for certification provided by many state laws. If a teacher can be certified under the laws of the state with very little college preparation, it becomes extremely difficult to induce the teacher to take more college work than is absolutely required by state law.

Emergency Certification

Although a majority of the states require four and a few even five years of college preparation for certification as a teacher, as can be seen from the table above, even these minimum requirements are often debased by the issuance of emergency or temporary certificates based on only a few semester hours of college work. In 1961-62, 97,348 emergency certificates were in force in the schools of the United States. This means that 6.7 per cent, or nearly one in fifteen of all teachers, were operating on a substandard preparation.

Slow Progress in Certification

Comparison of these requirements with those of the other established professions shows clearly why teaching has a long way to go to acquire professional status and recognition. Certification laws now reflect the popular misconception that anybody can teach, especially in the lower grades. As long as this popular belief is so widely held, it is obvious that in some states just "anybody" *does* teach.

Although historically the states have had the power to make and enforce regulations regarding the certification of teachers, and to issue teachers' certificates in accordance with these laws, from the time of our very earliest schools up until the first decade of this century the states generally left certification matters to the local school officials and boards. Within the last forty years, however, nearly every state has again assumed the certifying authority *at the state level*. In a very few states certificates may still be issued (under powers specifically granted by the states) by local authorities or by state colleges. In brief, while each state has ample authority to set up and enforce high standards for the certification of teachers, the problem still remains of getting many of the states to set their minimum standards at an educationally acceptable level.

Great progress is being made in raising minimum certification standards. State professional organizations of teachers, working in conjunction with the National Education Association and the Commission on Teacher Education and Professional Standards, have collected data on teacher certification, aroused public support for better certification standards, and worked closely with legislative committees to secure the passage of needed legislation. Many states which have not felt it possible to raise their standards immediately have by law adopted near-future deadlines which will require a minimum of four years of college work before any teaching certificate can be issued—and no temporary or emergency certificates will be permitted.

Weaknesses in certification laws.   Since, in the final analysis, the people of each state must speak through their elected representatives —the state legislature—to bring about improvement of teacher certification laws, it would appear that the basic problem is one of getting people as a whole to support favorable legislation. But there are many problems in certification laws besides that of securing additional legislation. For example, some states have passed certification laws so detailed and stringent that many educational leaders feel they have overdone a good thing. So many very specific courses may be required by the law that local districts will be prevented from hiring well-qualified teachers who have not had the particular courses required. Too, the laws may be so specific and so inflexible that needed adjustments cannot be made by the colleges and universities in their teacher-education curricula.

Another problem is lack of reciprocity between states. A teacher, well trained and with good experience gained in one state, may not be able to secure certification in another state because of different certification laws. Some way needs to be found, without lowering the standards of any state and without imposing a national pattern on all states, to make possible the free movement of good, well-qualified teachers from one state to another. The National Commission on Teacher Education and Professional Standards has had moderate success in encouraging many of the states to recognize for certification the preparation of teachers from NCATE-accredited institutions in other states, thus paving the way for complete national reciprocity. (See Figure III p. 272.)

In-Service Growth

One of the hallmarks of many recognized professions is the professional tradition of planned, effective in-service growth. Many doctors, lawyers, and engineers constantly study, both formally and informally, to increase their professional competence and keep their professional knowledge up to date. Teachers, too, must have a planned program of in-service training and growth to keep from getting in a rut, to keep from getting stale.

Necessity for In-Service Education

This is perhaps of special importance in teaching, since there is no profession, occupation, or job that has more inherent possibilities for in-service growth. No teacher ever reaches a point where he is teaching as well as it is *possible* to teach. Better programs of in-service growth are not only a step toward better professional status and recognition for teaching; they are absolutely necessary if we are to do good teaching. It is still possible for a teacher to avoid any effort that would result in professional growth, but many means of acquiring worthwhile and educative in-service experiences are now commonly available.

Means of In-Service Growth

One of the most important is additional formal college classes, taken in the regular college sessions, in summer school, or through

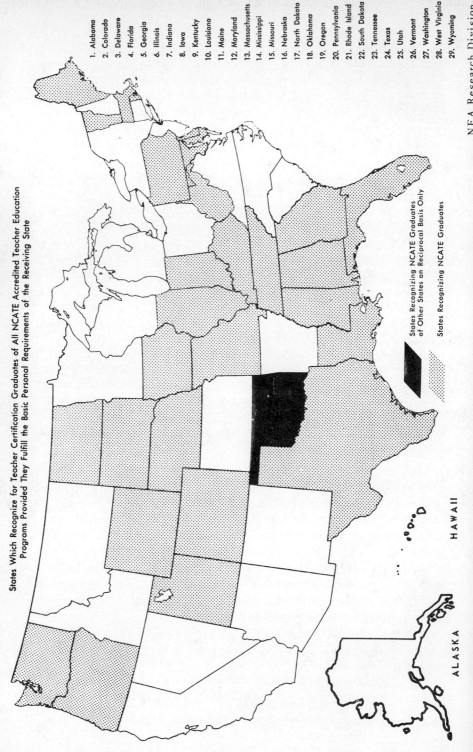

FIGURE III

States Which Recognize for Teacher Certification Graduates of All NCATE Accredited Teacher Education Programs Provided They Fulfill the Basic Personal Requirements of the Receiving State

1. Alabama
2. Colorado
3. Delaware
4. Florida
5. Georgia
6. Illinois
7. Indiana
8. Iowa
9. Kentucky
10. Louisiana
11. Maine
12. Maryland
13. Massachusetts
14. Mississippi
15. Missouri
16. Nebraska
17. North Dakota
18. Oklahoma
19. Oregon
20. Pennsylvania
21. Rhode Island
22. South Dakota
23. Tennessee
24. Texas
25. Utah
26. Vermont
27. Washington
28. West Virginia
29. Wyoming

States Recognizing NCATE Graduates of Other States on Reciprocal Basis Only

States Recognizing NCATE Graduates

HAWAII

ALASKA

NEA Research Division.

extension classes brought out to the school from a nearby college. Workshops, using a problem approach, and designed to help teachers work on their own school problems, are increasingly popular. But professional growth need not—should not—be expected to come from continuation of college level work alone. Planned educational travel, worthwhile community service projects, and other normal activities of teachers can be made a means of continued in-service growth.

Teachers can experience an extremely satisfying kind of in-service growth through work on school committees—formulating plans for curriculum improvement, improvement of marking and grading practices, development of new instructional materials, for example— through realistic but imaginative experiments and research conducted in their own classrooms. Taking an active part in the local teachers' organization or the local PTA can be professionally stimulating and educational.

Professional meetings of teachers at a local, state, regional, or national level provide many opportunities for teachers to get new and practical experience that will help them grow in knowledge and understanding of their work. Through attendance at such meetings, taking an active part in them, and reading the professional journals that many of the organizations publish at frequent intervals—through these and similar activities any teacher can keep growing professionally.

Each of these avenues of in-service growth can be, to a limited degree, made a requirement for the teacher through certification provisions that mandate continued formal graduate schooling, through local board of education regulations which demand a certain number of hours of advanced work for continued employment, and through salary scales which tie pay increments to definite educational or professional service requirements. In the final analysis, however, mandatory provisions for in-service growth are not the answer to the needs of the profession. Professional maturity for teaching will be achieved only when teachers recognize the inherent professional necessity of continuing to grow on the job, and accept the challenges of in-service growth as a personal obligation to be met willingly.

Better Continuity in Teaching

One of the criteria often mentioned as a distinguishing mark of the profession is lifelong, career service. It is unfortunate, surely, that so many teachers stay in the work only for a brief period until "something better" turns up. It gives teaching a reputation for itinerancy that is not in keeping with its desired professional status. Really, however, the situation is not as bad as it seems.

It can be expected that an occupation that attracts as many young women as does teaching will lose a great many of these women to an even more attractive enterprise, marriage and homemaking. But it is to be hoped that many of those who leave teaching to take up the responsibilities of marriage can be encouraged to return to the classroom at some future time, usually after their own children are old enough to be in school. The combination of a teaching career with marriage is now a very common practice; 67 per cent of all teachers (70 per cent of the men, 62 per cent of the women) are now married persons. Local boards which have a policy that forbids or discourages the hiring or rehiring of married women teachers should certainly re-examine the position they have taken; they will probably find it untenable. For it has been well established that married teachers make good teachers.

The economic factors and sometimes unpleasant working conditions that cause a large part of teacher turnover, and outright loss of teachers from the profession, will be discussed in a later section of this chapter. It should be sufficient to point out here that teachers' organizations in all states are working constantly and successfully through local and state committees on teacher welfare for the improvement of conditions that cause us to lose thousands of good teachers annually.

Teacher Competence

"A chain is no stronger . . ." runs the old proverb. Nor is the would-be profession of teaching any stronger than the weakest of those who make up the occupational group. There is a substantial amount of downright incompetent and ineffective teaching going on in the American public schools; some of it, unfortunately, goes undetected, but enough of it is so obvious to even the lay public as to constitute a serious problem in teaching.

Those of us who are already teaching have good reason to be proud, deeply proud, of our occupation and of our fellow teachers. The vast majority of teachers do a commendable job. In fact, when we view the relatively ineffective processes used in many institutions for screening and selecting prospective teachers, when we note the low value apparently placed on professional training by undemanding minimum certification laws in many states, when we see how many teachers are seriously underpaid—when we consider all of these things, the surprising fact is that teachers are as good as they are!

Improvements being brought about in teacher selection, certification, and salary schedules are definitely resulting in the raising of the general level of teacher competence. We cannot, however, absolve the teaching profession itself from some of the blame for conditions that exist. Doctors, lawyers, and certified public accountants, to name only a few of the recognized professional groups, have for a long time taken upon themselves the policing of their own organizations, and they deny membership or dismiss from membership those who are proved incompetent or unethical in the practice of the profession. Teachers have been slow in following the lead of the other professional groups in these matters.

Like other professions, ours of teaching has a code of ethics, a notable statement of what we expect of ourselves as a group. The code adopted by the National Education Association has also been adopted or paralleled by action of the local and state teachers' organizations throughout the nation. Any code of ethics is both highly idealistic and yet thoroughly practical—it works if we will it to work! Our trouble is not only that teachers often fail to live up to their professional-ethic ideals (that is true in the other professions as well) but that teachers' organizations have been extremely loath actually to enforce the provisions upon their members. We must quite ruthlessly weed out of the profession those who violate the self-imposed code of the profession—and incompetence is a *prima facie* evidence of violation. We must set our own house in order.

Better Economic Conditions for Teachers

The economic problems of teachers as a group are not insoluble, but the solutions seem a long way off. Part of the difficulty is simply the lack of adequate provision of funds by the people of the United States for their schools. But the basic fiscal problem is complicated by two difficulties that might be called psychological.

Psychological Barriers

First there is the almost neurotic self-pity that has developed in some segments of the teaching profession. Salaries are often unreasonably low and teaching conditions are not always pleasant. But we as teachers have sometimes spent so much time at the wailing wall that we have exhausted not only ourselves but public sympathy as well. Teachers who spend a majority of the time feeling sorry for themselves are a sorry lot indeed. We have painted such a black picture of teaching as a life work that prospective teachers have been frightened away from the profession.

At the other extreme is found the second psychological problem: some individuals and groups within the teaching profession seem to think it is unethical, grossly materialistic, and almost indecent for teachers to be concerned with money. We are interested, they say, in the higher things of life, not in mere material gain. Actually, these latter folk are forgetting that the economic concerns of teachers are not opposed to social and educational values; they are bound up with them. The adequately paid, secure, unworried teacher does a better job in the classroom than one whose life is an economic misery. Materialistic concerns—money matters—become *value* problems the moment they affect society at large. The great philosopher Berdyaev touched the heart of the problem when he said, "Bread for myself is a material question; bread for my neighbor is a spiritual question." [3]

If we as teachers are seriously concerned with the economics of teaching and the economic problems of teachers, we need have no cause whatsoever for embarrassment. How much teachers are paid is a social question, a value question in the highest sense.

Teacher Salaries

Although tenure and retirement provisions are of great importance to teachers, their primary economic concern is necessarily with cash salaries, their take-home pay.

Comparisons with other professions.   Compared with the already recognized professions, the emerging profession of teaching has very low salaries. But this comparison is not at all fair; the analogy is faulty. While it is true that the professions of medicine, dentistry, law, and engineering have average salaries of perhaps seven to twelve thousand dollars a year, whereas public school teachers' salaries average thousands of dollars lower, there are many reasons why the two are not comparable. First, the above-named professions have already gone through their period of struggling to gain public recognition and

[3] Nicolas Berdyaev, *Fate of Man in the Modern World* (London: Student Christian Movement Press, Ltd., and New York: Morehouse-Gorham Co.). Reprinted by permission of the publishers.

acceptance. Second, the recognized professions require many more years of college- and graduate-level preparation than does teaching at the present time. Third, members of these professional groups ordinarily work on a year-round basis, while most teachers work at their primary job only nine months—and are paid accordingly. Furthermore, the teacher, unlike members of other professions, does not have the heavy expenses of operating an office, and the teacher's clients are always plentiful! Nevertheless, average salaries in teaching are much lower than they should be to provide a modest but adequate standard of living, and to attract and hold the very best people in teaching.

Of course, the purchasing power of the dollar, rather than the salary figure itself, is what really counts, and it is very true that the cost of living during this last ten years has, in many places, increased as fast as or even faster than salaries. Still, the rate of salary increase continues to outstrip the rate of increase in living cost. Moreover, although teachers' salaries in times of recession or depression are usually reduced somewhat—even drastically—the reduction is seldom as much as the gains that have already been established. In other words, both the *relative* and *absolute* salaries of teachers are definitely on the increase.

Who determines salaries?   School systems in all states are constantly working toward salary goals which have been set up through professional teachers' organizations, often assisted by lay groups. These proposed salary schedules are suggestions only; local attitude and local finances dictate the actual salaries. State laws in 34 states now put a floor under salaries by establishing legal minimums, but the local district can and often does go well beyond these figures. States laws put floors under salaries, but local districts establish their own ceilings.

Salary schedules.   Perhaps the most encouraging improvement in the financial status of teachers is the widespread adoption of the "single" salary schedule with regular yearly increases, or increments. A "single" salary schedule is one that provides equal compensation for all teachers in the school system, men and women, elementary and secondary alike, based on years of experience and training. This is a great step toward putting pay-for-teaching on a sound basis.

Comparisons by geographic regions.   State-by-state comparisons of average salaries can be secured from research data current at any given time, but the yearly fluctuations make much data quite variable.

Also, within-state variations in salaries are obscured by the reported "average." Tremendous national variations can be found—from as little as $2000 per year in some poor districts to as much as $10,000 per year for classroom teaching in a few very wealthy and progressive districts. Therefore, the general regional comparisons given in the table below are useful in gaining a broad perspective of salary differences.

TABLE III

AVERAGE ANNUAL SALARY OF INSTRUCTIONAL STAFF

Region	1959-60	1960-61	1961-62
New England..........	$ 5,305	$ 5,599	$ 5,803
Middle Atlantic	5,771	6,091	6,314
Southeast	4,045	4,365	4,596
Middle	5,343	5,610	5,868
Southwest	4,784	4,868	5,388
Northwest	4,480	4,700	4,890
Far West [a]	6,233	6,653	6,945
Total, 50 states and Dist. of Columbia:	$ 5,159	$ 5,449	$ 5,716

[a] Includes Alaska and Hawaii.

NEA Research Division. Reprinted by permission.

Distribution of average salaries.   Even more significant than overall average salaries is the distribution of these salaries into the various dollar ranges. The table below indicates this information on a national basis for the past decade.

TABLE IV

CLASSROOM TEACHERS' PAY OVER A TEN-YEAR PERIOD

School year	Per cent of teachers paid		
	Below $ 3,500	$ 3,500- 4,499	$ 4,500 and over
1952-53	62.0%	25.0%	13.0%
1953-54	55.8	26.6	17.6
1954-55	48.5	29.2	22.3
1955-56	42.6	31.4	26.0
1956-57	35.0	33.0	32.0
1957-58	25.6	33.5	40.9
1958-59	17.0	31.7	51.3
1959-60	12.8	29.7	57.5
1960-61	9.2	26.0	64.8
1961-62	6.4	21.8	71.8

NEA Research Division. Reprinted by permission.

Rate of salary increase.   The national average salary in 1961-62 for all instructional personnel in the public schools stood at $5,716, an increase of 65.7 per cent in the decade 1951-1961. This rate of increase has not been even in all states and districts—average salaries in some states have more than doubled in the last ten years, and in other states or districts the rise has been less than spectacular.

The most flexible schedules are those expressed in terms of *index* or *ratio* rather than dollar figures. That is, once a base salary (usually based on a B.A. degree and no experience) is established, then all other steps and ranges are fixed in terms of that basic *index* salary, and are expressed in ratios thereof. A sample of such a schedule is given in Figure IV, below:

FIGURE IV

HYPOTHETICAL INDEX SALARY SCHEDULE

Base: $_____ ◄——

Base amount to be reviewed annually; NEA recommends $6000

Uniform increments; 6 percent of the bachelor's degree minimum

Salary step	Bachelor's degree	Master's degree	Sixth year M.A.+30	Doctor's degree
1	1.00	1.10 ◄	1.20 ◄	1.35 ◄
2	1.06	1.16	1.26	1.41
3	1.12	1.22	1.32	1.47
4	1.18	1.28	1.38	1.53
5	1.24	1.34	1.44	1.59
6	1.30	1.40	1.50	1.65
7	1.36	1.46	1.56	1.71
8	1.42	1.52	1.62	1.77
9	1.48	1.58	1.68	1.83
10	1.54	1.64	1.74	1.89
11	1.60	1.70	1.80	1.96
12	1.66	1.76	1.86	2.02
13	1.72	1.82	1.92	2.08
14	....	1.88	1.98	2.14
15	....	....	....	2.20

10 percent above base for each additional year of professional preparation; 15 percent for doctor's degree

12 increments for bachelor's degree class and 13 for master's degree class; typical of present practice

Twice the bachelor's degree minimum

NEA Research Division
Reprinted by
permission.

No salary schedule is without its errors and inequities, but an established yet flexible schedule can do much to assure that teachers are rewarded impartially for their experience and training. Whether other factors of "merit" should be also considered in establishing salaries is a perennially controversial topic of discussion between school boards, who often favor merit-rating plans, and teachers' groups, who almost uniformly oppose such proposals.

Tenure

More than three-fourths of the states now have some legal provision for "employment security" for the teacher, subject to his continued satisfactory performance of his job. The tenure laws usually provide for permanent employment of the satisfactory teacher after a probationary period has been served; continuing contract laws provide that a teacher is (after the probationary period) automatically continued in his contract unless notified otherwise by a certain date each year.

Does tenure protect poor teachers? It is important to note that the tenure laws do not in any sense relieve the local school board of the responsibility for, or opportunity of, dismissing poor teachers. Very briefly, all laws having to do with teacher tenure contain about the same three provisions: (a) a definite probationary period; (b) a requirement that any charges against the teacher must be made in writing; and (c) an opportunity for the teacher to reply to the charges in a hearing before the board and to appeal the local board's decision to the courts.

You will see that there is nothing in the tenure laws to protect the unsatisfactory teacher: the laws merely guarantee an orderly, open, and fair method for discharge of teachers who do not do satisfactory work. Really, the laws in the last analysis are not designed so much to protect the teacher as to protect the public which they serve. These laws give the public, the people who support the schools, assurance that good teachers will not be fired arbitrarily or with insufficient cause, and that poor teachers *will* be removed from the schools in an expeditious but scrupulously fair manner.

Abuses of tenure laws. There are certainly abuses in the administration of some tenure laws, and there are to be found both professional educators and laymen who doubt the wisdom of having such legislation in force at all. Teachers may sometimes try just to coast along, doing nothing either very good or very bad, hiding behind the law that requires definite charges of inefficiency or immorality before they can be dismissed. Some boards who "don't want their hands tied" (as they would say) by the tenure law make it a practice to dismiss each teacher as he nears the end of his probationary period; thus no teacher ever attains tenure! These and other difficulties found with the tenure laws represent faults in the administering of the laws, rather than faults with the basic idea of tenure legislation.

The professional ethics committees of the professional teachers' organizations—local, state, and national—have been alert to bring unfavorable public sentiment to bear upon either boards of education or teachers who violate the provisions or the spirit of the laws protecting tenure of teachers.

Retirement

It has taken over fifty years of educational legislation to provide for some form of retirement benefits for teachers in all states. New York first established the pattern with retirement legislation in 1894, and Idaho became the final state to provide for teacher retirement in 1947. The unfortunate part of this otherwise bright picture is that many of the states provide such small benefits that the teacher is really left without adequate provision for old age. Nevertheless, the basic idea is now found in all states, and the actual financial provisions are constantly being improved.

Pensions and annuities.   It is well to note that most of the states provide not pensions—a financial crumb thrown to the starving teacher, a pasture furnished *gratis* to the faithful, worn-out work-horse—but annuities, which are *earned* and *paid-for* benefits. Teachers in most states today are not *given* a pension; they *purchase* an annuity. This is important; teachers are not asking for something extra, an additional benefit from the local district or the state. The ideal retirement system, and the one in most common use, provides that the teacher *must* belong to the plan, *must* contribute a certain portion of his income each year (usually about 5 per cent) and that the state or local district (sometimes both) *must* contribute a matching amount. Although, under most systems, the money the teacher contributes may be withdrawn when he leaves teaching, the money put in by the school remains to enrich the retirement fund. Each state, and in many cases local districts within a state, has its own particular way of administering the retirement funds, but the majority of the systems permit retirement with full benefits after thirty years of service covered by the plan.

Unsolved problems.   As with all the other problems affecting teacher welfare, there are several unsolved questions regarding retirement systems. How can we arrange to transfer retirement credits from one state to another when the teacher moves? Reciprocity between states is needed here, as well as in certification practices. How can we tie in the benefits of Federal Social Security legislation with existing teacher retirement systems without detriment to the teachers involved? These and a host of similar questions are constantly being studied by teachers' organizations, working closely with legislative officials in each state. In this area of teacher welfare the professional organizations have worked very effectively, not only for the interests of the teacher, but for the public interest most of all. For teacher welfare is important primarily insofar as it promotes the *public* welfare.

Fringe Benefits

Other provisions for the improvement of the financial security of teachers are of perhaps less significance than salaries, tenure protection, and retirement benefits, but certain fringe benefits also play a part in making teaching more attractive as a life-long career.

Sick leave.   Nearly every district today makes contractual provision for a given number—usually 10 or 12—of days of sick leave, which may be taken without loss of pay. Ideally, but not always, this leave may be accumulated indefinitely, and is never lost if it is not used.

Disability pay.   For longer periods when the teacher, because of inability or accident, is unable to be on the job, many districts provide insurance covering such disability so that at least a portion of the regular salary can be received during the period that the teacher is incapacitated.

Hospitalization insurance.   Insurance covering at least a major portion of the costs of hospital and medical insurance is almost uniformly available at reduced cost to teachers, either through the local district or the teacher's professional association. Part of the cost of this insurance is often borne by the school district.

Leave with pay.   An increasing number of districts provide a specified number of days per year for personal leave without loss of pay to allow the teacher to be absent on account of illness or death in the family or to transact urgent personal business. And in a growing number of larger and more progressive districts sabbatical leaves, usually at half pay, are provided after a given number of years of service to enable the teacher to pursue advanced graduate study or otherwise improve himself professionally.

Public Recognition of Teaching

The last of the goals that the emerging profession of education must seek is, we have said, better public response to public education and to those who carry out its work. This goal has not been reached, but we are nearer to it than ever before. Teachers want not only economic recognition, but social recognition too. They want to be recognized as important people in the community, doing a socially significant work with professional competence.

This recognition is coming. Teachers are increasingly accepted as professional persons of importance to the community; teachers *matter* more than ever before in the history of our country. No longer are elementary teachers looked down on just because they teach the "common branches" of learning. Teachers take an increasingly large share of responsibility for community leadership in areas other than formal classroom teaching. They belong to the church organizations, youth agencies, chambers of commerce, service clubs; they are a vital part of the social life of the community.

Teachers are only rarely subject to the absurd social restrictions of dress, behavior, and entertainment that were so common a few years ago. In a recent study of the status of rural teachers, the National Education Association discovered only a very few teachers who felt that they were required to do or not to do special things just because they were teachers. Public recognition of teachers as important leaders and as human beings is gratifying in itself, but it is especially significant because public recognition and acceptance of teachers is an indication of public understanding of education—what it means, what it is trying to do, and how important it is to the life of the community. A major achievement of the professional organizations of teachers at local, state, and national levels has been the bringing about of better public understanding and appreciation of the teacher and his work.

Professional Organizations

In almost every community in America there is a local teachers' association. It is usually affiliated with the state organization which is found in every state in the union. These state teachers' associations are in turn affiliated with a national organization.

The NEA

The largest and most influential of the national groups is the National Education Association, with headquarters in Washington, D.C. Membership in the NEA is now close to the goal of "a million or more by '64." More than a million teachers are already members of the affiliated state education associations.

The NEA, originally the National Teachers' Association, was first organized in 1857, when leaders from existing state organizations met together in Philadelphia to weld the separate groups into an association at the national level. The original meeting was called for the announced purpose of forming an organization of those teachers "who are willing to unite in a general effort to promote the educational welfare of our country . . . and who are ready to devote their energies and contribute of their means to advance the dignity, respectability and usefulness of the calling. . . ." [4]

This has remained the basic purpose of the NEA and of its affiliated state and local associations as well: to advance the educational welfare of the country and promote the usefulness of the teaching profession. How well this purpose has been carried out at every level is seen in the tremendous growth of these organizations, both in membership and effectiveness. Not solely by the efforts of these groups, but in a large measure *aided* by the work of professional organizations, the status and welfare of the teacher have been vastly improved, new teaching techniques and materials developed, and the public brought to realize the tremendous importance of supporting and improving the American system of public education.

Special-interest departments of the NEA and affiliated state and local organizations provide an excellent opportunity for teachers to work with others who are interested in special areas such as improvement of instruction, curriculum revision, science teaching, music education, administration, and many other fields.

Other Teachers' Organizations

Organization of the teaching profession has taken other forms, too. Union-type organizations of teachers affiliated with the American Federation of Labor (AFL) and the Congress of Industrial Organizations (CIO) are active in some cities and states. A World Con-

[4] Quoted in Stinnett, *op. cit.,* p. 80.

federation of Organizations of the Teaching Profession (known as WCOTP) has been quite effective in bringing about a unification of existing educational associations throughout the civilized world.

Importance to the Beginning Teacher

Knowledge about the various professional associations of teachers is important to the beginning teacher, as is a knowledge of some of the problems of teaching as an emerging profession and the solutions that are being worked out to these problems. But most important of all for the beginning teacher is not just *knowledge* of these professional problems, but active participation in their solution. Effective professional activity is most likely if you join and work in your professional organizations—local, state, and national. A unified profession can do immeasurable good in advancing the cause of education.

The Legal Status of Professional Associations

Criticisms of professional associations of teachers are often voiced both within the profession and by outsiders. It is alleged that they are administrator-dominated, power-hungry, status-conscious, monolithic structures whose powerful influence on education was not envisioned by those who founded our school system or wrote our school laws. In short, these associations are alleged to fall into a category somewhere between the immoral and the illegal.

Actually, most of the criticisms seem to impartial but informed observers to be unjustified. The associations do exert a powerful extralegal influence on education (much like that of the accrediting associations described in Chapter Three above) but their firm establishment as a part of our system of education has been affirmed by the courts.

In a recent case, the appellate court of a midwestern state ruled against a teacher who had brought suit against his school board for requiring him to join the local, state, and national associations as a condition of his enjoying the regular salary increments provided by the adopted salary schedule. This specific decision may not be of great importance, but the opinion of the court in this case is most interesting:

> In the teaching profession, as in all professions, membership in professional organizations tends to improve the interest, knowledge, experience and over-all professional competence.

Membership in professional organizations is no guaranty of professional excellence, but active participation in such organizations, attendance at meetings where leaders give the members the benefit of their experience and where mutual problems and experiences and practices are discussed, are reasonably related to the development of higher professional attainments and qualifications. Such membership affords an opportunity for self-improvement and self-development on the part of the individual member. It is the duty of every school board to obtain the services of the best qualified teachers, and it is not only within their power but it is their duty to adopt rules and regulations to elevate the standards of teachers and the educational standards within their school district.[5]

Growing Maturity of Professional Organizations

Several clear indications that the professional organizations of teachers are by no means interested just in higher salaries and other direct benefits to teachers have become apparent in recent major developments of programs in the National Education Association and its affiliated state organizations.

"New Horizons" project in teacher education and professional standards. This project, mentioned previously in this chapter, affirms the determination of the profession to accept unhesitatingly its responsibility for assuming leadership and taking initiative to join with the public in setting and enforcing standards for entrance, preparation, and retention of teachers in the profession.

The professional autonomy movement. As part of the total "New Horizons" project, the teaching profession has taken a bold, if perhaps unpopular, stand on the issue of whether teaching has the right as a profession to make professional determinations in educational matters that call for professional expertness. This is not, it has been pointed out, so much a move towards autonomy as such as it is an avowal of responsible self-discipline.

Professional rights and responsibilities. A final indication of the growing maturity of the teaching profession is embodied in the relatively simple action of the NEA in terminating the existence of its committees on "defense" of teachers, tenure, and academic freedom and combining the work of these groups into a new Commission on Professional Rights and *Responsibilities* (italics added).

[5] National Education Association, *Research Memo* 1961-42, November, 1961.

Balancing Supply and Demand of Teachers

A persistent problem of the teaching profession has been that of getting an adequate supply of well-prepared teachers, trained in the needed fields, available in the right places at the right time.

Cyclic Nature of Supply and Demand

During the years of the Great Depression of the 1930's, there was an oversupply of teachers; the lack of other available jobs and the relative economic security of teaching, together with a decreased school enrollment brought about by a decline in birth rates—all of these factors operated to give us more teachers than there were teaching positions. Many teachers were unemployed, and hundreds of thousands of those who had jobs were teaching for very meager salaries. Then, with the manpower shortages brought about by World War II, with many teachers leaving the profession to accept jobs in defense industries and many others entering the armed services, a serious teacher shortage developed which has continued until today. In addition, rising birth rates during the 'forties resulted in an enormous increase in the number of children to be educated and in the number of teachers needed to staff new classrooms. Today there is a serious teacher shortage at both elementary and secondary levels, and it does not appear that there will be an overabundance of teachers within any foreseeable future.

The present teacher shortage is much more alarming than the general public seems to realize. Extensive and competent surveys [6] have been made of the teacher supply and demand for the past several years, and authoritative estimates in September, 1961, placed the teacher shortage at not less than 240,000 teachers; that many *new* teachers are needed annually to staff the schools adequately.

Why do we need so many teachers? There are five major reasons:

Need for New Teachers

1. *Enrollment growth.* Thirty-five thousand new teachers are needed to take care of the tremendous growth in school enrollment.

[6] See especially the annual "Teacher Supply and Demand Report," prepared by the NEA Research Division.

The total enrollment in public and private elementary and high schools has gone up at the rate of more than a million new students a year since 1950, and promises to continue at not less than that rate of increase indefinitely. The increase was felt at first in the lower elementary grades, but as these children have moved up through the grades to high school, and new ones have taken their place, the bulge is felt all through the school system.

2. *Replacements.* New teachers are needed to provide replacements. Every year thousands of teachers—in 1961, 120,000—are lost through retirement or death, or leave teaching to enter other work, or resign to get married.

3. *Relieve overcrowding.* Thirty thousand new teachers are needed to relieve overcrowded classrooms. Thousands of classrooms are woefully overcrowded, many of them to almost double their normal capacity. Even if enrollments should stay the same, which they obviously will not, many new teachers are needed to staff new classrooms as they are built.

4. *Enrichment.* Twenty-five thousand new teachers are needed to enrich the instructional program. Many schools are now unable to offer specialized instruction in health and safety education, crafts, music, art, and remedial courses simply because no teachers can be found or spared for these important areas. If teachers were available, they would be employed to provide instruction in these needed areas.

5. *Replacement for substandard teachers.* Another thirty thousand new teachers are needed to replace present substandard teachers. Many hundreds of schools are now employing many thousands of teachers on substandard certificates, teachers who ought to be and would be replaced by fully-qualified teachers if such were available.

Decreasing Supply

At the same time that this *need* is increasing, the supply of qualified teachers has been increasing only slowly—so slowly as to give the effect of a net decrease. For many trained college graduates do not even apply for teaching positions, further reducing the actual supply of teachers available. In 1960, only 75 per cent of the potential elementary teachers graduated by the colleges, and only 66 per cent of the potential secondary school teachers, actually entered teaching. In some fields, such as math and science, only 46 per cent of the trained graduates entered teaching.

Imbalance

Of equally serious import is the fact that teachers are not necessarily prepared for the "shortage" fields. In 1960, elementary vacancies outnumbered high school vacancies 8 to 5, but the supply of secondary teachers increased six times as much as the supply of elementary teachers. Moreover, specific field preparation often bears no relation whatever to the number of anticipated vacancies.

The picture of teacher supply and demand presented above is not very heartening, yet it does indicate that a person contemplating entering teaching today has every reasonable assurance of being able to find satisfactory employment, provided he is well prepared for teaching and has the personal qualifications necessary to make a good teacher. Furthermore, the somewhat bleak picture represents another of the unsolved problems of teaching as an emerging profession, another challenge that must be met if teaching is really to become recognized as a full-grown profession.

ELEVEN: TOPICS FOR STUDY, REPORT, AND DISCUSSION

1. Arrange, with your instructor's help, for members of the class to visit a meeting of some professional organization of teachers. Such groups as community education associations will normally be very glad to invite members of the class (perhaps, if the class is large, only a few at a time) to attend their meetings. See if you can determine the actual program and actual accomplishments of this group of professional educators.
2. If your college or university has a Student Education Association chapter, attend some of the meetings or, better yet, join the group and take an active part in becoming oriented to working in professional organizations. If there is no local chapter, work with your instructor to get one started.
3. State education associations will usually issue complimentary tickets to students in professional education courses so that they may attend state or regional meetings of these associations. If it would be possible for you to afford the necessary personal expenses of such attendance, ask your instructor how to go about getting tickets.
4. Secure a copy of the certification requirements of the state in which you expect to teach. How adequate, in your opinion, are these requirements in assuring that a high standard of professional competence will be demanded of all teachers?
5. As a committee project, secure from the state education associations of several surrounding states data on teacher salaries, retirement benefits, and tenure laws, and make a graphic comparison of teaching conditions in the states surveyed.

6. With your instructor's permission, invite one or more of these persons to lead a class discussion on *the professional future in teaching:* a) superintendent or principal who actually hires teachers; b) the director of your college or university placement bureau; c) a teacher who is an active member of several professional organizations. Or, put them all together on a panel for an interesting discussion!
7. Read several issues of some professional education journal, general or specialized in nature, to find out just what these magazines have to offer the teacher. List and briefly review the articles that could actually be used to contribute to your professional knowledge or growth as a teacher.

ELEVEN: BIBLIOGRAPHY

American Assocation of School Administrators, Department of Classroom Teachers of the NEA, and National School Boards Association, *Who's a Good Teacher?* Washington: National Education Association, 1961. This publication, the result of a study sponsored jointly by the three organizations named, summarizes recent research on teacher competency.

Armstrong, W. Earl, and T. M. Stinnett, *A Manual on Certification Requirements for School Personnel in the United States.* Washington, D. C.: National Education Association, 1961. The most useful available compilation of certification requirements state-by-state; even the latest edition, which should always be used, cannot always reflect the fast-changing requirements.

Brubacher, John S., *A History of the Problems of Education.* New York: McGraw-Hill Book Co., Inc., 1947. A fascinating historical account of the development of teaching is found in chap. 16; very readable.

Educational Policies Commission, *Professional Organizations in American Education.* Washington, D. C.: NEA, 1957. A first-rate summary of the problems facing the professional organizations with suggestions for future action.

Hodenfield, G. K., and T. M. Stinnett, *The Education of Teachers: Conflict and Consensus.* Englewood Cliffs, N. J.: Prentice-Hall, Inc., 1961. As the subtitle suggests, this is an analysis of the major agreements and disagreements in programs of teacher education today. Much of the book surveys the recent national conferences of the Teacher Education and Professional Standards Commission.

The Journal of Teacher Education, published quarterly by the National Commission on Teacher Education and Professional Standards of the NEA, is an excellent general source of information on current trends in the professionalization of teaching.

Lindsey, Margaret, ed., *New Horizons for the Teaching Profession.* Washington, D. C.: National Commission on Teacher Education and Professional Standards, NEA, 1961. Comprehensive report of the many-faceted professional program for the improvement of teaching and the teaching profession.

NEA Research Division, *Teacher Supply and Demand in Public Schools, 1962*. Washington: National Education Association, 1962. This, the latest available of a series of annual reports, details the current statistics of, and problems in, teacher supply and demand. Very useful for determining which teaching fields are over- or under-supplied.

Perrodin, Alex F., "Teachers Meetings," *NEA Journal,* Vol. 43, No. 8 (November, 1954), 490 f. Excellent brief suggestions for making staff meetings a means of in-service training and growth; puts the basic responsibility on the teacher, not the administrator.

Sarason, Seymour, Kenneth S. Davidson, and Burton Blatt, *The Preparation of Teachers: An Unstudied Problem in Education.* New York: John Wiley & Sons, Inc., 1962. A fresh, critical essay on the current status of teacher education. Moderately difficult, but rewarding.

Thomas, Lawrence G., Lucien B. Kinney, Arthur P. Coladarci, and Helen A. Fielstra, *Perspective on Teaching.* Englewood Cliffs, N. J.: Prentice-Hall, Inc., 1961. An excellent discussion of professional organizations may be found in chap. 16.

A well-planned classroom corner.
*Could planning such as is evidenced
here be done by the "administration"
alone?*

CHAPTER TWELVE

Administrative Specialization:
A Modern Development

There was a time, not too far back in American educational history, when the distinction between classroom teaching and educational administration did not exist; the teacher did the whole job himself.

Teaching and Administration Originally Combined

A contract executed in 1682 between the city officials in Flatbush, New York, and their Dutch schoolmaster has been preserved which gives a clear indication of the many duties required of classroom teachers in those days. The teacher was expected to perform these tasks (among others specified) under the general supervision of the civic officials: ring the bell for the opening and closing of school; conduct morning, noon, and evening prayer and catechism services daily; conduct special religious services on Monday, Wednesday, and Sunday; keep the church clean; ring the bell for church services three times; read the Scripture, the Articles of Faith, and the Ten Com-

THE TEACHER'S STAKE
IN ADMINISTRATION

mandments at Sunday services; lead the singing; read the sermons in the absence of the minister; provide the water for baptism and the sacraments for communion; keep birth records and the school census; toll the bell and dig graves for funerals; collect and account for school tuition charges; serve as messenger for the town officials; and, of course, teach school. For all of this he received a small salary, most of it in grain, plus the use of a "dwelling-house, barn, pasture, lot and meadows, to the school appertaining." [1]

The Development of Administrative Specialization

In the era represented by the illustration above, it was quite reasonable to expect that the "classroom" teacher could alone perform all of the educational services necessary in the community, including many ecclesiastical functions of the church which was so closely related to, and often housed, the school. Up until the beginning of the nineteenth century, in fact, it was quite customary in American education to make no distinction between teaching and administrative duties. No exact date can be given for the beginnings of formal school administration in this country, but it is significant that the first city superintendent of schools was appointed in Buffalo, New York, in 1837, the same year that the first really influential chief *state* school administrator, Horace Mann, was appointed in Massachusetts. So it can readily be seen that the specialization of educational functions in this country is not much more than a century old as a common practice.

Differentiation of Duties Breeds Conflicts

The specialized duties of school administration, as distinguished from teaching, developed largely as the result of two major influences: the increasing *size* and the growing *complexity* of the educational enterprise. Efficient, responsible, and effective administration demanded more time—more man-hours—than the regular teacher could spare from the classroom. But, as so often happens when different functions of a single enterprise—in this case, public education—become so complex and specialized that different groups of persons are given separate responsibilities, a rift between the two groups appears and

[1] Edgar W. Knight and Clifton L. Hall, *Readings in American Educational History* (New York: Appleton-Century-Crofts, Inc., 1951), pp. 17 f. Reprinted by permission.

sometimes widens to the proportions of a real schism. It sometimes seems today that the two groups in our schools—teachers and administrators—have very little in common; the rift between the two groups sometimes takes on the aspect of a major battle, one group fighting the other.

This should not be. While it is obvious that the *duties* of administrators and teachers are and should be different, the *purposes* of both groups are identical: better education of American children and youth. What happens to the children in the process of education is all that really matters. As the great American educator Thomas Briggs expressed it in his treatise on school supervision, "A school is organized that it may be administered; it is administered that it may be instructed." [2] All administrative, supervisory, organizational, fiscal, and legal aspects of public school work have one purpose: better teaching for better learning.

Beginning students in the field of professional teacher education sometimes evidence an unnecessarily modest and even self-deprecating attitude when problems of school administration are mentioned; they think and sometimes say, "But I'm just a beginner in the field, not even a teacher yet. And if I ever do become an administrator, it won't be for a long, long time." But the prospective teacher or the beginning teacher has a definite stake in school administration, even though he has no intention of making his professional career in this field. Knowledge of administrative problems helps the classroom teacher in his daily work of teaching, helps him as a community leader in educational matters, and helps make him an effective partner in the administrative work of the school.

The Conflicts Between Teacher and Administrator

Salary Differential

In spite of the logical reasons that can be advanced for considering the purposes of teachers and administrators as having a common goal, and for encouraging the study of administrative problems by classroom teachers, there are today evidences of a rift between the two groups that appears to be increasing. Perhaps one of the most unfortunate causes for this rift is the salary differential

[2] Thomas H. Briggs, *Improving Instruction* (New York: The Macmillan Co., 1938), p. 99.

that is properly found between the two groups. Some teachers are jealous of the distinctly greater remuneration that the supervisors, principals, and superintendents usually receive. It is undoubtedly true that in some, if not many, schools there has been an unjustifiably large salary differential between administrative and classroom-teaching groups, but these extreme cases are gradually being rectified by the adoption of salary schedules that more nearly reflect the responsibilities assigned to each group of educational workers. In the past quarter of a century, the gap between the average salaries of teachers and those of administrators has decreased by about 25 per cent. In fact, some educational authorities maintain that there is not enough salary differential today to reflect adequately the higher level of preparation, the more complex duties, and the greater responsibilities required of the school administrator.

The grass is always greener on the other side of the fence, and many classroom teachers look at the duties and responsibilities of the administrator and think, "What a snap! Boy, would I like to trade jobs with him!" It is undoubtedly true that some administrators don't really earn their keep (that's true of some teachers, too, of course), but the capable administrator—supervisor, principal, coordinator, or superintendent—has a responsibility that, if competently performed, is well worth the extra salary he gets. Administrative work (as compared with classroom teaching) generally requires many more years of experience, additional advanced training, specialized skills and abilities; the administrator is on call twenty-four hours a day, often seven days a week; he must coordinate the work of many other educational specialists (often including a few very rugged individualists); he must take the brunt of public criticism, not only for his own mistakes and those of his teachers, but often for decisions that are right but unpopular. The good administrator earns his money—and his ulcers.

Resentment of Authority

Another cause for conflict of interest (and sometimes for personality conflicts) between teacher and administrator is the unwholesome belief that the administrator is supposed to be the embodiment of authority—the absolute boss; someone, therefore, whose very viscera should automatically be hated by any self-respecting teacher. Both of the groups—teachers and administrators—are partially to blame for this feeling: some administrators for acting like martinets and despots, and some teachers for assuming that "all administrators are like that," and for being themselves autocratic in their own classrooms.

It is not surprising that the authoritarian concept of school administration still persists, however wrongly; for many centuries authoritarianism was the accepted *ideal* in education. In the year 1866, F. S. Jewell wrote:

> The authority of the teacher as a sovereign in the school is in no way derived from, or dependent on the will of the pupil as subject; nor is the teacher in any way amenable to the pupil for his mode of exercising it. So far as the pupil-subject is concerned, the teacher is, in the better sense of the term, a *true autocrat,* and may both take his stand and carry himself as such. . . .
>
> The teacher's authority as absolute, must be imperative, rather than deliberate or demonstrative. His requirements and decisions, in whatever form presented, whether that of request, demand, or mandate, must be unargued. *What he resolves upon and pronounces law, should be simply and steadily insisted upon as right,* PER SE, and should be promptly and fully accepted by the pupil as right, on the one ground that the teacher, as such, is governor.[3]

And as late as 1928, Professor Ross Finney suggested as proper for the American schools, a

> . . . system of school discipline as inflexible and final as that which obtains in the army. It should be kept out of sight for the most part, to be sure. On the surface of things the school should present the appearance of voluntary self-government by the students themselves. . . . But the compulsion is closeted with the faculty and board, to be used to the uttermost if necessary. And it should be brought to bear upon the lessons as well as upon school decorum and ordinary morals. Without such discipline it is hard to see how the schools of a democracy can conserve the necessary orderliness and the fundamental institutions of civilization.[4]

No wonder, therefore, that the American schools have only slowly been able to break away from the tradition of absolute authoritarianism, or that many teachers and administrators look upon the admin-

---

[3] Quoted by John T. Wahlquist, *Philosophy of American Education* (New York: The Ronald Press Co., 1942), p. 214. Reprinted by permission.
[4] Ross Finney, *A Sociological Philosophy of Education* (New York: The Macmillan Co., 1928), p. 480. Reprinted by permission.

istrative position as primarily one which gives one person or group the right to tell another group what to do—the voice from on high speaking to the assembled multitude.

Mutual Aloofness of Teacher and Administrator

There is still another factor which has created and sometimes widened the gap between teacher and administrator: this might be called the "let George do it" attitude. Some administrators have held themselves consciously aloof from the daily work of the classroom teacher, with its trials, frustrations, and rewarding moments: they feel that they have graduated into the higher realms of educational states-manship (for example, trying to reduce the school coal bill) and shouldn't be bothered with the problems of the classroom. On the other hand, there are some teachers who blithely assume that any problem outside of the daily routine of their own classroom is no concern of theirs: let the administration worry about school finance, the testing program, what should go on in faculty meetings, or the knotty problems of public relations. It would be very unfair to both teachers and administrators to give the impression that this cavalier "let the other man worry about that" attitude is by any means uni-versal. It would be equally unrealistic to deny that the shifting of responsibility to the other group is one of the chief causes of teacher-administrator friction.

The Teacher as Administrator

It is very difficult to present an accurate and realistic ap-praisal of the present status of teacher-administrator relationships in American education without seeming either hypercritical or insensi-tive to difficulties that really do exist. A fair statement might be some-thing like this: there was a long period in American educational history when the teaching and administrative functions were not dif-ferentiated. This was followed by a period of growing differentiation, which ultimately resulted in quite open conflict between the groups. Today, the recognition of the ultimate identity of interest of both teachers and administrators, together with an increasingly democratic outlook and practice in administration, has given even the beginning teacher a definite stake in administration.

The classroom teacher is an administrator himself; he administers, plans, directs, organizes, delegates authority, and carries out countless other functions of a basically administrative nature right in the classroom. The determination of what materials will be used in teaching, how they will be used, what learning activities will comprise a unit of study—all of these are part of school administration. The modern classroom teacher is reasonably autonomous in his own classroom administration: he sets up student committees, maintains classroom control, has a large voice in determining his own daily schedule, and makes decisions which are reflected in the grading, classification, and promotion of students.

The Teacher as a Partner in Administration

Even though a case can be made for the contention that the teacher *is* an administrator in his own classroom work, more important by far is the *partnership* which the teacher has in working with the regularly-designated administrative officers of the school in which he teaches. Let us look briefly at some of the areas in which the teacher does not so much assume or "take" responsibility, but in which he inevitably *shares* responsibility with the rest of the staff— teachers and administrators alike.

Public Relations

It is easy for some teachers to assume that the primary responsibility for maintaining good school public relations rests with the superintendent, the board of education, and the other members of the administrative staff. To some degree this is true. The board of education formulates and promulgates the official school policies which represent to the general public what the school is trying to accomplish. The superintendent's office customarily issues the press releases to the local newspapers, setting forth changes in and giving explanations of the all-school program. Principals often address PTA groups, civic clubs, and other representatives of the lay public to explain, as official spokesmen for the school, what is being done by way of curriculum changes, new vocational programs, or different emphases being given to certain aspects of the student activities program.

But the informal program of public relations is far from being the sole or primary prerogative of the school administrative staff. What the teacher says or does in the regular classroom work is carried home to the parents by the students and makes much more of an impact on community opinion of the school than do formal press releases or public statements of policy—actions speak louder than words. It is true in one sense that teachers are public servants, professional persons employed by the community to carry out the public's wishes in educational matters. But the teachers, by virtue of their special professional preparation and assignment, are more than mere public employees—they are also charged with the responsibility of advising laymen about the purposes and principles of modern education, about needed changes in the school curriculum, about the needs for improved and expanded teaching materials and school buildings, about the significance of modern educational research. The lay public in many communities expects that the teachers will be specialists in one or more of the phases of the educational program, and much of what the general public thinks and believes about education depends on how well the teachers fulfill their professional responsibility of being educational advisors to the community.

Another way in which the teaching staff shares with the administration the responsibility for good public relations is by their membership and activity in a variety of community groups. No one would suggest that the teacher should become an indiscriminate joiner, but in the natural course of events we can expect teachers to become active members of a wide range of organizations and societies. Teachers will normally be found in most of the organized groups in any community—the churches and Sunday schools, the luncheon clubs, the fraternal groups, veterans' organizations, patriotic societies, bridge clubs, chamber of commerce, labor and farmers' organizations— wherever normal people meet for fun, fellowship, worship, community service, or promotion of some worthy enterprise. As members of such groups, teachers should wear no academic halo, make no presumptions of being educational specialists ministering to the unenlightened, or attend the meetings conspicuously covered with chalkdust. That is, they belong to these groups as private citizens, but they can nevertheless be normally and naturally good spokesmen in these groups for the public enterprise that is closest to their hearts—the cause of better education for the children and youth of their communities.

When some aspect of the program of the school where you teach is under attack—when criticisms, say, of the new report cards are stirring up potential trouble between the school and its community, it is not enough for you to say, "Well, all I know is what the principal said; he claims it was the superintendent's idea." The teacher must be prepared to meet criticisms and attacks directed against the school program—to meet them honestly, to discuss them objectively, to explain the reasons behind certain perhaps unpopular school policies, and to carry valid criticism of the school back to the proper authorities. The only possible way a teacher can be prepared for such effective public relations work is to become deeply interested and directly involved with the "administration" of the school.

Teacher Welfare

No weighty academic arguments need be advanced to convince the classroom teacher that he has an interest in such administrative problems as how much teachers will be paid or how much sick leave will be granted. As with all other problems involving teachers and administrative officials, even in the most ideally "democratic" circumstances the final decisions must rest with the board of education; the board is ultimately responsible for the expenditure of the taxpayers' money and for compliance with the state school laws. Increasingly, however, teachers are being asked to serve on committees which study problems related to teacher welfare and make recommendations to the superintendent and the board of education. This is not mere lip service to the principle of democracy in administration; including teachers in the study of these problems is thoroughly realistic and practical.

Who is more deeply concerned than the teacher with how the salary schedule and its increments are set up, with the regulations governing eligibility for sick leave and payment of substitute teachers, the policy regarding observance of the tenure laws, provisions for rating teacher competence, or introduction of fringe benefits such as group insurance programs or credit unions? (Without being too cynical, we could suggest that it is easier to get 100 per cent attendance of the members of a committee of teachers appointed to discuss the salary schedule than it would be to get equally good attendance at a meeting of the committee on the school testing program!) A very practical reason for encouraging teacher participation in teacher welfare decisions is this: the administration and the school board will get better teacher support for whatever program is adopted—whether it is completely in accord with the faculty recommendations or not—simply because the teachers had a voice in the policy making.

Perhaps this is the best place to make one warning comment about difficulties sometimes encountered in securing good teacher participation in administrative problems: it might be called the antiadministration or "gimme" approach that some teachers use when discussing with the superintendent, principal, or board of education matters (especially salaries) which concern the teacher very directly and personally. While teachers have an undeniable right to make their wants known, it is most inappropriate and usually ineffective to come individually or in groups before the administrative officials or school board with demands or petitions or to engage in any practice that could be construed as lobbying. It doesn't make for harmonious relations within the school or the community, and what is more important, it just doesn't work as well as more cooperative approaches.

As an example of the ineffectiveness of pressure techniques, we may cite the experience of a group of teachers who asked for an audience with the board of education and demanded that a new salary schedule be instituted which would give them more money and place salaries on a more equitable basis. The board could have found the necessary money in the budget, as a matter of fact, but no positive action was taken; the board members, being human, resented being pressured by the teachers. The next year, a different approach was used. The superintendent was persuaded by the teachers to set up an official salary schedule committee which represented both teachers and members of the administrative staff. When the committee had made a thorough study of salary matters, keeping in mind the financial limitations under which the school operated, and had presented an oral and written report to the board through the superintendent, then the new salary schedule, providing higher salaries and more equitable distribution of salary funds, was unanimously adopted by the board.

School Budget

Another closely related administrative problem which is sometimes assumed to be the sole province of the school administrative officials is the budget. Actually, teachers have a number of very valid reasons for being interested in budgetary matters—it affects their salaries, their work in the classroom, and their own direct contribution to the support of education as taxpayers. It is impossible to say what is common practice in the schools of the United States regarding teacher participation in budget-making; there is a tremendous amount of variation in policy and procedure in the thousands of school districts. But this much can be said with assurance: it is becoming much more common today to ask the teachers to help with budgetary planning, and teachers can no longer assume that they are not concerned with problems of school finance. The well-prepared teacher does not, of course, have to be a specialist in school finance, but if he is to take his rightful place in the school system he must know something about where the money comes from and how it can most effectively be spent.

Teaching Materials

There was a time in the history of American public education when the teacher had no real personal concern with instructional materials, other than trying to make the best use of what was provided. The principal or some other administrative official selected and ordered the books, supplementary reading materials, maps, library supplies, charts and pictures, shop and laboratory equipment—everything that might be called instructional materials.

In some schools this is still the practice, but more and more teachers are being asked to share in the responsibility for the selection, purchase, use, and even storage of such materials. Encouraging such teacher participation is not so much the result of some nebulous, "liberal" feeling that we ought to have more democracy in educational administration: it is frank recognition of the fact that the well-prepared, competent teacher in a modern educational program must be consulted regarding the materials of teaching if the program is to be of maximum effectiveness. So no longer can the teacher assume that "the office" will automatically select and order the necessary teaching materials, which will then need only to be requisitioned or checked out of the supply room and put to use in the classroom. The teacher must, by the very nature of the teaching responsibility itself, be prepared to make wise judgments about instructional materials and to assume some of the responsibilities for selection, use, and care of this equipment. Here again, the teacher cannot just "let George do it."

Testing Program

It is still possible to find many schools where complete responsibility for the school testing program (other than the administration of regular teacher-made tests used ordinarily in day-by-day teaching) is assumed by the administrative staff, with the teacher having no part in it whatsoever. The principal (or superintendent) selects the tests to be used—intelligence, achievement, aptitude, and personality tests; he determines when they shall be given; he or a testing specialist administers and scores the tests; and the test results are recorded in the "front office." The teacher isn't even an innocent bystander in such a testing program. Increasingly, however, the teacher does take an active part in the planning and administering of the school testing program; again, not just because the school strives for democracy in administration, with the shared opportunities and responsibilities which that entails, but because the only way to *use* tests and test results intelligently demands full teacher participation in the program. The point of view expressed here does not deprecate the value of the services of test experts or other administrative officials in carrying out a good testing program; it simply emphasizes the part the teacher must play if the work is to have maximum worth.

Tests are given in the school for a variety of educational purposes: to analyze individual differences and determine individual needs; to motivate instruction and learning; to determine grade placement or classification of students; to see how well the curriculum of the school is actually functioning; to check on the effectiveness of various instructional materials and methods; to provide a basis for educational, social, and vocational guidance; to serve as the basis for cumulative school records and for reports made to parents on the educational progress of their children.

It is not possible, as some testing specialists have suggested, to divide these purposes of a testing program into two areas, "instructional" and "administrative." All of the purposes involve the work of the teacher as well as the work of the administrative staff; there is every good reason that the teacher should share fully in the selection of tests (the teacher understands whether the test "fits" the curriculum that is actually being taught; he knows the individual problems and needs of his students) and in the analysis and use of test results. The testing program cannot logically or with good effect be shrugged off by the teacher as a problem for the principal or superintendent to handle; the teacher is a necessary partner in this administrative responsibility. It is a responsibility, however, that the teacher can share only if he knows what he should about how good testing and evaluating instruments and procedures can contribute to a sound educational program.

Health and Safety in the School

The school health and safety program would appear, at first glance, to be an area of administrative responsibility in which the teacher would share only insofar as his own classroom and his own students were concerned. The broader policies, such as utilizing the services of school nurses, conducting periodic health examinations, providing for the physical health and safety of the student, keeping school health records, operating the lunch program, and providing for safety patrols and fire drills—all of these problems and many more would appear to be the primary responsibility of the principal, superintendent, school health officials, and ultimately of the board of education.

But these administrative officials cannot do the job alone. It does very little good to provide health records unless they are understood and used by the teachers. Periodic health examinations are important, but the individual teacher is responsible for the immediate reporting of suspected or obvious illness and indisposition of the students directly under his supervision to the school nurse or other authority. Safety patrols and fire drills, when they are established only by administrative decree, do not reflect the same effective safety consciousness and safety habits that can be built up when the classroom teacher has a voice in planning and operating these safety measures, and teaches safety education as a regular part of the classroom work. Here again, although primary responsibility for health and safety rests legally with the school administrative officials, it is the teacher's acceptance of responsible partnership with these officials for maintaining and promoting health and safety that makes the program really effective.

Faculty Meetings

"Faculty meetings *my* responsibility?" the teacher may say incredulously. "I'll come if I have to, but it wasn't my idea. The principal called this meeting; let him worry about what happens. All I ask is that they let us go by four-thirty; I've got to have my hair set tonight!" In the older, more traditional, more authoritarian type of school, such an attitude toward faculty or staff meetings was common among teachers. In schools today where these meetings are scheduled regularly or called on occasion merely for the purpose of announcing administrative decisions, distributing more work to the teachers, or making routine announcements, the teachers are quite justified in disclaiming any responsibility in connection with such gatherings.

More and more, however, it has become common in the better

schools to make faculty meetings an occasion for joint efforts to improve the school program; for real cooperative planning; for hearing the reports of faculty committees and acting on their proposals; and for meeting together to discuss such matters as the curriculum, the guidance program, better utilization of instructional materials, and other matters pertaining to professional improvement.

In this more effective type of faculty meeting, the teacher doesn't just come to listen or to be told; he just doesn't sit back and wait for the administrative officials to make plans and announce new procedures. The principal, supervisor, or superintendent must, of course, assume such responsibility for these meetings as his assignment in the school system makes appropriate, but if the faculty meeting is to become an occasion for real improvement of the school program, for real professional growth of the teachers, teacher responsibility cannot be shirked. Here is another instance of the futility of trying to get out of the responsibility that is rightly the teacher's by saying, "Let the administration worry about *that*. I've got enough worries of my own!"

Teacher Participation in Other "Administrative" Areas

Some other aspects of the school program which have traditionally been considered the province of the administrative staff are, in most modern schools, increasingly becoming matters of concern to the teaching staff as well. Planning of new school buildings, renovation of existing plants, and purchase of new desks, tables, and other room equipment often involve suggestions and decisions which can properly be made by the entire school staff. The educational philosophy of the school is meaningful and capable of being actually implemented in the school only when all of the professional workers have a part in its formulation. The curriculum is no longer merely a sequence of courses or subjects, a bare course-of-study outline handed down by higher authority, but a series of goals, experiences, activities, and materials which the whole staff plans cooperatively, often with the assistance of the students and the advice and suggestions of lay persons in the community. The daily class schedule can be worked out and duplicated by the principal, and simply placed in the teachers' mailboxes or announced at a faculty meeting, but in the modern school the schedule becomes a far better expression of educational purpose and plan if it is arrived at through the cooperation of the entire professional corps. Guidance services are not the province of the guidance specialist alone, but an integral part of the classroom teaching program. The student activity program (extracurricular activities) should not be designed by the principal or superintendent or "run" by a select group of coaches, directors, and sponsors, but should evolve from the cooperative planning of the whole staff.

And so on down the line: every part of the operation of the school demands the planning, the suggestions, and the active participation of all teachers. Policies regarding classification, promotion and retention of students; the emphasis which will be placed on homework; the use of supervised study periods; necessary record keeping; grouping of students according to abilities; policies which encourage home visitation by teachers; in-service training programs for the professional staff—these and numerous other phases of the educational planning of the school cannot be profitably assumed as administrative burdens to be borne by a portion of the staff alone; every teacher has a part in such "administrative" problems.

Teachers Work with Supervisors

"Administration" and "Supervision"

So far in this chapter we have not attempted to make any distinction between "administrative" and "supervisory" functions as such. In smaller schools there is no real distinction; the same personnel act in both administrative and supervisory capacity. In larger school systems, however, there is at least a tenuous distinction between the two functions, and between the duties of administrators and of supervisors.

The administrators are charged with the general operation of the school system (the superintendent's function) or of separate sub-organizations of the school (the principal's function). The supervisors are not so much concerned with school plant problems, over-all school policy, matters of school finance or school law, or the business and personnel problems that are the main concern of the administrator. The supervisor works directly with the instructional program, or a part of it, and directly with the teachers who carry on that part of the school's work. So, whether in a large school where the supervisory staff is designated as such, or in a smaller school where the administrator (principal or superintendent) acts also as a part-time supervisor, the teacher can expect to work directly under the guidance of someone who represents educational authority.

Inadequacies of Supervisory Programs

In all honesty it must be admitted that in far too many schools the supervision of instruction is very unsatisfactory. Ideally, supervision has a very concrete purpose: helping teachers do a better job of teaching—a worthy aim which most classroom teachers would applaud. In the better school systems, this aim is carried out very effectively; the supervisor devotes his entire professional time and effort to the *improvement of instruction*. All too often, however, the classroom teacher gets no real supervisory help. Sometimes no supervisors are provided in the staffing pattern of the school; the superintendent, assistant superintendent, or principal tries to squeeze in some time for supervision as he goes about his other duties, but he just can't get the job done. More than one teacher has taught for several years in the same system and never had a single supervisory visit made to her classroom. Of course, the principal sticks his head in and makes an announcement, or sees the teacher after school in the hall and asks how things are going—but that is not supervision!

Another difficulty with the current supervisory pattern is the lack of mutual understanding on the part of both teachers and supervisors —neither knows what to expect of the other. Some supervisors, unfortunately, believe that the job of supervision is synonymous with inspection, investigation, fault-finding, or telling the teacher what he *should* be doing. Some teachers look on all supervisors as "snoopervisors," critical or underhanded stooges of the administration, sent out to "get the goods" on a teacher presumed incompetent or unsatisfactory. Fortunately, in the modern school these mutual misunderstandings are gradually dying out; better patterns of supervision are fast emerging.

Getting the Most out of Supervision

In this transitional period, when older ideas of supervision are passing from the educational scene and newer ideas are coming into common practice, what does supervision mean to the classroom teacher? Just this: if the teacher builds up a favorable attitude toward supervision, rather than one of fear or distrust, his work will be made much easier. Often, the classroom teacher must *ask* for supervisory help; this seems like an admission of ignorance to many beginning teachers, but it is really the beginning of wisdom. Ask and it shall be given—many supervisors withhold suggestions for fear of seeming too bossy. If the teacher shows a readiness to accept supervisory help, then it will most likely be forthcoming.

A good supervisor can help the teacher in a multitude of ways: suggest sources of supplementary reading materials; help plan the use of audio-visual aids; assist in developing units of study; make suggestions for individualizing instruction and dealing with "problem" learners; guide the teacher in long-range planning of the year's work; help in problems of testing, evaluating, grading, and reporting; and in numerous other ways be a personal and professional helper, to the beginning teacher especially. One of the greatest benefits that comes directly to the classroom teacher from the whole administrative machinery and administrative personnel of the modern school is good supervision: seek it out, accept it willingly, make use of the help that is rightfully yours.

Teachers' Organizations and Administration

One of the most convincing of all of the good reasons that can be advanced for teachers' joining their professional organizations is that these groups are often extremely effective in promoting better school administration in ways that directly affect the teacher's work. The professional groups especially concerned with administrative problems have pioneered in developing better administrative practices: the National Association of Secondary School Principals, the National Association of Elementary Principals, the American Association of School Administrators, the Association for Supervision and Curriculum Development—all of these groups, affiliated with the local and national educational associations, have been tireless and effective workers for better schools. And the groups composed largely of classroom teachers have also embarked on extensive and effective programs for improving public education: local and community teachers' associations, the state education associations, and the NEA have collectively an effective voice in how the schools are operated.

Local or Community Education Associations

Some very significant improvements in school administration have been effected through the efforts of local professional groups which usually include both teachers and administrators. Often it is such a group that does the necessary research and compiles the appropriate data to bring about better provisions for teacher welfare—higher salaries, a single salary schedule, adoption of tenure regulations, provision for sick leave, and improvement of the retirement system. When the superintendent, the board of education, and the general public are informed, factually and convincingly, about the need for such improvements, it is far more likely that the desired gains will be achieved than as if a few of the teachers merely present a grievance to the board. The united voice of the profession, speaking thoughtfully and convincingly, and backing up their statements with carefully documented facts, will be listened to with respect by most administrators and boards of education.

The local association is often the starting place for effecting improvements in the local educational program itself. Such a group may undertake studies of the school testing program, the methods of reporting to parents, the philosophy and objectives of the school, the improvement of the curriculum, the needed provisions for the education of exceptional children, or any of scores of similar problems. Their findings, if carefully documented and forcefully presented, may well become the basis for changes in school administrative policy and procedure. It would be the rare administrative officer who would not accept such evidence of intelligent concern with the affairs of the school as a praiseworthy contribution to the solution of some of the problems that confront him as an administrator. Such professional efforts on the part of the staff, working through teachers' professional groups, tend to strengthen the common bonds of educational interest that ideally should characterize the teacher-administrator relationship.

State Education Associations

Like the local associations, the state teachers' organizations are composed of both teachers and administrators, though subsections representing the different specific interests of each group may exist within the association as a whole. Again, by presenting a united professional front, the teachers' and administrators' groups may bring about increased public support for the schools that will make the work of both groups more profitable and more productive.

For example, favorable legislation for financial support of the state school system must of course originate technically in the state legislature, but in many states it is the legislative committee of the state education association that provides the impetus and the research that "starts the ball rolling" in the statehouse. In some states, the professional organizations have done such a thorough and honest job in compiling data on educational matters that the state governmental and legislative officials accept without question the authenticity of the information provided by the state teachers' association. Another educational problem, teacher certification, is—like the fiscal problem—technically a matter for the legislature to decide; but again, in many states it is through the work of the state education association that the proposals for better certification laws are brought to the attention of the legislature and actually written into the state legal code. In such matters, and in many other educational problems as well, the state associations can, with complete forthrightness and with no taint of behind-the-scenes lobbying, influence public opinion and bring about enactment of laws favorable to the cause of education—a very necessary step in improving school administration, because in our democracy the schools are in a very real sense "administered" by the general public.

National Associations

The National Education Association and its affiliated special-interest departments and divisions have worked very effectively for better school administration. It has been said that the members of Congress often turn to the NEA Research Division for authoritative data on the school systems of the country, rather than to the official educational agency of the government, the U.S. Office of Education. This is not to deprecate in any sense the importance or competence of the latter office; it merely indicates that the Commissioner of Education and his staff have received such restricted appropriations from Congress that congressmen themselves have come to realize that their own governmental agency does not have the research facilities possessed by the NEA.

The Educational Policies Commission of the NEA has no official or legal status which would allow it to become the spokesman for our educational system either on a national or a state level, but as a matter of fact its deliberations and pronouncements on desirable policies for the operation of our public school system have had a direct and profound effect on the nation's schools. It is through such agencies of the NEA—and this commission is only one of many important divisions of the national association—that teachers can by virtue of their active professional membership in teachers' associations find still another way to make their collective voice heard when matters pertaining to school administration are discussed.

Direct Teacher Representation in Administration

Throughout the pages of this chapter we have discussed the specific interests the classroom teacher has in so-called administrative problems, and some of the ways he can make that interest effective in actual school practice. There are some educators who argue that teachers should have a much greater and much more direct representation in administrative matters. In some schools, the entire teaching staff constitutes the committee of the whole, and all of the teachers sit in on the discussions of major administrative policies and participate in the final decisions. In other schools, particularly the larger ones, the teachers elect certain of their numbers to be their official representatives in the discussions and deliberations of the administrative council. In still other schools, almost all of the formal teacher participation in administration comes through the work of regularly constituted special or standing committees. This is not the place to argue the relative merits of these systems; each has its advantages and its disadvantages.

What is most important is this: that teachers make a distinct effort to shoulder their responsibilities in connection with many matters formerly thought to be the job of the administration, and that administrators share with the members of the teaching staff some of the opportunities and responsibilities for policy determination and decision making that teachers were formerly excluded from even thinking about. In brief, the teacher has a very real stake in administration; it will take the combined and cooperative efforts of both teachers and administrators to achieve an effective working relationship.

If we really mean what we so often say, that the American public school must prepare its students for life in a democracy, then we must also believe that the school itself must exemplify the best of democratic principles in its own operation. At the risk of sounding hopelessly platitudinous, this must be said: only the school that practices democracy can teach democracy.

TWELVE: TOPICS FOR STUDY, REPORT, AND DISCUSSION

1. Would you like to become a school administrator? Try to think the question through seriously and completely, and be prepared to defend your answer!
2. Select a committee from the class (with your instructor's permission) and make arrangements through some cooperative school administrator to visit a school administrative office to find out just what goes on there. Report your findings to the class.
3. Study the official policy statements (legislative programs, reports of major committees, etc.) of your state education association to find out as precisely as you can just how teachers are working closely with administrative staff members in a joint effort to improve teaching and learning in your state.
4. Invite a good school administrator in to speak to the class on the topic, "What the school administrator expects of the teachers."

TWELVE: BIBLIOGRAPHY

Chamberlin, Leo M., and Leslie W. Kindred, *The Teacher and School Organization*, 3rd ed. Englewood Cliffs, N. J.: Prentice-Hall, Inc., 1958. This is one of the few books available which is primarily concerned with pointing out the teacher's concern with school administration. See especially Part V.

Leese, Joseph, Kenneth Frasure, and Mauritz Johnson, Jr., *The Teacher in Curriculum Making*. New York: Harper & Row, Publishers, 1961. Part I, less detailed than the rest of the book, provides both an overview and specific details regarding the teacher's part in bringing about curriculum change.

Robinson, Thomas E., and others, *It Starts in the Classroom*. Washington, D. C.: National Education Association, 1951. A brief pamphlet, easily read in an hour or two, but one of the very best sources of practical suggestions for the classroom teacher's effective working in public relations.

Swearingen, Mildred E., *Supervision of Instruction: Foundations and Dimensions*. Boston: Allyn and Bacon, Inc., 1962. An understanding of the teacher's concern with the supervisory process can be gained from reading chap. 4, "Major Functions of Supervision."

Willett, Henry I., "Cooperative Administration—Fact or Fancy?" *NEA Journal*, Vol. 44, No. 2 (February, 1955), 91-93. Discusses actual ways teachers may participate in administration without attempting to assume responsibilities that are necessarily administrative.

The most useful current information on the joint concerns of the teacher and the administrator is often available in the school administration journals. See recent copies of such periodicals as *The American School Board Journal, The Nation's Schools, School Management,* and *Overview*.

The rewards of teaching. *Could you
doubt that this teacher finds rewarding experiences in her work?*

CHAPTER THIRTEEN

The Popular View

How does the general public view teachers? Perhaps the following sample from recent popular fiction provides some insight into how teachers are regarded as people.

"Ah, poor Miss Dove!" thought the mothers of the outgoing sixth grade as they watched that seasoned mentor of youth descend the steps from the stage of the school auditorium. Ordinarily—try as they might to disguise the fact by poking fun at her bony figure, her sharp nose, and the tight little ball of hair at the nape of her rigid neck—they were afraid of Miss Dove. As children most of them had been exposed to her not-too-tender mercy. Forty-five minutes a day, five days a week, nine months a year for six notably impressionable years of their lives, they had spent in the geography room in the aura of Miss Dove's personality. There, life had been different from life at home. Nobody had cared if they were bored or entertained, gay or sulky. Nobody had asked them to be clever or charming. The teacher had required only that they be industrious and good—but steadily, all the time. "The *terrible* Miss Dove" they had called her, and their title for her had derived less from her dogmatic insistence upon such tiresome virtues as punctuality,

TEACHERS ARE PEOPLE

correct posture and neatness than from the awful suspicion that she knew all about *them*. She could put her finger on the snivelly, ignoble spots in their natures as unerringly, they felt, as she could touch with her long map pointer the capital of Bolivia or the source of the Danube.

To her pupils, past and present, Miss Dove was not so much a fellow creature of flesh and blood as a public conscience. But on this June morning some of them, rich and charitable in successful maternity, glimpsed infinite pathos in the spinister's life. . . .

At the tail end of the line came Miss Dove. She walked with her usual measured tread. She wore her usual dark dress. Her face was impassive. Her eyes—those dispassionate, undeluded eyes that could strike terror to mamma and moppet alike—were cool and gray and perfectly dry. She looked precisely as she always looked. But the mothers, regarding her through a haze of emotion, saw her with a difference. She was no longer the terror who had haunted their school days—who had made them wash out their mouths with soap when they chewed their pigtails or used inelegant language; who had forced them, through dread of her silent contempt, to sit still until the bell rang no matter how badly they needed to go to the bathroom; who had known, though she hadn't stooped to question their word, when they were fibbing. She was not even the cold-blooded monster who had, later, remained unenchanted by their own children's infantile graces—by Sistie's bashfulness, and Bubbie's imperfect articulation, and the adorable way Jackie-Boy stomped his foot, like a regular little man, when his will was crossed. She was Woman Bereft.[1]

These are the opening paragraphs of a heartwarming, sympathetic, fictional account of a teacher as presented in a story appearing in a popular household magazine and later upon the screen. Miss Dove is pictured in the narrative as an admirable teacher, a worthy person, someone to be admired for her professional competence—but still, typically a teacher: not quite normal, a little odd, a somewhat pitiable caricature of a real human being. And it is this popular misconception of the teacher as being somehow set apart from ordinary people that necessitates the positive statement which serves as the title and theme of this chapter: Teachers *Are* People!

One of the most amazing paradoxes of American society is the high regard the people of this nation have always had for education—its purposes, its power, and its importance—and the low regard they

[1] Reprinted by permission of Dodd, Mead & Company from *Good Morning, Miss Dove* by Francis Gray Patton. Copyright 1954 by Francis Gray Patton; Copyright 1954 by The Curtis Publishing Company.

have shown for teachers. The American public does not necessarily look *down* on teachers (though such a view has not been at all uncommon); rather, they look *askance* at teachers—view them with a critical, patronizing, often unfriendly eye. At best, the popular conception of the teacher reflects one or more stereotyped notions— teachers are peculiar, they are frustrated, they are congenital "old maids" (of both sexes), or they are either too incompetent to earn a decent living in business or too dense to understand that they could earn more money doing something else.

Of course, the public attitude toward teachers as a group is often much more favorable than that pictured above. Teachers are often loved, accepted, praised, imitated, and even venerated. But all too often the unfavorable stereotypes have been preserved in our national literature, our folklore, and in the general public sentiment. Teachers themselves have often helped perpetuate these misconceptions about themselves and their work by continual self-deprecation—"Oh, I'm just a teacher." Worse yet, some members of the teaching profession have given the general public good reason to accept and confirm these popular notions about teachers by living up to them—by being eccentric, odd in appearance and mannerisms, lacking in social graces and deficient in human relations skills.

Stereotyped Notions About Teachers

Unflattering and uncritical ideas about what teachers are like as a class or group have found their way into the writings of many notable authors [2] who were primarily concerned with some other problem and wrote about teachers only incidentally. Thus, these writings reveal popular, casual, offhand notions about teachers, rather than a studied opinion; they therefore indicate quite accurately persistent stereotypes that the general public uses when it thinks of teachers.

We all have read Irving's *Legend of Sleepy Hollow,* and remember the description of the teacher, Ichabod Crane—built like a scarecrow; a gangling, pin-headed, flat-topped oaf. But what could anyone expect? He was just a teacher. Perhaps you remember the picture Mark Twain gave of the teacher in *Tom Sawyer*—Old Dobbins, a ridiculous figure, his bald head covered with an ill-fitting wig which

[2] See articles by D. Charles and G. Dodds listed in bibliography at the close of this chapter.

sometimes came off; a man who had aspired to be a doctor but who had been forced by poverty to be "nothing better than a schoolmaster." Dickens described two "typical" teachers, the formidable Mr. Gradgrind, with his unimaginative, even stupid, devotion to the textbook, and Mr. Wackford Squares, "a vulgar, conceited, ignorant schoolmaster, overbearing and mean."

These are but some fairly familiar examples of the stereotyping of teachers that has found its way into our literary heritage. Many other examples could be cited; you might be interested in watching for the preservation of these fixed notions about how teachers differ from ordinary people as you read popular magazines, short stories, novels, or see teachers portrayed in the movies and on television programs. Not invariably, but with monotonous frequency, the teacher is presented in an unfavorable light, not as a real person but as a member of a slightly odd group known collectively (often with a slight snicker) as "just teachers."

One of the basic reasons that teachers in modern times have lacked the respect of the public is that teaching has been thought of as a part-time or short-term job, not a real life work. Brubacher cites as an illustration of this the preface of the sixteenth-century publication, Coote's *English Schoolmaster,* which was addressed "To the unskillful . . . and to such men and women of trade, as tailors, weavers, shopkeepers, seamsters, and such other as have undertaken the charge of teaching others. [With this textbook] thou mayest sit on thy shop board, at thy books or thy needle, and never hinder any work to hear thy scholars." [3]

Even today, however, when teaching is becoming recognized as a worthy career, even as an emerging profession, teachers are often still regarded as falling into various stereotyped classes. Sometimes they are simply thought of as *ridiculous*—dowdy, frumpish, old-fashioned in dress and appearance, unskilled in the social amenities, and (in the case of college professors at least) hopelessly absent-minded. In other words, they just look and act like teachers. Another standardized pigeonhole into which the public delights in fitting teachers is "frustrated"; a favorite term is "frustrated old maid." (As we indicated above, this does not necessarily imply any given age or sex—some people seem to have been *born* with old-maidish tendencies, and all of us have seen males who gave the distinct impression

---

[3] John S. Brubacher, *A History of the Problems of Education* (New York: McGraw-Hill Book Co., Inc., 1947), p. 501. Reprinted by permission.

of being old maids.) Still another category under which teachers are neatly filed by general public opinion is "ineffective"; we in the field of teacher-training sometimes get a little weary of hearing our colleagues repeating the old saw, "Those who can, do; those who can't, teach; those who can't teach, teach others how to teach." Very funny.

Another commonly held notion about teachers is that they are brutal sadists, who enjoy exercising physical or psychological domination over others. The long tradition of the teacher as an embodiment of physical brute force stems partly from the harsh and autocratic methods that for centuries delayed the progress of education. It used to be the mark of the successful teacher to be able to lick any boy in the room; one teacher in a German school in the eighteenth century established something of a professional record when he revealed that in his fifty-one years of teaching he had given "911,527 blows with a rod, 124,010 blows with a cane, 20,989 taps with a ruler, 136,715 blows with the hand, 10,235 blows on the mouth, 7,905 boxes on the ear, and 1,118,800 blows on the head." [4] This, you understand, is well above par for even those rugged days, but it indicates in part why the idea of the teacher as a physical or psychological brute has lingered in the popular mind.

We have been speaking so far largely about stereotyped notions of what teachers are like as these ideas have come down through several centuries. But modern education has produced some fictional ideas about the characteristics of teachers, too. You will sometimes hear that the modern scientific emphasis in education has reduced the educative process to a cold and heartless science, and that the modern educational practitioner is just a cold-blooded professional who views his students with clinical detachment. Another of the bits of current folklore surrounding modern education is connected with popular misconceptions about the nature of "progressive education." The "progressive" teacher is popularly caricatured as a mere helpless bystander, who cowers in the back of the room while the children take over—saying and doing nothing for fear of inhibiting the growth or harming the psyches of her little charges. Another closely related version of the same idea about teachers is this: in the modern school, there is no direction, no discipline, no order; all activities are carried on so "democratically" that the teacher is just "one of the boys," indistinguishable from the rest of the group. Another persistent popular idea about teachers is that they are all female. Both popular speech

[4] James Mulhern, *A History of Education* (New York: The Ronald Press Co., 1946), pp. 383 f.

and the professional books in teacher education reflect this idea—the teacher is commonly (almost universally, in fact) spoken of as "she." This has become so common that even the present writer has had to struggle to use both "she" and "he" interchangeably in this text when speaking of teachers. (It still comes out "she" most of the time; sheer habit!)

It would do no good to try to refute these standardized ideas about what teachers are like; we could take them one by one and argue that they are not true, but the arguments would not convince the people who cherish these quaint notions. About all we can do is this: we can try to make teaching the kind of work that will attract and retain a genuinely *normal* cross-section of our nation's men and women—well-adjusted people, happy people, effective people. Then perhaps these stereotyped notions will gradually atrophy, because there will be so much evidence that teachers *are* people that no one will think otherwise.

Characteristics of the Good Teacher

It seems almost futile, for our purpose here, to attempt to list in any detail the qualities that distinguish the good, successful, normal teacher. Such studies as those cited by Lee [5] are complete, revealing, and informative, but whether we base our list on what students have said, on what parents want their children's teachers to be like, on what we ourselves recall about the good teachers we have had, or on a scientific analysis of the personality and behavior traits of teachers who are accounted as successful by educational experts, we still run into the same difficulties. Either the lists get very mechanical (the good teacher gives assignments clearly, makes proper provision for individual differences in student ability and interest, etc.) or the lists produce only a catalog of rather intangible qualities ("tactful, sympathetic, good-natured, etc."). Worse yet, if we try to list all of the desirable characteristics we would like to find in a teacher we get something that sounds like a testimonial to the virtues of a saint, or a funeral eulogy delivered over the remains of some paragon of virtue, too good to be real.

Let us approach the problem of what makes a good teacher, then,

[5] See reference to book by G. Lee listed in bibliography at the close of this chapter.

not from the standpoint of recounting a list of desirable teacher characteristics or suggesting a rating scale for teachers (several of these scales are available, and would be well worth your perusal as a sort of self-check),[6] but rather by trying to see what there is about good teaching that makes it one of the most enjoyable, rewarding, and worthwhile of all occupations. In the process of getting maximum enjoyment out of teaching, the teacher will find that he is developing the qualities that distinguish the good teacher from the mediocre or the poor; what is more, the person who honestly and thoroughly enjoys doing a good job of teaching cannot help developing as a person—becoming "not just another teacher," but an individual in his own right.

How to Enjoy Teaching

It is almost axiomatic that a person must approach any job with real enthusiasm before he can fully expect to enjoy what he is doing. Chaucer had a telling phrase for this when he wrote his highest praise for the medieval scholar, "and *gladly* wolde he lerne, and *gladly* teche." If a person simply doesn't enjoy making the effort to learn to become a teacher, or if he cannot teach gladly, then the possession of all the appropriate skills and personality traits in the world cannot make him a good teacher.

Academic and Intellectual Demands of Teaching

In the early sixteenth century, the Englishman Thomas Elyot began one chapter of his treatise on teaching, *Book Named the Governor,* with an exasperated remark that has become quite famous, "Lorde god, howe many good and clene wittes of children be nowe a days perisshed by ignorant schole maisters." [7] The language of this old writer may strike us today as being a bit intemperate, but Elyot's observation is sound: the ignorant person makes a mighty poor teacher.

Persistent suspicion of scholarship. In recent years, it has become quite popular in professional circles to reiterate that bookworms

---

[6] Such scales are to be found in chapters of books by G. Lee and E. Reinhardt listed in bibliography at the close of this chapter.

[7] Quoted by Brubacher, *op. cit.,* p. 499. Reprinted by permission.

don't make good teachers; that the best scholars are not necessarily the most successful in either elementary or high school classrooms. This is very true, but overemphasis on the truth of these statements has led us to make a completely fallacious assumption that we can reverse the statement and still make sense: that if the best students don't always make the best teachers, the poorest students will be the best teachers! Some superintendents have made it a fetish in hiring teachers to avoid even interviewing the Phi Beta Kappas and other honor students, and consciously to seek out students with just average grades. The theory seems to be, in part, that since superior scholarship sometimes handicaps the teacher who must deal with those who learn slowly, *ergo,* inferior or mediocre scholarship will make the teacher more sympathetic and understanding with those who, like himself, find intellectual effort rather difficult. One superintendent with whom the writer was acquainted went so far as to say that he would not hire any teacher who hadn't failed at least one subject in college! (It so happened that the superintendent himself had a college record that on several counts would thus make him eminently eligible for employment in his own school system!)

The problems of the "scholar."   Let us look at the problem a little more closely. Why do persons with very superior academic records sometimes fail to make the best teachers? There are several possibilities. Such a student may have overconcentrated on one phase of college life—scholastic achievement—to a degree that he unbalanced his over-all preparation for teaching. He may have avoided becoming involved with the student activities and the normal social affairs which are part of the professional background of the good teacher. The supreme effort represented by superior academic achievement may have been a form of compensation; many a student who has suffered from real or imaginary inferiorities has tried to compensate for this lack of ability to make friends, get dates, play basketball, or be cast in the college dramatic productions by saying, in effect, "I'll show them! At least I can make better grades than those social butterflies, those muscle-happy athletes!" Still another problem faced by the exceptionally able student is this: he *does* learn easily, solve problems readily, read with superior speed and comprehension, and retain what he has learned; this sort of person is sometimes woefully impatient with ordinary people who simply do not operate on his intellectual level. Thus, the slow rate of the average or below-average learner frustrates and annoys him; as a teacher he lacks the patience and insight into normal learning difficulties which are needed to make him a success in the classroom.

Now, all of the above explanations of the difficulties sometimes encountered by students of high intellectual endowment or achievement when they attempt to teach might seem to confirm the theory that the average student makes the best teacher. This is not necessarily so; the average student will probably make an average teacher, and if he works hard at the job, he can rise many levels above mere mediocrity as a teacher. But the intellectual demands of teaching as a profession are high, and they are getting higher all the time. It does not matter whether you teach in kindergarten or at the graduate level in a university: really good teaching demands a high degree of intellectual ability. What are these intellectual requirements?

Intellectual skills required. First of all, good teaching demands that you know your subject; no matter how skillful you are in interpersonal relations, how well you understand the stages of development in children and youth, how much you know about the learning process, or how charming you are when you address the PTA—if you don't *know* your subject-matter field too, you can't teach at anything higher than a routine level. Don't misunderstand; we are not speaking now of the storehouse concept of knowledge, or of the ability to recite obscure facts in the field of your specialty. The kind of knowledge the teacher needs is that which can clearly explain facts, derive and formulate generalizations, see implications, understand and explain cause-and-effect relationships, test hypotheses, solve problems, verify information, and make applications of what is known to everyday living. That is academic scholarship at its best—and those who possess it have one of the major qualifications for teaching.

Intellectual curiosity. Another intellectual demand of teaching is intellectual curiosity; you must like ideas, like to think, have the capacity to wonder, and enjoy learning, yourself. There is no quicker way to grow stale as a teacher, no surer way to find teaching a barren and disheartening task, than to settle back into a fixed mental rut and teach the same old facts and same old ideas in the same old way, year after year.

Study. The last of the intellectual demands which we might mention here is a liking for and ability to study—yes, just plain *study*. Again, no one would suggest that you prepare for teaching—or for anything else in life, for that matter—by becoming a bookworm. But the person who actively dislikes studying or who has never developed study skills can have a rough time trying to teach. There are always new books to evaluate, new materials to go over, new findings in your field to keep up with. If in college you have not developed the inclination toward such intellectual effort, you may be able to scrape by as a teacher; that's about all. And since one of the chief difficulties in any type of studying is actually getting to the job and sticking with it, the prospective teacher needs to develop to a high degree the ability to do his work on schedule—not just when he feels like it or gets around to it; he needs also to develop what might be called the seat-to-the-chair facility. The teacher will spend many hours sitting and working at his desk, at home or at school. Sitting and working, period.

Self-Improvement

It is probably possible, theoretically, to enjoy teaching to some degree, and even to be a fair-to-middling teacher, without ever making any conscious effort toward self-improvement. But it is hard to think of a successful football coach, for example, who would be satisfied with going through season after season with no change in his repertory of plays, or of a band director who could stand to hear generations of beginning clarinetists squeaking through identical musical passages, or of a fifth-grade teacher being happy with dragging out the same old units of study year after year for each new class.

One of the clichés of American folklore is that you've got to move ahead or you'll slip backward. Cliché or not, this statement has real application in the work of the teacher. It is almost impossible to stand still in teaching. New methods, new materials, new testing instruments, new understandings of child development, and new goals for the school are constantly being developed. The teacher who sits back on his life certificate cannot possibly hope to enjoy the work of teaching as well as one who keeps up with the changes going on around him.

Nothing can kill the job (or effectiveness) of teaching more quickly or more thoroughly than becoming bogged down in a dread and deadly routine. Since some of the work of the teacher is, frankly, repetitious and routine, special effort has to be made to keep from letting the necessary routine of teaching dominate the life of the teacher. What we are suggesting here is not some supreme effort at intellectual, professional, or personal improvement—a self-conscious "Operation Bootstrap" that will lift you out of the morass of the mediocre in one noble attempt. People who embark on overly ambitious programs of self-improvement, as such, often alienate their friends and end up feeling like deflated martyrs.

Let us look at this problem of self-improvement for teachers in terms of the requirements of teaching itself, not in terms of the teacher's own personality. For example, modern education at every level is becoming more and more a highly technical matter, with constant change in aim, methods, and materials being based on new research and experimentation and writing. This fact suggests several reasonable ways the teacher can engage in a program of in-service growth: attendance at summer session classes in a good college or university; participation in workshops; membership in work-study committees; attending professional-group meetings at a local, state or national level; and writing up for publication his own classroom experiences or projects, so that others may try what he has found to be successful. You will notice, perhaps, that none of these activities is basically self-centered; the teacher does not engage in the in-service programs out of a sense of pride or of duty, but because these activities for teachers provide avenues to more successful—and more enjoyable—teaching.

Another illustration of how professional growth can be job-centered rather than self-centered may be seen in the kind of reading a teacher does. If the teacher reads "highbrow" magazines and "serious"' books because he feels he *ought* to, the process of self-improvement gets a little stuffy. But if the teacher reads regularly and widely outside his own field because he *wants* to, then real professional and personal growth is being encouraged.

The well-read teacher is not likely to find teaching dull. Out of his fund of information and ideas, gained from wide and intelligent reading, can come new ideas of how to make classroom work more meaningful—the more the teacher knows of the world outside the school, the better can he follow that maxim that education should be related to life. Wide reading gives the teacher a store of illustrations and applications and points of reference that make good teaching more possible. If the teacher believes that education should center around the problems of life, including the controversial issues of our present society, the teacher needs to know what important writers are saying about these problems and controversies.

In like manner, modern concepts of education demand that the teacher be a person of rich experience and background not gained from books alone. The teacher who has lived and worked with people of various races, economic levels, and culture patterns has a better experience background for teaching than one who has led a routine, sedate, and sheltered life. The teacher who has worked with his hands or done some of the menial jobs that people do for a living has a better understanding of the "life" to which we claim we are trying to relate education. And if the teacher has not had this rich and varied background of experience in living and working with all kinds of people, of seeing life at its worst as well as its best, then perhaps a summer spent as a clerk in a store or a worker with a construction crew would be more profitable than amassing nine more hours toward the master's degree!

Now, no self-conscious "slumming," please! It's just that if we are to live up to the contention of this chapter that teachers are people, teachers must first of all *be* people. And if we are to understand that teaching can be fun, we must first of all find out that *people* can be fun. We need to have something of the serious but matter-of-fact attitude of the old Swiss educator, Pestalozzi, who explained his years of working with the downtrodden in this simple phrase, "I lived for years among beggars, in order that beggars might learn to live like men."

Personal Appearance

An important part of successful and enjoyable teaching is what we might call "dressing the part." One of the common stereotypes of teachers, as we indicated earlier in this chapter, revolves around the popular idea that teachers just naturally *look* peculiar, that they are set apart from ordinary folk in manner, dress, and appearance. There is enough possibility of this stereotype becoming true that we need to take special precautions against it. We would not suggest that the women teachers look like pages out of *Vogue* magazine or that the men try to emulate the sharp styles suggested in *Esquire*. But ordinary, appropriate, tasteful dress and meticulous personal grooming are possible even on the often inadequate salaries of teachers. It is not only possible, it is important: first, to make teachers appear, as they are, normal members of the human society; second, to keep up the morale of the teacher. Untidy appearance not only creates the impression of an untidy intellect, but is conducive to it. Most important, the dress and appearance of the teacher are reflected directly in the attitude of the student. In your own school experience you can probably remember some teacher whose only claim to permanence in your recollection was some personal mannerism or peculiarity in dress, and still other teachers whose very appearance became part of a pleasantly recalled learning situation.

Special Behavior or Ethical Requirements for Teachers

If we plan to enjoy teaching, we might as well face the fact that to some degree in all communities and to a greater degree in some communities, the teacher is popularly considered to be bound by special rules and customs in matters of personal behavior. Frankly, there *is* some limitation on the personal freedom of teachers in most communities. But except in isolated instances, it isn't nearly as bad as it sounds.

Teachers as a group aspire to professional status and recognition; this status and recognition places certain demands upon the members of the profession. The professional ethics of teaching, for example, require that the teacher be close-mouthed and discreet about confidential matters of many sorts. One kindergarten teacher with whom the writer is acquainted claimed that she could retire any day and live comfortably on the blackmail money she could extort from the parents of the little ones who had revealed the most intimate and embarrassing family secrets in school! She was joking, of course; no reputable teacher betrays professional confidences, but no thoughtful teacher would consider this limitation on freedom of speech any cause for concern.

All professions have special requirements. All persons who seek and achieve that special form of public recognition known as professional status have some of the same problems as teachers. A physician must, in most communities, conform to the community idea of how a doctor should deport himself if he expects to gain and keep the respect of his patients. A doctor in a small community a few years ago took advantage of his status as an attractive bachelor to carry on rather flagrant affairs with some of the young women in the town. After advising with and warning him, the local medical association dropped him from membership in the professional group, thus making it impossible for him to be on the staff of the local hospital; in effect, he was no longer able to practice his profession of medicine. He went to court to have the dismissal action rescinded by legal order, maintaining that his private love-life was his own affair (so to speak). The fact that he had a reputation as a notorious wolf did not, he said, lessen his medical skill. The court ruled against his petition, on the grounds that the profession of medicine had acquired a status of public prestige, honor, and trust that could not be violated with impunity. If he wanted to be a doctor, he had to act like one.

Some of you may not agree with this court decision. "Freedom to act is a personal matter," you say, "and what a person does is his own business so long as he stays within the law and does an honest day's work at his job." Before we attempt to answer that argument, let us look at the case of the small-town banker who began to spend all of his spare time at the horse races, wagering (and losing) very large sums of money on the nag he fancied. The board of directors of the bank finally dismissed him, despite his statement—which was true— that he was using only his own money, performing his banking duties faithfully, and minding his own business. But he had failed to see this important point: his actions, which would have caused no comment or suspicion had he been, say, a plumber or an architect, were a source of real concern to the bank and its depositors; he could not help arousing suspicion on the part of the townsfolk that he was using the depositors' funds to finance his inveterate gambling at the race track.

One more example. Employees of the Federal government who are employed in positions covered by the "Hatch Act," which forbids certain types of political activity, do not lose their basic rights as citizens; they do, however, definitely lose certain privileges that other citizens enjoy. They cannot solicit campaign funds, be precinct chairmen, or make political speeches—not so long as they wish to enjoy the protection of the Civil Service laws.

How to react to special requirements.   If we intend to enjoy teaching, we might as well face the fact that teaching has—like any other job performed under careful public scrutiny—certain occupational hazards; we learn to live with them, or we quit teaching. (Or, if we don't have the nerve to quit, we just sit around and complain about the sad plight of teachers.) No one in his right senses would suggest that teachers ought to be spineless, mousy creatures (the figure of speech is a bit mixed, but you understand what we mean) who just put up with anything to keep their jobs. There are three perfectly legitimate ways of reacting to special demands in the areas of manners, morals, appearance, recreation, or personal habits which the community may make of its teachers.

First, if the matter isn't really important, if it does not involve personal or professional integrity, you might as well play the game according to the local ground rules. The writer is acquainted with a high school teacher who spent an entire school year in extreme personal misery and emotional uproar because the local custom—ground rules—required that the men teachers wear coats and ties in the classroom. He wanted to wear a sport shirt. His arguments were most convincing—sport shirts are cooler, a coat binds one about the shoulders, a tie constricts the neck. Most men would agree with him that traditional male clothing doesn't really make much sense. It is very difficult to agree, however, that such a minor point was worth a year of professional and personal upset. We say that as teachers we try to teach tolerance and acceptance of individual differences; common sense requires us to practice what we preach—to be tolerant of the peculiar customs in certain communities, and appreciative of the fact that communities are as individually different as children are.

Second, if the restriction on personal or professional freedom *is* really important, the teacher might well use his professional skill as an educator to try to change, quietly but effectively, community ideas and behavior patterns. If anybody ought to know how to bring about change in behavior patterns—to motivate the desire to change, to use the psychology of group dynamics to produce new ideas and new learnings—it's the teacher. Educators, who of all people should know better, have been guilty of using bulldozer tactics in trying to change community opinion on matters of manners and morals, when they should be using the very educational techniques that they believe work so well in the classroom. Physician, heal thyself.

Finally, if the restriction is of such importance that one cannot honestly abide by it during the period when change might be effected in the community, the teacher should have the visceral courage to resign. For example, if the rules of the school or the customs of the community should demand that one suppress honest evidence, teach a falsehood, lie to a parent, or hurt a child (and these things happen), then the teacher must have the integrity—and enough backbone—to resign. But these cases requiring immediate resignation are very rare; hasty decisions are not really very becoming for a teacher, anyway. As a teacher, you are committed to find out all the facts, to know the whole truth; don't become upset or send in your resignation until all the evidence is in. What may look like a blatantly dishonest or evil practice may be something you don't really understand. And finally, the teacher is morally committed to a belief in education as a gradual change in behavior. Maybe one could sometimes serve the cause of right better by staying and working on the problem than by simply running away from it.

Academic Freedom

A teacher cannot really enjoy his work unless he feels free. He needs more than just personal freedom; he needs what we have come to call academic freedom—that is, intellectual freedom to teach the truth as he sees it. Unfortunately, most of the difficulties that arise in securing and maintaining academic freedom come from a misunderstanding of the meaning of the term itself.

First of all, there is no such thing in a democracy as a complete freedom. All freedoms are relative and limited, even freedom to teach. Under our laws and customs, no one is free to advocate the overthrow of the government by force or violence, or free to incite riot. In our schools no one is free to force his opinion down the throat of someone else, or free to disregard scientific evidence and teach just what he "feels in his bones" to be true. No one is free to indoctrinate, to lie, or to distort. No one is free to inflict hurt or to disregard the rights of others—in highway traffic, in business practices, or in teaching. The idea of absolute freedom is ridiculous.

Second, academic freedom is not a right possessed by teachers as a special privilege, or granted to them by society for their personal protection or pleasure. Academic freedom belongs to the public: *they* set up the rules and the limits and the applications of it for the protection of society itself. The teacher does not *own* academic freedom as a special prerogative of his calling; he is simply the trustee of this freedom that belongs to the public. The purposes of academic freedom are to make democracy workable by assuring that the public will have freedom to learn, freedom to get the facts, freedom to make up their own minds, and freedom *from* indoctrination and thought control.

So whenever a question arises that concerns academic freedom, the teacher's first thought should be not "What are they trying to do to me?" or "How will this affect my freedom?" but rather "What does this mean to the freedom of society as a whole; to the freedom of the children whom society has placed under my care?" In the light of such questions, many of the so-called problems of academic freedom will look a lot different to teachers, or even disappear altogether.

For example, loyalty oaths. As soon as such oaths are proposed many teachers immediately rebel with bitter cries about "violations of academic freedom." Is this really the question? Often not. Admittedly,

such special oaths that single out teachers as objects of public suspicion and distrust are discriminatory, unfair, and generally useless.
But unless the oath represents a "clear and present danger" to the
freedom the public enjoys in a democracy, the insult that it seems to
slap on teachers might profitably be ignored. We are not primarily
concerned with freedom for the teacher, but with intellectual freedom
for those we teach. We don't like these oaths, but in many cases we
are better off to accept them as just another occupational hazard.

We have not attempted in any sense to offer here a complete
analysis of the problems of academic freedom. Especially in times of
national and international stress, teachers and schools will be faced
with special problems in securing for their students the right to hear
all sides of controversial issues and to discuss certain important but
"ticklish" social, political, and economic questions freely and openly.
But we would like to submit that teachers will have less difficulty with
such problems, and more pleasure in teaching, if they think in terms
of *academic responsibility* rather than being oversensitive to alleged
violations of their own academic freedom. If teachers assume the
responsibilities that are rightly theirs—of seeing that all sides of controversial issues are presented fairly, of resisting any attempts by
pressure groups to stifle honest discussion, and of doing such a demonstrably good job of fair and impartial teaching that no one can question their competence or their motives—the problem of curtailment
of academic freedom will be minimized.

Intrastaff Relations in the School

If we accept the major premise of this chapter—that teachers are
normal human beings—we cannot ignore the problem of friction between members of the teaching staff and between teachers and
administrators. Since teachers are indeed human, they will evidence
the same human frailties that cause friction wherever people live and
work together.

This need not, however, be so serious a problem as to dim the real
enjoyment you can find in the work of teaching. We must be willing
to recognize that the same characteristics of human behavior that we
observe in children will also be found in the teachers and administrators with whom we work—and in our own personalities and behavior
patterns. If we do as good a job of applying our knowledge of human
psychology to ourselves and our co-workers as we do to the children

and youth we teach, one source of much friction and disappointment in teaching could be minimized, if not avoided.

We know, for example, in working with children that *status feelings* are of great importance. Teachers, like children, need recognition and praise; they want to be accepted by their peer group. The beginning teacher can't very well do a sociogram on his colleagues, but he can observe intelligently and sympathetically how the group works together—note the aggressive and the submissive, the constructive critic and the destructive griper, the various roles played by each member of the staff in their normal working relationships. And, sensitized to the dynamics of the behavior of the group in which he is a new member, he can consciously avoid actions and comments that will unnecessarily deflate egos, upset balances already achieved, or rub someone's fur the wrong way. The new teacher, especially, must do the "fitting in"; it is simply not psychologically realistic to expect the existing group to try to adapt themselves to *his* peculiarities. As Robert Owen remarked to his Quaker colleague, William Allen, "All the world is queer save thee and me, and even thou art a little queer." Let's be realistic. We expect individual differences in children; we will find them characteristic of adult groups, too.

Does this mean slavish conformity to the behavior patterns, mores, likes and dislikes of the older teachers? Not at all. It means that the teacher who goes into a new job with the honest expectation of enjoying teaching must use consummate skill in human relations. For example, the new teacher may be subject in some schools to a certain amount of suspicion or even hostility; fortunately, this is the exception rather than the rule. But the new teacher who knows something of the psychology of group behavior can be prepared for this treatment if it comes; it's just what happens to the new child in the classroom or on the playground, or to the stranger who moves into a settled community. Or again, the new teacher may be surprised at how emotionally some of his colleagues react when certain topics or problems are mentioned. He need not be startled; everybody has his emotional "sore spots"; everybody's actions are to some degree controlled more by how he feels than by what he rationally knows.

So, the beginning teacher, or the experienced teacher moving into a new school or new community, can learn to enjoy his work and his co-workers even if they do seem a little peculiar; he probably seems that way to them. Conformity to the group patterns and group mores already established among the teachers in the school is not weak or cowardly; it is realistic. We say that we accept each child as he is, that we start with the class "where they are." Such acceptance of the *status quo* does not imply weak resignation. Progress with children comes slowly, but if the teacher is any good, it does come. Progress with adult groups is even slower—they lack the plasticity of youth—but the wise teacher accepts things as they are among his co-workers, and builds on that basis.

The Mental Health of the Teacher

Good mental health is extremely important to teachers. First, it saves them from submission to the popular stereotype of the teacher as "different" from ordinary folk. Too, good mental health contributes immeasurably to the enjoyment of teaching; teaching is not an easy job, but it becomes a nightmare for the teacher who is emotionally upset, insecure, disturbed. And finally, good mental health is important to the effectiveness of teaching. Mental health is, figuratively, communicable; it's catching. The teacher's good mental health is reflected in the students, in their happiness, their growth, their achievement.

The Mental Strains of Teaching

Teaching isn't an easy, relaxing job. It is hard work—but infinitely satisfying and richly rewarding to the teacher who has the right combination of personality characteristics, behavior patterns, and training for the job. Teaching puts certain special stresses on the emotional and mental health—and on physical health as well. Many teachers are consistently overworked—the spirit may be willing, but the flesh is weak; constant strain takes its toll in human energy. The overwork may come in the form of crowded daily schedules, too many different class preparations, overlarge classes, or rooms poorly equipped, inadequately lighted, or lacking in proper ventilation. The insecurity some teachers feel in their jobs—actual fear of losing the job—is sometimes compounded by financial worries caused by distressingly inadequate salaries. Teachers who are not protected by an adequate retirement system work under the strain of worry about the future; teachers whose contracts provide for no sick leave are constantly under tension wondering what would happen to them in the case of serious illness. The ordinary teacher in the classroom must play several quite different roles daily—perhaps several at once: guide, advisor, judge, disciplinarian, confidant, enforcer of rules. The teacher must keep an even temper, be skilled in taking an impersonal attitude toward classroom disturbances, and yet be able to have a very warm personal rapport with each student—and they're all different.

The classroom teacher needs to be equipped with hydromatic drive, so that dozens of times a day he can shift gears silently, automatically, smoothly—changing pace, direction, and destination with the changing needs and activities of the class. In the elementary school the teacher must every day work intimately with very immature students; at the secondary level, the chronological age of the students is greater but the basic immaturity is still there. Small wonder that when teachers get out of the classroom into normal adult gatherings and activities they sometimes find it difficult not to seem condescending in their dealings with other adults, not to sound bossy, not to assume that their contemporaries need to be told what to do. The popular belief that the teacher can't put off the schoolroom manner when engaging in normal adult activities has some basis in fact.

Mental Health Needs

Despite all of these strains and stresses, most teachers seem to weather the storm pretty well. They need, and consequently develop, a high boiling point; humanly enough, they sometimes get irritated, but good teachers develop a special ability to react quietly, to live calmly in an emotionally-charged atmosphere. For good mental health the teacher needs to have a well-developed sense of humor—and an almost superhuman ability to keep from laughing at the wrong time. For to children and youth their own problems, mistakes, achievements, and embarrassments are as important as are these same things to adults; the teacher must take his students seriously.

Good mental health requires that each individual *value* himself, *like* himself, *accept* himself for what he is. At the same time, the mentally healthy person has a deep conviction of the worth and acceptability of other people, individually and in groups. The good teacher develops these abilities, skills, and feelings that make for harmonious and satisfying interpersonal relationships.

One trait of the mentally healthy person is his capacity for feeling, his ability to let emotions play a balanced part in his life. The good teacher, likewise, is emotionally stable without being emotionally rigid. Cheerfulness, alertness, friendliness, appreciation—all of these signs of sound emotional health are transmitted from the teacher to the children and set the emotional tone of the learning environment. But less desirable emotional reactions—fear, anger, self-pity, harshness—are also "catching"; they can pollute the classroom atmosphere as surely and insidiously as a noxious gas.

This is only a partial sketch of the qualities of emotional and mental health we can expect to find in the teacher who is a normal human being, who really does a good job of teaching, and who is convinced from personal experience that teaching can be fun. The emotionally healthy teacher is a person who has attained psychological maturity without getting old, who understands and appreciates himself and others, whose behavior pattern is at the same time both stable and adaptable.

The Rewards of Teaching

If teachers are, as we have maintained, normal people, then they have a normal need to find some reward in their work. They must enjoy teaching so much that they would rather do it than anything else. That is the only sound basis on which one may reasonably choose a life work.

It seems almost impossible to discuss the rewards and satisfactions of teaching without sounding stuffy; it is hard to discuss intangible, personal, emotional feelings about teachers without having the paragraphs drip with gooey sentiment. But, for the person who has the ability and competence and skill to become a really good teacher, teaching offers rewards and satisfaction that no other career can afford. You will notice that we used the phrase, "a really good teacher." This is important; only the teacher who is a success in the work of teaching can reap the rewards. Poor, halfhearted, ineffective teaching has no rewards. If you can't be a *good* teacher, do something else—anything else. But don't teach.

Material Rewards

It may strike you as peculiar to start a listing of the rewards of teaching with the one which is the least defensible and perhaps, in the long run, the least important. Because today, as you well know, nobody can get rich teaching; anybody who puts money at the top of the list of the things he hopes to get out of teaching is not being realistic. But since many people who would make good teachers are frightened away from the profession because they are afraid it won't offer a decent living, we might as well start with this problem.

In many school systems, salaries are pitiably, shamefully low; retirement provisions are but a pittance; tenure policies provide shaky job security at best; and sick leave and other marginal or fringe benefits are meager or nonexistent. But in the better school systems, salaries and other benefits of a material nature are fully adequate; the financial rewards compare favorably with those available in almost any other type of employment. The encouraging point is this: these "best" systems are becoming the patterns for education everywhere; what is more, the best teachers can expect to find employment, if they are fully qualified, in such school systems. If you are a competent teacher, you can expect that during your professional career you will become a member of the staff of the rapidly increasing number of schools that have excellent salary schedules, retirement systems comparable to the best in private industry and government service, and the so-called fringe benefits which add much to the financial rewards of teaching.

Personal Freedom

As we indicated above, teachers are still occasionally subject to some anachronistic personal restrictions, and as professional workers and public servants, they will never have, perhaps, the degree of untrammeled freedom that some people enjoy. But the more absurd special restrictions are fast disappearing from teaching. Teachers are free to be real people, full-fledged citizens. And because schools exist in every community in the United States, job opportunities are to be found almost wherever the teacher may go. You can (especially since *good* teachers are always in demand) pick the geographic area in which you want to work and live to a much greater degree than most workers. And although the work-load of teachers is heavy, there is a freedom and flexibility in the work schedule that many workers do not enjoy; you can adjust your work during out-of-school hours to times that suit your convenience, with no thought of a time clock to punch. And with salaries getting more nearly adequate, the long summer period for study, rest, recreation and other employment is not to be disregarded as one of the joys of the job of teaching.

Challenge

There is no great amount of mere routine in the work of the good teacher; the work never becomes saturated with sameness if the teacher really tries to do a good job. Every day is different, every individual, every class meeting, every new activity and project. The best minds in teaching are always facing new challenges; intellectual horizons are unlimited. There has never lived the teacher who knew it all; nobody has ever taught as well as it is possible to teach. We are in no sense just trying to glorify the work of teaching when we say that the tasks of education are never done, the work of the school is never complete, the challenge of teaching never fully met.

Prestige

Gone are the days when the teacher was "low man on the totem pole." Again, we speak of the better schools in the more advanced communities educationally when we say that teachers have a place in the respect and affection of the community that is matched by few other groups of workers. In a public-opinion survey conducted by Elmo Roper a few years ago,[8] a cross-section of the general public rated teachers as the most important workers in society. This feeling is by no means universal, but as we of the profession give our best efforts and set our own house in order—work to get rid of substandard teachers, to weed out the incompetent, to win greater public support for better schools and more financial support for education—every indication is that the popular respect for teachers will continue to rise.

Certainly, parents as a group hold teachers in quite high regard; the teacher is, next to the parent, the most important adult in the life of the child, and parents as a rule cherish the welfare of their children above all else. The teacher tends to bask in the reflected glow of the warmth the parent feels for the children he has entrusted to the teachers. And children and youth have a fine sense of judgment and discrimination, generally, in their appraisal of teachers; they despise and ridicule the poor ones, but more often than not they take the best of their teachers and virtually enshrine them in their hearts as saints or supermen whose every word is authority personified. This may sound silly to you, but just wait till you are teaching and experience the feeling of being a VIP to some student. It helps!

[8] Cited in Emma Reinhardt, *American Education—An Introduction* (New York: Harper & Brothers, 1954), p. 431.

Job Satisfaction

There is tremendous personal satisfaction in doing a competent teaching job. When you see the plans that you have made take shape as a significant and creative project for the students, when you see the light that dawns in the eyes of a child for whom you have made a difficult concept clear, when you see the self-assurance that blossoms when you have helped a student master a skill, when you see children or youth become more secure, more mature, happier under the influence of your teaching—then you will experience the thrill (that's a horribly sentimental word, but there is no other!) that makes all the drudgery and frustration that so often accompany teaching eminently worthwhile. Along with these major achievements that make teaching so satisfying are the little day-by-day successes that are al-almost inevitable, even with the dullest classes: Jimmy made his "O's" better today—not much better, but some; in music class, Johnny-one-note cracked his own private sonic barrier by showing a little departure from his usual monotone; Mary, the sophomore who can't think about anything but boys and never reads anything but movie magazines, showed a small but positive gleam of interest in the discussion in American history class. Sometimes the gains are small—infinitesimally small—and sometimes they are stupendous, but the good teacher achieves something every day.

Service

The very existence of a modern, complex human society indicates quite clearly that despite our apparently innate core of human selfishness there *is* a facet of human nature we call altruism, the desire to do something for someone else without thought of personal gain or aggrandizement. In teachers, the desire to render social service seems unusually strong, and in teaching the opportunities to realize that desire to serve are unlimited. Teaching *matters* in our civilization; education is demonstrably important, socially useful beyond the shadow of a doubt. It is a constructive work, one that makes a difference in the lives of individual students, of social groups, of communities. Is it too much to say in these troubled times that education is the one good hope we have for the future of national and international civilization itself?

The service rendered by teachers is not all of cosmic importance. We can see this in the following quotation, a whimsical answer to the question, "What is a teacher?"

To a child thrust into a strange world, a good teacher is the best thing that can possibly happen.

A teacher is Courage with Kleenex in its pocket, and Patience with papers to grade.

Teachers spend 12 hours a day searching for truth and the other 12 hours searching for error.

They are incorruptible, indispensable, infallible, invincible, and nearly inexhaustible.

A teacher does not really mind sniffles, squirmings, stomach aches, spills, sloth, and sauciness. Neither does she disintegrate before tears, trifles, fights, futility, excuses, parents who spout, little boys who shout, and little girls who pout.

Most of all a teacher is somebody who *likes* somebody else's children—and still has strength enough left to go to the PTA meeting.[9]

Note especially the phrase, "Courage with Kleenex in its pocket." That epitomizes the service teachers give because they *like* somebody else's children. The teacher can serve by being the highest embodiment of an ideal—and also by having an extra Kleenex handy.

A Goodly Fellowship

Becoming a teacher, persevering as a teacher, and growing as a teacher has one final satisfaction we must mention: in being a good teacher, you join a great and goodly fellowship of others who since the dawn of human civilization have found a lifetime of satisfaction and reward in the cause of education. Joining such a group and upholding the best of its traditions may well be the most important thing you've ever done. Want to give it a try?

THIRTEEN: TOPICS FOR STUDY, REPORT, AND DISCUSSION

1. Read some current short story, play, or novel which is about teachers or uses a teacher as one of the important characters. What stereotyped notions about teachers are in evidence?
2. Write out a brief description of the best and the poorest teacher you have ever had. Try to include in the description the most significant qualities (both personal and professional) of each teacher.
3. What indications do you have that you possess the personal and intellectual qualifications for becoming a good teacher? Be honest, but don't underrate yourself.

[9] "What Is a Teacher?" *NEA Journal,* Vol. 41, No. 7 (October, 1952), p. 450. Reprinted by permission.

4. Have you already started on a program of continuing growth as a teacher? What books have you read recently, aside from those required in college courses, that have added to your general knowledge? What magazines do you read regularly? What special kinds of "learning experience" have you had—participation in extracurricular activities, pursuit of some hobby, working with youth groups, or employment in business or industry—that will contribute to your professional and personal competence?

5. With the assistance of your instructor, secure one of the self-check scales used to help teachers evaluate themselves. How do you rate?

6. Hold a panel discussion in class on the topic "Freedom in Teaching." Analyze what is said in the discussion and formulate your own opinion on how "free" teachers may realistically expect to be.

7. What do you expect to "get out" of teaching as a career? What do you expect to "give" in the course of a lifetime of teaching?

THIRTEEN: BIBLIOGRAPHY

Abraham, Willard, *A Handbook for the New Teacher*. New York: Holt, Rinehart & Winston Inc., 1960. A very clever but extremely penetrating brief series of essays about the personal-professional problems of the new teacher. Worth reading in its entirety.

Association for Supervision and Curriculum Development, *Creating a Good Environment for Learning*, 1954 Yearbook. Washington, D. C.: National Education Association, 1954. Chap. 7 discusses ways teachers can practice good human relations among themselves and in contact with children and the community.

Brembeck, Cole S., *The Discovery of Teaching*. Englewood Cliffs, N. J.: Prentice-Hall, Inc., 1962. A problem-oriented discussion of the job of the teacher from a personalized point of view; many case studies and case illustrations. See especially chaps. 1, 2, 3, and 18.

Caldwell, Sarah, "Teaching Is Hard Work," *The Atlantic Monthly*, Vol. 194, No. 5 (November, 1954), 40-44. Sympathetic, down-to-earth discussion of the job of teaching, very interestingly written by a former president of the National Education Association.

Charles, Don C., "The Stereotype of the Teacher in American Literature," *The Educational Forum*, Vol. XIV, No. 3 (March, 1950), 299-305. Very interesting listing of literary characters who portray stereotyped ideas of the teacher as "different."

Davis, Billie, "I Was a Hobo Kid," *The Saturday Evening Post*, Vol. 225, No. 24 (December 13, 1952), 25 ff. A fascinating, heartwarming account of how a migrant child found new meaning and purpose in life through the influence of just "ordinary" teachers.

Dodds, Glenn W., "Does Fiction Libel the Teacher?" *The Nation's Schools*, Vol. XCII, No. 4 (October, 1948), 41-43. The title question is answered affirmatively, with several good illustrations.

Lee, Gordon C., *An Introduction to Education in Modern America*. New York: Holt, Rinehart & Winston, Inc., 1953. Chap. 16 gives a good listing and discussion of desirable personality traits, and suggests ways for teachers to continue to advance in stature and wisdom.

Reinhardt, Emma, *America Education: An Introduction*. New York: Harper & Row, Publishers, 1954. Chap. 10 describes many of the studies of what makes a successful teacher, and chap. 12 contains a very encouraging account of the personal rewards that may be expected in a life of teaching.

Spickard, Jean G., "My Forty Children," *Woman's Home Companion,* Vol. LXXXII, No. 1 (January, 1955), 22 ff. An interesting account by a high school teacher of her work with forty freshmen. Indicates clearly the kind of information about teaching that reaches the public through popular magazines.

Van Dalen, Deobold B., and Robert W. Brittell, *Looking Ahead to Teaching*. Boston: Allyn and Bacon, Inc., 1959. The first five chapters, especially, give interesting insights into the concerns of the beginning teacher.
See also the self-rating scale in Appendix B.

Wynn, Richard, *Careers in Education*. New York: McGraw-Hill Book Co., Inc., 1960. Chap. 8, in particular, concerns itself with the teacher as a person, though other chapters are equally worthwhile.

EDUCATIONAL

PERSPECTIVE

Learning in process. *Does the learning here illustrated represent some of the basic truths which the educational platitudes oversimplify?*

CHAPTER FOURTEEN

Perspective and Platitude

Factual knowledge about the American school system is a necessity for anyone who expects to make the work of education his career, or for any parent or other lay citizen who hopes to make wise judgments or take wise action with respect to public education. But factual knowledge alone is not enough; equally important is understanding of educational plans, purposes, and programs—their real meaning and their often subtle interrelationships. It is this kind of mature understanding of American education that we should all seek. To be effective educational workers, professional or lay, we need educational perspective—the long view, the studied opinion, the careful judgment, the sense of relative value and importance that true perspective of any area of human endeavor gives us.

In getting and keeping this educational perspective, however, it is perhaps not wrong ideas that hinder and confuse us so much as it is the educational platitudes that many teachers and laymen persist in repeating. A platitude, you will recall, is a truth which has been literally flattened out by overuse, a truth with a worn-down appearance and little remaining vigor or flavor. It's a truth that is easy to

BEWARE THE
PRONGHORNED PLATITUDE

repeat—we've heard it often, it's always being said—but one which conveys very little real meaning; it's easy to say, but it doesn't say much.

Even more serious, these platitudes about education are often somewhat pompous and dogmatic. In repeating them, the speaker commits himself irrevocably to an untenable "either-or" choice, puts himself squarely on the *horns of a dilemma;* hence the term, "prong-horned platitude."

There are many of these statements in common currency, some of them favorable to modern education, some of them very critical. They all have some common features. Insofar as they are true, the real truth in them lies buried in the platitudinous phraseology; many of them are only half-truths at best; and all of them force the speaker to take an uncomfortable position of *absolute acceptance* of one point of view and *absolute rejection* of the opposite—the lack of opportunity for partial agreement or disagreement is truly a dilemma. Let us look at some of these trouble-making statements commonly made about modern education and modern schools.

"We Don't Teach Subject Matter; We Teach Children"

This is one of the favorite slogans of teachers who like to think of themselves as Progressives with a capital "P." It sounds like a bold, unfettered, and noble statement of purpose, an expression of supreme contempt for the older type of school which stressed teaching history, say, rather than teaching John and Mary. When it was first used as a rallying cry for the proponents of the newer education it had a great deal of force and meaning; it correctly decried over-emphasis on subject-matter-to-be-learned at the expense of concern with the learner himself. It had the unfortunate overtone, however, of suggesting that the teacher must make a definite choice between subject matter and children—as if by teaching one, you couldn't teach the other.

Like all of these educational platitudes, this one is true—up to a point. There can be no doubt that at the beginning of this century, when the new educational psychology, the new concepts of learning as a kind of living, and the new concepts of the social function of the school—all of these new emphases called rather generically "progressive education"—were set in opposition to the old, bookish, subject-centered education, the sharp distinction between "subjects" and "children" made sense. The statement had a further element of truth, which most of us recognize today: subject matter as such is not an end in itself, but a means to an end—better education. Moreover, even education is not an end in itself, but the means to a greater and more important end: a better life for children and the society in which they live.

Now, common sense and logic both tell us that we cannot really separate the means and the ends in any process, or set one over against the other, or ascribe to one *all* of the important virtues of the entire process. In the case of subject matter *vs.* child, we can easily see that any attempt to say which of the two is most important is patently foolish. If you are a music teacher, do you teach music or do you teach children? There can be only one reasonable answer: you teach children music, or you teach music to children, or you teach children through music. We completely miss the point of education if we try to separate the learner from what is learned.

Such a statement as "we teach children, not subject matter" leads to all sorts of very fuzzy thinking. It has allowed some teachers to try to justify their own lack of subject-matter knowledge: why study or try to teach something that isn't important anyway? It has made some teachers complacent about the poor showing of their students on achievement tests or other indices of learning: after all, says the teacher indignantly, we don't stress such learnings! *We* teach children, not subject matter! It has led to an underemphasis on kinds of learning that are important and easily overlooked if subject matter is constantly deprecated and pushed into the educational background. There is nothing in the tenets of modern or progressive education that would deny (actually, there is much that would emphasize) such kinds of learning as knowledge of the world about us, understanding of societies past and present, recognition of cause-and-effect relationships, command of fundamental skills, sense of continuity in human history, ability to get along with others—the list could go on. If modern education means anything at all, it means the kinds of learning suggested in the sentence above. It is inconceivable that such learnings could result, in the educational process, apart from subject matter; they *are* subject matter. When such subject matter has become a real part of the experience of the child, when it has become part of the means to his growth and is expressed in a changed behavior pattern, we say the child has *learned*.

The supposed conflict of subject matter *vs.* children is a wholly imaginary battle. Take out the *vs.* and we have the heart of the educational problem as it really is: how to take the formal and informal heritage of the human race and the present experiences of children and youth—all of this is what we really mean by "subject matter"— and use it in the process of education. There is no real conflict between teaching subject matter and teaching children.

"We Learn by Doing"

"Well," said a student indignantly to the writer not long ago, after a complex discussion about learning theory, "I don't see why you have to make learning sound so complicated; everybody knows that we learn by doing." This is one of the favorite educational platitudes. It is easy to say, simple to understand in a superficial sort of way, and pleasant for the teacher to believe. Because if it is true, there really is not much to teaching except to see that the students get a lot of chances to *do* things. Easy, isn't it?

"We learn by doing" is a true statement if we define *learn* and *doing* accurately and broadly. But there are lots of kinds of learning and lots of kinds of doing: the statement becomes true only insofar as it is made specific. For example, there exists in one of the large midwestern university training schools a room that is a peculiar monument to the enormous stupidity of one teacher who thought that the whole learning process could be neatly summed up in the "learn by doing" phrase. The classroom of this history teacher is crowded, jam-packed, with models of Trojan horses and Greek chariots. The history students who have "studied" under this teacher for the past decade have done almost nothing the entire year but build models. Why? The teacher says simply, "They learn by doing, that's why!" But in this unusual teaching-learning situation, what are they doing? Making models! What are they learning? How to make models! Now, let's be entirely fair with this teacher: she has the germ of a good idea. At the same time they are building models, the students *could* be doing many other things also, taking part in many other learning activities; there *could* be all sorts of incidental or concomitant learnings; *could* be, we say. Because unless the teacher and students together plan the *doing* so that the desired learnings have at least a chance of emerging, "doing" itself does not automatically result in learning—desired and worthwhile learning, that is.

The extreme example cited above is not what will necessarily occur as a result of the oversimplified, uncritical view of all "doing" resulting in learning or all learning coming from a certain kind of "doing." But it illustrates the fallacy of trying to compress learning theory or educational practice into one simple statement. In many of the earlier progressive schools, doing was thought of as synonymous with physical and vocal activity; the child was not assumed to be doing unless he was *up* and doing! The experience from which learning came was also often thought to be necessarily firsthand experience; the learner had to do whatever it was *himself,* or learning couldn't take place.

While we must agree that there is a very basic truth in the saying "we learn by doing," the difficulties with uncritical acceptance of this slogan as a complete explanation of the learning process are many. First, the phrase—useful as it was in the earlier days of educational change in this century as an antidote to a view of education that was almost exclusively passive—today seems largely outmoded. In most schools the complete passivity, the strict obedience to authority, and the severe limitations of pupil freedom against which the slogan raised its battle cry are largely practices of the past; to keep repeating a phrase that criticizes a kind of education no longer commonly accepted only serves to arouse objection to and suspicion of present-day education. Moreover, the phrase is at once too simple and too comprehensive; it seems to deny the doctrine of individual differences which is so widely accepted as fundamental to modern education. It seems to say that all learning is really the same for every child; if you just keep the children active, the experiences they have will be automatically and universally educative.

This oversimplification of the concept of experience as a teacher has led the authors of an ASCD Yearbook to caution, "Experiences have different meaning and intensity for each child. . . . No matter how carefully the teacher plans . . . the same experience has different meaning and intensity for different pupils." They go on to describe an actual classroom situation:

> Steven entered into the construction period with enthusiasm. He always pushed forward the group's work with his quick insight into problems. Denny seemed to move in a dream; the problems of measurement and accuracy which were challenging to Steven did not even exist for Denny. This surely was a vivid illustration of the principle that the same outcomes in learning cannot be expected for different children, since each perceives the same situation so differently. Once, thought Miss Jensen [the

teacher], she had been discouraged and felt her teaching a failure when it did not increase children's similarities. She had expected from all children the same answers, the identical understandings and responses to most school experiences. Since she had become sensitive to the many aspects of children's personalities and the variety of their past experiences, she realized that she must expect differences in learning. But there must be readily available a variety of materials and actvities so that each child may find something of meaning to him, if he is to grow and to learn.[1]

Just as there are all kinds of children, so are there all kinds of experiences, each with its special learning value to different students under different learning conditions. "Experience" or "doing" is too broad a word to be used exclusively and completely to describe all learning; it may *embrace* the whole truth of learning but it does not *express* the whole truth. We need to emphasize that reading, listening, contemplating, creating, appreciating, accepting, observing, forming hypotheses, trying to apply what has been learned, and recording these learnings are all types of "doing" which are part of the modern school curriculum.

The basic difficulty with the easy phrase, "we learn by doing," is the same one we will find with all of these other educational platitudes: it implies an either-or choice, a choice of the sort Chancellor Hutchins made when he said blandly, in discussing the function of higher education, "We may wisely leave experience to life and set about our job of intellectual training." [2] We can recognize at once the fallacy of assuming that the college must *choose between* experience and intellectual training; they are not opposites. And yet we who speak of the kind of experience we call "doing" as though it were the *opposite* of the more traditional forms of educational activity, instead of a part of learning, are being just as narrow. The simple phrase, even when we do not mean it as simply as it sounds, tends to give a public impression of a very limited educational perspective.

For learning is a very complicated process; only the uncritical teacher would suggest that all doing results in desired learning, or that all learning comes from *doing* in the plain, active sense that the term is generally used. Some experience, as Dewey pointed out in

[1] Association for Supervision and Curriculum Development, *Creating a Good Environment for Learning,* 1954 Yearbook (Washington, D.C.: National Education Association, 1954), p. 44. Reprinted by permission.
[2] Robert M. Hutchins, *The Higher Learning in America* (New Haven: Yale University Press, 1936), p. 70. Reprinted by permission.

the early days of the Progressive Education movement, is not educative at all; some of it is mis-educative; some of it is at best a grossly
inefficient way of learning. And some learning doesn't look like
"doing" in any active sense of the word. The modern school needs to
guard against becoming the "activity" school in a purely physical
sense. The alert teacher must be careful not to phrase his educational statements in a way that causes the general public to suspect
either the accuracy or adequacy of his theory of learning. We learn
through experience; we learn by doing. True—but not true *enough!*

"Education Is Life Itself, Not Preparation for Life"

This is another of the old rallying cries of the early "progressive" in education. The slogan was an outgrowth of the belief, certainly well founded, that the schools had ceased to be living institutions, had ceased to have any life in themselves and had settled back
complacently to "prepare" children for life. In such a school, the
students were not supposed to ask *why* they should be studying, say,
geometry. Geometry was not *supposed* to be of any immediate good,
but rather a part of the student's preparation for something ahead—
other mathematics courses, college entrance requirements, or "applications" of geometry that he would find out about in due time when
he grew up and "went out into life."

The trouble with this slogan—education is life, not preparation for
life—is that it represents a battle cry which has turned into a whim-
per. It started out as a statement of purpose and turned into an
apology. Using this statement, the educator could try to justify almost
any omissions in the curriculum ("After all, we are not preparing for
life; we are helping the children live now!") or any whimsical inclu-
sions of dubious school activities ("But the school must be a society
in miniature. The school is life itself; and life itself includes everything!").

Today, we must frankly admit two limitations of education in relation to life in general: education is in part preparation for life, and
education as carried on by the public school cannot hope to *be* life
itself in any reasonable meaning of the term.

Education is preparation for life; society sets up, controls, and supports the public school system, and makes it compulsory that all

children attend, just because the school is the best way we have found to prepare children for activities in later life. If the school did not prepare for life, it would have no basis for seeking and securing public support. And if we who teach really believed that education did not prepare for life, we might as well shut up the school and go home. We do want the school to be "life itself" at one stage of the child's development, for at least part of the day, five days a week, nine or ten months a year. But that fine concept of the school as a living institution and as a place for real living does not necessitate our saying that the school is not *also* a period of preparation. Why bother with the fundamental skills unless they are to be used in later life? Why teach the social studies unless we believe that they will help make the students better people and better citizens when they assume adult-life responsibilities? Why teach "getting along with others" unless we believe that this experience will have definite value as preparation for later living?

And we cannot maintain either, with any degree of accuracy and honesty, that the first part of our slogan—"education *is* life"—really means what it says. Education is at its best when it most fully includes the activities of normal life, when it is involved in what William James called "the thick of things," when it avoids any monastic withdrawal from the problems of life. This lifelike view of education, most of us believe, is very true; but such view is a long way from stating flatly that education is *identical with* life. Education, at least as it is carried on by the American school system (and that is what we are talking about here), cannot and should not try to duplicate life itself in every respect, or by any means become identical with life-as-a-whole.

The *purposes* of education are different from those of life in general; the *materials* of learning are different (planned, selected, graded in difficulty, arranged in order of importance, etc.); the *methods* of formal education are by no means the hit-or-miss, trial-and-error methods by which life educates; the *ground rules* are different (school cannot be conducted exactly like adult society); the *maturity* of the learner is not the same in school and in life itself.

As an alert reader, you have probably said to yourself as you've read these paragraphs, "Yes, but the school can *try* to be like life!" Certainly; the slogan under discussion here has done much to give to the formal system of education a sense of direction toward life-likeness. But the school, many educators and laymen today believe, is grossly in error if it tries to escape from its responsibility for being a specialized agency, performing a specialized function, and serving as the best means society has yet discovered of preparing for life—if it tries to hide behind the glib excuse, "Education is life, not preparation for life!"

"The Aim of Education Is Growth; the Aim of Growth Is Just More Growth"

This statement is a rough paraphrase of one of the most interesting statements ever made by Professor John Dewey,[3] whom many consider to be the founding father of modern progressive education. This identification of education with growth originated as an effort on the part of the pioneer progressives to convince other educators and the general public that earlier (and then current) concepts of education as simply a matter of "passing on the cultural heritage" or "filling the minds of the students with knowledge" were too static for a dynamic society. And saying that the aim of education was just growth and more growth, without any other specific purpose or aim, was a way of arousing professional and popular sentiment against an educational system that had become fixed and sterile in its aims. Once you set up fixed educational aims, the early progressives maintained, you have limited the scope of education and bound it to a slavish acceptance of predetermined purposes. Fixed aims are authoritarian aims; the way to bring freedom to education is to give it unlimited horizons. You stifle the very growth process that *is* education if you state in advance the *end purpose* of that growth.

Most educators today would agree that the aims and objectives of education must never again be allowed to become as fixed and static as they have often been in times past. Absolutism and authoritarianism are as out of place in a democratic educational system as they are in a democratic social system. But it is a grievous error for educators to suggest, directly or by implication, that the only way to keep from developing a fixed, absolute, authoritarian concept of the goals of education is to deny the existence of all educational goals. If all we can say is that education is growth, and the only direction we can give to education is a vague indication of "more growth," then the general public has every right to wonder whether we know what we

[3] John Dewey, *Democracy and Education* (New York: The Macmillan Co., 1916), pp. 59 f.

are talking about. An educational system that is aimless is also point-less.

Moreover, "growth" as a *synonym* for education is too vague. It implies a wholly natural development, an unplanned and undirected process—something that just happens. Education is a growth process, but to call it just plainly and simply "growth" is inadequate. It is a special kind of growth—normal and natural, to be sure, but also directed, scheduled, planned, compressed, and accelerated, as the needs of the learner may warrant. For example, one part of educational growth consists of growing in ability to get along with other people. The good school, elementary or secondary, cannot just "let" the children grow naturally in social development. Teacher-pupil planning is carried on; growth situations are consciously devised; skills in working with a group are taught directly; learning activities are planned which will "bring out" the shy child and teach the over-aggressive to curb his antisocial behavior. All of these activities are types of growth, but each is also a form of direct and quite sequential learning.

It is generally agreed among educators that learning is a developmental process which depends in large part for its effectiveness upon the "readiness" of the child to undertake the next step in learning. We speak for example of "reading readiness" as a developmental stage which must precede effective instruction or learning in reading. This does not mean, however, that the good teacher just sits around and waits until the child has automatically (and in his own good time) developed reading readiness. The skilled teacher *plans, devises,* and *contrives* kinds of learning experience which will speed up the process of achieving readiness to read.

You may object to this rather labored elaboration of the real meaning of the phrase "education is growth"; it all seems so obvious! That is just the difficulty; certainly it is obvious to skilled and well-trained teachers that the term "growth" has many overtones of meaning and many implications for educational practice that the word alone does not directly convey. That is precisely why we must avoid the use of the tired platitude, "education is growth." It misleads the general public; it does not convey the meaning that we intend. We need to develop new ways of explaining the growth concept in education that are more meaningful and more understandable. And when we can explain clearly to the general public what we really mean by growth in education, then the chances are much better that we will really understand just what we mean ourselves.

"The School Should Be Child-Centered"

We have touched briefly in Chapter Five on the inadequacy of this popular statement as a real explanation of the place that the child has in modern education. It is one of those unfortunate educational slogans that forces the speaker to take sides. If you agree with it, you are *for* the child and *against* something else—subject matter, or the teacher, or society; if you disagree with the statement, you are against the child and believe that the school should be centered around the subjects taught, the teacher, or what society demands. The unqualified, positive statement, accepted or rejected, leaves little room for compromise.

Historically, it is easy to see why this ringing challenge of "the child-centered school" was once so popular. The general public needed to be aroused to a realization that school children and youth had often become secondary to some impersonal concept called "education" and an impersonal institution called "the public school." In the early years of this century, when the present educational revolution was just starting, the child as an individual had come to be peripheral to the educational process; we had almost lost sight of the person being educated. Education was too much centered around subjects, courses of study, things to be learned—with very little consideration being given the *learner*.

But the phrase, "the child-centered school" soon lost its influence and importance as a reminder that we must not lose sight of the child; it became a doctrine, a dogma, almost a cult of child-worship. To a limited degree in actual school practice, and quite generally in the popular concept of "progressive" education, the child-centered school came to connote a highly individualistic kind of education, with each child "expressing his own personality," doing just what he wanted to at the moment, and clamoring to be the center of attention—the school an anarchy rather than a democracy, with all effort centered on the individual child and no attention paid to social values and the needs of society.

You will notice we said that this actually happened in only a very few schools; these were mostly private progressive schools which were frankly—and quite possibly this was necessary—experimenting with radical educational ideas and methods just to see what improvements could be made in traditional education. The trouble was that the extreme child-centered concept in education was popularly supposed to be common in all schools which were attempting even a little bit of "progressiveness" in their operation. Yet, the very large majority of American public schools during the first decades of this century, while giving increasing attention to the learner as a person, were by no means as child-centered as they were reputed to be. But the very term came to connote an educational radicalism and a cavalier disregard of the authority of society which made the general public suspicious of anything labeled "progressive."

The term, "the child-centered school," served its purpose of arousing educators and the general public to the importance of the learner as an individual, worthy in his own right as a human being, not just a "pupil" in an educational system. At the same time, it overemphasized extreme individualism in education and alienated a substantial portion of the general public, who suspected modern education of excesses never actually committed. Perhaps the expression should now be rephrased; it doesn't really say what we mean, anyway. What we really mean is more nearly this: The highest good we know in a democracy is neither the individual nor the society; it is the *individual in society* that we value most.

The best school we can conceive of for our democracy, therefore, is one that is centered in the individual-social relationship. We value the unique worth of each human personality as it functions in a society of other uniquely valuable personalities. Individual moral excellence reaches its highest expression in dealing with other people; individual academic achievement is important only as the knowledge and skill are put to use in society; intelligence as an individual possession has little value as compared with intelligence used as an instrument for improving society.

"Child-centered school" has become one of the educational clichés that confuses the present issue, annoys and disturbs many persons who want sincerely to understand and approve of what the schools are doing, and does not express what we really mean about the purposes of modern education. Let's retire it from our educational vocabulary.

"Students Really Learn Only When They Are Interested"

Down through the centuries of the historical development of formal education, alert educators have pointed out the importance of the doctrine of *interest;* it is no new or modern insight or theory that people seem to learn more easily, more quickly, and more permanently that which interests them most. Unfortunately, however, it is easier to make general statements about the importance of interest in learning than it is to understand specifically how interest affects learning. People tend to take sides on the question of interest, particularly on the question of the relative importance of interest and effort. In general, the educational conservative believes that *interest grows out of effort;* if the student is forced to do the assigned work he ultimately becomes interested. The educational liberal is likely to maintain that *interest must precede effective effort;* get the student interested and he will put forth the necessary effort to learn or achieve.

The basic difficulty with most statements about interest and effort is the attempt to oversimplify the complex relationships of the two factors in learning, to make an either-or, black-*vs.*-white choice. Then, this oversimplified reliance on either interest *or* effort becomes a stumbling block to educational understanding and agreement. Our task here is not to attempt to review all of the informative and detailed psychological evidence regarding the place interest has in learning; rather, we need to examine briefly some of the pertinent facts about interest and effort which will give us sufficient background to prevent our becoming uncompromising devotees of either the "interest" or "effort" school of learning.

First of all, interest itself is not a simple concept. There are *kinds* of interest, *degrees* and *levels* of interest that the student may have or acquire. Much depends on individual differences in background, experience, motivation, drive, or purpose. Interest does not automatically spring from a certain set of conditions; it does not necessarily either precede or follow effort as a matter of course. It may range from a mild, superficial curiosity, through transitory spurts of relatively deep involvement, to a lifelong, all-pervading passion. Whether interest plays a relatively large or a relatively small part in any particular learning situation or educational activity varies with the individual, the circumstances, and above all with the kind and degree of interest manifested.

If the school is to adhere conscientiously to its avowed purpose of being as lifelike as possible, it must recognize one inescapable fact about human existence and human society: people have to do a lot of things they don't particularly want to do at the moment, or at all. From the standpoint of the teacher, we can put it even more personally: teachers (like all other people), no matter how much they enjoy teaching, must often force themselves to do *what has to be done*. School is not lifelike if it pretends that every learning and every activity can be sufficiently motivated by present "natural" interest; effort must be made. The interest sometimes must come later. Bagley, one of the more conservative of twentieth-century American educators, was not just being stodgy and old-fashioned when he observed that "gripping interests often grow out of efforts not initially attractive." Bagley elaborated upon this belief in *effort* as intimately related to *interest* when he said:

> Now, obviously, the *freedom* of the immature to choose what they shall learn is of negligible consequence compared with their later freedom from want, fear, fraud, superstition, and error which may fetter the ignorant as cruelly as the chains of the slave-driver; and the price of this freedom is systematic and sustained effort often devoted to the mastery of materials, the significance of which must at the time be taken on faith.[4]

We cannot always start out with a built-in, natural, initial interest; such a strong interest is often the outcome of a fairly routine acceptance of responsibility. The school which is seriously trying both to be a good present learning experience for children and to prepare these children for the responsibilities of adult life must realistically teach the development of a sense of *deferred* values—rewards that can be reaped, not in terms of momentary or immediate pleasure, but at some later time.

We can believe very strongly in the importance of interest in education, and be wholly supported in that belief by a wealth of psychological evidence, but we still must remember to distinguish between true interest and mere *whim*.[5] One of the earliest and most understandable mistakes of the pioneer progressives in education was the easy assumption that whatever the child wanted to do, expressed a desire to do, or tried to do was an interest that deserved to be allowed full exploitation. Dewey himself warned his would-be followers that a child's whims could be quite as arbitrary as the authoritarian decisions of an adult.[6] Dewey's basic theory of interest was often very poorly understood by those who thought they had caught the real

[4] William C. Bagley, "An Essentialist's Platform for the Advancement of American Education," *Educational Administration and Supervision*, Vol. 24, No. 4 (April, 1938), p. 251. Reprinted by permission.
[5] John Dewey, *Experience and Education* (New York: The Macmillan Co., 1938), p. 83.
[6] John Dewey, in *33rd Yearbook, Part II*, NSSE (Chicago: National Society for the Study of Education, 1934) p. 85.

spirit of the new progressive education. This great educational philosopher saw clearly the heart of the interest-effort problem when he said, in effect, that we should be guided not by what the child *proposes,* but by what he *purposes.*

Purpose—which is not to be confused with transitory curiosity, mere whim, or spur-of-the-moment proposals for activity—real purpose is the vital connecting link between interest and effort. For if a purpose that has sufficient personal, social, or educational value motivates conduct or activity or learning, then it does not matter which comes first in accomplishing that purpose: interest or effort. As a matter of fact, neither one has to be put first or second in our thinking, neither one considered of greater or lesser importance in learning. Purpose makes interest and effort combine to yield effective learning.

"The School Curriculum Is As Broad As Life Itself"

In our previous discussion of the curriculum (see Chapter Six), we have suggested briefly that any single statement about curriculum is likely to be a misleading half-truth; curriculum is a big and complex subject. The broad-as-life concept of curriculum is another of those ringing, all-inclusive statements about education that first had wide currency in American education in the early decades of this century when educators singly and in groups were trying to rouse the public—and the schools—from their complacent academic lethargy. For hundreds of years the formal educational program of the school had been conceived of as a special kind of verbalistic, bookish, academic discipline quite properly removed from the workaday world and the affairs of real life. The idea that the school curriculum really includes all of life was advanced by educators, we may suspect, more as a device to break down existing artificial barriers between learning and living than as a carefully formulated definition of the curriculum. But some educators, and some laymen, took this sweeping statement quite literally and made it not only a battle cry but a defense for the inclusion of anything and everything in the term "curriculum."

Once we see the historical necessity for such a generalized definition of the curriculum, and realize that it served a purpose in the development of education, we probably ought to try to make a somewhat more modest appraisal of what the school curriculum really is. The sum total of learning activities, the total educational program of the school *is* very broad—but not as broad as life itself. That's expecting too much; it makes the purpose of the school sound random and unfocused; it gives the school an impossible task to perform; it is manifestly unrealistic, for even the most generous interpretation of the curriculum still leaves the school with only a certain segment of total experience as the school's province. Francis Bacon, the seventeenth-century English scientist, could say grandly, "I have taken all knowledge to be my province," but today there is so much to be known and learned that the school curriculum cannot even include all *knowledge*—to say nothing of everything else in life.

We would do well to shelve this sweeping educational platitude; it doesn't say what we mean, and it arouses public ire because it makes professional educators sound both vague and grasping—vague because the broad-as-life curriculum could mean anything (or nothing), and grasping because such a curriculum would arrogate to the school the work of all the agencies and institutions of society. Even the best school cannot do the whole job alone.

"Let's Cut Out the Frills in Education"

This is one of the familiar popular statements about education—so familiar, in fact, that we are justified in including it as one of the standard clichés about education. Surprisingly enough, it does not necessarily represent the viewpoint only of the overburdened taxpayer or of the confirmed opponent of the public schools; it is a favorite statement of some teachers and administrators who would like to see the school exercise a more conservative function in our society.

The meaningless (or at best half-truth) nature of this slogan is easily discovered when we try to identify what is meant by "frills." The extracurricular activities, maybe? Vocational subjects, with the special teachers and special shops they require? Modern school plants? Audio-visual teaching equipment? New books for the libraries? Good teachers? Inside plumbing?

All of these might be called frills—if by frills we mean the things that cost quite a bit of money, or the things we didn't use to have in the schools "when I was a boy!" But what some people think of as frills are looked upon by others as essentials. It is not possible to get either the general public or professional educators to agree among themselves—much less to reach agreement between the groups—as to what really constitutes these "frills" we ought to get rid of.

This statement about "frills," then, doesn't really mean much. Instead of putting it into our discard pile of superannuated slogans, however, maybe we should inject it with new meaning by redefining frills—luxuries we *can't* afford in our educational system. What are some of these frills we really ought to cut out? We could make some suggestions:

—the luxury of antiquated local control of schools, when localism interferes with efficient school operation

—the luxury of low tax rates, maintained at the cost of the educational future of our children

—the luxury of monolithic, impressive school buildings, built as monuments to civic pride

—an exclusively college-preparatory curriculum, because it's more "respectable" than vocational training

—maintenance of snobbish "scholastic" standards for grade promotion or high school graduation

—avoidance of school responsibility for such expensive or "difficult" instructional areas as driver education and family-life education

—overemphasis on one part of the school program to inflate local pride—a winning team, say, at the expense of laboratory equipment

—racial or religious bigotry condoned or implemented by school policy because we want to keep "our kind of people" together

As you read this list, you may be a bit puzzled; these are not the kinds of extras or luxuries people mean when they talk about cutting out the frills in education! Besides, some of the statements above are not really very clear! You are quite right; the list is meant to provoke discussion, to start a new train of thought. Try it for size on the next person who suggests we "cut the frills in education."

"Competition Is the Lifeblood of Achievement"

Critics of modern education are quite vocal in this complaint about the public schools; gone, they say, are the good old days when competition made each person strive to excel and raised the general level of school achievement. Nowadays, they would contend, the school has ruled out competition; everybody passes, nobody fails. How can the school prepare young American citizens to take their place in a competitive, free-enterprise economic system unless they get the habit of competing in school?

Thus, the critics complain, modern education is failing to develop good learners, good citizens, and good participants in our economic system—all because competition has been abandoned in the schools. How accurate is this charge? Again, the half-truth of the statement, "competition is the lifeblood of achievement," is even further devaluated by the tacit insistence that one must take an absolute position: either you are for competition or you are against it. The modern school (and the thoughtful modern teacher) does not find it necessary to approve or disapprove of competition as such. The either-or choice is simply not valid.

Competition is a good, a positive educational good, when it is *fair, healthy, controlled*. But competition as practiced in the school, and encouraged by the school, has often had these very serious faults:

1. It creates a false sense of values—grades, gold stars, honor rolls, or the various means of indicating "failure" are often mere extrinsic rewards or punishments; they have nothing to do with whether or not a student is really learning and growing to the best of his ability.
2. Competitive practices in education often result in a flat denial of the importance of individual differences. Why should the slow learner or the handicapped reader be placed in direct competition with the brighter, more able student— and judged according to how well he does in an unfair and unrealistic competition?
3. Competition may get in the way of the learning process. Cheap rewards in the form of grades, for example, make it likely that the able student will work only as hard as he must to get the recognition he cherishes; the less able student may give up trying to learn and concentrate on just passing.

The modern school has not discarded competition; it has made an effort to use the competitive spirit in more healthy, rewarding ways. For example, some critics deplore the passing of the old-fashioned spelldown. Nostalgic recollection pictures this peculiar teaching technique as a fine example of interesting, challenging, healthy competition. It *was* a certain amount of fun—for the better spellers. But the students who needed the spelling practice and experience the most (the poorest spellers) got the least of it; they soon lost out and quickly went to their seats. And the best spellers, who did not need the practice encouraged by the competition, stayed at the head of the class and got the practice needed by somebody else.

The tendency for the modern school to replace competition *in part* with cooperation, and especially the present-day emphasis on each student's competing with his own past record or his own best possibility—these are evidences not of weakness in modern education, but of progress. Cooperation can include humane and sensible competition; no absolute choice between the two techniques must be made.

"There's Too Much Progressive Education in the Schools"

The most thoroughly standardized educational platitude today would appear to be this: blame anything you don't like about the schools on progressive education. This is the large, economy-size, all-purpose criticism to make of education today. It shows that the speaker has thoroughly assessed the strengths and weaknesses of the American educational system, and has come to the scholarly conclusion that all of the troubles are attributable to what he has carefully distinguished as "progressive education." Or does it? Maybe it shows, more often, our human tendency to repeat what we have heard others say, to express dissatisfaction where we should be admitting ignorance, and to find a scapegoat for our own failures (individual and collective) to support and provide for a good system of public education.

When we hear the mistakes and weakness of the American schools blamed on "too much progressive education" we may be reminded of the apocryphal story about the cynic who maintained that Christianity was obviously impractical; "It just won't work," he said. "How do you know?" questioned his friend. "It's never been tried!" And so with progressive education; the basic insights, theories, and implication of this modern view of education we call "progressive" have never really been tried. Except in a scant handful of notable experimental schools, progressivism *as such* was never really given a real chance.

A great number of American schools, public and private, attempted to put into practice some of the ideas that underlay the general educational movement we have come to call "progressive," but most of the attempts were either superficial, partial, or inadequate. Progressivism was not so much a set of plans or detailed procedures as a point of view about education and society; emphasis upon personal, social, and intellectual freedom; emphasis upon education as a nat-

"Progressive education — Bah!!"

ural process, working *with* the grain of human nature, not against it; emphasis upon the social responsibility of education as a vital force in human living, both within and outside of the school itself. It was very easy for educators to see a part of this broad picture, or for schools to try certain of the instructional methods it suggested, without ever really getting at the heart of the progressive movement.

We must distinguish between early (or naïve) and later (or more mature) progressive education. The period from the turn of the century until the early 'thirties marked the rise of what might be called naïve progressivism; the period since the early 'thirties has given American education a more mature, more balanced kind of progressive education.

Early progressivism was marked by a distinctly negative outlook; it was a reaction against the sterile, authoritarian, book-centered, repressive educational practices common in American schools at the turn of the century. It was bold, brash, critical, and radical. It emphasized doing away with traditional practices rather than proposing specific new direction and new techniques in education. Its key word was *freedom*—freedom for the individual; freedom of activity; freedom from authority; freedom from established institutions, from established moral and social restrictions; freedom for each child to develop according to his own unique "life-style," and to grow and learn and experiment in his own way, and at his own rate.

Early progressivism, then, was essentially destructive rather than constructive, individualistic rather than social, radical rather than evolutionary. This is, of course, a generalization, and, like most such generalizations, a rather rash one. But as we note the fundamental changes in later or more mature progressivism, the basic accuracy of the characterization of early progressivism as "naïve" can be recognized.

The best way to help us see how the progressive movement developed would be to look at specific ideas that are generally associated with this movement and see how these ideas changed as schools had an opportunity to try them out and as educational appraisal of these practices resulted in the modifying of earlier doctrines.

For example, many of the early progressive schools tried out quite literally the idea that children should be allowed to do as they pleased. This obviously would not work in a social setting such as is found in the public schools. It was Dewey himself, as we mentioned previously in this chapter, who cautioned would-be progressives that unlimited freedom for children was neither practical nor of real educational value. Impulse and desire are not the same as purpose; the child can be as arbitrary as the authoritarian teacher, he said.[7] Freedom for the child, then, must in any social setting be limited by the rights of others and the basic needs of the child himself. Progressive schools learned this lesson in just the way that (according to their beliefs) all real learnings are brought about—by direct experience. Finding out how wrong they could be was not a pleasant experience for these schools. There were growing pains as the schools experimented with the concept of child freedom. The schools did learn, however, and as a result modified their practices so that today the ordinary public school allows a great deal more freedom for children and youth—infinitely more, in fact, than schools of an older generation would have thought permissible. But this freedom is not the complete, untrammeled, ridiculous "freedom" that the ordinary layman often associates with the term progressive education. The mistakes were corrected, but the popular misconception lingers on.

Another example: Dewey and the other most able proponents of

[7] Dewey, *Experience and Education*, p. 75. Reprinted by permission.

progressivism decried the overuse of adult authority, the (sometimes benevolent) despotism that so generally characterized the schools of the early part of this century. Some well-meaning but poorly-informed progressive experimenters took this to mean that all adult control should be abandoned in the classroom. A few radically progressive schools were characterized by an anarchic bedlam that was just as unsound educationally as the previous authoritarianism—and a lot worse for public relations. For although the modern schools gradually learned another lesson—that a degree of adult authority in the classroom is necessary to meet the real needs of the children—and although Dewey cautioned his followers that they must understand that it is *absurd,*[8] as he said, to exclude the teacher from the organization and operation of the learning process—even so, the general public got the idea that all progressive schools had been "turned over to the kids." Even though Dewey warned his fellow-experimenters in education that the teacher *has no moral right* [9] to withhold from the class the benefits of his greater wisdom and maturity, some teachers and a large segment of the lay public continued to believe that progressivism in education meant the complete abdication of the teacher. Progressivism came to be synonymous in public belief with the total withdrawal of adult authority and guidance.

One more example of how progressives in the early years (a) first overdid or misunderstood a basically sound principle, (b) later corrected their mistakes, but (c) are still blamed popularly for perpetuating and advocating an obviously untenable educational practice: the advocacy of "learning without planning." Certain of the early progressives took the valid progressive objection to adult *domination* of the learning activities to mean that there should be no planned learning activities whatsoever, no formal curriculum, no lesson plans, no scheduled activities, no subject matter, and—above all—no drill. The complete formlessness of the education advocated by such experimenters was, of course, a failure. Able leaders of the progressive movement again cautioned the radical element against misunderstanding the basic learning principles involved and against carrying a basically good idea to a ridiculous extreme.

Thoughtful proponents of progressivism pointed out that the concept of pupil-teacher planning did not mean less planning, but more; the teacher should *share* the planning of learning experiences and

[8] *Ibid.,* pp. 64-66. Reprinted by permission.
[9] *Ibid.,* pp. 32 f. Reprinted by permission.

activities, not just give up planning altogether. The curriculum of the more traditional school was entirely too limited, too formal, too verbalistic—but that did not mean at all that a good progressive school should try to throw out the whole concept of curriculum as a sequence of carefully planned materials and activities for learning. True enough, much of the drill found in the more traditional schools was useless or even harmful educationally and psychologically; but drill was still necessary—for drill is a part of many learning experiences, a kind of activity that fits in very well with progressive principles of education, if it is used correctly. Meaningless, punitive drill? No. Motivated repetition of usable skills? Absolutely yes! "The basic materials of study," warned Dewey, "cannot be picked up in a cursory fashion!" [10]

We have devoted several paragraphs to this one popular educational platitude, "There's too much progressive education in the schools today," for several important reasons. First, this is one of the commonest criticisms, and because it is so common, otherwise well-informed adults repeat it constantly without really—if we may be brutally frank—knowing what they are talking about. Second, early proponents of experimental and radical progressivism made some mistakes—they didn't really understand the basic principles of the new movement, and/or they pushed what was a sound practice to ridiculous extremes. We must honestly admit the many mistakes of early progressive education. And finally, it is important that we understand that whatever is wrong with American public education today is probably, in the vast majority of schools at least, not too much but *too little* sound understanding and application of the basic beliefs of progressive education *at its best*. Children and youth in American public schools today, we submit (and this is debatable, of course), do not have too much freedom; they have too little freedom—of the right sort, appropriate to their maturity, their needs, and exercised under competent adult guidance. The children and youth of today do not have an excess of opportunity to develop serviceable and satisfactory individual personalities—they have too little, in crowded classrooms with crowded schedules; personality development is being underdone, not overdone. And so with the whole list of the basic beliefs of modern, mature, *proved* progressive principles. Not too much, but too little; we need to try progressive education and see if it really *will* work!

[10] *Ibid.*, p. 96. Reprinted by permission.

"Let's Go Back to the Three R's"

This phrase is one of the most commonly heard in discussions of education today. It's a simple, easy thing to say; it implies that the speaker understands just what is wrong with our schools, and knows just what should be done to remedy all of the present educational deficiencies: go back to the three R's! So simple, so comprehensive— and so misleading! For we can't "go back" to something we have never left; there is very little evidence, except in the "feelings" some people have on the subject, that the modern school has ever quit teaching the fundamentals of reading, writing, and arithmetic.

The good old days never were so good as they are painted in rosy-tinted memory. The older generation has always looked back with nostalgic pride on their own educational experiences and achievement, and compared the younger generation's education unfavorably with their own. The author of a survey [11] of present-day criticism of the schools recounts the story of an ancient clay tablet recently discovered by archaeologists which contains the lament of a father concerning his son's poor education. In hieroglyphic characters the father spelled out his charges against the schools of his time: his son couldn't keep the accounts straight in the shop, couldn't write legibly, and couldn't get along with the customers; the money spent on his education had been wasted!

Down through the ages has come the complaint—no doubt often quite valid—that the schools aren't teaching the fundamentals, or at least the students aren't learning what the schools try to teach. Today, most of the alleged failures of education are blamed on progressivism, but there is considerable evidence that the problem existed long before any progressive influences were felt in the schools. In an 1894 report by a Harvard University committee on composition and rhetoric we find this complaint recorded: "At Harvard, as the committee demonstrates, the unhappy instructors are confronted with immature thoughts, set down in a crabbed and slovenly hand, miserably expressed and wretchedly spelled, and yet the average age of admission is 19." [12]

Since adults have never, apparently, been completely satisfied with how today's schools compare with the good old days, we should not

[11] Ann Usher, "Are the Schools Neglecting the 3-R's?" *Better Homes and Gardens,* Vol. 31, No. 10 (October, 1953), p. 204.
[12] *Ibid.* Reprinted by permission.

be surprised to find a continuing pattern of criticism of the newer education. But it is not very reassuring for teachers to tell the critics of modern education that we can't pay any attention to them because "people have always complained about the schools." We cannot very well dismiss the critics of modern education with the offhand statement that, after all, the schools have never been able to satisfy everybody. And in reply to the charges that the schools don't teach the fundamentals it is not very illuminating for defenders of the modern school simply to shout back, "We do *so* teach the fundamentals!"

There is, of course, no absolutely valid way of *proving* that the present-day schools are better than older schools, that the fundamentals are not being neglected, but we can make some interesting "then and now" comparisons that are at least indicative of educational progress. Much of this "comparative" research has been published in the educational and popular magazines in recent years; we have space here to report only a very few samples of the results.

A survey test originally given to a very select group of students in the Boston grammar schools in 1845 was again given to some 12,000 unselected students in cooperating school systems throughout the United States in 1919. The 1919 pupils did considerably (though not remarkably) better than the "cream of the crop" Bostonians of some 75 years earlier. In Cleveland, tests which had been given for admission to high school in 1848 were administered to a comparable group of students in the same school system 99 years later, in 1947. The scores of ten best students were compared, and it was found that the 1947 group scored more correct answers than the earlier group; the present-day students did a little better in word definitions, mental arithmetic, and practical arithmetic, but not so well as the earlier group in American history, grammar, and geography.[13]

Many other examples of the then-and-now studies could be cited but such comparisons are not really very significant. The tests which were given several generations ago covered different subject matters than are studied by present-day students; the earlier groups were in general much more selected (in 1850, for example, only 3 per cent of high-school-age youth were in high school; today the figure is nearly 85 per cent); and both the tests and the methods of scoring were insufficiently standardized to make statistical comparisons possible. Despite these handicaps, the modern student shows up surprisingly well. A spokesman for the NEA Research Division summarizes the

[13] Frank W. Hubbard, "Volleyed and Thundered," *NEA Journal,* Vol. 43, No. 7 (October, 1954), p. 339.

results of comparisons between the typical school children of the 19th and 20th centuries as follows:

> The following may be stated with substantial assurance in comparing "typical" school children of the 19th and 20th centuries:
>
> 1. In reading—The child of today in most instances reads silently more rapidly and with more understanding; he reads a larger variety of material; he reads many more publications. He may not read as well orally as Grandpa.
> 2. In spelling—With the words in common use, today's child spells better than the child of the past century. On uncommon words he isn't likely to do quite as well, and on rare and "spelling-demon" words he is definitely poorer than the typical school child of the past.
> 3. In arithmetic—Today's child does as well on processes in common use and a little better on "thought" problems. On processes that have become obsolete or have been postponed to later grades he does less well during the elementary school period; he usually "catches up" on the postponed items by the time he completes Grade IX.
> 4. In handwriting—Today's child doesn't do as well in the copy book writing so admired prior to 1910; he develops a simple style suitable for most purposes.
> 5. In history—The typical child today has more understanding of the meaning of history as related to the affairs of everyday life; he is less skilled in repeating lists of specific names and dates.
> 6. In geography—On the basic facts today's child does as well; he is likely to have a better grasp of the significance of geographical facts as related to commerce, air travel, and international affairs; he may be less able to repeat the names of countries, capitals, rivers, and other geographical features, formerly memorized in list form.
> 7. In English language—In oral and written expression the typical child of the 20th century far surpasses the child of the past century in originality and selfdirection; his scores on the basic rules of punctuation and grammar will be as high, if not higher. He may show less familiarity with the classics of prose and poetry, so often memorized in large amounts prior to 1900.
> 8. In the modern languages—The typical child today acquires some knowledge of one of the modern foreign languages; the typical child of the past century had little contact with modern languages in public schools.
> 9. In science—Today's typical child is so much better informed in science that it is a waste of time to consider any comparison with the typical school child of the 19th century who was given a smattering of "natural philosophy," some of which was true and had some possible use.

The foregoing is a telescopic view of what is true in general as far as can be determined on the basis of the studies up to the present. The gist simply is: The typical school child today does as well or better in the so-called "fundamental subjects" as compared with his typical predecessor of 40 or 50 years ago. And in addition, certain things are true:

1. He makes progress in the "three R's" more efficiently and by less expenditure of school time.
2. He has a better understanding and makes more use of the facts and skills acquired.
3. In the time saved he has more systematic instruction in a number of new fields such as healthful living, recreation, civics, science, intercultural relations, current events, international affairs, public speaking, music, practical arts, and fine arts. On these phases of modern education no comparisons can be made because they were given little or no attention in the earlier schools and because relatively few standardized tests exist.[14]

This statement, of course, would not be acceptable to many critics of modern education; they would simply reply that *of course* educators will defend their own practices! But there are real evidences that the good old days never really existed, that there is today more learning and better learning. The evidence is not all in, the battle is not won; but we have enough data so that we can give a reassuring reply to the popular challenge, "Let's go back to the three R's."

"Psychologists Tell Us . . ."

This is the opening gambit in a great number of the most popular of the educational platitudes. Many educators and laymen attempt to defend a particular—and sometimes untenable—point of view by claiming a broad authority which is specified only in the phrase "psychologists tell us." It is one of the most dangerous of the educational platitudes precisely because it does sound so authoritative—and may or may not be true. The science of psychology has made tremendously important contributions to the advancement of the cause of modern education, but careless quoting or easy acceptance of every new bit of psychological research or theory as gospel truth has been harmful and upsetting—to educators and to lay citizens alike.

The difficulties with uncritical acceptance of all that is called psy-

[14] *Ibid.*, pp. 399 f. Reprinted by permission.

chology are many. First of all, we are sometimes likely to assume that an *existing* popular belief or practice becomes demonstrably wrong just because it is challenged by a new psychological finding. The commonly accepted view is scorned, the new opinion accepted as "the latest thing." Another difficulty is that psychology is only in the process of becoming an exact science; it is entitled to its mistakes and its growing pains—and has had plenty of them. Still another danger in uncritical acceptance of each new psychological viewpoint is our failure to realize that psychology *does* change; what may have been the best thinking of psychological research in 1920 may now be entirely outmoded by recent findings.

This is not the place to discuss psychological theory in any detail —you will have ample opportunity to study psychology elsewhere in your program of teacher education—but it does give a certain needed balance to our psychological outlook if we remember that each of the great modern psychologists has made some mistakes as well as some tremendous contributions. Each of the "schools" of psychology has been important in adding to our understanding of human behavior, but there is scarcely an educator today who would care to commit himself heart and soul to being an unswerving disciple of Watson, Thorndike, Freud, or any other great psychologist.

Parents, too, have been confused by shifts in psychological viewpoint. First they were told by some psychologists to go all-out for a "permissive" attitude; more recently they have been warned *not* to be "neutral parents." At one point in twentieth-century psychological thinking, the child was not to be caressed at all; later he was held whenever he cried (the demand schedule); still later parents were advised to adhere to a strict by-the-clock schedule; and now a balance of flexibility and order in the child's schedule is advised. Small wonder that parents are sometimes confused and suspicious when the word "psychology" is mentioned.

But psychology and psychologists are not to blame; the blame rests with those of us (a) who have failed to assess the logic of new theories and new "discoveries," (b) who have failed to identify and check our "authorities" for what we say and what we believe about psychology, and (c) who have uncritically embraced any new idea and perhaps carried it to a ridiculous extreme just because it was labeled psychology.

The solution to the educational problems posed by that seemingly valid cliché, "Well, psychologists tell us . . ." is quite simple: more careful study, more critical thinking, more independence of judgment before we accept at face value the new (and changing) "truths" about human behavior.

"We Teach Them How to Think, Not What to Think"

Proponents of modern educational methods resort to this innocent-sounding platitude whenever they are confronted with a particularly pointed question about what the schools are teaching. It *sounds* innocuous enough, but this simple statement creates all sorts of trouble for the schools. The statement originally meant simply this: that the modern school is opposed to indoctrination and in favor of careful thinking. Unfortunately, it came to be used as an excuse for an inexcusable neutrality on important questions, an easy way out of taking a stand on issues that the school must face if it is to do its job well. The statement gives the unfortunate impression that modern education has, in rejecting any taint of authoritarianism in teaching, also rejected the idea of values, of the relative importance of different ideas, of significant goals and aims as central to education.

The either-or position implied is simply not tenable. "How to think" is *not the opposite* of "what to think." There is no point in knowing the techniques of using the intelligence unless that skill is put to use. The *how* and the *what* of thinking must operate together, not independently. Furthermore, the thought process is not complete if it results in the indefinite suspension of judgment. *Commitment* is part of thinking; if one thinks well and effectively he must reach conclusions, and those conclusions must result in specific actions. The modern school in a democracy must believe that certain values are important; living in a democracy is in itself a commitment to and acceptance of a democratic value system.

We betray our own lack of appreciation of the purpose of education if we try to deny that the school must do some teaching of what to think. What is more, we unnecessarily alienate the laymen who support and control the school if we insist that the school is intertested only in the "how" of thinking. Here again, as we have discovered in our analysis of some other statements above, is a statement that is so easy to make and so hard to defend. If we really believe that education is important, that it has a job to do, we will drop forever from our professional vocabulary such an oversimplification as this: "We teach them how to think, not what to think." We do both; and the platitude that so glibly denies the responsibility that is rightly ours should be quietly but firmly laid to rest.

FOURTEEN: TOPICS FOR STUDY, REPORT, AND DISCUSSION

1. Read some article of your choice in a current professional magazine and find and analyze any *educational platitudes* it contains.
2. What are some of the educational platitudes you have already run across in professional education courses you have taken?
3. Read some current criticism of modern public education and pick out the platitudes that the critic appears to be using to bolster his criticism.
4. How did you get "interested" in your favorite recreation or hobby? To what extent was effort involved in the building of this interest?
5. Jot down some of the most important truths about the psychology of human behavior that you can recall. Now, analyze the list to see how (a) authoritative, (b) logical, and (c) verifiable it is. Where did you get your information?
6. Ask several adults with whom you are acquainted, and whom you know to be quite critical of modern education, just what is wrong with present-day schools. Bring a list of the criticisms (but not of the critics!) to class and discuss them with other members of the class.

FOURTEEN: BIBLIOGRAPHY

Abraham, Willard, "Let's Clean Our Own House!" *Educational Leadership,* Vol. XII, No. 1 (October, 1954), 39-43. Penetrating self-analysis of some of the shortcomings of our educational "gobbledygook" by a writer who is himself a professor of education.

Association for Supervision and Curriculum Development, *Forces Affecting American Education,* 1953 Yearbook. Washington, D. C.: National Education Association, 1953. Chap. 5 reports on some of the "then and now" research that tends to refute popular, stereotyped criticisms that modern education is a failure.

Bode, Boyd H., *Progressive Education at the Crossroads.* New York: Newson & Co., 1938. One of the landmarks in the development of progressive education; Bode was one of the first to warn against the common oversimplifications of the movement. Brief and readable.

Dewey, John, *Experience and Education.* New York: The Macmillan Co., 1938. An excellent summary of the views of mature progressivism by its most authoritative spokesman. Warns against easy misinterpretations of what progressivism means. Brief and not too difficult.

Ernst, Frederic, "How Dangerous Is John Dewey?" *The Atlantic Monthly,* Vol. 191, No. 5 (May, 1953), 59-62. Middle-of-the-road defense of Dewey-type progressive education.

Harris, Raymond, *American Education: Facts, Fancies, and Folklore.* New York: Random House, 1961. Discusses popular educational platitudes as "folklore," "fantasy," and "myth." Not uncritical, but well balanced.

Hill, Gladwin, "A Father Looks at Progressive Education," *The Atlantic Monthly,* Vol. 194, No. 6 (December, 1954), 55 ff. Describes the author's favorable reactions to mature progressivism, after his having been previously indoctrinated in what he calls the "anarchy-and-ignorance" views of progressive education popularly held.

Lynd, Albert, "Who Wants Progressive Education?" *The Atlantic Monthly,* Vol. 191, No. 4 (April, 1953), 24-34. Very critical appraisal of the influence of progressivism on American schools. Not very accurate.

Mayer, Martin, *The Schools.* New York: Harper & Row, Publishers, 1961. A somewhat journalistic survey of contemporary education, critical and not entirely free of the platitudes discussed in this chapter.

Trace, Arthur S., Jr., *What Ivan Knows that Johnny Doesn't.* New York: Random House, 1961. Purports to show the failure of contemporary U.S. education in contrast with that of Russia.

Walcutt, Charles C., *Tomorrow's Illiterates.* Boston: Atlantic-Little, Brown, 1961. Highly critical attack on modern reading methods; conclusions should be accepted with caution.

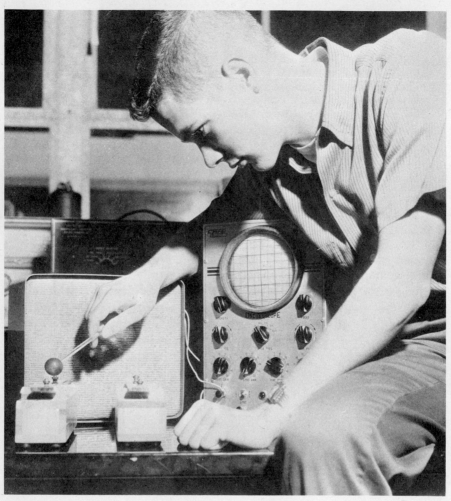

Individual vocational study. *How do
programs of specific vocational training help reduce the number of drop-
outs?*

CHAPTER FIFTEEN

The Importance of What Teachers Think

A leading educational psychologist has said that, in the long run, what teachers think about educational problems is more important than what they know about education. There are many questions and controversies in American education which depend for an answer or solution not so much on the acquisition and interpretation of specific facts as on society's answer to the basic question, "What do we want our schools to do?" The teacher is in an especially strategic position with respect to these questions and problems; what the teacher thinks about these matters is important. First, the teacher is a full-fledged *member* of the society which must think its way through these problems, come to a decision, and put that group decision into practice; as a citizen in our society, the teacher's knowledge and opinions are important. Second, the teacher is a *professional employee* of the society—community, state, and nation—that supports the school; as such, the teacher is literally duty-bound to carry out the collective will of the democratic society he serves. Finally, the teacher is a *professional leader;* he has the right and obligation to take a leadership role in educational matters, just as we would expect the busi-

SOME UNSOLVED
PROBLEMS

nessman to be an informed and effective leader in the economic life of the community.

Because it does matter what we as teachers *think* about educational problems, we shall examine in this chapter several important issues in modern education. There will be no attempt to present here all of the facts or opinions about these problems, or even to supply a neat list of the pro-and-con arguments which are used to support divergent opinions. We are not trying to decide these questions right now, or even to understand all of the implications or ramifications of each one of them. Rather, we as teachers need to be alerted, need to make ourselves aware of some of the larger issues in education. And the term "larger issues" is used here not just because it is a pious-sounding, mouth-filling phrase; quite literally the problems of this chapter are *larger* issues than the very important but relatively limited questions of school organization and support, new developments in curriculum, and the place of teachers' organizations in our professional growth and welfare.

You may begin to suspect, at this point, that you are about to be given a quick overview of the philosophy of education. Not at all; the questions to be discussed in this chapter are, it is true, basically philosophical questions, but the treatment of them here could not be dignified by the name "philosophy." Perhaps all we can present here is a brief introduction to some of these educational problems, an introduction that will make us want to pursue some of the basic issues involved 'way back to their philosophical bases in cosmic views of the nature of man, of society, of truth, and of God. But not right here!

Who Shall Be Educated?

At first glance, this may not seem like a realistic question to ask about our own American system of education. The answer appears obvious: everybody! That's the great American dream, translated into educational opportunity and educational policy; in our country, education is universal, compulsory, free. It is not limited to a chosen few or to those who by fortune of being wellborn or financially well-off can afford the prestige and luxury of going to school.

That's the American educational ideal, all right, and we have a real right to be proud to claim it as our own. (We recognize, of course, that many other countries have similar educational ideals, and in talking about these ideals as *ours* we do not deprecate the educational systems of other peoples of the civilized world.) Not only are these ideals commendable features of our national educational policy, but they are surprisingly well translated into practice. Each of the 50 states has laws designed to insure that education will be free, universal, compulsory, and open to all children and youth regardless of economic status or social "class." But there are still several problems in determining who shall be educated *in actual practice*.

Not Everyone Goes to School

We usually think of the years 5-19 as school-age years; it is easy to assume that all children and youth of school age—well, *nearly* all —are in some sort of school. Nationally, about 90.2 per cent of all school-age persons *are* in school, though in some states the percentage is nearer 70 than 90. Pretty good, we may say, especially in comparison with some other countries. The 90 per cent figure *is* good— for those in school. But what about the 10 per cent who are not in school? This group constitutes a continual rebuke and challenge to our American school system. Many of those not in school are members of minority groups—mostly Puerto Ricans, Spanish Americans, American Indians, and Negroes—many of them citizens, but economically, socially, and educationally, men without a country. Others of the not-in-school group are staying home because they have no decent clothing or no shoes, or are needed to help earn a living for the family. Others of our children and youth are in institutions for the mentally or physically handicapped, or—bitter shame to them and to the American educational system—in prison. Others are not in school simply because they have "dropped out," as the records will show—why, we often do not know.

The Problem of "Drop-outs"

We are all generally aware that a good many students who start high school drop out before completion of their secondary school work, but it is a bit startling to see how serious this problem is, viewed state-by-state or nationally. (See Figure V, p. 381.) The percentage of eighth-grade students who do *not* complete high school ranges from a low of 6.9 in Wisconsin to a high of 66.4 in Mississippi.

In nineteen of the states, more than 40 per cent of high school students drop out before graduation. In general, these states with a high drop-out percentage are in the South, but so advanced a state educationally as Pennsylvania loses nearly 35 per cent of its high school students prior to completion of their secondary school work.

It is interesting, if disheartening, to note that the states with the highest drop-out rates are, almost without a single exception, the states which have the highest percentage of draft registrants rejected for educational deficiencies. Simply in terms of national defense, can we afford to have up to 56 per cent of the otherwise eligible draft registrants in a given state excused from military service largely because the public schools are somehow unable to qualify these young men *educationally* for service in the armed forces?

The loss in defense potential is just one of the problems created, at least in part, by a high incidence of drop-outs. The economic losses are even more significant. It is almost universally true that economic conditions are distinctly better in those states which have the most effective educational systems. Tens of thousands of these high school "drop-outs" are perfectly able young men and young women intellectually; the economic loss represented by their failure or inability for some reason to complete even a secondary-school program is, in an economy desperately in need of well-trained and technically-trained workers, a tragic waste of manpower and economic potential. The social problems caused by these "early leavers" from school are also very serious. Many of these young folk who leave high school early do quite well in later life, but thousands of them have lost forever their opportunity to prepare for maximum participation in the complexities of modern life. As persons, as parents, and as voting citizens they are not nearly so well prepared for adult responsibilities as they would be had they finished high school. The educational waste represented by the failure of these young men and women to take advantage of their opportunities in school is much less important to our society than the economic and social losses that are caused by the drop-out problem.

Should Everyone Complete High School?

As you have been reading the preceding paragraphs, you have probably been translating these statements about the tens of thousands who do not complete high school into more understandable and prac-

FIGURE V

HIGH-SCHOOL GRADUATES IN 1955-56 AS A PER CENT
OF EIGHTH-GRADE ENROLLMENT IN 1951-52

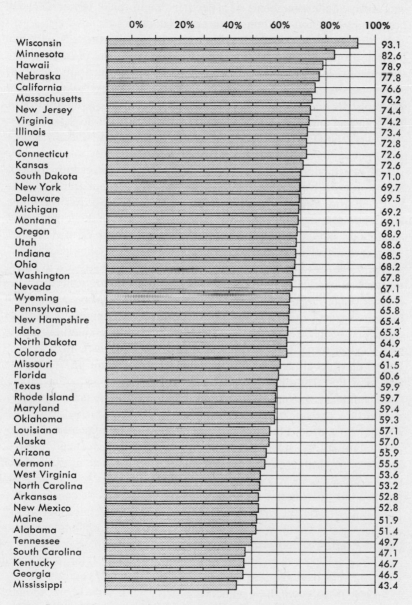

State	0% 20% 40% 60% 80% 100%	Value
Wisconsin		93.1
Minnesota		82.6
Hawaii		78.9
Nebraska		77.8
California		76.6
Massachusetts		76.2
New Jersey		74.4
Virginia		74.2
Illinois		73.4
Iowa		72.8
Connecticut		72.6
Kansas		72.6
South Dakota		71.0
New York		69.7
Delaware		69.5
Michigan		69.2
Montana		69.1
Oregon		68.9
Utah		68.6
Indiana		68.5
Ohio		68.2
Washington		67.8
Nevada		67.1
Wyoming		66.5
Pennsylvania		65.8
New Hampshire		65.4
Idaho		65.3
North Dakota		64.9
Colorado		64.4
Missouri		61.5
Florida		60.6
Texas		59.9
Rhode Island		59.7
Maryland		59.4
Oklahoma		59.3
Louisiana		57.1
Alaska		57.0
Arizona		55.9
Vermont		55.5
West Virginia		53.6
North Carolina		53.2
Arkansas		52.8
New Mexico		52.8
Maine		51.9
Alabama		51.4
Tennessee		49.7
South Carolina		47.1
Kentucky		46.7
Georgia		46.5
Mississippi		43.4

tical terms. Instead of thinking in national percentages, you have perhaps been remembering specific drop-outs of your own acquaintance, people who started out in high school with you but "quit" before graduation. A few moments of reflection should recall to mind several —perhaps dozens—of young men and women of your own age—your grade school and junior high school friends and classmates—who got sidetracked somewhere in the early or even later years of high school. Try to remember them: "Where is old Jim now, do you suppose? Whatever happened to Emily, the girl who sat next to me in the sophomore home room? And are Bill and Jerry still hanging around the pool hall and beer joints—they were suspended from school when they were juniors, and never did come back. Never did get steady jobs, either; just bums, maybe. But now Roberta got married when she was a sophomore; she left school and has a couple of kids, I think. She didn't much care for school anyway, and her husband's a good guy who runs the service station on Main Street. She did all right. And Billy left high school when he was a senior; joined the Army, came out a sergeant, got a good job in the radio shop. He did all right too—better than some of the dopes that did get high school diplomas."

And so it goes. As you actually think of the "drop-outs" you know, not just the statistics and percentages that spell out the national picture, a serious question may arise in your mind. Maybe a sort of natural weeding-out process occurs during high school, a sort of Darwinian "survival of the fittest." Maybe everyone shouldn't try to or be expected to finish high school. Maybe we have oversold ourselves on this American ideal of universal education, "secondary education for all American youth."

It could be. As our high schools have become so heterogeneous, so almost completely unselective, the problem of providing a curriculum or, more accurately, a series of learning activities and experiences—suitable for everybody and designed to keep everybody in high school until graduation has provided some king-sized headaches for the secondary school. Yet, almost any kind of high school experience for the students is better than no high school at all; if we can just keep them under the slight and part-time influence of the school, keep them off the streets, let them at least *grow up* before the school loses its last slim hold on them—even these minimal goals of secondary education are preferable to just giving up and saying, "Here's the high school; if you don't like it, get out."

Trying to keep youth in school who don't want to be there, though, has serious difficulties. We must agree with the critics of modern education that *in some cases* secondary education for everybody has meant a watering-down of the legitimate high school curriculum to a point of academic thinness that cannot be justified. It has meant that as the high schools no longer cater to a select group, and the average ability of high school students—by the operation of the inexorable law of averages—goes down (and it surely has), the schools themselves have responded to this change by lowering standards and pitching the work of the high school at the level of the lowest common denominator—and that can be pretty low! Moreover, if the school emphasizes the custodial function of just "keeping" the youth in school, the educational function may be neglected. Moreover, those who are merely "kept" in school can have, and often do have, "educational" experiences that are definitely harmful. The student who is not at all interested in staying in high school can develop habits of intellectual and moral slovenliness, outright physical and/or emotional rebellion against all forms of authority, order, and discipline, or what is perhaps the most serious of all, a deep and all-pervading apathy toward the people and the life around him.

Most educators and laymen, therefore, are in general agreement that we should first of all try to adjust the high school curriculum to the real needs of youth and of society, not to some academic tradition or set of artificial "standards" left over from a previous period in our culture when secondary education was frankly a privilege for a relatively select few or primarily a type of education designed to prepare for college entrance. Three aspects of the high school program need especial attention: (1) more meaningful and more appropriate vocational education (including preparation for the vocation of marriage); (2) more attention to individual differences in the academic curriculum (so that we will not always be operating at the level of the lowest common denominator); and (3) a better guidance program so that the high school can help individual students to meet their own needs and make their own adjustments at the same time that they become better prepared to assume adult responsibilities for group living and national citizenship.

At the same time that most educators and laymen are quite unanimous in suggesting these improvements, they find general agreement in the statement that everyone should stay in school only so long as that school experience is the most profitable that can be provided. When a student can no longer profit from continuing his high school education, then he should do something else. The difficulty is this: how can we determine when a student has reached the point of no-further-profit in his formal education? And who should make the determination to terminate the student's formal educational career? And what kind (if any) of part-time continuation education should be provided for those whose continued attendance in the regular high school has been deemed no longer profitable? These questions cannot be answered now; we simply do not know the answers. But the problem of who should be educated and for how long is one of the major educational issues to which teachers and other citizens must be alert, one which makes a tremendous difference in the kind and extent of education which our society is willing to provide.

What Is Society's Responsibility for "Free Education"?

Closely related to the problem of who shall be educated is this one, "How free should education be?" We often assume that public education is indeed free, just as our national ideals say it should be. As a matter of fact, however, free public education is still only a partially realized ideal; education is by no means universally and completely free, even up through elementary and high school.

Direct and Hidden Costs

All of the states do provide free tuition, in the sense that no direct charge is made against the children or their parents for instruction as such. Many states, however, provide free textbooks only in the elementary school, if at all; many school systems make a charge for instructional extras like workbooks and laboratory materials; the so-called extracurricular activities almost universally require special fees, direct or indirect, to be paid by the parents through their children.

Harl Douglass, one of the most eminent students of our educational system, has described the present status of free public education graphically when he writes:

> Starting first with admissions to athletic events and to plays, class pins, and a modest school annual, the costs in some schools have increased to more than a hundred dollars per pupil, including costumes, dues in clubs, school parties and dances, subscriptions to school papers and to periodicals for use in classes, rental fees for typewriters, laboratory fees, library fees, school

jewelry, initiation into fraternities and sororities, use of automobiles for school functions, workbooks and materials for shop and instruction, and a school annual, copies of which sell for as much as college annuals used to, but which involves also costs for pictures, usually running into several dollars.

As a result of these increased costs of participation in the normal activities of the high school, American secondary education is no longer free. It has been rapidly becoming a commercial commodity. When one also takes into consideration the increased costs of the clothing, cosmetics, and extraschool social life of high-school pupils, one understands how it is that many splendid boys and girls, guilty of nothing more culpable than having been born to poor fathers and mothers, are made to feel most uncomfortable while attending high school. Not only are the effects upon self-assurance and the other aspects of personality development undesirable, but unfavorable attitudes toward the school and public education, toward American "democracy," and toward more fortunate classes of society are developed.[1]

In addition to the expenses enumerated for specifically high school activities, the costs of education for families with children in the elementary schools are often a considerable burden. It is quite common for schools to charge special fees for kindergarten, for materials such as construction paper and finger paints, for locker fees, for weekly newspapers required in class work, and for admission to elementary school events. The charges, considered individually, are usually quite modest, but cumulatively, especially for families with several children in school at once, the effect may constitute a real financial burden. As someone has said, the American public schools have "two-bitted" the parents to death! It is the dime and quarter and dollar fees that add up to real hardship for many families.

Another hidden cost of education is the loss in family income or earning power occasioned by having to keep the children in school rather than having them at work. For many farm families, and for the great majority of migrant farm laborers, this loss in family income is very substantial. It is easy for us who have lived in more fortunate circumstances to wonder why migrant workers, in particular, don't send their children to school; after all, it's free! Not for them; each child big enough to pick up potatoes or work in the beet fields represents a real contribution to a pitifully meager family income. Many families of the laboring classes find that the income from the work of

[1] Harl R. Douglass, *Modern Administration of Secondary Schools* (Boston: Ginn and Co., 1954), p. 181. Reprinted by permission.

a single high-school-age boy or girl, though perhaps very inconsequential by adult-worker standards, is enough to help keep the family from actual starvation. These families simply cannot afford the luxury of continued education for their children.

The Expansion of the Concept of Free Schools

It is true, of course, that the modern elementary or secondary school is continually expanding its services, both the directly educational ones and the social and economic benefits that make education more nearly free. This development has been a very slow one, historically; it has been less than a century since the basic *concept* of free tuition (i.e., instruction) was finally adopted for both elementary and secondary schools.

Instructional materials. Not more than fifty years ago it was still quite common for parents everywhere to provide at their own expense whatever textbooks were available; the idea of completely free texts for all grades is only slowly coming into general public acceptance. Although by the beginning of the present century it was generally agreed that such instructional materials as globes, maps, and blackboards were legitimate expenses to be charged to the public purse, even such materials as these were often furnished, throughout the three hundred years of American educational history, for the most part by interested parents and citizens. Even today, many school boards which will buy *books* without any question, as long as the money holds out, react with startled unbelief and considerable indignation to any proposal that such "frills" as motion picture machines, record players, or musical instruments should actually be purchased from school district funds.

Health services. Basic health services are provided as a part of free education in the great majority of schools today—at least in theory. Again, as long as the money is available in the budget, most public schools have no qualms about providing free medical examinations (or at least examinations of sight and hearing), free inoculations and vaccinations, and free emergency nursing service for common ailments such as sore throats or cut knees. But beyond this the school hesitates to go. Physical ill health, for example, may be treated by the school physician, but problems of mental health treatment, requiring the services of a psychiatrist, are not generally thought to be within the range of legitimate school services. Even services for physical health are limited. Eye examinations, yes; eyeglasses, no! Definitely not! If the child can't read because he can't see, the school will make sure that he is referred to an oculist, or at least that his parents are told that he probably needs glasses. But to provide glasses from school funds? Heavens, no! It is the job of the school to teach the child to read, but the job of the parent to see that the child has glasses. If the parents are too poor to buy glasses, the Kiwanis Club or the Elks Club, or some other philanthropic group or agency of public assistance to the needy should take over from there. That, at least, is the general public attitude.

Food services.   Food services are provided by many schools on a subsidized basis, most generally by indirect federal subsidy under the National School Lunch Act. This is a great help to many low-income families; it not only relieves them to a large degree of financial responsibility for the noon meal (and for even a family of moderate means, with several children in school, this can be very important in the family budget), it guarantees the kids at least one square meal a day. Hence, breakfast and "dinner" can be pretty skimpy—and often are. This aid surely helps make education more nearly free (and more nearly possible) for tens of thousands of school children. But what if the family can't afford even the few cents that the subsidized lunch costs? Most schools try to find some way the child can earn his lunch (or preferably, his lunch *money;* he feels a lot better if he can "pay cash" just like the rest of the children), but there is just no provision for paying *out of school funds* the school lunch expenses of the poverty-stricken child.

Clothing.   For thousands, perhaps tens of thousands of school children—there is really no way of knowing how many—lack of adequate clothing makes the "free" public school system inaccessible; for all practical purposes, if a child does not have shoes to wear to school, the public school for him just doesn't exist. We hear very little about this problem because very few families are willing to admit just how "hard up" they are—"poor but proud" is not just a figurative expression. It is much easier to write to the teacher that Jimmy was home last week with a cold than to admit that he stayed out of school because he didn't have a warm enough coat, and there just wasn't any money to get one till Daddy got paid at the end of the week. It is difficult for us, many of whom have never known real want, to realize how many little children stay away from school for days—even weeks and months at a time—because the family cannot afford clothing that will keep them warm and dry. It is difficult, too, to understand how many youth of high school age drop out of school because they are ashamed of their clothes; at this age nothing, not even educational opportunity, is so important in the minds of many of the adolescents as being dressed "like the others." Foolish pride, we may say, but having to wear patched overalls when the rest of the boys are wearing more formal attire is enough to make the teen-ager decide to quit school and go to work.

Higher education.   We have been discussing so far in this section some of the ways in which the traditionally free public school really isn't free at all—to those who can't afford it. What of the levels of our school system that do not pretend to be free—colleges and gradu-ate schools, in particular? Should everyone really have an unlimited opportunity to get at least free *instruction* for as many years as he can study with profit to himself and society? We have given, as a society, a partial affirmative answer to this question in:

1. providing many junior colleges of local or regional nature in which all *instruction* is free to youth (or adults) who care to attend;
2. supporting many state colleges and universities which offer instruction at both the undergraduate and graduate levels for tuition charges that pay only a minor fraction of the actual cost;
3. giving public support to the provisions of the G.I. Bill of Rights, which guarantees to certain veterans (a special group, but a very large one) not only free tuition but sub-sistence (room and board) payments for a specified number of months, based on the length of military service rendered; and
4. offering scholarships and low-cost loans for undergraduate and graduate students through the National Defense Edu-cation Act, National Science Foundation, and other gov-ernmental agencies.

There are some who would propose that higher education be made more nearly completely free, with tuition charges at all public institu-tions of higher learning abolished entirely, as they have been in public secondary schools. Still others propose that we not only offer free tuition for undergraduate and graduate instruction, but free room and board, and perhaps even cash payments to the parents of the college student to make up for the loss of his contributions to the family income while he is in college. This last, of course, would be

of them. This is perhaps as it should be. The ultimate answers must
only for the very able student who has been selected on some sort of
national or state-wide "scholarship contest" basis, and who would not
otherwise be able to afford the luxury of a college education.

Limitations

In the preceding paragraphs we have raised a good many questions
about how free public education ought to be, and answered very few
come from the expressed wishes—and financial support—of the
citizens of our democracy itself. No professional educator can say
with any certainty what our society *ought* to do about making education free. Take the problem of providing eye examinations, but not
glasses. If the school started supplying glasses, would it also supply
dental fillings, hearing aids, and artificial limbs—as to some degree
the government does in a rather thoroughly socialized nation such as
Great Britain? Or is it better to leave these matters to the individual
family, to organized charitable and philanthropic organizations, service clubs and fraternal groups, or public agencies for assistance to
the impoverished, needy, and disabled? And so with the problem of
inadequate clothing for school children: where would the public
school draw the line if it started spending public school funds for
overshoes and overcoats for the needy school child? Likewise, with
the problem of free higher education: if we were to subsidize completely the college education of all the needy youth who were able to
profit most from attending college, who would make the selection?
Would we here in America, as has been done in some other countries,
allow the state or the national government to conduct competitive
examinations which would determine eligibility for free higher education, the students not securing a sufficiently high score on the examination to be "sidelined" into vocational work? Would this create more
class consciousness and social tension than a democracy can well
afford?

Lots of good questions, you see; very few adequate answers, as
yet. Again, it seems quite clear that the professional educator who is
to have an accurate and realistic perspective of the larger issues in
education must be thoroughly aware of these problems, and alert to
possible solutions. It is not reasonable to assume, however, that the
professional educator will be the one to announce the decisions of
what *ought* to be done—decisions only society as a whole can make.

Should the Teacher Take a Stand on Controversial Issues?

As we discuss this problem, two basic concepts should be taken for granted. First, the modern school, alert to individual and social needs, realistic in its curriculum, believing that each person in the social system has both individual rights and social responsibilities, and recognizing that learning takes place most effectively through planned activities and experiences—such a school must teach about many things, some of which are bound to be "controversial" issues. Second, such a school is by its very nature and purpose unequivocally committed to the principle that in good teaching there will be no indoctrination, in the ordinary sense of the term.

So the question is not whether the school should teach about controversial issues, as they come up naturally in the work of the school, or whether the school or its teachers should indoctrinate. It is simply this: can the teacher be expected to be neutral on these issues? Is the danger of neutrality greater than the danger of taking a stand?

Or we might put it this way: the problem at hand is how to teach or present controversial issues and still assure the teacher's freedom as an individual, his intellectual freedom, and the fulfillment of his professional responsibility to his students, his school, and his society.

The Obligation of the Teacher

In anything he teaches, controversial or not, the teacher is obligated first of all to know whereof he speaks. He needs to know the subject under discussion with reasonable thoroughness (no one can know all there is to know about anything), to know on what authority *statements* are presented as *facts,* on what scientific or research basis *beliefs* may be introduced as *evidence,* on what grounds reasonable people may rightly hold to a view opposite his own—in short, to know what he is talking about.

Another obligation of the teacher is to restrict classroom teaching and discussion to legitimate issues—that is, to problems and questions that are related to the learning activities at hand. This is not an authoritarian limitation, just a common-sense one. If issues about which there is bound to be controversy—crucial issues, debatable issues, issues charged with strong emotional feelings—if these are dragged into the classroom discussion or activities "by the heels," so to speak, justified criticism of introducing extraneous material may be made by the public. Moreover, controversial issues which are discussed at times and in classes where they do not really belong, where they are not legitimately related to the learning activities at hand, are not usually treated very fully or very carefully; everybody just says what he thinks, which results in a slapdash attempt to let everybody have his say rather than in a true learning situation.

Another caution the teacher should observe in dealing with controversial issues is to speak as an authority only in his field of specialization or competence. In doing so, he should of course label his opinions, his facts as facts, and carefully distinguish between the two; but even this is not sufficient. Just because the teacher is the only adult in the room, he is not necessarily entitled to be considered an expert in fields outside of his own. He may be an authority—in some degree at least—in one or more fields; that does not make his opinions in other or even related fields authoritative. It is the same with any other "professional" worker. A Bureau of Reclamation engineer, for example, might be entitled to an authoritative opinion about *how* a dam should be built in a specific location; whether Congress *ought to* authorize public funds for the construction of the dam is a matter in which his engineering training and experience do not qualify him to have any "better" opinion than the next man.

The final precaution in discussing controversial issues in the classroom consists mostly of abiding by the elementary rules of fair play. Reports of different opinions, relevant "facts" which are in actual or seeming conflict, and expressions of feeling and attitude should not only be permitted but sought out and encouraged. No one should be hindered from expressing his own beliefs, so long as he too follows the rules of fair play, listens as well as speaks, and respects the right of individuals to differ from but still be accepted by the group.

Objectivity Is Not Neutrality

Now back to our original question (after what may seem to you like a rather roundabout discussion of some of the techniques and ground rules for teaching controversial issues): should the teacher take a stand on these issues, or should he be perfectly neutral so he will not influence unduly the opinions of the students, so they will be free to make up their own minds? The answer to this question, you may see, is embodied in our discussion of *how* to present controversial issues. For if the teacher is a free and responsible person, he has an inalienable *right* to his own opinions and an *obligation* to express them. Neutrality is at best just a pose, and a poor one at that. At its worst, detached neutrality is an admission of ignorance, or an implication that the problem so interesting to the students really isn't worth the teacher's consideration, or even an indication that the teacher is afraid and insecure.

The teacher must take a stand on controversial issues; as teachers, we must accept the risks involved or our whole concept of democratic values goes down the drain. The teacher must take a stand on such issues, or our cherished values of personal freedom and social responsibility will disappear.

How Can We Balance the Values of Local Educational Control with the Economies of Centralization?

Consolidation of schools into larger attendance and administrative units and centralization of school control, both at the local and state levels, are developments in American education which have come about in the last quarter-century not just for purely educational reasons alone. Changing cultural beliefs and changes in other institutions and agencies of our society have had an effect on the growing centralization of educational control and the diminishing of local grassroots control of the small, local school that used to be so characteristic of the American educational scene.

Respect for Bigness and Efficiency

As a people, we have come to worship size—"the bigger the better" seems to be a typically American motto. We like big cars, big supermarkets, big newspapers, colossal movies, and supercolossal olives. Partly this is just a whimsey, but we take pretty seriously the idea that smallness is the equivalent of inadequacy, that size is an index of quality. This has affected the pattern and organization of American public schools.

Efficiency, some observers of American cultural patterns have pointed out, is almost an object of veneration in our land. We stand in awe of what we like to call "businesslike efficiency" in any activity, whether it be a merchandizing operation, a church, a club, or a school. In many ways we have sought for our schools the accolade of businesslike efficiency even at the cost of losing educational values. The highest praise we can have for a board of education is that they are good, sound, practical businessmen; the pinnacle of achievement for a school administrator is to earn the reputation of being businesslike. Of course, this is not wholly true, but true enough to have been one of the factors in developing the kind of school system we now have.

Trend Toward Centralization

As was pointed out previously in this text (see Chapter One), our present-day American economy, whether we like the change or not, is becoming more of a planned economy and decreasingly an unplanned or laissez-faire way of life. As a people, we have encouraged centralization and control of a number of the activities of our economic, governmental, and personal lives under various agencies, offices, and authorities. The Rural Electrification Authority (REA) has replaced the ruggedly individualistic system of personally owned kerosene lamps and lanterns on better than 90 per cent of the farms in rural America; only the most conservative and suspicious of critics would call this development "socialism." Social Security legislation affecting vast segments of our population has outmoded the familiar "over the hill to the poorhouse." Public health clinics, state and municipal health services, and voluntary prepaid sickness and hospitalization insurance plans have been so widely accepted that few would want to return to the days when individual and family health problems were thought to be of no public concern. Most people would no more want to replace municipally owned and operated water and sewage systems with the backyard pump and the vine-covered outhouse than they would want to give up the U.S. Post Office system and go back to Pony Express and the Wells-Fargo stagecoach. These changes toward centralization of services and controls in the hands of various governmental units—city, county, state, and federal—are accomplished facts; for better or for worse, they have affected our earlier concepts of individualism and localism in education as well.

Persistence of Localism and Laicity

Despite our near-worship of the ideals of size and businesslike efficiency, and despite the cultural and economic trend toward centralized direction of human affairs, *localism* and *laicity* are still rather distinctive features of American education. Basically, we believe that our schools can serve the children and youth of our society best when they are controlled and operated at the local level by local citizens and the professional educators whom they employ. We believe that ultimate control of the schools must rest with the layman, not with the professional expert. Again, these beliefs may not be wholly logical or wholly in keeping with some of our other beliefs, but they persist with almost undiminished strength. Most American citizens do not want the schools to become big, impersonal, heartless organizations, run by experts far removed from the school, unaware of and unresponsive to local needs, desires, and customs. Overemphasis on mere size of the school (either as an administrative or an attendance unit) and overcentralization may quite conceivably weaken the American public school system beyond repair.

There are, beyond the shadow of a doubt, increases in economy and effectiveness of our educational system that can be brought about by increased centralization of the controls of the schools and of the schools themselves. It is patently obvious that the old one-room district school *in most areas* has been rendered obsolescent, if not actually obsolete, by shifts in population, modern means of transportation, and changes in the educational program itself. It is simply not reasonable to continue poor and inefficient schools under the guise of encouraging local control. The children are cheated and the taxpayers are robbed if we insist that an antiquated system of education must be continued just because some people believe, mistakenly, that it is in keeping with American traditions of "grass-roots" democracy.

Some Hopeful Trends

Neighborhood schools.   There is no easy answer to the question: "How can we balance the values of local educational control with the economies of centralization?" There are, however, certain straws in the wind that indicate directions in which we can be and perhaps should be moving. One is the currently popular plan of "cottage schools," as they are called: small, neighborhood elementary schools with separate rooms for each of the first three grades. Thus, the children can attend school close to home, walking safely to and from school in their own familiar neighborhood; they can have many of the advantages of the homey feeling so often found in the really good one-room rural school without the disadvantages of a poor building, inadequately trained and overworked teachers, and limited availability of materials for learning.

Localized attendance centers.   Another way that has been found to keep the schools close to home and close to the people is to devise larger administrative units without making any radical change in the attendance units. For example, all of the schools in a whole county (including in some cases also certain schools in adjoining counties that are so located as to make a single administrative unit feasible) can be placed under one board and one administrative staff, but most of the children will continue to "go to school" in the same places as they did before. If the existing school buildings are adequate from the standpoint of health, comfort, safety, size, space for learning activities, and convenience of location, there is no earthly use of abandoning them and "bussing" all of the children to a large consolidated school. But by consolidating the *administration* of the schools of the area, many economies and improvements can be effected. The people of the new, larger district still control the schools directly by election of a representative board of education, but this local control is more efficient on a large scale than a small one. One superintendent of schools can serve a half-dozen local high schools scattered over the district, and a dozen or two elementary schools; before, each district had to have its own superintendent, business office, and record system. Purchases of school supplies can be centralized with resulting economies in expenditure of school funds. Each little school may not have been able to afford a music teacher or a shop teacher or certain special equipment such as motion picture projectors; now, under one "management" the schools can get together and share the services of special teachers and the use of special equipment.

Advisory groups.   Another way that has been developed to keep the schools close to the people, without giving up the economy and educational effectiveness of centralized control, has been to enlist more citizens directly in the work of the school. One common criticism of any form of consolidation is that, whereas before the change there were, say, forty-five school board members on the fifteen boards, now the new board for the combined districts has only seven members. Centralized control! Taking the schools away from the people! To counteract this, many schools are enlisting the help of citizens committees for the public schools—groups of citizens widely representative of the interests and concerns of all of the various sections of the district. These groups work with and advise the school board on policies and procedures, thus in effect (though not in a legal sense) vastly increasing the size and representative nature of the board of education.

Encouraging parental leadership. Still another way to make the schools responsive to the will of the lay public for whom the schools really exist is to make a conscious effort to balance lay and professional leadership. Education has in the past few decades become much more technical and highly specialized than it used to be. The teaching of reading, for example, is a task requiring extensive professional training and consummate professional skill. There was a period in American educational development during the last two or three decades when many professional educators became overly imbued with a sense of professional superiority and told the parents, directly and indirectly, to quit meddling with the teacher's business. "Don't question our methods of teaching," the parents were told in effect—and sometimes directly and bluntly. "Times have changed since you went to school; you wouldn't understand what we are doing; we're professionals and we know our business." Parents were urged not to let their children read at home before they were taught how to read in school. Parents were sometimes directly forbidden to help their own children in any way with their homework; Mamma or Papa might upset or even destroy the very delicate learning process that the teacher was trying to carry on.

Today, most professional educators are willing to admit that such extreme banishment of the parent from the educational process was quite wrong. The professional educator has a professional duty to the child, but the parent has a parental duty to the child, too—and it's his own child, after all. So, many schools today are holding discussion groups to help parents see the why and the how of modern education, to win parental support and get parental suggestions for improvement of the educational program. Many schools are trying to teach parents how to help the child at home, rather than flatly forbidding such help. And many schools are including parents on committees charged with selecting books for children, determining curricular aims and content, and devising satisfactory testing and reporting programs. Now, some of our best friends are parents!

Not all of these present tendencies—which seek to hold on to the gains we have made in economy and efficiency through centralization of educational control at the same time we seek to keep the people close to their schools—are the "right" answers to the problems. But it would appear that we can maintain in our public school system a thoroughly democratic emphasis on localism and laicity without going back to the older inefficient provincialism in education.

How Much Can We Really Afford to Pay for Education?

In 1940, 3.4 per cent of our national income was spent for education; in 1952, only 2.5 per cent. During the same period, from 1940 to 1952, the actual cost of education increased nearly 150 per cent, but national income increased so much faster than did expenditures that we are actually investing a much smaller portion of our income in education than we did at the close of the Great Depression period. National averages are, of course, deceiving; extreme variation exists among the different states, as a review of the figures presented in Chapter Three above, will reveal. Such figures, of course, may be misleading; relatively low expenditures may reflect efficiency as well as penury, and relatively high expenditures may result from the operation of many small, inefficient school districts, from unusual burdens caused by sparsity of population, or from more willingness of the taxpayers to "buy" good education for their children. But, at best, to spend only 2¼ to 2½ per cent of our national income on one of the most important agencies of society—education—seems a pitifully small investment in our nation's future.

Yet, the cost of education is indubitably high. The total cost of education, public and private, kindergarten through college, has been estimated at over eighteen billion dollars annually. Some states and some local districts are making an almost superhuman effort to support their schools out of very meager resources; the school tax can be, and occasionally is, a crushing burden to the average property owner. It isn't just what many people would consider the "frills" that have caused the cost of education to soar. Direct instructional costs still account for more than two-thirds of the total spent for education. With increasing numbers of children to be educated, rising costs for salaries and other legitimate school expenses, and expanding curricula and increasing scope of school services demanded by the public, no let-up is in sight. So it is necessary that we again, and constantly, raise the question, "How much can we afford to spend for education?"

Frankly, no one knows. Many suggestions have been made, but they tend to represent wishful thinking, rather than a realistic appraisal of the facts. For example, one advocate of a militant restructuring of the entire American public school system states flatly that the nation should budget approximately *ten per cent* of the national income for education now and for many years to come.[2] How he arrives at this figure is not made clear; certainly, it seems like a nice round figure, adequate and generous—to say nothing of the fact that it might have a faint overtone of scriptural authority as a tithe of our national income! Other proposals would limit taxes for education to a flat one per cent of assessed valuations, or some other figure gratuitously provided, or call for a hold-the-line budget that would keep school expenses the same as they are now regardless of changing needs or increased educational responsibilities.

It is evident that we need studies to determine (on local, state, and national levels) answers to questions like these: How can educational costs be reduced, without impairing educational services, by more efficient school management? How can educational costs be most equitably distributed, so that one segment of the economy, one tax-paying group, or one source of revenue does not bear an unfair share of the burden while others escape paying a just share? What services now performed by the school should be expanded, what continued, what curtailed? Should some school health services, for example, be taken over by public health agencies? What is the optimum portion of a state's income that ought to be allocated to educational services, and what to other public services such as roads, conservation, old-age pensions, and care of the mentally ill—all extremely important services provided by the state?

Educators need to undertake these studies as a start, even though other citizens and appropriate governmental agencies should really take most of the initiative. If for no other reason than sheer self-defense professional educators need to encourage such studies; for as it is now, many lay citizens look upon educators and their professional organizations as an unprincipled group that will ask for all they can get—the "school bloc," it is called in many legislative circles.

2 Theodore Brameld, *Patterns of Educational Philosophy* (Yonkers-on-Hudson, N. Y.: World Book Co., 1950), p. 655.

If we are to escape the charge of self-seeking "grabbiness" and shameless lobbying in our own interest, we "school people" must be prepared to back up our requests for money with real facts.

How much can we afford for education? The answer must come, ultimately, not from professional educators but from the people as a whole. We simply don't know—but we had better find out!

Should the Public School "Reflect" or "Lead" Society?

This is a difficult question, reaching far back into educational history and deep down into educational philosophy. Like the other basic questions about the function and operation of an educational system in a democratic society, the answer lies not in what we as teachers think (though we are obligated to know what we think and are entitled to express our opinions) but on what the members of our society as a whole decide is best.

Some persons believe that the school should just reflect or mirror the society that supports it. The school, these persons say, is a creation of society, it is answerable to society, and it must merely pass on to the students the cultural heritage, approved facts, and all value systems cherished by the society it serves. As one eminent conservative in American educational circles has put it,

> Society is, in fact, prior to the individual, and the school is an agency for promoting stability and adapting the individual to the environment in which he lives. . . . For society establishes schools to provide a firm basis for itself and to sustain the common interest. Schools are a part of the environment which they serve; they are not autonomous or insulated against the social forces and influences around them; nor can teachers on the basis of a guess as to the active forces of the day help to build a new social order. *Society changes first and the schools follow.*[3]

Others take a view diametrically opposed to this; they advocate that the school should lead society—that the school should be at the forefront of every new social frontier, a pioneer social agency leading society as a whole toward new horizons. George Counts, the most militant leader of this group, proposed once that the schools ought

[3] Isaac L. Kandel, *Conflicting Theories of Education* (New York: The Macmillan Co., 1938), pp. 79-86. Reprinted by permission.

actually to build a new social order—if they had the courage! [4] He maintained that teachers "should deliberately reach for power and then make the most of their conquest." [5] He suggested that teachers, "instead of shunning power, . . . should rather seek power and then strive to use that power fully and wisely in the interests of the great masses of people." [6] These statements are cited here not because they represent the views of any great number of American educators (perhaps, since they were written more than three decades ago, they do not accurately represent even Counts' position today), but to show how extreme is the variation of opinion of the social function of the school.

You may perhaps wonder why, since the general public must make the decision anyway, we as teachers must concern ourselves with the problem of whether the school is to reflect and maintain the social order as it is or take the lead in changing where social change is necessary or desirable. Why don't we just sit back and wait for the decision? The answer is quite simple: we can't wait because education won't wait. The educational process under the supervision and control of the school is going on day by day; the social effect of the school is being felt daily in every community in America. Inevitably, the school and its teachers are having some effect on society—an effect which may be conservative, middle of the road, liberal, or even radical. In the absence of any clear-cut decision by the general public, the school itself, and the teachers themselves, must make at least a temporary decision—adopt an operating hypothesis subject to later revision—on the question of the primary objective of the school in relation to society.

Can the School Teach Moral and Spiritual Values Without Religion?

We have indicated previously in this text some areas of rather general agreement among educators and laymen about this question. The public school is prohibited from teaching religion *as such* by American constitutional law, American tradition, and public opinion. Yet, the school must seek to inculcate in all children and youth a sense of moral and spiritual values. Without relying on specific religious

[4] George S. Counts, *Dare the School Build a New Social Order?* (New York: John Day Co., 1932). Reprinted by permission.
[5] *Ibid.*, p. 28.
[6] *Ibid.*, p. 30.

sanctions or appeals (*e.g.,* the Ten Commandments, church doctrines, or personal appeals to be "saved") it is difficult, psychologically, to secure personal commitment to a set of ethical ideals or rules of moral conduct.

The problem of the public school as a contributor to the teaching of moral and spiritual values (for surely no one would expect to absolve the churches, the home, and the culture from all responsibility in this area, and assign the whole task to the school) has been pointed up by two major developments of relatively recent occurrence. One has been the postwar increase in all forms of juvenile delinquency and misbehavior, ranging from youthful impudence and scorn for authority to serious breaches of the law. The other is a decision of the United States Supreme Court which would appear, at first glance, to make it absolutely impossible for the school to have anything to do with moral and religious teachings just at the time the school is being frantically urged to get busy and do *something* about the apparent lack of morality in the younger generation.

The "Released Time" Controversy

The McCollum Decision (as it has come to be called) of the Supreme Court was widely accepted as directly prohibiting the public schools' having anything to do with religious or moral teachings. This decision, issued by the court in 1949, was really not nearly so far-reaching in its meaning as many people thought. What actually happened was this: A Mrs. Vashti McCollum, a professed atheist, had protested to school authorities, and then in court action, that her seven-year-old son was being subjected to ridicule and scorn because he would not leave the schoolroom when the other children did to take part in religious exercises and training currently provided by the churches of her city on time *released by the schools* for this purpose. She protested that such release of school time for religious education conducted by the churches constituted a violation of the constitutional provision for separation of church and state—as well as a source of unwarranted embarrassment to her son, who had to stay behind in the room and be called an atheist. The school authorities, and then a series of lower courts, ruled against her plea that released-time practices be outlawed.

The case finally went to the Supreme Court, which at length ruled against the released-time practices in this particular school (Champaign, Illinois) on these grounds:

1. Time was released only to specific churches; the school thereby was supporting certain denominations or sects.
2. School time and school buildings were being used for purposes other than public education.
3. The churches were enjoying the use of the police powers of the state (to certify teachers, take roll, and treat absence from religious instruction as truancy from school) to advance their own sectarian programs.

The decision was both acclaimed and lamented by teachers and laymen throughout the United States, depending on individual points of view. Some looked on it as a bolstering of the historical wall of separation between church and state, others as a direct affront to religion and the work of the churches. Many schools, unfortunately, leaped to the conclusion that they must leave religious and moral matters strictly alone in order to stay within the law. In one school, singing of Christmas carols was immediately forbidden; in another, the primary-grade children were not permitted to take any notice of the approaching Christmas season by having a tree or making decorations for their rooms. Other schools forbade their glee clubs or choruses to sing the classical compositions of such great church musicians as Bach, and others forbade reference to religion in history courses.

Of course, this was all quite unnecessary. All that the Supreme Court had decided was that *released time* practices, common in thousands of schools, were unconstitutional. The court decision had stated that the high tribunal itself was not hostile to religion: "Both religion and government," said the justices, "can best work to achieve their lofty aims if each is left free from the other within its respective sphere." Furthermore, the court recognized that the public school could not do an adequate job of teaching history, art, music, drama, and other fields if the place of religion in man's cultural development were ignored. Justice Jackson wrote:

> Nearly everything in our culture worth transmitting, everything which gives meaning to life is saturated with religious influences derived from paganism, Judaism, Christianity—both Catholic and Protestant—and other faiths accepted by a large part of the world's peoples. One can hardly respect a system of education that would leave the student wholly ignorant of the currents of religious thought that move the world society for a part in which he is being prepared.[7]

[7] Quoted in C. C. Morrison, "The Concurring Opinions," *Christian Century*, Vol. 66, No. 24 (June 15, 1949), p. 737. Reprinted by permission.

A subsequent Supreme Court decision (Zorauch vs. Classen) modified to a degree the McCollum decision; and on matters pertaining to Bible reading, free textbooks and bus transportation for parochial school students, and other issues involving religion and the schools, the courts have handed down inconclusive and often seemingly contradictory rulings. One conclusion is clear: constitutionally, the public schools cannot directly teach or support formal sectarian religious doctrines.

Even the widespread practice of engaging in completely nonsectarian and essentially nondoctrinal public prayer in school assemblies and classrooms has seemed to come under the stern disapproval of the Supreme Court. The Court's renowned New York prayer decision, in 1962, actually forbade only *mandated* prayer in public schools— that is, public and audible prayer which had been required by law. In no way did the decision suggest that prayers could not be offered in schools, though such was the interpretation of many who feared that the Supreme Court was systematically and viciously attempting to remove all vestiges of our religious heritage and traditions from the public schools.

What CAN the School Do?

There are several ways the school can emphasize moral and spiritual values without violating the spirit—or the letter—of the Constitution as interpreted in Supreme Court rulings, especially the McCollum decision. Note first of all that the decision was against devotional, creedal religious exercises—not against the *study* of religion, but against the advocacy under school auspices of a specific religious faith. The school can, and should, teach religious literacy. The school can recognize the importance of great religious writings and leaders and events and ideals—and teach them as a part of the understanding of modern man, his history and his problems, his failures and his dreams.

The school can encourage not mere *toleration* of religions other than the one accepted by a student individually or accepted by the community as a whole, but real *respect for* and *acceptance of* religious differences as normal and wholesome in a democratic society. The school must also teach respect for religious nonconformity as an individual right.

Most of all, the school can teach moral and spiritual values directly and indirectly without basing them on any religious doctrine whatsoever. Not "directly" in the sense of the famed Elgin plan of a couple of decades ago, in which the schools of this town in Illinois had a regular schedule for teaching honesty on Monday, thrift on Tuesday, purity on Wednesday, and so on. But "directly" in the sense that such teaching is not left to mere haphazard chance, but is a specific part of the curriculum and aims of the schools. Sharing, helping, working together, being honest, respecting the opinions and rights of others, maintaining individual integrity—these and countless other moral and spiritual values can be made a part of the daily experience and learning activities of the children and youth in our public school. And most of all—the teacher who is himself or herself a living example of moral values (not a dispenser of specific creeds, nor a sentimentally pious or sanctimonious kill-joy) is the best possible inspiration for moral growth and spiritual vitality in the classroom.

Finally, the school has a special reason for being interested in this problem. Many people feel that modern education—because it is generally liberal, pragmatic, and suspicious of authoritarianism in all of its forms—is without any sense of values. We must prove that we do have a sense of values or public confidence in the school system will be seriously—and justifiably—undermined. If we can actually do a good job of teaching moral and spiritual values to the children and youth for whom we have undertaken both a professional and a personal responsibility, then public faith in the American school system will be immeasurably increased.[8]

The Public School and Segregation

The question of racial segregation has been "decided" by the Supreme Court of the United States, but the decision is only a beginning. The judicial ruling outlawing segregation can hardly come as a surprise to any careful student of constitutional law, or to anyone who believes that the fundamental personal and social rights of all men, regardless of race, creed, or previous condition of servitude must be respected and safeguarded in a democracy. But the actual implementation of this decision is up to the schools just as much as it is to the

[8] For an excellent discussion of the values that the school affirms, and how they may be taught, see Educational Policies Commission, *Moral and Spiritual Values in the Public Schools* (Washington, D.C.: National Education Association, 1951).

courts. The courts will rule, and governmental agencies will enforce, but the success of desegregation in American education will depend in large measure on how the schools do their part.

What Is the Job of the School?

First, the schools must obey the law, regardless of the personal feelings of school boards, administrators, teachers, or the community. It is quite possible, perhaps even logical, for an *individual* to practice the overt kind of civil disobedience advocated by Henry Thoreau (who went to jail rather than obey a law he thought unjust), but an *agency of society* cannot rebel against the laws of the society it serves.

Second, the schools, in the trying days ahead, in the tumultuous and sometimes dangerous period of unrest and upset that will doubtless (in some areas at least) accompany the painful process of adjusting old customs and beliefs to the new constitutional interpretation —the schools must really practice what they preach. Administrators and teachers have long maintained that the way to solve any serious social problem is through education; we need to approach the problem of desegregation as an educational task of the first magnitude. We know that all learning is gradual, that all behavior changes must come slowly. Let us remember this. We know that early experiences are often of lasting importance; let us try to make the early experiences with integration as satisfying as possible. We know that old habits and ways of living are learned behavior; let us be both patient and optimistic as we attempt to help people unlearn behavior that is no longer acceptable. We know that emotion plays a large part in the learning process—that it can be used to motivate good learning, or that it can be such a disruptive force as to make learning impossible; we need to remember this as we work in an educational area charged with the most explosive of human emotions—race prejudice.

Third, we need to commit ourselves to seeing that the new program does work. If we cannot make it work, we are not adequate to our task as teachers. Unless we want it to work, all we have said about the importance of individual differences, the cherished values of democracy as a way of life, and the supreme worth of human personality as the highest good we can know on earth—all of these are vanity, and a striving after vain things.

FIFTEEN: TOPICS FOR STUDY, REPORT, AND DISCUSSION

1. Defend or criticize the great American ideal of "secondary education for all American youth."
2. Hold a panel discussion in class on the question, "How Free Should Public Education Be?"
3. What does it cost you to attend college? How much of the cost is borne by the institution (if it is a private college) or by the taxpayers of the state (if it is a public college)? Don't answer this part of the question aloud—but are those who are subsidizing your college education getting their money's worth?
4. If possible, invite to the class some public school official (administrator or board member) who has been directly involved in a program of school consolidation and reorganization of districts to discuss the problems and advantages of redistricting our public school system.
5. If there is a local Citizens Committee for the Public Schools in operation, see if you can secure permission for a group from the class to visit one of their meetings, and report back to the class on how the group operates and what it is accomplishing.
6. Find out, by consulting the school laws of your own state, just what the exact legal status of the public school is with respect to teaching of religion. Are Bible reading and prayer required, encouraged, or forbidden? Are any practices being carried on that are of doubtful legality?
7. What would constitute a good, workable, defensible, and completely legal program of education in moral and spiritual values in the schools of your state?
8. Consult current newspapers and magazines to discover what progress is being made in carrying out the Supreme Court ruling on desegregation in the public schools.

FIFTEEN: BIBLIOGRAPHY

Conant, James B., *Slums and Suburbs*. New York: McGraw-Hill Book Co., Inc., 1961. A brief but penetrating study of the problems of providing education for all in the urban setting.

Educational Policies Commission, *Moral and Spiritual Values in the Public Schools*. Washington, D. C.: National Education Association, 1951. One of the best statements available regarding the values the school tries to teach, and the ways these values may be taught in the ordinary classroom.

————, *Public Education and the Future of America*. Washington, D. C.: National Education Association, 1955. A thoughtful and thought-provoking policy statement about the directions that American education might well take in the next decades of our country's development.

Hansen, Kenneth H., *Philosophy for American Education.* Englewood Cliffs, N. J.: Prentice-Hall, Inc., 1960. Presents the philosophical bases for an understanding of some of the unsolved problems in education.

Hodgkinson, Harold L., *Education in Social and Cultural Perspectives.* Englewood Cliffs, N. J.: Prentice-Hall, Inc., 1962. Brings to bear some fresh and revealing findings from the behavioral sciences on some of the most exasperatingly difficult unsolved problems in education.

Kerber, August, and Wilfred Smith, eds., *Educational Issues in a Changing Society.* Detroit: Wayne State University Press, 1962. An excellent selection of critical articles on some of the major unsolved problems of current American education.

Lieberman, Myron, *The Future of Public Education.* Chicago: The University of Chicago Press, 1960. A provocative and frequently provoking attack on the complacency of the American educational system and its professional organizations.

Mason, Robert E., *Educational Ideals in American Society.* Boston: Allyn and Bacon, Inc., 1959. A scholarly and thoughtful analysis of the basic American educational ideals which must give perspective to our search for solutions to educational problems.

National Education Association, *High School Dropouts.* Washington, D. C.: Research Division and Department of Classroom Teachers, NEA, rev. September, 1959. Discusses the nature and extent of the drop-out problem and proposed remedial measures; includes excellent bibliography.

"School Dropouts," symposium in *NEA Journal,* Vol. 51, No. 5 (May, 1962), 51-59.

A

INDEX